International Criminal Justice Series

Volume 8

Series Information

The *International Criminal Justice Series* aims to create a platform for publications in the whole field of international criminal justice. It, therefore, deals with issues relating, among others, to:

- the work of international criminal courts and tribunals;
- transitional justice approaches in different countries;
- international anti-corruption and anti-money laundering initiatives;
- the history of international criminal law.

The series concentrates on themes pertinent to developing countries. It is peer-reviewed and seeks to publish high-quality works emanating from excellent scholars, in particular from African countries.

Editorial Office

Prof. Dr. Gerhard Werle
Humboldt-Universität zu Berlin
Faculty of Law
Unter den Linden 6,
10099 Berlin, Germany
gerhard.werle@rewi.hu-berlin.de
moritz.vormbaum@rewi.hu-berlin.de

More information about this series at http://www.springer.com/series/13470

Koen Vriend

Avoiding a Full Criminal Trial

Fair Trial Rights, Diversions and Shortcuts in Dutch and International Criminal Proceedings

ASSER PRESS

Springer

Koen Vriend
Law Faculty/Criminal Law
University of Amsterdam
Amsterdam
The Netherlands

ISSN 2352-6718 ISSN 2352-6726 (electronic)
International Criminal Justice Series
ISBN 978-94-6265-152-4 ISBN 978-94-6265-153-1 (eBook)
DOI 10.1007/978-94-6265-153-1

Library of Congress Control Number: 2016951656

Published by T.M.C. ASSER PRESS, The Hague, The Netherlands www.asserpress.nl
Produced and distributed for T.M.C. ASSER PRESS by Springer-Verlag Berlin Heidelberg

Printed on acid-free paper

This Springer imprint is published by Springer Nature
The registered company is Springer Science+Business Media B.V.
The registered company address is: Van Godewijckstraat 30, 3311 GX Dordrecht, The Netherlands

For my parents
For Tim

Acknowledgements

This book is based on a dissertation that was defended at the University of Amsterdam. I am truly grateful for the support of my two supervisors, Profs. Tom Blom and Göran Sluiter. I would also like to thank Profs. Jan Crijns, Ward Ferdinandusse, Rijnhard Haentjens, Adriënne de Moor-Van Vugt and Harmen van der Wilt for their willingness to be members of the doctoral committee.

Contents

Abbreviations

A. Ch.	Appeals Chamber
ACHR	American Convention on Human Rights
AJ	Appeals Chamber's Judgement
BGH	Bundesgerichtshof (German Federal Court of Justice)
C	Constitution
CC	Criminal Code
CCP	Code of Criminal Procedure
ECHR	European Convention on Human Rights
ECLD	Extraordinary Criminal Law Decree
ECLI	European Case Law Identifier
ECtHR	European Court of Human Rights
ECtHR (GC)	European Court of Human Rights, Grand Chamber
GVG	Gerichtsverfassungsgesetz (German Code on the Organisation of the Judiciary)
HR	Hoge Raad der Nederlanden (Dutch Supreme Court)
HRC	Human Rights Committee
ICC	International Criminal Court
ICCPR	International Covenant on Civil and Political Rights
ICTR	International Criminal Tribunal for Rwanda
ICTY	International Criminal Tribunal for the former Yugoslavia
LJN	Landelijk jurisprudentienummer (Dutch case-law identifier)
NJ	Nederlandse Jurisprudentie (Dutch case-law journal)
NOR	Naoorlogse Jurisprudentie (Dutch case law journal)
OM	Openbaar Ministerie (Dutch Public Prosecution Service)
par	paragraph
RPE	Rules of Procedure and Evidence
SCSL	Special Court for Sierra Leone
Sr	Wetboek van Strafrecht (Dutch Criminal Code)
Stb.	Staatsblad (Dutch Official Bulletin of Acts and Decrees)
Stcrt.	Staatscourant (Dutch Government Gazette)
StPO	Strafprozessordnung (German Code of Criminal Procedure)

Sv	Wetboek van Strafvordering (Dutch Code of Criminal Procedure)
T. Ch.	Trial Chamber
TIC	Taken Into Consideration
TJ	Trial Chamber's Judgement
UN	United Nations
UNICRI	United Nations Interregional Crime and Justice Research Institute

Chapter 1
Full Criminal Proceedings in Decline

Abstract Full criminal proceedings are avoided on many occasions. Criminal cases may be diverted from the courts and handled in administrative procedures, cases may be handled solely by the prosecutor or they are handled in a simplified manner by the court. A distinction is made between diversions and shortcuts. Diversions are avoidance mechanisms that infringe upon the principle of *nulla poena sine iudicio*. Shortcuts to proof infringe upon the full criminal trial because they allow for an abbreviated presentation and discussion of the evidence in front of the trier of fact. Diversions and shortcuts, also referred to as avoidance mechanisms, have to comply with the notion of fairness in criminal proceedings. The notion of fairness is derived from the case-law of the European Court of Human Rights. This book examines avoidance mechanisms that infringe upon the ideal type of conducting full criminal proceedings in Dutch and international criminal proceedings.

Keywords Diversions · Shortcuts to proof · Fair trial · Full criminal trial · European court of human rights

Contents

K. Vriend, *Avoiding a Full Criminal Trial*, International Criminal Justice Series 8, DOI 10.1007/978-94-6265-153-1_1

The contested trial is only the presentational surface of the criminal justice system, a surface which masks the reality of the criminal justice process.[1]

1.1 The Full Criminal Trial

This book is based on an archetype: the full criminal trial. In archetypical criminal trial proceedings, the charges against the accused are presented in open court, they are supported by evidence that can be challenged, and the proceedings are concluded by the reasoned judgment of the court. The *ius puniendi*, the right to punish, rests firmly with the court: the court metes out punishment after it has conducted adversarial proceedings ('une procédure contradictoire') in which the guilt of the accused has been determined.[2] This implies that evidence is both presented and challenged: the factual basis for the judgment must be the result of the close scrutiny of incriminating and exonerating evidence. Considering the interests of the accused, it is essential that the accused is able to participate effectively in the proceedings. In order to ensure this, the accused is provided with all kinds of procedural rights that enable him to participate during the proceedings. These rights are properly categorized under the notion of a fair trial which is the basic notion that criminal proceedings against an accused must be conducted in a fair and decent manner. The importance of fairness in criminal proceedings is proclaimed consistently by the most authoritative judicial body on the interpretation of the right to a fair trial: the European Court of Human Rights.[3]

To study the characteristics of the full criminal trial in isolation from the 'law in action' would result in a distorted view on the manner in which criminal cases are processed in modern societies. Criminal cases are often diverted from full criminal proceedings: offences are decriminalized and handled in administrative procedures, they are handled solely by the prosecutor or handled by the court in a simplified manner. When being handled by the prosecutor, cases can be diverted by way of an out-of-court settlement, or by the imposition of a sentence by the prosecutor. Even when cases are brought before the courts, numerous shortcuts to proof can be discerned that speed up the proceedings. This book focuses on such avoidance mechanisms that either divert from or speed up the proceedings, thereby avoiding the full criminal trial.

Efficiency considerations play an important role in the rise of avoidance mechanisms; specifically, bargaining with the accused to settle the case without involving

---

[1] Duff et al. 2004, p. 10.

[2] For the purpose of this study, the notions of 'adversarial proceedings' and 'une procédure contradictoire' refer to the opportunity for the accused to challenge the evidence during the proceedings.

[3] E.g. *Delcourt v. Belgium*, in which the Court held: 'In a democratic society within the meaning of the Convention, the right to a fair administration of justice holds such a prominent place that a restrictive interpretation of Article 6 para 1 would not correspond to the aim and purpose of that provision.' ECtHR, 17 January 1970, App. No.: 2689/65, (*Delcourt v. Belgium*), para 25.

the court reduces the costs of the criminal justice system considerably. The rise of 'consensualism' in criminal matters, which entails that the accused consents to a particular procedural outlook of the proceedings, also contributed to the decline of the full criminal trial. The notion that criminal (procedural) law is first and foremost *public* law, which provides a procedural model that is not for the parties to decide upon, is eroded when private law notions such as party autonomy or *pacta sunt servanda* become more prominent regarding the handling of criminal cases.[4]

The full criminal trial is both the 'epistemic engine' that strives to produce accurate fact-finding and the best context in which the accused can exercise his fair trial rights.[5] Any derogation from this optimal setting or ideal type must be accounted for. The focus of this study is on the fair trial implications of such derogations. Although the epistemological context is important, it is not suitable for a fruitful analysis: this would require an objective standard of accuracy that allows us to determine whether the diversion or shortcut to proof infringed upon the fact-finding tasks of the court. Because no such standard exists, it would be inappropriate to evaluate the avoidance mechanisms in the light of accurate fact-finding. It is, however, submitted that accurate fact-finding is greatly enhanced when evidence is processed in a manner that allows for challenges and adversarial debate ('un débat contradictoire').[6] In this sense, there is a relationship between accurate fact-finding and the fairness of the criminal proceedings. This should not be misunderstood: providing the accused with a fair trial does not necessarily result in accurate fact-finding. It does, however, enhance the chances that the final result will be in conformity with the truth.

Fairness has its own intrinsic value. Criminal cases should be processed in a fair manner; in other words, diversions and shortcuts do not operate in a context in which efficiency reigns supreme. They are *legitimate* only when they provide for a fair handling of the case. This perspective is the primary evaluating perspective of this study. Although fairness is normally associated with regular trial proceedings, it is argued that its normative scope reaches further than the trial context as such. Fairness permeates the whole criminal justice system and is a principle underlying the enforcement of criminal law. In their seminal study *The Trial on Trial*, Duff et al. stated:

> Given that the trial is one of the central ways in which the rights of the accused are adequately protected, there is at least good reason to consider other aspects of the criminal justice process against the standards set by the criminal trial, properly understood and properly theorized.[7]

---

[4] Such private law notions can play a role in determining whether the accused has validly waived particular procedural rights. If he has done so out of his own free will, the waiver is valid and cannot be revoked easily.

[5] Laudan observed: 'It thus seems fair to say that, whatever else it is, a criminal trial is first and foremost an *epistemic* engine, a tool for ferreting out the truth from what will often initially be a confusing array of clues and indicators.' Laudan 2006, p. 2. Emphasis in original.

[6] Cf. ECtHR (GC), 15 December 2011, App. No.: 26766/05 and 22228/06, (*Al-Khawaya and Tahery v. United Kingdom*), (French translation) para 118. As confirmed in: ECtHR (GC), 15 December 2015, App. No.: 9154/10, (*Schatschaschwili v. Germany*), (French translation), para 103.

[7] Duff et al. 2004, p. 12.

Regarding the protection of the fair trial rights of the accused, the full criminal trial sets the proper standard.

1.2 Purpose and Scope of the Study

Avoidance mechanisms can be discerned in a great number of national as well as international criminal justice systems. The common law practice of plea-bargaining, the Italian *patteggiamento* and the German practice of *Verständigung* all provide fascinating ways to avoid the full criminal trial.[8] These mechanisms have been studied extensively, with most such research being comparative in character; in these studies researchers compare particular criminal justice systems, describing the differences and similarities regarding these avoidance mechanisms.

This study has a different scope. This book examines avoidance mechanisms that infringe upon the ideal type of conducting full criminal proceedings in Dutch and international criminal proceedings. Such avoidance mechanisms are pervasive and entrenched in current criminal justice systems and they are not limited to particular categories of criminal offences. Both minor and serious violations of (international) criminal law can be processed outside the context of the full criminal trial. The heterogeneous character of avoidance mechanisms entails that a classic comparative approach does not suffice: to compare avoidance mechanisms that operate in different criminal justice systems would add little to our understanding of the phenomenon. Even avoidance mechanisms that can be discerned in both the Dutch and the international criminal justice system have particular features, which makes a classical comparison of limited interest. It will not provide a framework for the evaluation of the avoidance of a full criminal trial. What is of interest, however, is the question what the consequences are for the position of the accused when an avoidance mechanism is used to divert the case from the court or to speed up the proceedings. It is this perspective that is of primary interest in this book: the normative implications, in terms of fairness, of the avoidance of the full criminal trial.

Considering that avoidance mechanisms can be discerned regardless of the category of criminal offences, it is necessary to present an overview in order to outline the diversity and flexibility of these mechanisms. The avoidance mechanisms that are discussed in this study provide examples that are critically evaluated in the light of the fair trial rights of the accused. Sometimes, the examples cover 'common ground', such as in the case of facts of common knowledge and appeal proceedings. Those mechanisms can be discerned in both the Dutch and the

[8] From the rich and voluminous literature on plea-bargaining in common law criminal justice systems, see inter alia: Turner 2009, pp. 7–72. For the concept of *patteggiamento*, see inter alia: Langer 2004, pp. 46–53. For the concept of *Verständigung*, see: Volk 2010, pp. 281–285.

international context. There is, however, also room for the discussion of 'outliers': avoidance mechanisms that are typical for a particular criminal justice system, such as the Dutch punitive order or the international practice of taking judicial notice of facts that have been adjudicated in other proceedings. The aim of the examples discussed in this study is to show that, despite their differences, the normative framework that is chosen can be applied to the great diversity of avoidance mechanisms.

The Dutch and international criminal justice systems have been chosen because together, they provide for a good representation of the great variety of avoidance mechanisms. The context of international criminal proceedings is of particular relevance because the nature and complexity of the crimes that are processed before the international *ad hoc* Tribunals (the International Criminal Tribunal for the former Yugoslavia and the International Criminal Tribunal for Rwanda) and the International Criminal Court almost inevitably lead to the avoidance of the full criminal trial. International criminal proceedings are lengthy, costly and complex. Measures to enhance the efficiency of such proceedings are to be welcomed, provided the accused is still able to participate effectively.

The avoidance mechanisms that can be discerned in the proceedings before the ICTY, ICTR and ICC are discussed. The proceedings at the ICTY and ICTR have resulted in a considerable amount of case law, which allows for a proper analysis of the avoidance mechanisms that operate at these two Tribunals. Other international criminal tribunals, such as the Special Court for Sierra Leone, have not produced a similar amount of case law; as a result, they are not included in the analysis, apart from a single anecdotal reference. The ICC is included because the manner in which this permanent international court will handle complex and time-consuming cases is of great importance. The legitimacy of the ICC depends to a significant extent on the question whether the Court is able to process cases efficiently and within a reasonable time.

As previously mentioned, the choice for the international criminal context is primarily based on the type of cases they process: complex and lengthy proceedings regarding the most heinous crimes. The *sui generis* character of the international criminal proceedings stimulates the search for efficient ways to handle such cases. In order to show the broad spectrum of avoidance mechanisms, it is necessary to include a domestic criminal justice system in the analysis as well. Domestic criminal justice systems provide for other examples of avoidance mechanisms, such as diversions regarding minor offences (which are absent in the international criminal context) and shortcuts in regular criminal proceedings, in most cases due to the existing caseload. Whereas the international context provides for avoidance mechanisms due to the type of cases, in the domestic context, ways are explored to efficiently handle the great number of criminal cases.

The Dutch criminal justice system provides for such a criminal justice system. The Dutch system is of particular relevance because, alongside out-of-court settlements based on consensus, it also provides for a special diversion from the full criminal trial: the punitive order. This diversion entails that the prosecutor can unilaterally impose a sentence and thereby avoid the criminal trial. Another important reason for the inclusion of the Dutch criminal justice system is the fact that the Dutch system has been deeply influenced by the case law of the European Court of Human Rights. The normative framework of the ECtHR that is used in this study is, therefore, of particular relevance for the Dutch criminal justice system.

In the chapters on Dutch and international criminal proceedings, the particular diversions and shortcuts of the respective systems are discussed. They are critically evaluated in the light of the fair trial rights of the accused. How should the concept of fairness regulate and limit avoidance mechanisms in criminal proceedings? To what extent is the accused able to participate properly in the handling of his case when a diversion or shortcut is applied? The normative framework that is used for the evaluation is the concept of fairness in criminal proceedings, in particular the manner in which the European Court of Human Rights has interpreted the concept of fairness in its rich and voluminous case law. The question is answered to what extent avoiding the full criminal trial infringes upon the fair trial rights of the accused, in particular his ability to participate effectively regarding his case.

This study does not address administrative procedures in which decriminalized offences are processed: rather, the focus in this study is on the context of proper criminal law and criminal procedure. It is noted, however, that the normative framework presented is applicable to such administrative procedures as well, when the proceedings concern the determination of a criminal charge. This autonomous concept has been defined by the European Court of Human Rights in the famous *Engel* case.[9]

Another topic that is not included in this study is the (emerging) practice of mediation in criminal cases. Although cases can be diverted from the court this way, they do not result in any form of punishment. Avoidance mechanisms discussed in this study are essentially punitive in character. Finally, it is noted that the avoidance mechanisms discussed in this study are not exhaustive. Similar mechanisms can be found in other criminal justice systems, and it is also possible to discern other shortcuts in the criminal justice systems that are discussed in this study. The mechanisms chosen for examination in this study provide a representative overview of the diversity of these mechanisms.

1.3 Terminology: Diversions, Shortcuts and a Full Criminal Trial

In this study, a distinction is made between diversions and shortcuts to proof, although both allow for the avoidance of the full criminal trial.

---

[9] ECtHR, 8 June 1976, App. No.: 5100/71; 5101/71; 5102/71; 5354/72 and 5370/72 (*Engel and Others v. The Netherlands*).

Diversions are avoidance mechanisms that infringe upon the principle of *nulla poena sine iudicio*. This principle entails that punishment can be meted out only by an impartial and independent court, after regular proceedings have been conducted. Diversions are those mechanisms that divert the case from the court, such as out-of-court settlements and guilty pleas.

Shortcuts to proof infringe upon the full criminal trial because they allow for an abbreviated presentation and discussion of the evidence in front of the trier of fact. In other words, shortcuts do respect the *nulla poena sine iudicio* principle, but do not allow for a regular presentation and discussion of the evidence before the court. The principle of immediacy in the formal sense, the notion that all evidence is fully presented in front of the trier of fact, is infringed upon.[10]

Essentially, a full criminal trial is the handling of a case through proceedings before a court, in which all the relevant evidence is presented and discussed in order to allow the accused to participate effectively. Thus, the accused is able to object to any incriminating evidence and to present his arguments to the court. In order to inform the accused on how the court has considered his arguments, the judgment contains the reasons for the court's decision. The definition of the full criminal trial is closely related to the manner in which incriminating evidence is processed when a diversion or shortcut is used. For this reason, a more detailed discussion of the full criminal trial in the respective criminal justice systems is presented in Chaps. 3 and 4. Particular attention is paid to the manner in which the evidence is admitted, how the evidence is weighed and how the court accounts for its factual findings in the judgment.

1.4 The Normative Framework

The European Court of Human Rights has, over the past decades, developed an unprecedented amount of case law in which the notion of fairness in criminal proceedings has been defined in great detail. The diversity of the legal systems in the signatory states of the Convention provided the Court the opportunity to define the concept of fairness in criminal proceedings regardless of the particularities of a specific criminal justice system. The Court's interpretation transcends the classical inquisitorial-adversarial dichotomy and provides for an overarching notion of fairness in criminal proceedings. The interpretation of Article 6 of the Convention in relation to criminal proceedings has been one of the primary tasks of the Court.

---

[10] A distinction can be made between the principle of immediacy in the formal sense and in the substantive or broad sense. The first notion entails that all the evidence is presented in court (including second-hand or derivative evidence). The principle of immediacy in the broad sense entails that the court is provided with the original evidence. Damaška argued that this second notion can be equated with the common law 'best evidence'-rule. Damaška 1992, pp. 446–448; Cf. Nijboer 1979, pp. 821–823.

Considering this and the fact that the criminal justice systems that are discussed have been deeply influenced themselves by the interpretation of the right to a fair trial by the Court, the Court's interpretation of fairness in criminal proceedings is the proper normative framework.

To take the concept of fairness in criminal proceedings as the normative framework has an important advantage; to be specific, the evaluation of the diversions and shortcuts will not be limited to particular minimum rights contained in Article 6 of the Convention. Instead, a holistic approach is taken in which the minimum rights are incorporated. This provides for a comprehensive framework that does not focus solely on the relationship between an avoidance mechanism and a particular minimum right.

1.5 Outline of the Book

The outline of the book is as follows. In Chap. 2, the concept of fairness in relation to diversions and shortcuts is discussed. This chapter provides the framework that is used to evaluate the diversions and shortcuts in the following chapters. The case law of the European Court of Human Rights regarding the concept of fairness in criminal proceedings provides the basis for the normative framework that is used to evaluate the avoidance mechanisms. In particular, the participatory model of proof, as developed by legal scholars John Jackson and Sarah Summers, is presented and justified as the suitable normative framework for the analysis.

In Chap. 3, the diversions and shortcuts in the Dutch criminal justice system are discussed. In order to fully understand how the full criminal trial is avoided, the chapter starts with an overview of the characteristics of the Dutch full criminal trial. The manner in which evidence is processed is of particular relevance: adversarial proceedings enhance the quality of fact-finding. After the characteristics of the full criminal trial have been discussed, three diversions from the full criminal trial are analysed: the punitive order, the transaction and the conditional dismissal. These diversions are mechanisms that divert the case from the court and enable the prosecutor to impose a sentence or reach a consensual settlement with the accused. The chapter concludes with a discussion of the shortcuts to proof.

In Chap. 4, a similar approach is taken within the context of international criminal proceedings. First, an overview is provided of the full criminal trial in international criminal proceedings. Subsequently, the chapter presents a discussion of the diversions from the full criminal trial: the guilty plea and the admission of guilt. Finally, the use of shortcuts to proof is discussed. Chapters 3 and 4 provide the examples of avoidance mechanisms in the different criminal justice systems. In order to fully grasp the workings of these mechanisms in the respective systems, they are described in some detail.

In Chap. 5, the diversions and shortcuts that have been discussed in the two previous chapters are evaluated in the light of the normative framework that was presented in Chap. 2: the participatory model of proof. The chapter focuses on the question of to what extent the accused can properly participate when the full criminal trial is avoided by a diversion or a shortcut. In the final chapter, general conclusions are drawn.

The research for this study was concluded on 1 January 2016.

References

Damaška MR (1992) Of hearsay and its analogues. Minn Law Rev 76:425–458

Duff A, Farmer L, Marshall, S, Tadros V (eds) (2004) The trial on trial vol 1: truth and due process. Hart Publishing, Oxford

Langer M (2004) From legal transplants to legal translation: the globalization of plea bargaining and the Americanization thesis in criminal procedure. Harvard Int Law J 45:1–64

Laudan L (2006) Truth, error and criminal law. An essay in legal epistemology. Cambridge University Press, New York

Nijboer JF (1979) Enkele opmerkingen over de betekenis van het onmiddellijkheidsbeginsel in het strafprocesrecht. Nederlands Juristenblad 36:821–823

Turner JI (2009) Plea-bargaining across borders: criminal procedure. Aspen Publishers, New York

Volk K (2010) Grundkurs StPO. C.H. Beck, Munich

Chapter 2
Diversions, Shortcuts and the Concept of Fairness

Abstract This chapter assesses the applicability of human rights standards to diversions and shortcuts to proof. The case-law of the European Court of Human Rights provides the most authoritative interpretation of the concept of fairness in criminal proceedings. Fairness is regarded as a principle that underlies the enforcement of criminal law. This entails that fairness applies in case of the full criminal trial, when the case is diverted, and when a shortcut to proof is used. More specifically, the concept of fairness in criminal proceedings is rooted in the idea of participation. Proceedings may be called fair if the accused has been able to participate effectively in the handling of his case, either by way of a diversion or a shortcut to proof. Four aspects of participation in criminal proceedings were identified and discussed in detail: non-compulsion; informed involvement; the ability to challenge the evidence, and the right to a reasoned judgment. These four aspects were derived from the participatory model of proof, as described by legal scholars Jackson and Summers.

Keywords Fairness · European court of human rights · Participation in criminal proceedings · Procedural justice · Article 6 ECHR · Diversions

Contents

K. Vriend, *Avoiding a Full Criminal Trial*, International Criminal Justice Series 8, DOI 10.1007/978-94-6265-153-1_2

2.1 Introduction

This chapter provides the normative framework for the following chapters on Dutch and international criminal law. It assesses the applicability of human rights standards (in particular the right to a fair trial) to diversions and shortcuts to proof. The applicability of the notion of fairness to diversion mechanisms is not self-evident. Fairness is regarded as a fundamental principle underlying criminal proceedings, which also permeates the rules of evidence of the different legal systems that are discussed in the other chapters. Fairness is defined based on the case law of the European Court of Human Rights. The interpretation of the concept of fairness by the European Court of Human Rights has been chosen as the normative framework, because the Court has, over the past decades, created an authoritative account of the concept of fairness in criminal proceedings. Both in qualitative and in quantitative terms, the Court has established, compared to other human rights bodies, the most detailed and sophisticated concept of fairness.[1] Moreover, the case law of the Court has deeply influenced the criminal justice systems that are discussed in this book.[2]

It is argued that the analysis of the Court's case law should, for present purposes, eschew trying to define the *principle* of fairness as such. Although such an analysis is in itself not without merit, an abstract notion of fairness does not provide the desired normative framework that is useful for the evaluation of the chapters on diversions and shortcuts to proof. The analysis should equally eschew the opposite approach in which fairness is dissected into particular rights and analysed from a rule-level or micro-perspective. Instead, an approach is chosen in which particular rights are interpreted in light of the overall concept of fairness and *vice versa*. The chapter concludes by presenting the participatory model of proof, which is used to evaluate the chapters on Dutch and international criminal law.

2.2 Fairness and Evidence Law

Rules of evidence seem to have escaped direct supervision by the European Court of Human Rights. The Court held in the famous *Schenk* case that the admissibility of evidence is 'primarily a matter for regulation under national law': Article 6 of

[1] Cf. Roth and Tulkens 2011.

[2] The Netherlands ratified the Convention in 1954. The international tribunals and courts have to operate in conformity with internationally recognized human rights standards (cf Article 21(3) ICC Statute). Along with the ICCPR and ACHR, the European Convention on Human Rights is regarded as an authoritative source regarding human rights standards. Fedorova observed on the standing of the ECtHR within the case law of the *ad hoc* tribunals: 'Although starting off with a somewhat dismissive approach to the case law of the ECtHR in the first, infamous, *Tadić* case, *ad hoc* tribunals came to embrace references to this human rights body's jurisprudence.' Fedorova 2012, p. 29. On the applicability of human rights norms in international criminal proceedings, see Gradoni 2009, pp. 74–94; Vasiliev 2014, pp. 89–158.

the Convention does not, as such, lay down any rules on the admissibility of evidence.[3] Considering the holistic approach of the Court regarding the fairness of the proceedings, this is not surprising: detailed rules on the admissibility of specific means of proof would not sit well with the overall determination of the fairness of the proceedings. Evidence that has been obtained in breach of domestic law will not automatically result in unfair proceedings: the use of illegally obtained evidence does not, as such, render the proceedings unfair.[4]

Not only does the Court refrain from stipulating general rules on the admissibility of evidence, but it also refrains from weighing the evidence presented before the domestic courts. Considering the Court's fourth instance doctrine, it is not in a position to evaluate and weigh the evidence presented in the domestic proceedings unless the evidence infringes upon a right protected under the Convention:

> The Court recalls that the admissibility of evidence is primarily a matter for regulation by national law and that, as a general rule, it is for the national courts to assess the evidence before them. The Court's task under the Convention is rather to ascertain whether the proceedings as a whole, including the way in which evidence was taken, were fair.[5]

According to Trechsel, the Court guarantees that 'procedural justice' has been done: the right to a fair trial does not include the right to an accurate factual outcome of the case. 'Outcome-justice', as Trechsel put it, is concerned solely with the outcome of the procedure as such.[6] One of the few dissenters to this view is former ECtHR judge Loucaides, who argued that the right to a fair hearing encompasses the right to a fair result.[7] He argued that it would be contrary to the *raison d'être* of Article 6 to be unable to challenge proceedings that have been fair, but have resulted in an unjust outcome.[8] Manifestly unjust judgments should be declared unfair.[9]

Loucaides ignored the important distinction between the two central aims of criminal proceedings: fairness and factual accuracy. Both aims are interdependent (e.g. fairness requires that witness evidence be contested in open court, which arguably also enhances the accuracy of the court's factual findings) but remain autonomous, in the sense that fair proceedings may result in an inaccurate

---

[3] ECtHR, 12 July 1988, App. No.: 10862/84, (*Schenk v. Switzerland*), para 46.

[4] ECtHR (GC), 1 June 2010, App. No.: 22978/05, (*Gäfgen v. Germany*) para 163. With references to other case law.

[5] ECtHR (GC), 13 July 2000, App. No.: 25735/94, (*Elsholz v. Germany*), para 66. Cf. ECtHR (GC), 21 January 1999, App. No.: 30544/96 (*Garcia Ruiz v. Spain*), para 28. 'In particular, it is not its [the Court, KV] function to deal with errors of fact or law allegedly committed by a national court unless and in so far as they may have infringed rights and freedoms protected by the Convention.' Cf. Goss's argument that the fourth instance doctrine is 'incoherent and internally inconsistent'. Goss 2014, pp. 42–58.

[6] Trechsel 2006, p. 83. Trechsel 1997, p. 102.

[7] Loucaides 2003, p. 31.

[8] ECtHR, 2 July 2002, App. No.: 33402/96, (*Göktan v. France*), Partly Dissenting Opinion of Judge Loucaides, p. 15.

[9] Loucaides 2003, p. 32.

outcome and *vice versa*.[10] The criminal trial is indeed, as Rawls observed, a classic example of imperfect procedural justice: even if all the rules of evidence and fair trial guarantees have been observed, the outcome of the trial may be unjust (i.e. a factual inaccurate outcome).[11] Therefore, to 'apply' standards of fairness to factual accuracy, or to evaluate the fairness of the proceedings by referring to the outcome of the proceedings, is misconceived. This seems to be at odds with the idea that the law of evidence has been shaped and deeply influenced by fair trial standards. If we regard the law of evidence as the category of rules that promote the factual accuracy of the verdict, then it would be useless to *evaluate* evidence law using fair trial standards. It is suggested, however, that although the outcome *as such* does not come within the ambit of Article 6 (or within any fair trial standard, for that matter), the manner in which the outcome has been reached, including the use that has been made of rules of evidence, is deeply influenced by fair trial considerations. In other words, if one were to argue that rules of evidence are fundamentally epistemic rules aimed at guaranteeing an accurate outcome of trial proceedings, fair trial considerations have adapted those rules in order to provide for a fair determination of the outcome of the proceedings.

The case law of the Court on evidentiary matters has been interpreted traditionally as a hands-off approach: evidentiary matters are for the domestic courts to decide. However, this analysis has obfuscated the fact that the Court has made significant inroads in the law of evidence of domestic jurisdictions.[12] To give a well-known but telling example, the Court has ruled on several occasions that the manner in which Dutch courts handled the testimony of witnesses in court was in violation of Article 6(3)(d). The Court ruled in *Kostovski* that the applicant was convicted on the basis of evidence that to a decisive extent consisted of anonymous witness statements and found a violation of Article 6(3)(d), taken together with Article 6(1).[13] In *Van Mechelen*, the use of anonymous statements from police officers was found to be incompatible with Article 6(1) and Article 6(3)(d).[14] In the more recent *Vidgen* case, the Court ruled that the mere appearance of a witness in court cannot, without more, be equated with an opportunity for the defendant to have examined the witnesses against him.[15] The Dutch Supreme

---

[10] Cf. Rawls's characterization of criminal proceedings as 'imperfect procedural justice': the rules of procedure do not guarantee the desired outcome (an accurate verdict). Rawls 1999, pp. 74–75.

[11] 'The characteristic mark of imperfect procedural justice is that while there is an independent criterion for the correct outcome [a factual accurate verdict, KV], there is no feasible procedure which is sure to lead to it.' Rawls 1999, pp. 74–75.

[12] In this respect, it is telling that the book edited by Roberts and Hunter starts with a chapter called 'The Human Rights Revolution in Criminal Evidence and Procedure'. Common law legal scholars have paid significantly more attention to the influence of the Court's case law on the rules of criminal evidence and procedure than Continental scholars. Roberts and Hunter 2013.

[13] ECtHR, 20 November 1989, App. No.: 11454/85, (*Kostovski v. The Netherlands*), para 43–45.

[14] ECtHR, 23 April 1997, App. No.: 21363/93; 21364/93; 21427/93 and 22056/93 (*Van Mechelen and Others v. The Netherlands*), para 62–63.

[15] ECtHR, 10 July 2012, App. No.: 29353/06, (*Vidgen v. The Netherlands*), para 47.

Court had to reconsider its position on the examination of witnesses following the Court's judgment.[16] To analyse these cases in isolation, i.e. as cases that are relevant only for a specific (procedural) right under the Convention (the right to examine witnesses), would be wrong. A piecemeal approach does not do justice to the manner in which the Court has, over several decades, created an intriguing and complex framework regarding evidentiary issues.

The Court's approach to the specific guarantees under Article 6(3) (such as the right to be informed of the accusation, the right to defend oneself in person or with the assistance of counsel and the right to examine witnesses) is a holistic and principled one:

> The Court recalls that the guarantees in paragraph 3(d) of Article 6 are specific aspects of the right to a fair hearing set forth in paragraph 1 of this provision which must be taken into account in any assessment of the fairness of the proceedings.[17]

The Court emphasized that whether a trial has been fair can be determined only by evaluating the proceedings as a whole.[18] Therefore, the Court's case law should not be analysed from the perspective of a particular right. One should not primarily look at particular rights (the rule-level, or the micro-perspective) or the notion of fairness as such (the principle-level, or the macro-perspective), but one should rather try to distil from the detailed case law elements that constitute the notion of fairness. When one regards the specific rights under Article 6 as rules that have to be interpreted and applied in the light of the fundamental principle of fairness, it becomes clear why an analysis focused on the general notion ('fairness') or any specific right ('the right to…') is either too broad or too narrow. It obfuscates the hermeneutic manner in which the specific rules and the principle of fairness interact with each other.

2.3 Principles and Rules

The concepts of principles and rules deserve some closer analysis before examining the model that will be used to analyse the Court's case law. Commenting on the distinction between principles and rules, Vasiliev observed:

> principles be defined as fundamental and absolute provisions permeating the legal system (some would say 'capturing its spirit'), formulated at such an abstract level where they cannot be detracted from by any exceptions, qualifications or reservations. Generality and intolerance to exceptions appear distinctive and inherent features of a principle. By contrast, rules are always accompanied by explicit or implicit exceptions, restrictions of scope, or conditions for application.[19]

[16] HR 29 January 2013, *ECLI*:NL:HR:2013:BX5539. Trechsel 2006, p. 317 and further.

[17] ECtHR (GC), 15 December 2011, App. No.: 26766/05 and 22228/06, (*Al-Khawaya and Tahery v. United Kingdom*), para 118.

[18] ECtHR (GC), 15 December 2011, App. No.: 26766/05 and 22228/06, (*Al-Khawaya and Tahery v. United Kingdom*), para 118.

[19] Vasiliev 2009, p. 51.

Abels argued that principles will never be completely realized and are open-ended.[20] They are also non-conclusive, in the sense that they will never have the definite answer to a particular (factual) situation.[21] Dworkin observed in this respect:

> Only rules dictate results, come what may. When a contrary result has been reached, the rule has been abandoned or changed. Principles do not work that way; they incline a decision one way, though not conclusively, and they survive intact when they do not prevail.[22]

Vasiliev observed that rules are more 'concrete provisions' than principles and are 'action-orientated'.[23] The relationship between rules and principles is hierarchical: a rule is a *lex specialis* of the underlying principle.[24] Whereas principles do not allow for any exceptions to them, 'rules are always accompanied by explicit or implicit exceptions, restrictions of scope, or conditions for application.'[25] This is an important insight because it helps to explain the distinction between an analysis on the principle-level and on the rule-level. Although one can legitimately analyse the Court's case law concerning a particular rule (e.g. the right to examine witnesses, or the right to legal assistance), such an analysis does not provide the answer to whether or not the proceedings as a whole were fair: this requires an analysis on the principle-level. Similarly, to analyse the Court's case-law solely from the principle-level (i.e. by asking, 'What does fairness entail?') is a legitimate and interesting approach but does not reveal much about the specific aspects of fairness.

To illustrate the distinction between principles and rules, four categories of cases can be discerned. The first category consists of cases in which a rule has been infringed upon, but where the principle of fairness has not. An example can

---

[20] Abels 2012, pp. 190–191.

[21] Abels 2012, p. 193. Cf. Sluiter et al. 2013, p. 21.

[22] Dworkin 1978, p. 35.

[23] Vasiliev referred to the work of Stephen Perry, who argued that rules 'specify a course of action to be followed in a particular type of circumstance.' Perry juxtaposed action-orientated rules with value-orientated principles. Perry 1997, p. 788.

[24] Vasiliev 2009, p. 46. Vasiliev noted that *lex specialis* should not be equated with *lex superior*: as such, a rule cannot prevail over a principle. *Idem*, p. 47.

[25] Vasiliev 2009, p. 51. An interesting example is the Court's reasoning on the 'sole and decisive rule', regarding examination of witnesses. The Court's Grand Chamber held that: 'It would not be correct, when reviewing questions of fairness, to apply this rule in an inflexible manner. Nor would it be correct for the Court to ignore entirely the specificities of the particular legal system concerned and, in particular its rules of evidence, notwithstanding judicial dicta that may have suggested otherwise […]. To do so would transform the rule into a blunt and indiscriminate instrument that runs counter to the traditional way in which the Court approaches the issue of the overall fairness of the proceedings, namely to weigh in the balance the competing interests of the defence, the victim, and the public interest in the effective administration of justice.' ECtHR (GC), 15 December 2011, App. No.: 26766/05 and 22228/06, (*Al-Khawaya and Tahery v. United Kingdom*), para 146.

be found in the case of *Al-Khawaya and Tahery*, where the right to examine witnesses had been infringed upon (in Mr Al-Khawaya's case, the witness was dead, while in Mr Tahery's case the witness was absent due to fear). Although the applicants' rights under Article 6(3)(d) had been infringed upon, in the case of Mr Al-Khawaya, the Court found no violation of Article 6(1) in conjunction with Article 6(3). The unavailability of the witness did not result in a violation of the principle of fairness: sufficient counterbalancing factors were in place to compensate for not hearing the witness.[26]

The second category consists of cases in which the infringement of a rule, results in the violation of the principle of fairness. For example, the right to access to a lawyer may be restricted to such an extent that it amounts to a violation of the principle of fairness.[27] Similarly, the Court has found a violation of Article 6 when no convincing reason was provided by the domestic court for the absence of a witness: assessing Article 6(3)(d) in conjunction with Article 6(1) resulted in a violation of the right to a fair and public hearing.[28]

The third category includes the cases in which no particular rule has been infringed upon as such, but where, nevertheless, the proceedings as a whole were found to be unfair.[29] In the case of *Barberà, Messegué and Jabardo*, the applicants complained that their rights under Article 6(1) in conjunction with paras 2 and 3 had been violated by the Spanish authorities. The Court found a violation of Article 6(1), due to the fact that the applicants were confronted with a sudden change in the composition of the Spanish court (although this did not, in itself, amount to an infringement of the right to an impartial tribunal), the brevity of the trial proceedings and the fact that certain evidence was not properly assessed in the presence of the accused and the public in general. Therefore, the Court concluded, the proceedings taken as a whole were unfair.[30]

The fourth category is included for the sake of completeness: conceptually, there are cases in which neither a particular rule nor the principle of fairness has been violated (such cases are likely to be declared inadmissible).

---

[26] ECtHR (GC), 15 December 2011, App. No.: 26766/05 and 22228/06, (*Al-Khawaya and Tahery v. United Kingdom*), para 153–158. In Mr Tahery's case, the Court found that the counterbalancing factors did not compensate for the handicaps under which the defence laboured. (para 159–165).

[27] Cf. ECtHR (GC), 27 November 2008, App. No.: 36391/02, (*Salduz v. Turkey*), where the Court held that the applicant's rights under Article 6(3)(c) in conjunction with Article 6(1) were violated.

[28] ECtHR, 26 July 2005, App. No.: 39481/98 and 40227/98, (*Mild and Virtanen v Finland*), para 45–48; ECtHR, 8 June 2006, App. No.: 60018/00, (*Bonev v. Bulgaria*), para 43–45; ECtHR, 12 April 2007, App. No.: 11423/03, (*Pello v. Estonia*), para 34–35.

[29] Cf. Rainey, Wicks and Ovey: 'Compliance with specific rights set out in Article 6 will not alone guarantee that there has been a fair trial. It is not possible to state in the abstract the content of the requirement of a fair hearing; this can be considered only in the context of the proceedings as a whole, including any appeal proceedings.' Rainey et al. 2014, p. 263.

[30] ECtHR, 6 December 1988, App. No.: 105990/83, (*Barberà, Messegué and Jabardo v. Spain*), para 89.

Having described the interaction between the specific rights of Article 6(3) and the overall requirement of fairness, the following section turns to the normative framework that will be applied in this study.

2.4 Participation in Criminal Proceedings

As illustrated above, analysing the European Court's case law on either a principle-level or a rule-level is not very helpful in describing a normative framework based on the notion of fairness. In this paragraph, the focus will be on the notion that fairness in criminal proceedings is routed in the idea of participation: proceedings may be called 'fair' if, and only if, the accused has been able to participate effectively in the proceedings.[31] Moreover, the participation model offers the possibility to evaluate diversions, despite the fact that case law of the Court on diversions is virtually absent.[32] The notion of participation has the benefit of simplicity: it seems quite straightforward and it has an intrinsic appeal to our sense of (procedural) justice. However, upon closer inspection the notion of participation is more complex and requires a detailed discussion. In this paragraph, the various aspects of participation will be discussed.

In the article 'Procedural Justice', Solum argued that the participation principle consists of two basic rights: the right of notice and the right to be heard.[33] The first right guarantees that the accused is duly notified of the charges brought against him, while the second right guarantees that the accused has standing in court and can object to the charges and the evidence collected against him. Although Solum's observations were concerned with U.S. civil procedure, his conclusions are relevant for the participatory model for criminal cases.[34] Solum argued that the right to participate in proceedings is essential for the legitimacy of the proceedings as such. He argued that any outcome-related or subjective aim, such as accurate fact-finding or respecting the dignity and autonomy of the litigant does not suffice to provide the normative underpinning of the participation principle.[35]

[31] Cf. the remarks of the Court in *Stanford*: '[…] Article 6 (Article 6), read as a whole, guarantees the right of an accused to participate effectively in a criminal trial.' ECtHR, 23 February 1994, App. No.: 16757/90, (*Stanford v. United Kingdom*), para 26.

[32] ECtHR, 27 February 1980, App. No.: 6903/75, (*Deweer v. Belgium*) is an interesting, but rather a-typical, exception.

[33] Solum 2004, p. 308.

[34] Solum argued that his model can, with some necessary modifications, be used for criminal procedure as well. Solum 2004, pp. 240–241.

[35] 'Because a right of participation must be afforded to those to be bound by judicial proceedings in order for those proceedings to serve as a legitimate source of authority, the value of participation cannot be reduced to a function of the effect of participation on outcomes; nor can the value of participation be reduced to a subjective preference or feeling of satisfaction.' Solum 2004, p. 275.

He further asserted that these basic rights are essential and are often found in authoritative judicial opinions.[36] The value of Solum's arguments lies predominantly in his observation that participation *legitimizes* the proceedings. This entails that any outcome-orientated approach will simply not suffice: to argue that the lack of participation by the litigant or the accused did not result in a less accurate outcome than with his participation is missing the point. This (which Solum aptly coined the 'participatory legitimacy thesis') needs, however, some more elaboration. The right of notice and the right to be heard are indeed very important aspects of any participatory model, but are insufficient as a coherent normative participatory framework.

In their search for a proper normative framework for the criminal trial as such, Duff et al. argued that criminal trials that result in a guilty verdict can be regarded as legitimate only if the verdict has been reached by 'communicative participation.'[37] Although their analysis focused primarily on the concept of the criminal trial within the common law tradition of England and Wales, they claimed that their model of communicative participation is applicable to adversarial and inquisitorial systems as well (with the necessary modifications).[38] The model of participation they envisaged, requires from all trial participants an active attitude: not only is the defendant encouraged (but not forced) to participate actively in the proceedings, but the same also holds true for the prosecution, witnesses or victims and the fact-finder.[39] The goal of this model is to attain 'normative knowledge': the court, after participatory proceedings, declares the truth about the accused's conduct. In this way, they argued, participation also has an epistemic aspect to it.[40]

[36] Solum 2004, pp. 308–309. Solum referred solely to US courts. His observations, however, transcend the specifics of US civil procedural law. Cf. Lord Bingham who noted: 'a long established principle of the common law that the defendant in a criminal trial should be confronted by his accusers' in: Dennis 2010, p. 255.

[37] '[...] it is essential to the trials' character that truth or knowledge is to be pursued by a process in which the defendant is invited (but not required) to participate: allowing such a role to the defendant is not important merely as a means to establishing the truth, or as a side-constraint on the pursuit of a kind of truth or knowledge that could in principle be established without giving the defendant any such role, but as integral to the process as one of calling the defendant to answer to the charge.' Duff et al. 2007, p. 119.

[38] Duff et al. 2007, pp. 200–201.

[39] Duff et al. 2007, Chap. 7. See also Weigend who observed: 'We have seen, however, that a trial is not necessarily the ideal mechanism for searching for and finding the 'truth'. As has been pointed out above, an administrative-style 'inquisitorial' investigation potentially provides a broader information base for the judgment because it enables the investigator to take his time in collecting the evidence and places lesser emphasis on the least reliable and most volatile form of evidence, that is, live witness testimony. The participation rights of the parties, including the right to be heard, the right to present evidence and the right to confront adverse witnesses, would of course have to be scrupulously respected even in an investigatory, non-trial process of proof-taking.' Weigend 2006, p. 220.

[40] Duff et al. 2007, p. 218.

Although the possibility for the participant to contest evidence may very well result in more accurate fact-finding (based on the idea that *contested* evidence is *better* evidence), participatory rights should be seen primarily as aspects of fairness.

The Dutch legal scholar Peters also referred to the importance of an adversarial setting, or 'procédure contradictoire', in criminal proceedings. Such proceedings enhance accurate fact-finding and, more importantly, institutionalize the conflicting interests of the State and the accused.[41] This entails that the adversarial trial protects the accused against a State that strives for an efficient handling of the case. Adversarial proceedings allow the accused to exercise his (fair trial) rights to the greatest extent and also provide for the accused's participation in the criminal justice system. Peters emphasized the importance of the 'ethics of conflict': the interests of the State and the accused differ fundamentally, which necessitates an adversarial procedural setting in which the accused can challenge the accusations of the State.[42] In order to effectively challenge the charges, legal assistance at all stages of the proceedings is essential.[43] Peters argued that, in bureaucratized criminal justice systems, the ability of the accused to participate and to influence the outcome of the proceedings may be jeopardized.[44]

Jackson and Summers discerned more specific aspects of participation in criminal proceedings in their impressive study *The Internationalisation of Criminal Evidence*. They distinguished four aspects that, taken together, form the 'participatory model of proof' as developed by the European Court of Human Rights. They argued that the Court has constructed a normative framework, which transcends the old dichotomy of civil and common law legal traditions, including the emphasis the respective traditions place on inquisitorial and adversarial elements.[45] The first aspect of this framework is non-compulsion: the accused cannot be forced to participate in his own trial. This notion is closely related to the possibility of waiving particular procedural rights, which will be discussed in further detail below. The second aspect entails that the accused must be sufficiently informed about his procedural rights. Third, the accused must, in order to be able to participate effectively, be able to challenge the evidence that has been collected against him. Finally, the accused is entitled to a reasoned opinion of the court, which can be challenged.[46] All four aspects, or 'strands' as Jackson and Summers coined them, will be discussed in some more detail below.

---

41 Peters 1972, pp. 284–285.

42 Peters 1972, pp. 283–285.

43 Peters 1975, p. 105.

44 Peters 1975, pp. 103–105.

45 See also Jackson 2005, pp. 737–764; Jackson and Summers 2013, pp. 114–130.

46 Jackson and Summers, pp. 103–106.

2.4.1 Non-compulsion

The first aspect entails that the accused cannot be forced to participate in the proceedings. This is evident in the privilege against self-incrimination, which the Court regards as a fundamental right of the accused.[47] As Jackson and Summers readily acknowledged, this notion seems to be at odds with any participatory model: how can a model of participation allow the accused to *not* participate? They argued convincingly that the right to participate should not be construed as a duty to participate: instead, it should respect the procedural autonomy of the accused. This entails that the accused may indeed not use his procedural rights and remain silent or act non-cooperatively. In this regard, participatory rights can be seen as subjective rights that the accused may wish to use or not.[48]

Besides simply not using procedural rights, the accused may also waive his procedural rights. The notion of waiver implies a well-informed accused who voluntarily decides to abstain from using his rights. The Court has emphasized that, in order to accept a valid waiver, the domestic court must ensure that the waiver complies with certain guarantees. Rights under Article 6 may be waived either expressly or tacitly. A tacit waiver may be accepted if the accused could reasonably have foreseen the consequences of his conduct.[49] The Court has held that an accused has (tacitly) waived his right to examine a witness who fears to testify in open court, if the fear can be attributed to the accused.[50]

An express waiver must be 'established in an unequivocal manner and be attended by minimum safeguards commensurate with its importance. It must not run counter to any important public interest.'[51] If an accused deliberately and knowingly chooses not to attend trial proceedings, he may have validly waived his right to be present during the proceedings.[52] Similarly, an accused who wishes not to put any questions to a witness present in court waives his right to examine such a witness. Not all rights under Article 6 can be waived, though. It would be hard to

---

[47] 'As regards the use of evidence obtained in breach of the right to silence and the privilege against self-incrimination, the Court observes that these are generally recognized international standards which lie at the heart of the notion of a fair procedure under Article 6.' ECtHR (GC), 11 July 2006, App. No.: 54810/00, (*Jalloh v. Germany*), para 100. For a detailed analysis of the scope of the privilege, see: ECtHR (GC), 29 June 2007, App. No.: 15809/02 and 25624/02, (*O'Halloran and Francis v. United Kingdom*).

[48] Note however that not every fair trial right can be regarded as a subjective right: the rationale of certain fair trial guarantees, such as the right to a public hearing, transcend the interest of the accused. The integrity of the criminal justice system as such may be challenged when such rights are not respected.

[49] ECtHR, 9 September 2003, App. No.: 30900/02, (*Jones v. United Kingdom*). Cf. ECtHR (GC), 18 October 2006, App. No.: 18114/02, (*Hermi v. Italy*).

[50] ECtHR (GC), 15 December 2011, App. No.: 26766/05 and 22228/06, (*Al-Khawaya and Tahery v. United Kingdom*), para 123.

[51] ECtHR (GC), 17 September 2009, App. No.: 10249/03, (*Scoppola v. Italy No. 2*), para 135.

[52] ECtHR (GC), 1 March 2006, App. No.: 56581/00, (*Sejdovic v. Italy*), para 82.

imagine to waive, when trial proceedings have been initiated, the right to be tried by an independent and impartial tribunal. This right not only protects the accused, but it also aims to uphold the integrity of trial proceedings in general: an important public interest.[53] Whether certain procedural rights can be waived relates to the distinction between the notion of fair trial rights as subjective rights, which are attributed to the accused, and the notion of fair trial rights as manifestations of systemic features that have to be respected regardless of the position of the accused.[54]

It is noted that the right not to participate undermines the idea that participatory rights also have a significant (some even argue: predominant) epistemic aspect: participation in this view is required in order to ensure an accurate factual outcome. However, the European Court has regarded the guarantees under Article 6 of the Convention as fair trial guarantees *as such*. Although fairness is deeply intertwined with the need for an accurate factual outcome, the two notions should be clearly separated on a conceptual level. Fair trials can indeed have inaccurate factual outcomes and *vice versa*. It is hard to agree with Redmayne's observation on the examination of witnesses that:

> To date, most of the indications are that the ECtHR understands the value of confrontation [of witnesses, KV] in purely epistemic terms.[55]

The Court has consistently held that the right to examine witness [the same holds true for the other minimum guarantees of Article 6(3)] is a specific aspect of the right to a fair hearing in Article 6(1). The Court did not state that these rights are aspects of the need to guarantee an accurate factual outcome of the proceedings. When an accused has threatened a witness against him and the witness refuses to testify in open court, the Court has held that the accused has waived his right to examine this particular witness.[56] This means that a potentially valuable witness who can testify against the accused will not be examined in open court by the accused. From an epistemic perspective this is unacceptable. From a fair trial perspective, however, the court could not do otherwise: it would be highly unjust to have the accused benefit from his criminal acts regarding the witness. The value of examining witnesses lies primarily in considerations of fairness.

This is, of course, not to argue that fair trial rights do not contribute to accurate fact-finding (on the contrary, they certainly do). However, the rationale for these rights should not be found in epistemic considerations but rather in the concept of fairness as a fundamental principle underlying criminal proceedings.[57]

[53] For an analysis of US practice on waiving constitutional rights, see: Stuntz 1989.

[54] Cf Jackson 2009, pp. 5–6.

[55] Redmayne 2013, p. 290.

[56] ECtHR (GC), 15 December 2011, App. No.: 26766/05 and 22228/06, (*Al-Khawaya and Tahery v. United Kingdom*), para 123.

[57] The right to a fair trial is so fundamental that it has acquired the status of international customary law. See: Fedorova 2012, p. 27.

2.4.2 *Informed Involvement*

The second aspect entails that the accused, in order to participate effectively, should be well informed about his rights and the consequences of any procedural choice he may wish to make.[58] Jackson and Summers argued that disclosure obligations and the right to legal assistance enable the accused to make well-informed decisions regarding his trial.[59] Article 6(3)(a) and (e), for example, ensure that the accused is put on notice of the charges formulated against him. Trechsel argued that the wording of sub-paragraph (a) creates the obligation to automatically render any relevant information to the accused. This is, however, not how the Court has interpreted this provision: the question is whether the accused actually had the information relevant for the proceedings and not whether the authorities fulfilled their duty to provide the accused with this information.[60]

The aspect of informed involvement is closely related to the right to have adequate time and facilities for the preparation of the defence, protected under Article 6(3)(b). An effective defence presupposes full knowledge of the evidence that has been collected against the defendant. The Court held:

> The right to an adversarial trial means, in a criminal case, that both prosecution and defence must be given the opportunity to have knowledge of and comment on the observations filed and the evidence adduced by the other party. [...] In addition Article 6 § 1 requires [...] that the prosecution authorities disclose to the defence all material evidence in their possession for or against the accused.[61]

Exceptions to this right are allowed under certain specific circumstances (such as the need to withhold evidence due to national security interests or in order to protect the legitimate interests of vulnerable witnesses) and it is, in principle, for the domestic courts to assess whether a restriction on disclosure is strictly necessary. The Court confines itself to its well-known holistic approach and determines whether the proceedings as a whole were fair. An important factor in this regard is which counterbalancing measures were taken to compensate the accused.

---

58 Jackson and Summers 2012, p. 103.

59 Jackson and Summers 2012, p. 103.

60 Trechsel 2006, pp. 203–204. 'The guarantee is interpreted in a simply functional perspective—instead of insisting on a clear act of the authorities which informs the defendant in a reliable way of the accusations against him or her, the Court lets it suffice if the accused, with due diligence, had the possibility of acquiring the information necessary for his or her defence, or if a circumspective strategy of the defence had in any case covered the point which was missing in the information.'

61 ECtHR (GC), 16 February 2000, App. No.: 28901/95, (*Rowe and Davis v. United Kingdom*), para 60. Cf. ECtHR (GC), 27 October 2004, App. No.: 39647/98 and 40461/98, (*Edwards and Lewis v. United Kingdom*); Trechsel 2006, pp. 238–242.

2.4.3 Challenging the Evidence

The third aspect of the participatory model of proof is the most important: every accused must be provided with sufficient time and facilities to challenge any incriminating evidence. It is a fundamental right of each accused to be able to question and challenge the reliability of any incriminating witness statements or non-testimonial evidence. The right to challenge the evidence is closely related to the principle of equality of arms, in the sense that the latter prescribes that the accused must be allowed to present exonerating evidence: 'The Court recalls that under the principle of equality of arms, as one of the wider features of the concept of a fair trial, each party must be afforded a reasonable opportunity to present his case under conditions that do not place him at a disadvantage vis-à-vis his opponent.'[62] In *Edwards*, the Court held that 'it is a requirement of fairness (…) that the prosecution authorities disclose to the defence all material evidence for or against the accused'.[63] The Court's observation was made regarding the non-disclosure of evidence within the trial context. However, the fundamental importance of disclosure should not be limited to trial proceedings only: disclosure is also important within the setting of out of court agreements.

The right to challenge the evidence is most problematic with regard to witness evidence: restrictions on the scope of the right to challenge the evidence occur most frequently in relation to witness evidence.[64] This stands to reason, because witnesses and victims may have legitimate interests not to be questioned by the accused or his counsel. Balancing between the accused's right to confrontation and any legitimate interests that witnesses may have, the Court has over several decades developed a rather complicated framework. In *Al-Khawaya and Tahery*, the Court set out the scope of the right to examine witnesses as protected under Article 6(3)(d). In principle, all evidence must be produced in the presence of the accused at a public hearing with a view to adversarial argument.[65] This is not controversial and has been held consistently by the Court.[66] This entails that good reasons must be presented for the non-attendance of a witness: failure to provide such reasons

62 ECtHR, 22 February 1996, App. No.: 17358/90, (*Bulut v. Austria*), para 47.

63 ECtHR, 16 December 1992, App. No.: 13071/87, (*Edwards v. United Kingdom*), para 36.

64 Challenging non-testimonial evidence often requires calling (expert) witnesses that may testify on the reliability of such evidence.

65 ECtHR (GC), 15 December 2011, App. No.: 26766/05 and 22228/06, (*Al-Khawaya and Tahery v. United Kingdom*), para 118.

66 E.g. ECtHR, 27 February 2001, App. No.: 33354/98, (*Lucà v. Italy*), para 39; ECtHR, 31 October 2001, App. No.: 47023/99, (*Solakov v. the Former Yugoslav Republic of Macedonia*), para 57; ECtHR, 20 November 1989, App. No.: 11454/85, (*Kostovski v. The Netherlands*), para 41; ECtHR, 6 December 1988, App. No.: 105990/83, (*Barberà, Messegué and Jabardo v. Spain*), para 78.

may, *without more*, result in a violation of the right to a fair trial.[67] If a good reason has been provided, the question must be answered whether the untested evidence is the sole or decisive evidence against the accused.[68] When the untested evidence is indeed the sole or decisive evidence, the Court must then verify whether sufficient counterbalancing factors have been put in place to compensate the accused for not being able to examine the witness. Such counterbalancing factors may result in the conclusion that although the accused was not able to examine the witness, the proceedings as a whole were fair. This means that the sole or decisive-rule is not absolute: the evidence against the accused may consist solely or to a decisive degree of the statement of a non-examined witness.[69] The Court observed that 'the question in each case is whether there are sufficient counterbalancing factors in place, including measures that permit a fair and proper assessment of the *reliability* of that evidence to take place.'[70] The use of the term 'reliability' implies that the non-examination of an important witness has implications not only for the fairness of the trial, but also for the factual accuracy of the final verdict. This way, the Court directs the domestic courts to provide for specific counterbalancing factors that enable the accused to question the veracity of the witness statement.

---

67 'Even where the evidence of an absent witness has not been sole or decisive, the Court has still found a violation of Article 6 §§ 1 and 3(d) when no good reason has been shown for the failure to have the witness examined.' ECtHR (GC), 15 December 2011, App. No.: 26766/05 and 22228/06, (*Al-Khawaya and Tahery v. United Kingdom*), para 120 (with references to relevant case law).

68 Decisive evidence is defined, somewhat circularly, as follows: '"Decisive" (or "déterminante") in this context means more than "probative". It further means more than that, without the evidence, the chances of a conviction would recede and the chances of an acquittal advance, a test which, as the Court of Appeal in *Horncastle and others* pointed out [...], would mean that virtually all evidence would qualify. Instead, the word "decisive" should be narrowly understood as indicating evidence of such significance or importance as is likely to be determinative of the outcome of the case.' ECtHR (GC), 15 December 2011, App. No.: 26766/05 and 22228/06, (*Al-Khawaya and Tahery v. United Kingdom*), para 131.

69 ECtHR (GC), 15 December 2011, App. No.: 26766/05 and 22228/06, (*Al-Khawaya and Tahery v. United Kingdom*), para 147.

70 ECtHR (GC), 15 December 2011, App. No.: 26766/05 and 22228/06, (*Al-Khawaya and Tahery v. United Kingdom*), para 147 (emphasis added). In a later case the Court (the fourth section) held: 'As the Grand Chamber indicated in *Al-Khawaya and Tahery*, the problems posed by absent witnesses, at issue in that case, and anonymous witnesses, as in the present case, were not different in principle. The underlying principle is that the defendant in a criminal trial should have an effective opportunity to challenge the evidence against him. That principle requires not merely that a defendant should know the identity of his accusers so that he is in a position to challenge their probity and credibility but that he should be able to test the truthfulness and reliability of their evidence, by having them orally examined in his presence' ECtHR, 10 April 2012, App. No.: 46099/06 and 46699/06, (*Ellis, Simms and Martin v. United Kingdom*), para 74.

2.4.4 Reasoned Judgment

The fourth and final aspect of Jackson and Summer's participatory model of proof concerns the right to a reasoned judgment that can be challenged. The authors did not elaborate extensively on this aspect and presented it almost as a given: every criminal trial should, in order to be fair, result in a reasoned judgment. On the face of it, jury trials cannot comply with this standard, but, as the Court has held, as long as the reasons for the verdict can be distilled from the proceedings as such (such as the summing-up of the judge before the jurors go into deliberation), the right to a reasoned judgment is respected. There is, however, a bit more to say on this aspect in particular with regard to the right to challenge the reasoned judgment.

The right to a reasoned judgment is part of the right to a fair hearing, protected under Article 6(1).[71] Although this does not entail that the domestic court must provide answers to every single argument the parties have raised during the proceedings, the court must address the essential issues of the case.[72] The Court has noted that, in order to guarantee a fair trial and to avoid arbitrariness, the accused and the public must be able to understand the verdict.[73] The right to a reasoned judgment is the logical final aspect of the participatory model of proof: the court has to account for its decisions and, in doing so, enable the accused to verify whether his arguments have been duly considered by the court.[74]

[71] ECtHR, 19 April 1994, App. No.: 16034/90, (*Van de Hurk v. The Netherlands*), para 61; ECtHR, 9 December 1994, App. No.: 18390/91, (*Ruiz Torija v. Spain*), para 29. The right to a reasoned judgment does not require the domestic court to provide a detailed answer to every argument raised during the proceedings. The nature of the decision determines the required detail of the reasoning. The Court's Grand Chamber held: 'The Court reiterates that Article 6 § 1 of the Convention obliges courts to give reasons for their decisions, but cannot be understood as requiring a detailed answer to every argument. The extent to which this duty applies may vary according to the nature of the decision. It is moreover necessary to take into account, *inter alia*, the diversity of the submissions that a litigant may bring before the courts and the differences existing in the Contracting States with regard to statutory provisions, customary rules, legal opinion and the presentation and drafting of judgments. That is why the question whether a court has failed to fulfil the obligation to state reasons, deriving from Article 6 § 1, can only be determined in the light of the circumstances of the case.' ECtHR (GC), 20 March 2009, App. No.: 12686/03, (*Gorou v. Greece (No. 2)*, para 37. The nature of an appeal decision, dismissing the appeal by the accused may result in simply confirming the reasons stated in the lower court's judgment. ECtHR, 27 September 2007, App. No.: 6301/05, (*The Estate of Nitschke v. Sweden*), para 39.

[72] ECtHR, 15 February 2007, App. No.: 19997/02, (*Boldea v. Romania*), para 30.

[73] ECtHR (GC), 16 November 2010, App. No.: 926/05, (*Taxquet v. Belgium*), para 90.

[74] 'The Court emphasises that a further function of a reasoned decision is to demonstrate to the parties that they have been heard.' ECtHR, 1 July 2003, App. No.: 37801/97, (*Suominen v. Finland*), para 37.

The right to a reasoned judgment is often linked to the right to a remedy, such as the possibility of initiating appeal proceedings: in order to estimate any chances on appeal, the accused must know the reasons for the verdict of the first-instance court.[75] It is obvious that any effective appeal procedure requires a reasoned judgment by the first-instance court. It is, however, a different question whether the right to a reasoned judgment should be linked automatically with the right to challenge that judgment or even whether the accused has a right to challenge the judgment at all. The right to appeal is, as such, not absolute. Article 2 of the 7th Protocol to the ECHR states that convicted persons have the right to appeal their conviction or sentence, but subject to the following exceptions.[76] No right of appeal exists in relation to offences of a minor character. Similarly, no appeal has to be provided for convictions handed down in first instance by the highest tribunal, nor for convictions on appeal after an acquittal in the first-instance proceedings.[77] Besides the guarantees in the Additional Protocol, no general right to appeal can be derived from the Convention itself. The Court has held that neither Article 6 nor Article 13 obliges member States to provide for appeals in criminal cases.[78] Under the ICCPR, however, a general right to appeal does exist. Article 14(5) of the ICCPR holds that everyone convicted shall have the right to have his conviction and sentence reviewed by a higher tribunal.[79] This does not preclude leave to appeal proceedings, as long as these procedures provide, rather contradictorily, for a full and substantial review of the conviction and sentence.[80]

---

[75] Cf. ECtHR, 22 February 2007, App. No.: 1509/02, (*Tatishvili v. Russia*), para 58.

[76] The Netherlands has not ratified this Protocol.

[77] In the case of abbreviated proceedings, the right to appeal may be waived. Cf. ECtHR, 29 April 2014, App. No.: 9043/05, (*Natsvlishvili and Togonidze v. Georgia*), para 90–98.

[78] ECtHR, 22 February 2011, App. No.: 26036/08, (*Lalmahomed v. The Netherlands*), para 34; ECtHR, 9 June 2011, App. No.: 16347/02, (*Luchaninova v. Ukraine*), para 37 (with reference to case law).

[79] The right of appeal is not limited to the serious offences, according to the Human Rights Committee. 'As the different language versions (crime, infraction, delito) show, the guarantee is not confined to the most serious offences. The expression "according to law" in this provision is not intended to leave the very existence of the right of review to the discretion of the States parties, since this right is recognized by the Covenant, and not merely by domestic law.' Human Rights Committee, *General Comment No. 32*, UN Doc. CCPR/C/GC/32 (2007), para VII. The Dutch Minister of Justice observed during the parliamentary debates on the new system of appellate review, that minor offences may be excluded from appellate review.

Kamerstukken II, 2005/06, 30320, 3, p 17. The Netherlands has not made a reservation to Article 14(5) regarding the nature of the offence.

[80] HRC, 30 April 1999, Communication No 662/1995, U.N. Doc. CCPR/C/65/D/662/1995, (*Lumley v. Jamaica*), para 7.3; HRC, 24 August 2010, Communication No. 1797/2008, U.N. Doc. CCPR/C/99/D/1797/2008 (2010), (*Mennen v. The Netherlands*), para 8.3; HRC, 3 April 2002, Communication No. 802/1998, U.N. Doc. CCPR/C/74/D/802/1998 (2002), (*Rogerson v. Australia*), para 7.5.

Despite the close relationship between the right to a reasoned judgment and the possibility to challenge the judgment, it is argued that a reasoned judgment is an important element of the concept of fairness in criminal proceedings. Especially when no remedy is available, it is essential to provide the accused with a reasoned judgment.

2.5 Diversions and the Concept of Fairness

The normative framework of participation rights described above applies without more to proceedings conducted before a court: any shortcut to proof cannot evade the test of fairness. The question remains, however, how the participatory model of proof relates to diversions: on the face of it, it is not obvious that this model applies to diversions that strive to avoid the context of the full criminal trial as such.[81]

From the perspective of Article 6 itself, the protection of the Article is triggered by the notion of the 'criminal charge': the moment someone is charged, the rights under Article 6 have to be respected. In its well-known case law, the Court has stated that its autonomous interpretation of 'criminal charge' consists of three components: the classification of the offence under domestic law, the essential nature of the offence and the nature and degree of the penalty imposed.[82] More specifically, the Court held that 'charge' should be understood as 'the official notification given to an individual by the competent authority of an allegation that he has committed a criminal offence'.[83] Besides such a notification, the Court also held that, when the situation of the suspect is 'substantially affected', the provisions of Article 6 come into play.[84] It follows that, regard being had to any prose-

[81] Diversion mechanisms are used in most ECHR member states. This entails that criminal law is to a significant degree enforced outside the classical court setting. The case law of the ECtHR on Article 6 with the typical court setting in mind, does not fully capture the enforcement of criminal law in member states. See also Turner, who favours more judicial involvement in plea agreement procedures. Turner 2006, pp. 501–570. See also Peters 2012.

[82] ECtHR, 8 June 1976, App. No.: 5100/71; 5101/71; 5102/71; 5354/72 and 5370/72 (*Engel and Others v. The Netherlands*), para 82. The criteria are not cumulative. When a State Party has labelled an offence as criminal, the guarantees of Article 6 apply without more. ECtHR (GC), 9 October 2003, App. No.: 39665/98 and 40086/98, (*Ezeh and Connors v. United Kingdom*), para 86.

[83] ECtHR, 27 February 1980, App. No.: 6903/75, (*Deweer v. Belgium*), para 46.

[84] Such was the case in *Deweer*, where the applicant was faced with an offer for friendly settlement by the Belgian public prosecutor for violations of economic regulations. If he would refuse, a closure order for the applicant's shop would come into force. ECtHR, 27 February 1980, App. No.: 6903/75, (*Deweer v. Belgium*). See also, ECtHR, 15 July 1982, App. No.: 8130/78, (*Eckle v. Germany*), para 73; ECtHR, 10 December 1982, App. No.: 7604/76; 7719/76; 7781/77 and 7913/77, (*Foti and Others v. Italy*), para 52.

cutor's competence *ratione materiae*, a notification sent by a prosecutor is based on the assumption that the person concerned has committed a particular criminal offence.

It is against the object and purpose of the protections of the Convention to regard fairness as a principle that should be respected solely during trial proceedings conducted before a judge. It is unacceptable to have diversions operate in a normative vacuum: this would allow States to circumvent fairness considerations by simply using diversion mechanisms on a massive scale. As the Court noted, the use of such mechanisms by decriminalizing petty offences cannot result in the exclusion of the principle of fairness.[85] This does not mean, however, that all guarantees of Article 6 are applicable to diversions: on the contrary, such mechanisms were put in place to avoid public hearings by an independent and impartial tribunal, which is one of the essential rights of Article 6(1). The accused can waive certain fair trial guarantees, provided he has been able to participate effectively in the diversion proceedings. This relates to the principle of *nulla poena sine iudicio* that was discussed in the Introduction. This principle can be interpreted strictly ('no sanction without a judicial order'), or more leniently: every sanction should be eligible for judicial review. The last reading of the principle corresponds with the participatory model described above and the Court's stance on the content of this right. The moment someone is notified of a criminal charge, he is entitled to the guarantees of Article 6. However, he can choose to waive certain rights under this Article, notably the right to be tried by an independent and impartial tribunal; in other words, the accused can choose to divert from full criminal proceedings and reach some sort of extra-judicial (not: extra-legal) settlement with the prosecutor.[86] In fact, after the prosecutor has offered the accused the chance to opt for a diversion mechanism it is imperative that the accused makes his choice in full cognizance of his position and the consequences of his choice.[87]

The Court has held that, for a bargain to be valid under the Convention, the following requirements must be met. First, the accused must be fully aware of the facts of the case (arguably, this includes the evidence against him) and the legal

---

[85] ECtHR, 21 February 1984, App. No.: 8544/79, (Öztürk v. Germany), para 49.

[86] In a similar vein, the Court held: 'Where a penalty is criminal in nature there must be the possibility of review by a court which satisfies the requirements of Article 6 § 1, even though it is not inconsistent with the Convention for the prosecution and punishment of minor offences to be primarily a matter for the administrative authorities.' ECtHR, 4 April 2013, App. No.: 21565/07; 21572/07; 21575/07 and 21580/07, (*Julius Kloiber Schlachthof GmbH and Others v. Austria*), para 28.

[87] The initiative to opt for a diversion mechanism lies normally with the prosecutor. The rather exotic possibility of 'submission' (Article 74a CC) will not be discussed here. Submission entails that someone offers to pay the maximum fine for an offence that is punishable only by a fine. The prosecutor can, in such cases, not refuse the offer of the person involved.

consequences of striking a bargain (most importantly, waiving the right to have the case fully determined before an independent and impartial tribunal). Second, the acceptance of such a bargain must be 'genuinely voluntary'.[88] Moreover, the Court held that 'the content of the bargain and the *fairness of the manner in which it had been reached between the parties* had to be subjected to sufficient judicial review.'[89] This means that the parties, when operating in the shadow of full trial proceedings, should make sure fairness is respected during the negotiations. Considering the different legal and institutional positions of the parties, this requirement is primarily directed to the prosecutor. The observation by the Court entails that not only is the concept of fairness applicable to diversions, but also that any issue regarding fairness should be capable of judicial review. In other words, whether the accused entered voluntarily and informed into an agreement and whether a sufficient factual basis existed for the agreement does not suffice: the manner in which the agreement was reached should also be part of the judicial review.

The notion that fairness applies to diversions is not only to be derived from the perspective of the Convention itself. From a rule of law perspective, it would be unthinkable that public authorities could operate outside any normative framework, especially when their actions result in (minor) penalties or limitations on the accused's freedom.[90] The principle of legality makes it explicit that public authorities may exercise their powers only within the realm of the law: regarding the Dutch context, both the Dutch Constitution and the Code of Criminal Procedure stipulate that criminal proceedings must be based on the law. The prosecutor can exercise his powers only when he is convinced that a criminal offence has been committed: to do otherwise would result in abuse of power. In order to effectively protect the accused from such abuse, the prosecutor must comply with certain norms when he opts for a diversion mechanism. Especially in the case of the transaction and the conditional dismissal, a solid normative framework is required: neither the Criminal Code nor the Code of Criminal Procedure provide a detailed framework of procedural guarantees for the accused. The punitive order, in contrast, is embedded in the Code of Criminal Procedure and has been categorized as a modality of prosecution.[91] This categorization entails that the punitive order has to be regarded as a criminal charge, which results in the applicability of the guarantees of Article 6.

In case of the transaction and the conditional dismissal, the protection stems from the fact that the prosecutor can offer a transaction or conditional dismissal

---

[88] ECtHR, 29 April 2014, App. No.: 9043/05, (*Natsvlishvili and Togonidze v. Georgia*), para 92.

[89] ECtHR, 29 April 2014, App. No.: 9043/05, (*Natsvlishvili and Togonidze v. Georgia*), para 92. Emphasis added.

[90] Hildebrandt argued that fair trial considerations should function as normative guidelines for diversion mechanisms. Hildebrandt 2002, p. 388.

[91] The specific paragraph in the CCP in which the provisions on the punitive order are placed is called 'prosecution by way of a punitive order' ('vervolging door een strafbeschikking').

only when he is convinced that the person concerned has committed a criminal offence.[92] The first *Engel* criterion requires that the guarantees of Article 6 are applicable if an offence is classified as criminal by domestic law. Offering a transaction or conditional dismissal may then be regarded as 'the official notification given to an individual by the competent authority of an allegation that he has committed a criminal offence.'[93] The question then arises whether the person involved has validly waived his right to an independent and impartial tribunal. The procedural guarantees of Article 6 are, aside from the guarantees that the person involved explicitly or implicitly waived, fully applicable to these mechanisms.

Commenting on the notion of fairness in relation to the work of international prosecutors, Mégret observed that fairness is a 'crucial quality' of the international prosecutor.[94]

The *Standards of Professional Conduct for Prosecution Counsel* of both the ICTY and ICTR stipulate that prosecution counsel is expected:

> to respect, protect and uphold the universal concepts of human dignity and human rights […].[95]

Referring to a decision by the ICTR Appeals Chamber, Côté observed that the duty for the prosecutor to act fairly extends to all stages of the proceedings.[96] However, negotiations preceding a plea agreement between the prosecutor and the accused can hardly be called a 'stage of the proceedings'. Stages of proceedings commonly refer to, the pre-trial, trial and appeal stages. Although not acting in a proper stage of the proceedings, the normative appeal on the prosecutor to abide by the notion of fairness when opting for a diversion mechanism does not diminish. On the contrary, one could argue that, devoid of any direct judicial supervision, the prosecutor must ensure, as an authority with public power, that the basic notions of fairness are respected. The fact that prosecutors should be able to

---

92 Cf. Reijntjes 2010, aant. 17.2 and aant. 18.6. See also for the *Berufsethos* of the prosecutor: De Doelder and De Meijer 2013, pp. 127–143. See also Den Hartog, who argued that Article 6 guarantees are applicable to transaction proceedings. The first *Engel* criterion applies in such cases. Den Hartog 1992, p. 252.

93 ECtHR, 27 February 1980, App. No.: 6903/75, (*Deweer v. Belgium*), para 46.

94 Reydams et al. 2012, p. 437. See also the Chapter 'Independence and Impartiality' by Côté in the same volume, at p. 363.

95 Article 2(f) Standards of Professional Conduct for Prosecution Counsel, *ICTY Prosecutor's Regulation No. 2* (1999). Article 1.7 of the draft Code of Professional Conduct for Prosecutors of the International Criminal Court contains a similar provision. The draft was prepared by the International Association of Prosecutors and the Coalition of the International Criminal Court. The Regulations of the Office of the Prosecutor, as currently in force, do not contain a similar provision. Noteworthy, however, is Regulation 62 (1), concerning admissions of guilt (a diversion mechanism). The relevant part of the Regulation reads: 'The Office shall make its own assessment of any admission of guilt by an accused […]. The Office shall bring to the attention of the Trial Chamber any credible information or evidence indicating that the admission of guilt was not informed, voluntary or supported by the facts pleaded.'

96 Reydams et al. 2012, p. 364.

exercise their duties independently and impartially and that they should function autonomously *vis-à-vis* the executive or the judiciary comes at a price: it is precisely because the prosecutor acts independently and impartially, that he must also act fairly.[97]

Fairness should permeate the (international) prosecutor's decisions and, he should have an eye for any exonerating evidence he comes across. Acting in a fair manner is regarded here as a desirable professional attitude of the prosecutor, which underlines the importance and applicability of fair trial notions regarding diversion mechanisms.[98] This means that acting in a fair manner is not confined to the trial stage: in the exercise of any public power, the notion of fairness should be respected. To refrain from conducting trial proceedings, either with or without the informed consent of the accused, means that no independent and impartial tribunal will hear the case. It does not, however, result in the non-applicability of fairness as such: the forum in which the prosecutor operates differs, but the level of fairness should not.

In international criminal proceedings the diversion mechanisms are rather uniform, as discussed in more detail in Chap. 4. The plea agreement procedure before the *ad hoc* Tribunals and the admission of guilt procedure before the ICC both allow for a negotiation process.[99] The validity of the reached agreement is determined by the court, which decides eventually whether or not to accept the agreement.[100] The judicial supervision of such agreements aims to ensure that they are reached in a fair way.

2.6 Conclusion

The participatory model presented above provides the normative framework to evaluate the diversions and shortcuts to proof that are described in Chaps. 3 and 4.

Regarding diversions, the participatory model provides a useful framework to evaluate such mechanisms in the light of the Court's case law. Although the Court

---

[97] On the notions of independence and impartiality regarding international prosecutors, see: Reydams et al. 2012, pp. 319–415.

[98] Cf. the observations made by Cleiren, who argued that principles of due process apply to every agent of the State in the exercise of any public power attributed to him. She argued that such principles do not only apply within a formal trial setting. Cleiren 1989, p. 263. De Meester argued that fair trial standards are not only applicable to proper trial proceedings, but are also applicable to pre-trial investigations: '[…] it (the right to a fair trial, KV) cannot be doubted that it applies to all stages of criminal proceedings, including investigations.' De Meester 2014, p. 67.

[99] ICC judges have to take into account the interest of victims when deciding on the admission of guilt [Article 65(4)]. A similar provision is absent in the RPE of the *ad hoc* Tribunals.

[100] Rule 62bis ICTY RPE; Rule 62 ICTR RPE; Article 65 ICC Statute. Interesting in this regard is the obligation for the Prosecutor at the ICC to verify *proprio motu* whether the admission of guilt is voluntary and informed, and whether the admission is supported by the facts pleaded. Regulation 62 ICC Regulations for the Office of the Prosecutor, ICC-BD/05-01-09.

has, for obvious reasons, not been able to produce extensive case law on diversions, a useful framework can be distilled from the Court's case law. The main question is to what extent the accused has been able to participate effectively in the out of court proceedings. The four different elements that Jackson and Summers identified in the Court's case law are regarded as guidelines here: compliance with every element is not necessary. Rather, the evaluation will focus on whether the accused has been able to participate effectively, where the possibility of challenging the evidence is of primary importance.

References

Abels D (2012) Prisoners of the international community. T.M.C. Asser Press, The Hague

Cleiren CPM (1989) Beginselen van een goede procesorde. Gouda Quint, Arnhem

De Doelder H, De Meijer ME (2013) Het Openbaar Ministerie als magistraat. In: Muller ER, Cleiren, CPM (eds) Rechterlijke Macht. Rechtspraak en rechtshandhaving in Nederland, 2nd edn. Kluwer, Deventer, pp 127–143

De Meester KFG (2014) The investigation phase in international criminal procedure: in search of common rules. PhD-thesis, University of Amsterdam

Dennis I (2010) The right to confront witnesses: meanings, myths and human rights. Crim Law Rev 4:255–274

Den Hartog A (1992) Artikel 6 EVRM: grenzen aan het streven de straf eerder op de daad te doen volgen. Maklu Uitgevers, Antwerpen

Duff A, Farmer L, Marshall S, Tadros V (eds) (2007) The trial on trial vol. 3: towards a normative theory of the criminal trial. Hart Publishing, Oxford

Dworkin R (1978) Taking rights seriously. Harvard University Press, Cambridge

Fedorova M (2012) The principle of equality of arms in international criminal proceedings. Intersentia, Cambridge

Goss R (2014) Criminal fair trial rights: article 6 of the european convention on human rights. Hart Publishing, Oxford

Gradoni L (2009) The human rights dimension of international criminal procedure. In: Sluiter GK, Vasiliev SV (eds) International criminal procedure: towards a coherent body of law. Cameron May Publishing, London, pp 74–94

Jackson JD (2005) The effect of human rights on criminal evidentiary processes: towards convergence, divergence or realignment? Mod Law Rev 68:737–764

Jackson JD (2009) Autonomy and accuracy in the development of fair trial rights. In: UCD working papers in law, criminology & socio-legal studies, research paper no. 09/2009, University College Dublin

Jackson JD, Summers SJ (2012) The internationalisation of criminal evidence: beyond the common law and civil law traditions. Cambridge University Press, Cambridge

Jackson JD, Summers SJ (2013) Confrontation with Strasbourg: UK and Swiss approaches to criminal evidence. Crim Law Rev 60(2):115–131

Hildebrandt M (2002) Straf(begrip) en procesbeginsel: een onderzoek naar de betekenis van straf en strafbegrip en de waarde van het procesbeginsel naar aanleiding van de consensuale afdoening van strafzaken. Kluwer, Deventer

Loucaides LG (2003) Questions of fair trial under the European convention on human rights. Hum Rights Law Rev 3:27–51

Perry S (1997) Two models of legal principles. Iowa Law Rev 82:787–819

Peters AAG (1972) Het rechtskarakter van het strafrecht. In: Buruma Y (ed) (1999) 100 Jaar strafrecht. Klassieke teksten van de twintigste eeuw. Amsterdam University Press, Amsterdam, pp 271–287

Peters AAG (1975) Individuele vrijheid en de positie van verdachten in het strafproces. In: Gunning M. et al (eds) (1993) Recht als kritische discussie: een selectie uit het werk van A.A.G. Peters. Gouda Quint, Arnhem, pp 79–106
Peters LJJ (2012) Vonnisafspraken in strafzaken. Een rechtsvergelijkende studie naar een vorm van onderhandelingsjustitie in Italië, Duitsland en Frankrijk. Wolf Legal Publishers, Nijmegen
Rainey B, Wicks E, Ovey C (2014) Jacobs, White & Ovey: the European convention on human rights. Oxford University Press, Oxford
Rawls J (1999) A theory of justice, rev edn. Oxford University Press, Oxford
Redmayne M (2013) Confronting confrontation. In: Roberts P, Hunter J (eds) Criminal evidence and human rights: reimagining common law procedural traditions. Hart Publishing, Oxford, pp 283–307
Reijntjes JM (2010) Art. 167 Sv. In: Melai/Groenhuijsen e.a., Wetboek van Strafvordering
Reydams L, Wouters J, Ryngaert C (eds) (2012) International prosecutors. Oxford University Press, Oxford
Roberts P, Hunter J (eds) (2013) Criminal evidence and human rights: reimagining common law procedural traditions. Hart Publishing, Oxford
Roth R, Tulkens F (2011) The influence of the european court of human rights' case law on (international) criminal law, introduction. J Int Crim Justice 9:571–575
Sluiter GK et al (eds) (2013) International criminal procedure: principles and rules. Oxford University Press, Oxford
Solum LB (2004) Procedural justice. South Californian Law Rev 78:181–321
Stuntz WJ (1989) Waiving rights in criminal procedure. Va Law Rev 75(4):769–842
Trechsel S (1997) Why must trials be fair? Isr Law Rev 31:94–119
Trechsel S (2006) Human rights in criminal proceedings. Oxford University Press, Oxford
Turner JI (2006) Judicial participation in plea negotiations: a comparative view. Am J Comp Law 54:501–570
Vasiliev SV (2009) General rules and principles of international criminal procedure: definition, legal nature and identification. In: Sluiter GK, Vasiliev SV (eds) International criminal procedure: towards a coherent body of law. Cameron May Publishing, London, pp 19–89
Vasiliev SV (2014) International criminal trials: a normative theory. University of Amsterdam, PhD-thesis
Weigend T (2006) Why have a trial when you can have a bargain? In: Duff A, Farmer L, Marshall S, Tadros V (eds) The trial on trial vol. 2: judgment and calling to account. Hart Publishing, Oxford, pp 207–222

Chapter 3
Diversions and Shortcuts in Dutch Law of Criminal Procedure

Abstract In this chapter diversions and shortcuts to proof in the Dutch criminal justice system are discussed. First, the concept of a full criminal trial within the Dutch criminal justice system is explained. Three diversions are discussed: the punitive order, the transaction, and the conditional dismissal the characteristics of each diversion is discussed, as well as the procedural safeguards that exist in respect to each diversion. Finally, five shortcuts to proof are discussed in the context of the Dutch criminal justice system: facts of common knowledge, chain evidence, confessions, cases ad informandum, and appeal proceedings.

Keywords Diversions · Shortcuts to proof · Dutch criminal justice system · Punitive order · Transaction · Conditional dismissal · Facts of common knowledge · Chain evidence · Confessions · Cases ad informandum · Appeal proceedings

Contents

K. Vriend, *Avoiding a Full Criminal Trial*, International Criminal Justice Series 8, DOI 10.1007/978-94-6265-153-1_3

3.1 Introduction

In order to understand the manner in which full criminal proceedings are avoided, it is essential to discuss first the main characteristics of the criminal trial in the Dutch criminal justice system. The Criminal Code and the Code of Criminal Procedure are based on the notion that a sentence can be imposed only after trial proceedings have been conducted before the court: this is the *nulla poena sine iudicio* principle.[1] In the past decades, however, this principle has eroded: out of court settlements, such as the transaction and conditional dismissal, have been used to enhance the efficiency of the criminal justice system. The introduction of the punitive order in 2008 was a milestone in the search for even more efficiency in the criminal justice system.

Efficiency considerations are, as such, legitimate: a criminal justice system in which criminal cases are processed in a swift and just manner is of general interest. However, it is at least equally important to ensure that criminal proceedings (including diversion mechanisms) do not infringe upon the rights of the accused. As the Minister of Security and Justice stated in the context of the upcoming revision of the Code of Criminal Procedure, the law of criminal procedure must also protect the accused from undue interference in his personal life. This applies in particular when criminal proceedings are shortened.[2]According to the Minister, however, a differentiation between cases concerning minor offences and serious offences is necessary. The latter category has to be handled by the courts, but minor offences can be handled by the prosecutor without judicial involvement.[3]

Before the diversions and shortcuts are discussed, the main characteristics of the full criminal trial will be analysed: one has to know what is avoided in the first place. This is also done in order to place the diversions and shortcuts in the proper context. Avoiding the full criminal trial has to be accounted for, especially from the point of view of the fair trial rights of the accused.

There are several ways of describing how a full criminal trial is conducted in a particular system. One way is to look at the role of the different actors in the criminal proceedings. Such an analysis focuses on the legal position of the different actors and the relationship between them. In the following pages, another perspective is chosen. In Chap. 2, the participatory model of proof was discussed and presented as the normative framework for the diversions and shortcuts in Dutch and international criminal procedure. The model emphasizes the importance

---

[1] Nijboer 1987, p. 98. One could also refer to the principle of *nulla poena sine processu*: only after proceedings have been conducted can a sentence be imposed. The *nulla poena sine iudicio* principle, however, is more appropriate because it refers to the actor that imposes the sentence: the judge.

[2] Ministry of Security and Justice, 'Kamerbrief over modernisering Wetboek van Strafvordering', 30 September 2015, p. 7.

[3] Ministry of Security and Justice, 'Kamerbrief over modernisering Wetboek van Strafvordering', 30 September 2015, p. 7.

of participatory rights regarding evidence; in other words, it seeks to answer the question: has the accused been able to participate effectively during the proceedings? In the following pages, the full criminal trial will be presented with a focus on the law of evidence. Three aspects will be discussed: the admissibility of evidence, the weighing of evidence and the obligation to provide a reasoned judgment. These aspects allow for a comparative approach: they provide a framework which can be used to analyse any particular system of criminal law. In this framework, three basic questions are of primary importance: what is the evidentiary input (the rules of admissibility), how is the input weighed and how does the court have to account for the conclusions it draws?

The concept of admissibility of evidence refers to the question of which evidence the court may use for the determination of the guilt or innocence of the accused. Rules of admissibility are prominent in systems that consist of a bifurcated court, where the fact-finder can be effectively shielded from unreliable, prejudicial or illegally obtained evidence. Bifurcated courts are courts in which the fact-finder does not rule on the admissibility of evidence but solely on the assessment or weighing of the admitted evidence (such as the typical common law judge-jury setting). In unitary courts, the court decides on both the admissibility of evidence and the weight that should be attached to the evidence.[4] Although one can safely state that bifurcated courts are characteristic of common law criminal proceedings concerning serious crimes, it would be wrong to equate unitary courts with civil law proceedings. French and Belgium criminal proceedings concerning serious crimes, for example, are held before a *court d'assizes*, which resembles a judge-jury setting. Dutch and German criminal proceedings are conducted before unitary courts: the court decides on the admissibility and evaluation of the evidence.[5]

Weighing the evidence refers to the question of how the court determines the probative value of evidence that has been presented. Particularly relevant in this regard is whether the court is in any way restricted by statutory rules on the weight of the evidence. Since the time of the French Revolution, the idea that the

---

[4] Damaška 1992, pp. 426–427.

[5] It is noted that unitary courts are not necessarily composed of professional judges: the German *Schwurgericht*, which hears homicide cases, consists of both professional and lay judges. Volk observed on the distinction between lay and professional judges: 'Die Schöffen üben als ehrenamtliche Richter "das Richteramt in vollem Umfang und mit gleichem Stimmrecht" aus wie die Berufsrichter (§§ 30, 70 Abs. 1 GVG). Sie entscheiden über die Schuld- und Straffrage gemeinschaftlich und Tatfragen ebenso wie Rechtsfragen. Bei entscheidungen ausserhalb der Verhandlung wirken sie aber nicht mit (§§ 30 Abs. 2, 76 Abs. 1 S. 2 GVG). Das Gericht hat es allerdings nicht in der Hand, ob innerhalb oder ausserhalb der Hauptverhandlung entschieden wird. Nur bei zwingenden Gründe darf ausnahmsweise ausserhalb der Hauptverhandlung entschieden werden. Die Schöffen sollen sich ihre Überzeugung allein auf Grund der Hauptverhandlung bilden und haben deshalb kein Recht, Einsicht in die Gerichtsakten zu nehmen. Das macht es sehr schwierig, der Hauptverhandlung zu folgen (weshalb der *BGH* allerdings Ausnahmen zulässt).' Volk 2010, p. 12, 14.

legislator is able to determine *ex ante* the probative value of various types of evidence (e.g. witness statements, confessions or real evidence) and their cumulative weight (e.g. three witness statements result in conclusive evidence; a confession is regarded as *regina probationis* and, therefore, conclusive evidence) has been gradually abandoned.[6] Stein argued that the last two centuries have been characterized by what he called an 'abolitionist wave': the tendency to abolish as many rules of evidence as possible.[7] That is to say: rules that conflict with, what Stein called, the epistemic confidence doctrine. During this process, rules of evidence that prescribe how fact-finders should evaluate the evidence are abolished, while rules on the exclusion of evidence on grounds extraneous to accurate fact-finding (e.g. exclusionary rules regarding illegally obtained evidence) are kept in place.[8] The decline in statutory rules of evidence favours a system of evidence law in which the available evidence is weighed freely by the court.

When the legislator provides no guidance on how to weigh the evidence, one could conclude that the system is best characterized as a system of free proof: the court is free to weigh the evidence as it wishes and is not obstructed by any statutory provision. This is misleading, though, because it could well be that the legislator has clearly regulated *which* evidence the court may take into account: the evidentiary output is not regulated in such a system, but the evidentiary input is. In other words, there is a notable difference between the free *admission* of evidence and the free *evaluation* of evidence.

The final element concerns the manner in which the court has to account for its factual findings: after deciding on the admissibility of the evidence, the court weighs the available evidence and decides whether it is convinced of the guilt of the accused. The result of the deliberations of the court have to be accounted for. The right to be provided with a reasoned judgment ensures that the court is, in fact, explaining how it has weighed the evidence presented.

3.1.1 Rules of Admissibility

Dutch law of evidence, as such, does not provide for rules of admissibility. The Code of Criminal Procedure contains the legal means of proof that the court may consider, namely the observation of the court during the proceedings, the statements of the accused, witnesses and experts and documentary evidence.[9] These legal means of proof stem from 1926, when the Code of Criminal Procedure was

---

6 Damaška 1995, pp. 343–344; Stein 2005, p. 108; Jackson and Summers 2012, pp. 20–21.

7 Cf. Jeremy Bentham (1748–1832) who favoured the abolition of exclusionary rules and rules on weighing the evidence. Rupert Cross (1912–1980) is believed to have stated that he worked for the day his subject is abolished. Twining 1990, p. 1 and 39.

8 Stein 2005, pp. 112–113.

9 Article 339 CCP.

adopted. The fact that the legal means of proof have never been amended shows their flexibility. In fact, every piece of information can be categorized as a legal means of proof. This means that no category of evidence is inadmissible *ex ante*: the legislator gives the court considerable freedom to determine which evidence it takes into consideration. The fact that no category of evidence is inadmissible must not be misunderstood: it refers solely to the kind of evidence. Evidence can be inadmissible due to the manner in which it was obtained; for example, a statement of the accused that was obtained under torture will be inadmissible evidence.[10]

The exclusion of evidence in criminal proceedings shields the court from unreliable, prejudicial or illegally obtained evidence. It stands to reason that the doctrine of exclusionary rules (or, rules of non-admissibility) has been developed primarily in systems with a bifurcated court system.[11] In such systems, rules of exclusion can function in *optima forma*: the judge determines whether certain evidence is admissible in the absence of the fact-finder (i.e. the jury). This way, the fact-finder is effectively shielded from non-admissible evidence. The definition of exclusionary rules given by Roberts and Zuckerman is worth quoting here, because their definition encompasses both exclusionary rules aiming at the enhancement of accurate fact-finding and rules aiming at other objectives:

> Exclusionary rules of evidence might be conceptualized as evidentiary standards purporting to encapsulate – or at least serve as durable proxies for – good epistemic or normative reasons for ignoring relevant information in criminal adjudication.[12]

Damaška divided these rules into two categories, intrinsic and extrinsic exclusionary rules. Both types will be discussed briefly.

3.1.1.1 Intrinsic Exclusionary Rules

Intrinsic exclusionary rules are described as rules that exclude evidence in order to 'enhance the accuracy of fact-finding'.[13] Intrinsic exclusionary rules are meant to shield the fact-finder from unreliable or prejudicial evidence.[14] The common law rule against hearsay is an example of an intrinsic exclusionary rule: the risk that the (lay) fact-finder will overestimate the hearsay evidence justifies its exclusion.[15] Such rules, then, oblige the judge (who can be characterized as an evidentiary

---

[10] For other examples, see HR 19 February 2013, *ECLI*:NL: HR:2013:BY5321.

[11] Damaška 1997, p. 12; Stein 2005, pp. 117–118.

[12] Roberts and Zuckerman 2010, p. 98.

[13] Damaška 1997, p. 14.

[14] The exclusion of illegally obtained evidence is not primarily justified on the ground that exclusion enhances accurate fact-finding. On the contrary, illegally obtained evidence can be highly probative.

[15] Zuckerman 1992, p. 179; Tapper 2010, pp. 553–555.

gatekeeper in this regard) to exclude evidence that is easily misinterpreted by lay fact-finders or is notoriously unreliable. Intrinsic exclusionary rules are largely unknown in systems consisting of a unitary court, where the court rules on both the admissibility and the probative value of the evidence presented. Evidence regarded as antithetical to accurate fact-finding will, in unitary systems, not be excluded but be ignored by the court. When, for example, hearsay testimony is admissible in a criminal justice system but the court finds a particular witness statement unreliable it will not be excluded; instead, it will simply not be used in the determination of the guilt or innocence of the accused. If, in a particular unitary court system, hearsay testimony is not admissible as a *general rule of evidence* and is therefore excluded, the court is still aware of the contents of the hearsay testimony. In such a system the legislator has made an *ex ante* assessment of the probative value of hearsay evidence.

The Dutch Code of Criminal Procedure does not contain intrinsic exclusionary rules: the court has to decide itself whether the evidence presented is reliable.[16] When the court concludes that a particular piece of evidence is not reliable, the evidence will be ignored. Exclusion of evidence occurs when an extrinsic exclusionary rule applies, which will be discussed below. Although the legislator has not formulated intrinsic exclusionary rules, the Supreme Court has: a witness statement obtained under hypnosis has no probative value.[17] Such a statement cannot be used as evidence.

3.1.1.2 Extrinsic Exclusionary Rules

Extrinsic exclusionary rules as such do not exist in Dutch evidence law. Instead of a statutory rule, the court has discretionary power to exclude evidence. Evidence that has probative value may be excluded when such evidence is the result of procedural irregularities in the pre-trial phase. Such procedural irregularities must have had a substantial impact on an important principle of the law of criminal procedure.[18] The Supreme Court held that evidence obtained in violation of the *Salduz* criteria (regarding the assistance of a lawyer during police interrogations) must, in principle, be excluded.[19]

---

[16] Corstens and Borgers argued that composing the *dossier*, or case-file, is a dynamic process. Corstens and Borgers 2014, p. 250. During the pre-trial investigations the prosecutor is responsible for the composition of the case-file. The accused and the victim can request the prosecutor to include particular documents to the case-file. The investigating judge can add documents to the case file. During the trial phase, the court can order the presentation of documents or other evidence, which is included in the case-file. However, it is common practice that the case-file is, to significant extent, composed by the prosecutor.

[17] HR 17 March 1998, *NJ* 1998, 798, m.n.t Reijntjes, para 5.4.

[18] HR 19 February 2013, *ECLI*:NL:HR:2013:BY5321, para 2.4.2.

[19] HR 30 June 2009, *ECLI*:NL:HR:2009:BH3079.

To speak of the *exclusion* of evidence in Dutch criminal proceedings is somewhat misleading. Exclusion of evidence, or its non-admissibility, presupposes a bifurcated court system in which the person that decides on the admissibility of the evidence is not the same as the fact-finder that decides upon the probative value of the evidence. In the words of Damaška:

> Even when a party is successful in alleging a violation of an evidence rule, the exclusion of information obtained in judge-driven examination is an infrequent sanction in Continental courts. The demand to exclude probative information to which the fact-finder already has been exposed is criticized as conducive to undesirable, artificial decision-making [sic]. One cannot unbite the apple of knowledge: *factum infectum fieri nequit*'[20]

Although Dutch legal doctrine and case law speak consistently of the exclusion of evidence ('bewijsuitsluiting'),[21] the court, in fact, does not exclude the evidence from the proceedings but attaches a fixed probative value (namely, none) to that evidence.[22] This resembles what is called in German legal doctrine a *Beweisverwertungsverbot*: the court is precluded from taking the illegally obtained evidence into account in the judgment.[23] Illustrative is a judgment of the Supreme Court in which it held that statements made by defence counsel during the proceedings are not a legal means of proof. Therefore, they cannot be taken into account in the judgment.[24] In another case, the Supreme Court held that the reports of probation officers cannot be used as evidence, because the information contained in such reports is gathered in a relationship of trust between the accused and the probation officer. Such information may be used only to determine the appropriate sentence for the accused, but not as evidence against the accused.[25]

Melai argued that it is only human, and therefore inevitable, that judges will be influenced by evidence that they have excluded from the case file themselves.[26] He favoured the possibility for the accused to file a complaint in the pre-trial phase

---

[20] 'A thing done cannot be undone'. Damaška 1990, p. 96. Emphasis in original. Cf. Damaška 1992, p. 427.

[21] Article 359a CCP does not speak of 'bewijsuitsluiting' (exclusion of evidence), but the term was used during parliamentary debates. *Kamerstukken II*, 1993/94, 23705, 3, (MvT).

[22] Cf. Krikke 1983, p. 276.

[23] 'Die Beweisverwertungsverbote lassen es nicht zu, dass alle vorhandenen Informationen verarbeitet werden, zwingen den Richter also dazu, sein Wissen partiell auszublenden und hindern ihn so an einer umfassenden Beweiswürdigung.' Volk 2010, p. 260.

[24] HR 15 September 1980, *NJ* 1981, 13. This also applies to the written pleadings of defence counsel. HR 31 October 2010, *LJN*: AX9178, para 4.2.

[25] HR 18 September 2007, *NJ* 2008, 192, m.nt. YB, para 3.3. In another case, the probation officer was questioned by the court of appeal on the probation report. The probation officer did not invoke the right to remain silent (based on the professional privilege of Article 218 CCP). The Supreme Court held that statements of a probation officer during the proceedings may be used as evidence against the accused. HR 25 September 2012, *NJ* 2013/127, m.nt. T.M. Schalken, para 2.4 and 2.5.

[26] Melai 1975, p. 161; Cf. Cleiren, who spoke of 'dissociation' in this regard. Cleiren 2010, p. 267.

concerning illegally obtained evidence with a judge who is barred from hearing the case on the merits.[27] Such a procedure would enable the effective exclusion of tainted evidence. This would also enhance the adversarial character of the investigatory phase of criminal proceedings.[28] However, the Code of Criminal Procedure does not allow for such a division, and it is highly unlikely that this will change in the near future. Courts are required to leave out the excluded evidence from their deliberations.

3.1.1.3 The Principle of Immediacy

Rules of admissibility do not hold a prominent place in Dutch criminal law: the law of evidence favours the free admission of evidence, with some minor exceptions that were described above. The free admission of evidence does not mean that every piece of evidence is discussed extensively during the trial proceedings. The principle of immediacy (i.e., the notion that every piece of evidence has to be presented and discussed during the proceedings with a view to adversarial argument) does not apply unconditionally.[29] According to Article 338 CCP, the court may declare the charges proven only after the close of the trial proceedings in which the evidence was presented. The principle of immediacy resembles the common law 'best evidence rule', which entails that the court should be provided with the best evidence available (i.e. preferably primary sources).[30] The principle of immediacy in Dutch criminal proceedings has been restricted significantly by the famous *De auditu* judgment of the Supreme Court. In this judgment, the Supreme Court approved the use of (written) hearsay evidence. The importance of this judgment for the manner in which trial proceedings are conducted can hardly be overestimated: the courts are allowed to base their factual findings on derivative evidence. Moreover, the hearsay testimony is normally included in the case file in written form. An adversarial debate during trial proceedings, in which the live testimony of a witness is challenged by the defence is, therefore, rather exceptional. One can only agree with the statement by Pompe, who observed that the *De auditu* judgment was more important for the law of criminal procedure than the adoption of the CCP itself.[31] Over the last decades, however, the interpretation of the ECtHR regarding the right to examine witnesses in criminal proceedings has

---

[27] Melai 1975, p. 165; Melai 1992, p. 77.

[28] Cf. Peters 1972, pp. 17–18. Also: HR 7 December 1971 (de Marconist), m. nt. A.A.G. Peters. Cf. Embregts 2003, pp. 110–111.

[29] For a detailed analysis of the principle of immediacy in Dutch criminal proceedings, see: Garé 1994. The ECtHR held that 'all evidence must normally be produced in the presence of the accused at a public hearing with a view to adversarial argument'. ECtHR, 2 July 2002, App. No.: 34209/96, (*S.N. v. Sweden*), para 41.

[30] Cf. Stein 2005, p. 39.

[31] Pompe 1959, p. 15.

resulted in a renewed appreciation of the principle of immediacy.[32] The influence of the ECtHR's case law on the manner in which Dutch criminal proceedings should be conducted in order to be fair, will be analysed in Chap. 5.

The court is, apart from some minor exceptions, free to admit any evidence it deems relevant. Not every piece of evidence is discussed extensively during the trial proceedings. The question then arises how the court evaluates or weighs the evidence presented. The notion of free proof can be divided into the *admission* of evidence and the *weighing* of the evidence. The manner in which Dutch courts weigh the evidence is of utmost importance: when a court is allowed to include any relevant piece of evidence in its decision, the weighing of such evidence becomes more prominent. This is related to the fact that the Dutch rules of evidence are regarded as an example of a negative statutory system of evidence law. In such systems, the court is left considerable discretion in the weighing of the evidence presented. In a positive statutory system, the legislator has determined *ex ante* the probative value of certain categories of evidence. For example, two witness statements that corroborate each other are regarded as conclusive evidence. In such a system, one can easily predict the outcome of the proceedings: the court is under an obligation to convict the accused when two similar witness statements are available. It is therefore a moot question how the court weighs the evidence: it simply has to apply the rules of evidence. In a negative statutory system of evidence law, the court has discretion in weighing the evidence. The legislator has not attached a fixed probative value to particular means of proof, but leaves it to the court to decide whether the applicable standard of proof has been met. Such systems do not oblige the court to convict the accused when a certain quantity of evidence has been presented; rather, it is the quality of the evidence that counts, and this is for the court to determine. Such systems, however, may require the court to base a conviction on a minimum number of means of proof: the *nuda confessio* rule and the *unus testis, nullus testis* rule are prime examples. Both rules are codified in the Dutch Code of Criminal Procedure and are discussed in some more detail below.[33]

3.1.2 Weighing the Evidence

Dutch courts enjoy considerable freedom regarding the evaluation or weighing of the evidence. It is within the court's discretion to select and weigh the evidence presented.[34] Article 338 CCP states that the court may declare the charges proven

[32] Dubelaar 2015, Opm. 6.

[33] Article 341(4) CCP and Article 342(2) CCP.

[34] E.g. HR 21 September 1999, *LJN*:ZD5186. The fact that the court has discretion in this regard, should not be confused with arbitrariness: the court cannot *randomly* select and weigh the evidence. The court must account for its choices in the judgment: this is why a reasoned judgment is so important.

when it is convinced that the accused is, in fact, guilty as charged. This *conviction* or persuasion must be based on the legal means of proof that have been presented during the proceedings.[35] The freedom of the court to weigh the evidence is encapsulated in this notion of *conviction*[36]: on the basis of the legal means of proof that are discussed during the trial proceedings, the court must determine whether it is convinced that the accused is guilty. Cleiren described the personal belief of the judge as a *conditio sine qua non* for a conviction.[37] Although the judge has considerable freedom to weigh the evidence, two statutory restrictions should be mentioned.

First, it follows from Articles 338 and 339(1) CCP that the *conviction* may be based only on a limited number of means of proof that have been presented during the proceedings, namely the observation by the judge, statements made by the accused, witnesses and experts and documentary evidence.

Second, the law of criminal procedure contains evidentiary thresholds. In order to convict, a minimum quantity of evidence must have been presented to the court. A distinction can be made between explicit and implicit statutory thresholds. The court must acquit the accused when the evidence consists solely of the statement of the accused or of a single witness statement. The *nuda confessio*-rule and the *unus testis, nullus testis*-rule are explicit statutory rules. The same holds true for evidence that consists solely, or to a decisive extent, of statements made by anonymous witnesses. In such cases, the court is barred from convicting the accused.[38] Similarly, when the evidence consists solely of the statements of witnesses that have testified on the promise of a sentence reduction, the court cannot convict.[39] Finally, documentary evidence which cannot be brought under one of the categories of Article 344(1)(1) to (4) CCP may be used only when it is combined with other evidence: it is, as such, insufficient evidence to convict the accused and it must be corroborated by other evidence.[40]

Implicit statutory evidentiary thresholds require the court to base its factual findings on several independent sources; in order to convict, the court needs at least two means of proof.[41] The Code of Criminal Procedure does not explicitly preclude the court from convicting solely on the basis of the court's observations during proceedings, the sole statement of an expert or the categories of documentary evidence summed up in Article 344(1) to (4) CCP. However, the requirement that a conviction must be based on multiple sources is implied. The observation of the court is restricted to the observations *during the proceedings*. The sole

[35] Article 339(1) CCP contains the means of proof.

[36] A differentiation between *conviction intime* and *conviction raisonnée* will be made below.

[37] Cleiren 2010, p. 260.

[38] Article 341(4) CCP; Article 342(2) CCP; Article 344a CCP.

[39] Article 344a(4) CCP.

[40] Article 344(1)(5) CCP.

[41] Nijboer argued that corroboration is indeed a principle underlying the law of evidence. Nijboer 2011, p. 77.

statement of an expert cannot suffice either: experts are asked to give their opinion on a particular aspect of the case based on a certain expertise (e.g. forensic psychiatry, forensic statistics etc.). The aspects of the case upon which the expert testifies are never equal to the charges the accused is facing. Therefore, it is impossible to base a conviction on an expert statement alone. The same holds true for the categories of documentary evidence under Article 344 CCP because such documentary evidence can never cover the whole charge. The only exception to this rule is Article 344(2) CCP, which states that the court may convict on the basis of the written statement of an investigating officer. In practice, however, this rule applies only to cases concerning minor (mostly traffic) offences.[42]

Regarding the rules of weighing evidence, the multitude of evidentiary sources and (implicit) statutory restrictions, it is useful to discuss the principle of corroboration. Nijboer argued that this principle permeates the Dutch law of criminal evidence: charges can be proven only on the basis of a multitude of sources.[43] As Nijboer acknowledged, this does not mean that every aspect of the charges has to be corroborated or confirmed by two or more means of proof.[44]

It is important to be clear about the scope of the principle of corroboration. One could define corroborating evidence as means of proof that relate to the same *factum probandum*. Two witnesses that state they both saw an accused shoplifting, for example, is corroborative evidence relating to the same *factum probandum*: the accused took away certain goods. The statement of witness A is then confirmed or corroborated by the statement of witness B (provided that both witnesses testified independently from each other). Another definition of corroboration entails the following. Witness A testified that she saw the accused grabbing something from a shop, and witness B testified that he saw the accused running away from the same shop. Although such witness statements are often regarded as corroborating each other, they are not; instead they supplement, rather than corroborate each other.

The latter example is in fact what is meant by the phrase ‘a multitude of sources’. The court cannot convict on the basis of one witness statement, but when the statements of witnesses A and B are combined there is sufficient evidence to convict (provided that the witness statements are reliable). Dutch law of criminal procedure requires that the conviction of the accused is based on several sources: a single statement simply does not suffice. It is, however, not required that every *factum probandum* is corroborated by two or more means of proof. When one speaks about the principle of corroboration, it is important to keep this distinction in mind. The first definition would introduce a high burden of proof for the prosecutor (he has to present corroborating evidence regarding every fact), whereas the second definition would allow for very formal reasoning. As long as the prosecutor presents several means of proof that relate to particular facts in the charges, the accused can be convicted.

---

[42] Nijboer 2011, p. 76.

[43] Nijboer 2011, p. 77.

[44] Nijboer 2011, p. 77.

In recent years, the Supreme Court has introduced a new criterion regarding the *unus testis, nullus testis*-rule, contained in Article 342(2) CCP. This criterion resembles the principle of corroboration: in cases in which the statement of a witness is the decisive evidence, the courts are required to specifically address the question whether there is sufficient other evidence that supports the witness statement.[45] In a typical sexual assault case, in which the evidence consists predominantly of the statement of the victim, the court is required to indicate which evidence supports the statement. Although the new criterion does not require that two or more means of proof corroborate each other completely, it does require the courts to consider carefully whether the *unus testis, nullus testis*-rule is observed.

The conclusion must be that the court is required to base its finding of guilt on a multitude of sources. When the evidence consists predominantly of the statement of the accused or the statement of a witness, the court is obliged to provide sufficient reasons when it convicts the accused.[46]

3.1.2.1 Conviction Intime and Conviction Raisonnée

When the court weighs the evidence, it has to decide on the probative value of each particular piece of evidence. Moreover, the court must determine whether the applicable standard of proof is met by answering the question: is there sufficient evidence to convict the accused? The applicable standard of proof in Dutch criminal proceedings is the *conviction* of the court: it must be convinced that the accused is guilty as charged. Defining the standard of proof is notoriously difficult. Sometimes references are made to what the standard is *not*: the preponderance of probabilities, the subjective belief of the court or absolute certainty. For present purposes, the degree of belief that the court must have for a conviction is that of a very high degree of probability that the accused is, in fact, guilty. This resembles the common law standard of proof beyond reasonable doubt.

In Continental criminal justice systems, including the Dutch, reference is often made to the distinction between the *conviction intime* and the *conviction raisonnée*. These two concepts can be discussed from two perspectives: the standard of proof and the obligation to provide reasons in the judgment. In both concepts the subjective belief of the fact-finder is regarded as the standard of proof. The term 'fact-finder' was chosen deliberately because it refers to both lay fact-finders

[45] HR 30 June 2009, *ECLI*:NL:HR:2009:BH3704; HR 30 June 2009, *ECLI*:NL:HR:2009:BG7746; HR 6 March 2012, *ECLI*:NL:HR:2012:BQ6144; HR 6 March 2012, *ECLI*:NL:HR:2012:BS7910 and Borgers 2012, pp. 873–893; Bleichrodt 2011.

[46] Corstens and Borgers argue convincingly that the new criterion regarding the *unus testis, nullus testis*-rule also applies to the *nuda confessio*-rule. Both rules aim to improve accurate fact-finding by precluding the court from convicting on the basis of a single statement. It is immaterial whether the statement stems from the accused or from a witness. Corstens and Borgers 2014, pp. 773, 799–800.

and professional judges. The question of how certain the fact-finder must be (his *degree* of personal belief) in order to convict refers to the notion of *conviction*. The second perspective is the obligation to provide reasons: when the standard of proof is met, must the fact-finder account for his subjective belief that the accused is guilty? In criminal justice systems that are based on the *conviction intime* this is not necessary. In fact, it is undesirable. The fact-finder (mostly lay fact-finders in a typical jury setting) is asked to determine whether he is convinced of the guilt of the accused. Reasons for his personal belief are not required. In systems that are based on the *conviction raisonnée*, such as the Dutch criminal justice system, the subjective belief must be accounted for. The court must provide reasons why it is convinced that the accused is guilty as charged.

In their commentary on the 1926 Code of Criminal Procedure, Blok and Besier argued that systems of free proof are often associated with the *conviction intime*: when the fact-finder is not constrained in any way by statutory rules regarding the admission and the weighing of the evidence, his personal belief is the applicable standard of proof.[47] Corstens and Borgers argued that the difference between *conviction raisonnée* and *conviction intime* is the existence of evidentiary thresholds in *conviction raisonnée* systems. The court must acquit when there is insufficient evidence, even if it is convinced of the guilt of the accused.[48] Nijboer agreed: evidentiary thresholds and other legal impediments to the free evaluation of evidence are absent from systems based on the *conviction intime*.[49] This is why admissibility rules are so prominent in such systems: first, sufficient evidence has to be presented to meet the applicable standard of proof and, more importantly, admissibility rules can effectively shield the fact-finder from tainted evidence. This way, evidence with probative value can be kept away from the deliberations of the fact-finder.

3.1.2.2 Statutory and Free Systems of Evidence Law

When the two types of *conviction* are discussed, reference is often made to the different systems of evidence law. Traditionally, systems of evidence law are divided into free and statutory systems of evidence law. The latter category is then subdivided into positive and negative statutory systems.

In the archetypical free system of evidence law, no rules of admissibility or rules regarding the evaluation of evidence exist. It is completely up to the court to select the relevant evidence and to determine whether it is convinced of the guilt of the accused. It is obvious that in such systems the court has been given a large amount of discretion regarding the determination of guilt; in fact, critics might

---

[47] Blok and Besier 1925, pp. 126–127.

[48] Corstens and Borgers 2014, p. 758.

[49] Nijboer 2011, p. 48.

argue that this is nothing more than an arbitrary system. Prominent proponents of the abolishment of technical legal rules of evidence include Jeremy Bentham and Rupert Cross. They favoured a system in which the fact-finder is left considerable freedom to assess any relevant evidence.[50]

In statutory systems of evidence law, the legislator has defined rules regarding the admission and evaluation of evidence. In such systems, evidence is divided into particular categories (the legal means of proof) with all kinds of technical rules attached to it. The evaluation of the admissible evidence is regulated to a greater or lesser extent. In positive-statutory systems, the legislator has determined that a certain quantity of evidence suffices for a conviction; the court is then obliged to convict the accused, even if it is not convinced of the accused's guilt.

Positive-statutory systems are at odds with both the *conviction intime* and the *conviction raisonnée*. Guilt or innocence follow almost mechanically from the evidence presented. This entails that there is no need to provide the accused with a reasoned judgment: it is simply superfluous to give reasons for a decision that is inevitable. To oblige judges in a positive-statutory system to account for their decisions is providing an appearance of accountability at best. The judgment will consist of a summing up of the evidence, without any substantive reasoning. It is therefore rather immaterial which type of persuasion is chosen in positive-statutory systems: the end result is an unreasoned judgment.

In negative-statutory systems, the court must be convinced in order to convict. In such systems, the court is never obliged to convict when a certain amount of evidence has been presented. What is of importance is the quality and probative value of the evidence.

Negative-statutory systems are characterized by the emphasis on the conviction of the court. When sufficient evidence has been presented to meet any evidentiary threshold and the court is convinced of the accused's guilt, the importance of a reasoned judgment comes to the fore. The leap from the evidence to the final judgment requires a solid justification. It is this final step in criminal proceedings that favours a combination of the negative-statutory system and *conviction raisonnée*: without a reasoned judgment, the accused would be left in the dark on how the court conducted fact-finding and determined his guilt.

Dutch law of criminal evidence is characterized as a negative-statutory system of evidence law.[51] The court is bound by legal means of proof (although it resembles a system of free admission of proof, in practice), and it has to observe evidentiary thresholds. Crucially, the *conviction* of the court is of primary importance: the court is never under a statutory obligation to convict. Nijboer argued convincingly that the Dutch system of evidence law is deeply influenced by the case law

[50] See Murphy 2003, pp. 2–6.

[51] Corstens and Borgers 2014, p. 757; Keulen and Knigge 2010, p. 474.

of the Supreme Court.[52] Examples include the *De auditu* judgment and the case law on the *unus testis, nullus testis*-rule, discussed above.

Considering the weighing of evidence, the Dutch law of criminal evidence can be characterized as a system of conditional free evaluation. When the evidentiary thresholds are met, the court is free to weigh the evidence as it wishes (provided, of course, that no epistemological errors are made). The court has to account for the outcome of the deliberations: the right to a reasoned judgment is a vital safeguard to verify how the court has evaluated the evidence and whether any factual errors have been made.

3.1.3 Reasoned Judgments

The rationale for providing the accused, and the public in general, with a reasoned judgment is uncontroversial. By providing reasons, the court accounts for its findings and explains its conclusions regarding the facts. A reasoned judgment enables the parties to verify whether all procedural rules, including the rules of evidence, have been observed. From the perspective of the ECtHR, the domestic courts must 'indicate with sufficient clarity the grounds on which they base their decisions'.[53] The rationale for this obligation found the Court, *inter alia*, in the fact that the accused must be able to understand the judgment and to demonstrate that the arguments of the parties have been taken into consideration. Moreover, a reasoned judgment obliges the court to base its findings on 'objective arguments'.[54] This way, arbitrary decisions are avoided.

Article 121 of the Constitution states that judgments must be reasoned. Corstens and Borgers argued that providing reasons ensures that the court takes the rules of procedure and evidence into account. The accused, the prosecutor and the public in general are properly informed of the court's reasoning. A reasoned judgment also allows for effective supervision by a higher court.[55]

The assessment of evidence is a mental process that, as such, cannot be verified by others. Ideally, after the evidence has been weighed the court juxtaposes the result to the applicable standard of proof. This process is often described as a leap: the judge takes a leap from the evidence presented to the final judgment. The CCP stipulates which evidence may be considered, but the *conviction* is obscured from others.[56] Although this mental process cannot be verified (we do not know, for instance, at which moment the court considers itself convinced) the outcome can.

---

[52] Nijboer 2011, pp. 39–52. Similarly: Van Dorst 2015, pp. 274–299.

[53] ECtHR, 16 December 1992, App. No.: 12945/87, (*Hadjianastassiou v. Greece*), para 33.

[54] ECtHR (GC), 16 November 2010, App. No.: 926/05, (*Taxquet v. Belgium*), para 91.

[55] Corstens and Borgers 2014, pp. 742–743.

[56] Cleiren 2010, pp. 260–269; Clermont 2008–2009, p. 470; Damaška 1997, p. 42.

Considered this way, the importance of a solid motivation in the judgment becomes clear: the legislator has, as far as possible, described the means of proof that the court may consider, but the ultimate issue remains for the court to answer. To underline the importance of a reasoned judgment, it is useful to refer again to bifurcated and unitary court systems. Damaška observed that bifurcated court systems produce judgments without reasons: a typical judgment consists of the jury's apodictic verdict on the guilt or innocence of the accused. The reasons for this finding are left in the dark because juries are not obliged to explain how they have reached their verdict and which evidence they have found persuasive.[57] Damaška emphasized that in such proceedings, the admissibility stage of the proceedings gains in importance: the evidentiary basis upon which the fact-finder must decide is in fact the only way parties can influence the ultimate decision and, at least equally important, can determine whether the proceedings were fair:

> If the rational support for the output of their decision-making process eludes supervision, the rational support for the input can be subject to attack.[58]

The lack of reasoning in the final judgment is then compensated by meticulous debates on the admissibility of evidence. Judgments of bifurcated courts gain their legitimacy *ex ante*: during the proceedings and before the final verdict is handed down. In unitary courts with their flexible, or even absent, admissibility standards, the legitimacy is gained only *ex post*: it is in the final judgment that the court accounts for its findings regarding the evidence.[59]

The Court has held that the absence of reasons in a judgment handed down by a lay jury is not in itself contrary to the Convention.[60] However, in order to prevent arbitrariness, the accused and the public as a whole must be able to understand the judgment.[61] This understanding can be provided in various ways, which can all be brought under the *ex ante* justifications Damaška discussed. In *Papon v. France*, for example, the Court held that the unreasoned judgment by the French Assize Court did not violate the Convention because the jury had answered 768 questions put to it by the president of the Assize Court. These questions 'formed a framework on which the jury's decision was based.'[62] Regarding proceedings before professional judges, the Court held that 'the accused's understanding of his conviction stems primarily from the reasons given in judicial decisions.'[63] The observations of Damaška fit well within these rulings of the Court; in bifurcated court

---

[57] Ashworth and Redmayne 2010, p. 377.

[58] Damaška 1997, p. 44.

[59] Damaška 1997, p. 46.

[60] ECtHR, 2 February 1999, App. No.: 31913/96, (*Saric v. Denmark*), pp. 14–15.

[61] ECtHR (GC), 16 November 2010, App. No.: 926/05, (*Taxquet v. Belgium*), para 90.

[62] ECtHR, 7 June 2001, App. No.: 64666/01, (*Papon v. France (No. 2)*), p. 28.

[63] ECtHR (GC), 16 November 2010, App. No.: 926/05, (*Taxquet v. Belgium*), para 91.

systems, the understanding of the judgment occurs during the proceedings, and in unitary court systems, it occurs in interlocutory and final judicial decisions.

Article 359 CCP obliges the court to hand down a reasoned judgment. Although not limited to the question of whether the accused is guilty (the ultimate issue), the obligation to provide reasons in case the court concludes that the accused is guilty is of particular relevance. Article 359(3) CCP states that this decision must be based on legal means of proof that have probative value. The court must indicate which means of proof it has used. Besides the obligation of the court to provide reasons *proprio motu*, the court must respond when one of the parties has specifically addressed a particular issue. When the court is not persuaded by the arguments of the accused or the prosecutor, it must account for that decision in the judgment. Article 359(2) CCP requires the court to respond specifically to such arguments.[64]

Other instances in which the court must specifically address a particular issue in the judgment concern the use of chain evidence; in case of a '*Murray*-situation'; the use of false testimony of the accused, and the use of statements of particular witnesses.[65] When the court uses chain evidence in its judgment, solid reasoning is required; specifically, the court must provide sufficient reasons why and how chain evidence was used in a particular case.[66] The court must indicate the similarities between the charges and why it is convinced that the accused is guilty. A '*Murray*-situation' is a situation in which an adverse inference is drawn against the accused when he remains silent in the face of a significant amount of incriminating evidence.[67] In such cases, the court must address this issue in the judgment.[68] Similarly, using any false testimony of the accused in order to convict him is allowed when the court provides sufficient reasons for doing so.[69] Finally, Article 360 CCP states that the court must provide specific reasons when use is made of statements of particular categories of witnesses.

---

[64] On the scope of this obligation: HR 11 April 2006, *ECLI*:NL:HR:2006:AU9130. See also: Dreissen 2014. The Minister of Security and Justice stated that, in the forthcoming revision of the Code of Criminal Procedure, one single criterion will be introduced on the obligation to provide reasons. Ministry of Security and Justice, 'Kamerbrief over modernisering Wetboek van Strafvordering', 30 September 2015, p. 111.

[65] Cf. Schoep 2015, Opm. 4.

[66] HR 14 March 2006, *ECLI*:NL:HR:2006:AU5496.

[67] ECtHR (GC), 8 February 1996, App. No.: 18731/91, (*John Murray v. United Kingdom*). The Court held, *inter alia*: 'On the one hand, it is self-evident that it is incompatible with the immunities under consideration to base a conviction solely or mainly on the accused's silence or on a refusal to answer questions or to give evidence himself. On the other hand, the Court deems it equally obvious that these immunities cannot and should not prevent that the accused's silence, in situations which clearly call for an explanation from him, be taken into account in assessing the persuasiveness of the evidence adduced by the prosecution.' (para 47).

[68] HR 3 June 1997, *ECLI*:NL:HR:1997:ZD0733.

[69] E.g. HR 3 July 2012, *ECLI*:NL:HR:2012:BW9968, para 4.2.

There are also instances in which the court may refrain from handing down a reasoned judgment.[70] The court may hand down an abridged judgment, in which no reasons are given for the conviction.[71] Such a judgment contains the charges, the facts for which the accused is found guilty and the reasons for the sentence that is imposed. The means of proof are not included, nor any reasoning on the weighing of the evidence by the court. However, when appeal or cassation proceedings are initiated, the abridged judgment must be supplemented with the means of proof on which the court relied.[72] In case the accused confesses unconditionally to the charges, it suffices for the court to sum up the means of proof; in this case, it is not necessary to provide a fully reasoned judgment.[73] The confession of the accused must be clear, unconditional and not equivocal.[74]

3.1.4 Conclusion

The full criminal trial in Dutch criminal proceedings can be characterized as follows. The court can take into account virtually all evidence that it deems relevant for the case. The weighing of the evidence is within the court's discretion (provided the evidentiary thresholds are met), for which the court must account in the final judgment. It can be concluded that the court holds a prominent place in the Dutch criminal justice system. The principle of *nulla poena sine iudicio* is mirrored in the manner in which criminal proceedings are conducted: the court is entrusted to ensure that trials are fair and result in accurate fact-finding. In order to do so, the legislator has left the court considerable freedom regarding the admissibility and weighing of the evidence. However, this freedom is not unlimited: the court must account, sometimes in great detail, for its factual and legal conclusions.

The following pages present a discussion of the diversions from the full criminal trial, addressing the question: what are the mechanisms that deviate from the *nulla poena sine iudicio* principle? After the diversions are discussed, the use of shortcuts will be analysed. Shortcuts to proof do not deviate from the *nulla poena sine iudicio* principle; rather, they operate within the procedural context of criminal proceedings. They deviate, however, from the notion that every part of the evidence has to be discussed during the proceedings in order to provide for an adversarial trial.

[70] In case of a single judge bench, Article 378 (CCP) applies (in case of proceedings before the court of appeal: Article 425(3) CCP). These articles allow the single judge to deliver the judgment orally, directly after the close of the proceedings.

[71] Article 365a CCP.

[72] Article 365a(2) CCP.

[73] Article 359(3) CCP.

[74] See e.g. Duker 2012.

3.2 Diversions in Dutch Law of Criminal Procedure

3.2.1 Introduction

Three ways of diverting a case from the full criminal trial will be discussed here: the punitive order, the transaction and the conditional dismissal. These diversions enable the prosecutor to react to criminal offences without bringing the case to court. He can either impose a sentence (in case of the punitive order) or try to reach an agreement with the accused, in which the accused agrees to comply with certain conditions that are punitive in nature (in case of the transaction and the conditional dismissal). The punitive character of these different ways to divert from the full criminal trial is important: the accused has to comply with the conditions imposed or agreed to. If he fails to do so, the prosecutor will most likely initiate regular criminal proceedings. The fact that the accused reaches an agreement does not alter the punitive character of the conditions that are agreed to. This is why mediation is not regarded as a diversion mechanism for the purposes of this study: mediation concerns primarily the relationship between the accused and the victim. The prosecutor is absent in this relationship, which means that the concept of mediation does not have a punitive character.[75] On the contrary, reconciliation is the most important goal.

The diversions that are discussed here will be evaluated in Chap. 5, where the participatory model of proof will function as the normative framework. In order to provide fruitful results, the analysis of the diversions is done with this framework in mind. Specifically, these sections will address the following questions: What are the main characteristics of each diversion mechanism? What is the legal position of the accused when he is confronted with a diversion from the full criminal trial proceedings?

3.2.2 The Punitive Order

The punitive order was introduced in 2008.[76] The prosecutor can issue a punitive order for certain, relatively minor, offences.[77] This entails that the prosecutor can impose sentences unilaterally without the involvement of the court. The punitive order can be imposed in case of crimes ('misdrijven') that are punishable by a

[75] The fact that, according to Article 51h CCP, the prosecutor promotes mediation between the victim and accused, does not alter the fact that mediation is aimed at reconciling the victim and the accused. For an analysis of several recent mediation pilots in Dutch criminal proceedings, including the theoretical background of mediation in criminal cases, see: Lens et al. 2015.

[76] Wet OM-afdoening, *Stb*. 2006, 330.

[77] Article 257b and Article 257ba CCP state that other public officials may also issue a punitive order. This is subject to detailed regulation.

maximum sentence of 6 years' imprisonment and in case of minor offences ('overtredingen').[78] This is the same range of offences for which transactions can be offered.[79] Punitive orders can, for example, be imposed for theft, simple assault or vandalism.[80]

The sentences that can be imposed by way of a punitive order are community service, a fine, the seizure of certain goods, the payment of a sum to the State (which is then transferred to the victim) and the prohibition to drive vehicles for a maximum period of six months.[81] Moreover, the following measures can be imposed: the surrender of certain objects, the handing over of certain objects to the State or paying the value of those objects, the confiscation of illegal proceeds, the payment of a sum to victim organizations and any other measure, provided that such a measure does not restrict the constitutional and religious freedoms of the accused.[82]

During the parliamentary debates, the Minister of Justice argued that the introduction of the punitive order was necessary to increase the crime control capacities of the judicial authorities.[83] The introduction of the punitive order changed the position of the prosecutor *vis-à-vis* the judiciary within the criminal justice system profoundly. The Minister of Justice envisaged that cases should be brought before the courts only if they are of a certain gravity, warrant imprisonment or should result in higher sentences than can be imposed by the punitive order. Contested cases, in which the prosecution and accused differ regarding the guilt of the accused, should also be brought before the courts.[84]

With the introduction of the punitive order the traditional prerogative of the judge, his *ius puniendi*, is abandoned. Considering the implications for the position of the judiciary and the prosecution regarding sentencing, intense debates were held over the past decades. Since the 1960s, several proposals have been drafted that argued in favour of allowing the prosecutor to impose sentences unilaterally.[85]

One of the major objections against the punitive order concerned this prosecutorial authority to impose sentences without judicial involvement. According to Article 113 of the Constitution, the judiciary is responsible for conducting criminal proceedings. Article 113(3) of the Constitution states that only the judiciary may impose sentences that consist of the deprivation of liberty. Although

[78] Article 257a CCP.

[79] Article 74 CC.

[80] Article 310 CC, Article 300 CC, Article 350 CC.

[81] Article 257a(2) CCP. See also Article 36 Economic Crimes Act.

[82] Article 257a(3) CCP. Cf. Crijns 2015.

[83] *Kamerstukken II*, 2004/05, 29849, 3, p. 1.

[84] *Kamerstukken II*, 2004/05, 29849, 3, p. 1.

[85] Cf. the enumeration given by the Minister of Justice in the Senate during the parliamentary debates. *Kamerstukken I*, 2005/06, 29849, C, pp. 1–2.

imprisonment is not a sentence that can be imposed in a punitive order, the constitutional implications that arise by expanding the *ius puniendi* of the judiciary have been discussed extensively.[86] To allow the prosecutor, or other public officials, to impose sentences is a significant departure from the *nulla poena sine iudicio* principle and profoundly changed the original framework of the CCP. Nijboer argued that this principle is the cornerstone of both the Code of Criminal Procedure and the Criminal Code.[87] Crijns emphasized that the justification for this expansion of the *ius puniendi* has not been discussed profoundly during the parliamentary debates.[88]

Although the prosecutor may impose a sentence unilaterally, the accused has the possibility to file a notice of disagreement against the punitive order.[89] This entails that the prosecutor must reconsider the case and decide either to withdraw the punitive order or to send the case to court. In the latter case, regular first-instance proceedings will be initiated. The possibility of filing a notice of disagreement ensures that the accused's right of access to a court is guaranteed. Unlike the transaction, which is discussed below, the initiative for involving an independent and impartial judge lies with the accused. Normally, the judge will not review whether the punitive order was issued correctly, i.e. whether all procedural safeguards have been complied with.[90] The judge will determine whether the accused is guilty as charged, applying the rules of criminal procedure regarding regular first-instance proceedings.[91]

The fact that sentences can be imposed implies that the accused is in fact guilty of the offence for which the punitive order is issued. The prosecutor must determine whether the accused is guilty; in this regard the determination of the ultimate issue shifts from the court to the prosecutor. The prosecutor must determine

---

[86] Cf. Crijns 2010, pp. 24–27; Crijns 2006, pp. 51–70; Groenhuijsen and Simmelink 2005, pp. 171–197; Hartmann 2005, pp. 84–96; Crijns 2004, pp. 225–236; Mevis 2004, pp. 353–367; Kamerstukken II, 2004–2005, 29 848, nr 3, pp. 55–60; Sikkema and Kristen 2013, pp. 179–205.

[87] Nijboer 1987, p. 98.

[88] Crijns 2006, pp. 59–62.

[89] Article 257e CCP.

[90] Cf. Crijns who argued that in exceptional circumstances the judge will review the manner in which the punitive order has been issued. When the imposition of the punitive order violates the principle of due process, the judge will take this into account (for example, by ruling that the prosecutor no longer has standing in court). Crijns 2014, p. 270.

[91] A comparison with plea bargaining is instructive: in such procedures, the plea bargaining procedure as such and the factual basis of the plea are supervised by a judge. Cf. Rule 62*bis* ICTY RPE: 'If an accused pleads guilty in accordance with Rule 62(vi), or requests to change his or her plea to guilty and the Trial Chamber is satisfied that: (i) the guilty plea has been made voluntarily; (ii) the guilty plea is informed; (iii) the guilty plea is not equivocal; and (iv) there is a sufficient factual basis for the crime and the accused's participation in it, either on the basis of independent indicia or on lack of any material disagreement between the parties about the facts of the case, the Trial Chamber may enter a finding of guilt and instruct the Registrar to set a date for the sentencing hearing.'.

whether there is sufficient evidence and whether there are any legal impediments to the imposition of the punitive order. The main difference between this and the other diversions is this determination of guilt; specifically, the other diversions are based on an agreement or consensus between the accused and the prosecutor.

3.2.2.1 Safeguards

The accused must be heard by the prosecutor when the punitive order consists of community service, a driving disqualification, measures or a fine or damages of more than 2000 €.[92] Hearing the accused in such cases has a threefold rationale. First, the manner in which the prosecutor determines the accused's guilt will be more accurate when the accused is able to present his side of the story. Second, the prosecutor will be able to evaluate the consequences of the sanctions he wishes to impose; before doing so, the accused can inform the prosecutor about his personal circumstances and the effect that any punitive order may have on his personal life. Finally, it enhances effectiveness: if the accused states during the hearing that he will file a notice of disagreement, the prosecutor might as well summon the accused immediately.[93]

When the views of the prosecutor and the accused differ, the prosecutor is obliged to provide the accused with reasons why he is not persuaded by the arguments of the accused. According to Article 257c(3) CCP, this obligation arises only when the accused has specifically addressed certain issues. This is similar to the obligation for the court to respond to issues that the accused has specifically addressed during the proceedings. When the court disagrees, it must provide reasons for this decision.[94]

The rationale of hearing the accused to increase the accuracy of the punitive order is somewhat problematic. The diversion is designed to entrust the determination of guilt to the prosecutor, and it should, therefore, be rather irrelevant whether the accused is heard or not. Currently, hearing is mandatory when the punitive order concerns certain sentences or measures. It would stand to reason to oblige the prosecutor to hear the accused in cases in which the evidential basis is rather small. In such cases, hearing the accused contributes to the accuracy of the determination of guilt. If the prosecutor is unable to determine the guilt of the accused due to insufficient evidence, the only appropriate reaction is to withhold the punitive order or to bring the case to court and let the court decide whether the accused is guilty.

---

[92] Article 257c CCP. In case of a fine or damages of more than 2000 €, the presence of the lawyer of the accused is required. Article 257c(2) CCP. Article 36(2) Economic Crimes Act stipulates that the presence of a lawyer is required when the punitive order consists of a fine or damages of more than 10,000 € and is issued for an economic crime committed by a corporation.

[93] *Kamerstukken II*, 2004/05, 29849, 3, p. 31.

[94] Article 359(2) CCP.

In order to ensure that filing a notice of disagreement against the punitive order is effective, it is necessary that the accused knows on which evidence the prosecutor relies. This way, the accused is able to formulate his objections against the punitive order in a detailed and effective manner. Article 33 CCP states that the accused has the right to acquaint himself with the case file when the prosecutor has issued a punitive order. The right to file a notice of disagreement entails that the accused is able to bring the case before a judge. According to the Minister of Justice, this is sufficient to comply with the requirement that sentences can be reviewed by a court, which is contained in Article 6 ECHR.[95] The right of access to a court is, therefore, guaranteed.[96] As stated above, the court will consider the case as a regular first-instance case.[97]

The implications of the punitive order for the (constitutional) position of the prosecutor and the judiciary raises the question of how the prosecutor determines whether the accused has committed a particular offence. Articles 257a through 257h CCP do not specifically address the question of how the prosecutor should determine the guilt of the accused. Article 257a CCP merely states that the prosecutor may issue a punitive order when he *determines* that a certain offence has been committed.[98] During the parliamentary debates, it remained unclear how the prosecutor should determine the guilt of the accused. The Minister of Justice argued that the right of the accused to file a notice of disagreement will ensure compliance with the CCP, including the rules of evidence. In other words, the prosecutor must be convinced that the case, if brought to court, will result in a conviction.[99] This is, in fact, the essence of this diversion from the full criminal trial: the prosecutor must act as if he were an independent and impartial judge.

3.2.2.2 Judicial Supervision

When a notice of disagreement is filed and the prosecutor sends the case to court, the court will not review the punitive order as such, but will determine itself whether the accused is guilty. The manner in which the prosecutor determined the guilt of the accused is not relevant because the court will process the case just as it would any other first-instance case. This means that the question of whether the prosecutor has complied with the safeguards contained in the CCP, such as the obligation to hear the accused, is *as such* not subject to judicial supervision. Apart

95 *Kamerstukken II*, 2004/05, 29849, 3, p. 42.

96 In *Deweer v. Belgium*, the Court held that the right to a court is 'a constituent element of the right to a fair trial'. ECtHR, 27 February 1980, App. No.: 6903/75, (*Deweer v. Belgium*), para 49.

97 Article 257f(3) CCP.

98 Article 257a CCP.

99 *Kamerstukken I*, 2005/06, 29849 C, pp. 31–32. Kooijmans argued in his inaugural address that the rules of evidence, contained in the CCP, must be taken into account by the prosecutor when he issues a punitive order. Kooijmans 2011, pp. 44–45.

from exceptional circumstances, the manner in which this diversion mechanism operates in practice is not supervised by the courts. The fact that the prosecutor can withdraw the punitive order after a notice of disagreement has been filed is not without relevance in this respect: the prosecutor effectively controls the access to the court.

Although the court will process the case in conformity with the rules on first-instance criminal proceedings, this does not necessarily mean that the manner in which the punitive order was issued is completely irrelevant. Crijns argued that the manner in which the punitive order was issued can be regarded as part of the pre-trial phase.[100] This entails that any procedural errors that have been made can be taken into account during the trial proceedings. This way, the court is able to respond to procedural errors that the prosecutor made when he issued the punitive order. In *Imbrioscia*, the Court emphasized that the rights contained in Article 6 may also be relevant before the case is sent to trial. An initial failure to comply with the procedural guarantees of Article 6 during the pre-trial proceedings may have consequences for the fairness of the trial as such.[101]

The legislator envisaged that the court would not determine whether the punitive order was issued correctly.[102] The Council of State, the Dutch advisory body on legislation, expressed profound critique on this point. The fact that the court is, in principle, not allowed to assess the legitimacy of the punitive order, combined with the 'quasi-judicial function' of the prosecutor, is incompatible with the constitutional position of both the prosecutor and the judiciary.[103] This is particularly troublesome in cases that cannot be categorized as petty crimes, such as shoplifting. Article 257a CCP gives the prosecutor the authority to issue punitive orders for crimes with a maximum sentence of 6 years' imprisonment. This entails that punitive orders may also be issued for more serious offences in which an accurate and concise determination of guilt is even more essential.[104]

The internal directive of the prosecution service on the punitive order states that cases in which sufficient evidence has been collected and where no legal impediments exist are diverted from the courts. In such cases, a punitive order will be issued.[105] This means that, in principle, the courts will handle only contested cases, cases in which the prosecutor wants to have the accused imprisoned and cases concerning offences for which no punitive order can be issued. The result is that a significant number of criminal cases are handled outside the traditional trial

---

100 Crijns 2015, Opm. 4c.

101 ECtHR, 24 November 1993, App. No.: 13972/88, (*Imbrioscia v. Switzerland*), para 36.

102 *Kamerstukken II*, 2004/05, 29849, 3, p. 21.

103 *Kamerstukken II*, 2004/05, 29849, 5, pp. 5–6.

104 This does not imply that the accuracy of the determination of guilt should depend on the gravity of the offence: every determination of guilt should be as accurate as possible.

105 Aanwijzing OM-strafbeschikking (2015A004), *Stcrt.* 2015, 8971.

context.[106] To enforce criminal law to a significant extent outside the realm of trial proceedings has consequences for the normative framework in which criminal law is enforced. Trial proceedings must be conducted in a fair manner; in its case law, the Court has developed a sophisticated and detailed framework regarding the fairness of trial proceedings. It is essential that when cases are diverted from the court they are still handled in a fair manner. In Chap. 5, the notion of fairness will be applied to the practice of diversions, including the punitive order.

3.2.3 *The Transaction*

With the introduction of the punitive order, the future of the transaction as a diversion is somewhat uncertain. The Minister of Justice envisaged that the transaction will be abolished after the punitive order has been implemented completely.[107] The annual reports of the prosecution service show that the number of punitive orders has risen significantly in the period 2009–2013. This to the detriment of the number of transactions. It is, however, possible that, after the full implementation and evaluation of the punitive order, both diversions will co-exist.[108] It can be questioned whether it is desirable to abolish the category of special transactions all together. Such transactions consist, for example, of out of court settlements with large corporations for fraud offences. This way, the prosecutor can avoid complex and time-consuming trial proceedings with an uncertain outcome. Transactions that do not fall into this category will be replaced by the punitive order (this is the category of relatively minor offences, such as shoplifting or simple assault).

3.2.3.1 The Legal Nature of the Transaction

Article 74 CC enables the prosecutor to offer a transaction to the accused. A transaction is best characterized as a consensual out of court settlement between the prosecutor and the accused.[109] This is the main difference to the punitive order: the transaction requires that the accused consents to the conditions stipulated by the prosecutor, whereas the punitive order can be imposed without the consent of the accused.

---

106 The Annual Report of the prosecution service shows that the punitive order is on the rise, to the detriment of the transaction. In 2009, 76,400 cases were diverted from the courts: 3900 punitive orders were imposed, 65,800 transactions were offered and accepted and 6700 conditional dismissals were reached. In 2013, the prosecution service diverted 61,700 cases from the courts: 34,300 punitive orders; 17,600 transactions and 9800 conditional dismissals. Openbaar Ministerie, *Jaarbericht 2013*, The Hague 2014, p. 62.

107 *Kamerstukken II*, 2004/05, 29849, nr 4.

108 *Kamerstukken I*, 2005/06, 29849, C, p. 22.

109 For a detailed analysis of the legal character of the transaction, see: Crijns 2010, pp. 173–182.

When the accused complies with the conditions stipulated by the prosecutor, the prosecutor forfeits the right to prosecute and no longer has standing in court.[110] The current practice of transactions stems from 1983 and, according to Osinga, consists of two elements: a sanction and a procedure.[111] Considering the procedural element, Osinga argued that the principles of due process ('beginselen van een goede procesorde') function as the normative framework. When the prosecutor offers a transaction, he must ensure that no due process principle, such as the prohibition to act in an arbitrary manner, is violated.[112]

It is important to keep the punitive character of the transaction in mind: although the transaction requires the consent of the accused, this should not detract from the fact that the conditions the prosecutor offers to the accused have a punitive character.[113] From the perspective of the Court, the transaction has to be regarded as a 'criminal charge'. In *Deweer*, the Court held that:

> The 'charge' could, for the purposes of Article 6 para 1, be defined as the official notification given to an individual by the competent authority of an allegation that he has committed a criminal offence.[114]

Hartmann discussed the hybrid character of the transaction and concluded that the transaction is best characterized as a mechanism that encompasses both punitive and consensual elements.[115] Crijns emphasized that the transaction is often regarded as a typical public law concept, in which private law notions such as freedom of contract and party autonomy are mostly absent.[116] Considering the consensual character of the transaction, reminiscent of private law contract theory, this is remarkable. Although consensualism is a constitutive element of the transaction, it does not fundamentally alter its punitive character.

3.2.3.2 Conditions

Transactions can be offered for a limited number of offences. A transaction can be offered for all minor offences and for crimes for which the statutory maximum term of imprisonment does not exceed 6 years. The prosecutor may include the following conditions in the transaction: payment of a sum between 3 € and the

---

110 Article 74(1) CC.

111 Osinga 1992, pp. 119–169, pp. 197–198.

112 Osinga 1992, pp. 198–199.

113 Consent is not the mere acceptance of the offer by the prosecutor: it also consists of complying with the conditions in the transaction. Cf. Crijns 2010, p. 175.

114 ECtHR, 27 February 1980, App. No.: 6903/75, (*Deweer v. Belgium*), para 46. See also: ECtHR, 8 June 1976, App. No.: 5100/71; 5101/71; 5102/71; 5354/72 and 5370/72 (*Engel and Others v. The Netherlands*), para 81.

115 Hartmann 2004, p. 98.

116 Crijns 2010, pp. 181–182.

maximum fine of the offence, surrendering confiscated goods or payment of the value of non-confiscated goods, confiscation of illegal proceeds, payment of damages and, finally, community service with a maximum of 120 h.

One of the main rationales for the transaction is to increase efficiency in the enforcement of criminal law. Trial proceedings are costly and the criminal justice system becomes overburdened when minor offences are brought before the courts. Closely related is the effect on law enforcement: when a significant number of minor offences are left unpunished, the legitimacy of such laws may be questioned. It is obvious that these rationales are primarily beneficial for the State, in particular for a State that considers the criminal process as an instrument to implement state policy.[117]

From the perspective of the accused, it may be in his best interest to accept the offered transaction. By accepting the transaction and complying with the conditions, he avoids a public trial with an uncertain outcome. Especially in the case of more serious offences, the transaction can be attractive for the accused to divert the case from the court and the general public. Similarly, the prosecutor can avoid lengthy proceedings and an uncertain outcome by offering the accused a transaction in such cases.

3.2.3.3 Safeguards

The prosecutor who offers the transaction must be sure that the accused actually committed the offence for which the transaction is offered. The transaction may be offered only when there is sufficient evidence and when there are no legal impediments.[118] This entails that no transaction may be offered when the prosecutor is not convinced that he could bring the case successfully before the court. Similar to the practice of the punitive order, the prosecutor must act like a quasi-judge when he offers a transaction to the accused. Although the prosecutor must ensure that a conviction could follow, complying with the conditions of the transaction does not result in an official determination of guilt. The determination of guilt can only be done within the context of a full criminal trial or by the imposition of a punitive order.

Considering that the prosecutor has no standing in court when the accused complies with the conditions stipulated in the transaction, there is no judicial supervision regarding the manner in which transactions are offered and accepted. Unlike the punitive order, there is no explicit obligation to hear the accused in case the transaction involves the payment of a sum exceeding 2000 €. When the accused does not comply with the transaction, or does not respond to the transaction offer, the prosecutor cannot enforce the conditions in the transaction. The prosecutor must then bring the case to court.

---

[117] Cf. Damaška 1986, pp. 147–180.

[118] This includes, for example, the existence of any justification or excuse.

The accused will be informed for which offence the transaction is offered, with a description of the underlying facts. This way, the accused is notified for which particular fact the transaction is offered. It is important to make a distinction here between normal transactions (which have been replaced by the punitive order) and special transactions. The last category consists of all transactions above 500,000 € and transactions above 50,000 € that are not included in the internal directives of the prosecution service. Transactions that are offered in controversial cases, such as cases that have attracted substantial media coverage or concern ethical issues, are also labelled as special transactions.[119] In case of a special transaction the prosecutor and the accused can enter into negotiations in order to settle the case and reach an agreement that is acceptable to both parties.[120] The evidence that has been collected will most likely be part of the negotiations; as a result, such evidence will be disclosed to the accused. This enables the accused to determine whether it is in his best interest to settle or not. Informing the accused about the evidence that has been gathered enables the accused to make an informed decision: by complying with the transaction, he waives his right to a fair trial. This is acceptable only when he has done so voluntarily and on an informed basis. The generally accepted procedural safeguards regarding plea-bargaining procedures are instructive in this regard: a valid guilty plea has to be informed, voluntary and not equivocal. Waiving the right to have the case determined by an independent and impartial judge requires solid procedural safeguards in order to enable the accused to make a well-informed decision.

Corstens and Borgers, authors of the leading text book on the Dutch law of criminal procedure, have argued that controversial transactions, such as cases that have attracted substantial media coverage or cases in which a transaction is offered for a crime that would normally lead to trial proceedings, should be brought before a court for judicial approval.[121] This resembles the guilty plea procedure, in which the court determines whether the plea has been reached in conformity with the law.

3.2.4 The Conditional Dismissal

The conditional dismissal resembles the transaction, but it has a broader scope: the conditional dismissal can be offered for a wider range of offences than the transaction.[122] In fact, the conditional dismissal can be offered for any offence.

---

[119] Aanwijzing hoge en bijzondere transacties (2008A021), *Stcrt.* 2008, 209 and *Stcrt.* 2013, 22031.

[120] The accused's lawyer can play an important role in such negotiations. Cf. Franken 2002.

[121] Corstens and Borgers 2014, p. 857.

[122] The transaction can be regarded as a *specialis* of the conditional dismissal.

In order to be effective, the cooperation of the accused is required: the prosecutor cannot impose the conditional dismissal. The accused has to be willing to fulfil the conditions that are stipulated by the prosecutor. If the accused is not willing to do so, the prosecutor cannot enforce them. The only alternative left is to bring the case to court and request the court to impose a conditional sentence in which a similar condition is included. The consensual character of the conditional dismissal resembles the transaction and is the most striking difference when compared to the punitive order.

3.2.4.1 Legal Basis

The legal basis for the conditional dismissal is Article 167(2) CCP, which gives the prosecutor the discretionary power to not bring the case to court when the accused complies with the conditions stipulated by the prosecutor. If the accused complies, the prosecutor will not pursue the case and the case will accordingly be dismissed. The prosecutor can offer a conditional dismissal only if the case, when brought before the court, would likely result in a conviction.[123] This is similar to the requirements for offering a transaction and imposing a punitive order.

The conditional dismissal will exist alongside the punitive order and can be offered for any offence.[124] This entails that the prosecutor may issue a conditional dismissal for offences above the 6 years' imprisonment range. In cases in which the maximum term of imprisonment exceeds the term of 6 years, no punitive order can be imposed, nor can a transaction be offered. Normally, the prosecutor will bring the case to court and initiate regular trial proceedings. If, however, the prosecutor concludes that a full criminal trial is inappropriate in a given case (for example, when the accused shows sincere remorse and the victim is not in favour of trial proceedings), he may opt for the conditional dismissal and stipulate the conditions the accused has to comply with. This may, for example, include the prohibition to contact the victim or to be present in a certain area.

Compared to the other diversions, the conditional dismissal is not strictly regulated.[125] Originally, the authority to dismiss a case had to be derived implicitly from the CCP. With the implementation of the punitive order, an explicit statutory basis has been introduced by amending Article 167(2) CCP. Prior to this, the authority to offer a conditional dismissal was based on the notion that he who can do more (to summon the accused) is allowed to do less (to offer a dismissal with certain conditions).[126]

---

[123] Van den Biggelaar 1994, p. 54.

[124] *Kamerstukken I*, 2005/06, 29849, C, p. 22.

[125] This was already noted by Bleichrodt in 1996. Bleichrodt 1996, p. 203.

[126] For a critical analysis, see: Bleichrodt 1996, pp. 199–200.

The rudimentary legal framework of the dismissal makes it rather difficult to give a detailed description of the precise workings of this diversion. During the parliamentary debates on the introduction of the punitive order, the Minister of Justice explicitly stated that the conditional dismissal will exist next to the punitive order.[127] The punitive order can, according to Article 257a(3) CCP, also contain conditions that the accused has to fulfil. Considering that the punitive order is not dependent on the consent of the accused, conditions contained in punitive orders are more effective than conditional dismissals, for which the consent of the accused is necessary. Conditional dismissals may remain indispensable for those cases in which no punitive order can be imposed because the maximum term of imprisonment exceeds 6 years and in which a full criminal trial is undesirable.

3.2.4.2 Conditions

The conditions that have to be fulfilled by the accused are not, as such, codified. It is common understanding, however, that the prosecutor may formulate only conditions that comply with the articles on conditional sentences (Article 14a CC et seq.).[128] This means that any condition that consists of a deprivation of liberty cannot be included in the conditional dismissal, as Article 113(3) C states that the deprivation of liberty is the prerogative of the judiciary. Conditions that can be included in the dismissal are, for example, the payment of damages, the prohibition to be present in a certain area and the duty to report regularly to the authorities. The list of conditions is not exhaustive: Article 14(2)(14) CC states that any condition can be included that relates to the accused's behaviour. However, such conditions may not result in the restriction of the freedom of religion and other constitutional rights of the accused.

The manner in which the prosecutor determines that the accused has committed an offence is similar to the other diversions. The prosecutor must determine whether the case, when brought to court, would result in a conviction. Similar to the other diversions, the prosecutor must act as if he were a judge and determine whether there is sufficient evidence for a conviction and whether there are any legal impediments to a conviction. Crijns emphasized that, considering the consensual character of the conditional dismissal, it is likely that the prosecutor will consult the accused before issuing a conditional dismissal.[129] There is, however, no (detailed) legal framework for the correct and fair issuing of the conditional dismissal. This is similar to the practice of the transaction in that no legal framework exists to ensure that transactions are offered in a correct and fair manner.

---

[127] *Kamerstukken I*, 2005/06, 29849, C, p. 22. According to the public prosecution service, 11,700 cases were dismissed by a conditional dismissal in 2014. Openbaar Ministerie, *Jaarbericht 2014*, (The Hague 2015), pp. 86–87.

[128] Bleichrodt 1996, pp. 202–203; Corstens and Borgers 2014 p. 604; Valkenburg 2015, aant. 7.

[129] Crijns 2010, p. 188.

The most important safeguard regarding the accused is that the fulfilment of the conditions stipulated by the prosecutor is voluntary. The accused can refuse to comply with the conditions from the moment the conditional dismissal is offered. Moreover, even after the accused has informed the prosecutor that he wants to comply with the conditions, he can refuse to comply any longer with the conditions.

3.3 Shortcuts in Dutch Law of Criminal Procedure

3.3.1 Introduction

In the following pages, several shortcuts in Dutch criminal proceedings will be discussed. Shortcuts to proof infringe on the notion that the evidence is discussed during the proceedings in an adversarial setting, which allows the parties to comment upon the evidence in front of the court. Shortcuts are distinguished from diversions, because shortcuts to proof do not infringe upon the *nulla poena sine iudicio* principle: the criminal proceedings are conducted in front of the court. However, shortcuts do infringe upon the principle of a full criminal trial because a full criminal trial requires that the evidence is presented and discussed extensively with both the prosecutor and the defence in front of the trier of fact. The shortcuts that are chosen, vary in nature and legal character. First, there are shortcuts that allow for a comparative approach with shortcuts in international criminal proceedings, such as the use of facts of common knowledge and the manner in which appeal proceedings are conducted. Second, it is important to emphasize the variety of shortcuts, as this variety makes a comprehensive and coherent normative framework indispensable. Every time the full criminal trial is avoided, either by way of a diversion or a shortcut, it is essential from a fair trial perspective that the accused can participate properly in the (out of court) proceedings.

3.3.2 Facts of Common Knowledge and Contextual Facts

Every criminal law system allows the court to take notice of facts that are so notorious that they are, in fact, indisputable. It enables the court to focus the trial proceedings on contested facts: patently indisputable facts do not require evidence in criminal proceedings. Such facts are regarded as facts of common knowledge. Article 339(2) CCP states that facts of common knowledge do not require proof. The consequences in terms of probative value of such facts are clear and undisputed. Questions arise, however, when one has to *define* facts of common knowledge.[130] In this paragraph the character of facts of common knowledge will be

[130] Cf. Enschedé 1966, p. 509.

discussed, beginning with an overview of the place of facts of common knowledge within the Dutch law of criminal procedure. After this general introduction a detailed analysis will be presented on a particular type of criminal cases: cases in which the accused stands trial for crimes committed in the context of an armed conflict. These cases are chosen because they can be compared with the cases before the international tribunals, which is important because the use of facts of common knowledge in the Dutch and international contexts is comparable and raises similar questions regarding the fairness of the proceedings. The use of facts of common knowledge in respect of contextual facts, which will be discussed below, is of interest here.

3.3.2.1 Legal Framework

Prior to the introduction of the current Code of Criminal Procedure in 1926, no statutory provision existed regarding facts of common knowledge. The Codes of Criminal Procedure of 1838 and 1886 did not contain a provision like the current Article 339(2) CCP. Notorious facts did not require proof, however: the court could rely on its own knowledge of, for example, the laws of gravitation and geographical facts. The Code of 1926 provided for a statutory basis for court practice.[131] The 1926 codification put an end to the reliance on the subjective knowledge of the court and introduced a more objective standard.

Article 339(2) CCP states that facts of common knowledge do not require proof. This entails that it suffices for the court to identify facts of common knowledge without requiring formal proof of those facts. Unlike the provisions on facts of common knowledge in the Rules of Procedure and Evidence of the *ad hoc* Tribunals, Article 339(2) CCP does not oblige the court to judicially notice a fact of common knowledge.[132] This means that it remains within the discretion of the court to require formal proof of a fact when the court is not sure whether the fact is of common knowledge.

Facts of common knowledge do not fall under the enumeration of means of proof of Article 339(1) CCP. This entails that, according to Article 338 CCP, the charge cannot be proven on the basis of facts of common knowledge. More precisely: a component ('bestanddeel') of the statutory definition of the crime cannot

[131] 'Ontwerp tot vaststelling van een wetboek van strafvordering, der Koningin aangeboden door de Staatscommissie voor de herziening van het Wetboek van Strafvordering, ingesteld bij Koninklijk Besluit van 8 april 1910,' no. 17 deel II Toelichting, Landsdrukkerij, 's-Gravenhage 1913, p. 282. Cf. Blok and Besier 1925, pp. 133–134.

[132] Cf. Rule 94(A) ICTY RPE and ICTR RPE. As the ICTR Appeals Chamber held in *Karemera*, Chambers do not have any discretion to judicially notice a fact of common knowledge: when a fact is of common knowledge, the Chamber is obliged to take judicial notice of it. ICTR, Decision on Prosecutor's Interlocutory Appeal of Decision on Judicial Notice, Prosecutor *v. Karemera*, Case No.: ICTR-98-44-AR73(C), A. Ch., 16 June 2006, paras 22–23.

be proven by labelling it as a fact of common knowledge. It follows from Article 339(2) CCP that a fact of common knowledge falls outside the *probandum*, or the object of proof as formulated in the indictment. Criminal proceedings must concentrate on facts that are *not* of common knowledge (and are, mostly, in dispute between the parties) and require formal proof.[133] Moreover, the court's *conviction*[134] cannot be based to a decisive extent on facts of common knowledge, in fact, Article 338 CCP states that the court's *conviction* can be based only on legal means of proof.

An analysis of facts of common knowledge runs the risk of being fragmented and case-specific. Generally, courts do not state explicitly how they discerned a fact of common knowledge. In Germany, a distinction is made between facts of general common knowledge ('Algemeinkundigkeit') and facts that are common knowledge for the court ('Gerichtskundigkeit').[135] The last category is the factual equivalent of the *ius curia novit*-principle. 'Gerichtskundigkeit' is not to be confused with any particular knowledge of the court: facts must still be notorious in general. Stein has argued that specialized courts (such as courts that hear exclusively military or economic cases) should be allowed to rely on empirical facts ('gerichtskundige Erfahrungssätze') that are established in so-called 'Serienprozesse', or proceedings that concern the same factual basis with several accused that stand trial successively.[136] The use of such facts speeds up the proceedings significantly and may be useful in cases in which accused have committed their crimes within the context of a criminal organization or state apparatus. In fact, it resembles the practice of taking judicial notice of adjudicated facts, which will be discussed in detail in Chap. 4.

3.3.2.2 Different Categories of Facts of Common Knowledge

Attempts have been made to categorize facts of common knowledge. Nijboer divided them into unique historical facts (e.g. '1st of January 2015 was a Thursday'), factual situations (e.g. 'the Thames flows through the city of London') and empirical facts (e.g. 'Newton's laws of motion').[137] The CCP incorporates empirical facts in the general concept of facts of common knowledge, whereas the Dutch Code of Civil Procedure makes a distinction between facts or circumstances

133 Van Woensel argued that, because facts of common knowledge limit the *probandum*, the provision on facts of common knowledge should have been incorporated in Article 338 CCP. Van Woensel 1997, aant. 5. Similar: Nijboer 1982, p. 31.

134 In the meaning of *conviction raisonnée*.

135 Dreissen 2007, pp. 289–290.

136 Stein 1893, pp. 74–75.

137 Nijboer 2011, pp. 209–210. Cf. Nijboer 1982, pp. 19–23.

of common knowledge and empirical facts.[138] The distinction is more of academic than practical interest, though.[139]

Besides distinguishing between categories of facts or rules, one can also make a distinction between different grades of 'commonality'. Facts do not need to be universally known in order to be common knowledge; for example, locally known facts (that is, within the territorial jurisdiction of the court) can be regarded as common knowledge.[140] The Amsterdam District Court may regard the fact that one cannot walk from the Central Station to the Leidseplein in less than five minutes as common knowledge, where the Rotterdam District Court may not. To distinguish between locally and universally known facts is also common practice before the international criminal tribunals.[141]

Facts can be common knowledge for a limited number of people, such as professionals; for example, it is common knowledge for farmers that rules and regulations regarding agricultural issues, such as the use of certain types of fertilizer, often change (which obliges farmers to remain up to date regarding such issues).[142] During the Second World War, it was common knowledge for journalists that

[138] Article 149(2) Dutch Code of Civil Procedure: 'Feiten of omstandigheden van algemene bekendheid, alsmede algemene ervaringsregels mogen door de rechter aan zijn beslissing ten grondslag worden gelegd, ongeacht of zij zijn gesteld, en behoeven geen bewijs.'.

[139] Van Boom et al. 2010, pp. 36–43. In the '*All Cops Are Bastards*-case', the Supreme Court did make a distinction (without commenting on it) between facts of common knowledge and rules of thumb. HR, 11 January 2011, *ECLI*:NL:HR:2011:BP0291 para 3.2.1. In another case, both categories were regarded as very similar to each other. HR 12 July 2011, *ECLI*:NL:HR:2011:BQ6555, para 2.4.

[140] Cf. *McCormick on Evidence*: 'the oldest and plainest ground for judicial notice is that the fact is so commonly known *in the community* as to make it unprofitable to require proof, and so certainly known as to make it indisputable among reasonable men.' Cited in: Walton and Macagno 2005, p. 10. Emphasis added. Cf. the Advisory Opinion of Advocate-General Aben in HR 11 October 2011, *ECLI*:NL:HR:2011:BR2990, para 3.4.

[141] E.g. the power vested in Rwandan *Bourgmestres* is, within the jurisdiction of the ICTR, a fact of common knowledge. 'Moreover, the powers of the office of *Bourgmestre* is a proper subject of judicial notice because it falls squarely into the category of matters that are of common knowledge within the jurisdiction of this Tribunal and which may readily be determined by reference to such reliable sources as the written laws of Rwanda. It also bears noting that within the area of its territorial jurisdiction and within the sphere of its specialized competence, a court is allowed to take judicial notice of an even wider scope of facts of common knowledge and notorious history. Thus, the Chamber may take judicial notice of facts that are notorious within the territories of Rwanda, Burundi and other neighboring states.' ICTR, Decision on the Prosecutor's Motion for Judicial Notice and Presumptions of Fact Pursuant to Rule 94 and 54, *Prosecutor v. Semanza*, Case No. ICTR-97-20-I, T. Ch. III, 3 November 2000, paras 29–30.

[142] Rechtbank Zutphen, 17 October 2007, *ECLI*:NL:RBZUT:2007:BB5666.

Dutch conscripts were mobilized in a certain period.[143] This type of facts of common knowledge is often used in relation to a *Garantenstellung* for accused acting in a certain capacity.[144] In a case before the court of appeal, a farmer faced charges of soil pollution. He had dumped certain types of manure on his estate, without a proper cover or package.[145] According to the farmer, both the type and quantity of the manure could not have polluted the soil.[146] The court of appeal did not agree with the farmer: the court stated first that it is common knowledge that the total quantity of manure produced by Dutch farmers results in environmental problems. Although these environmental problems are mostly associated with other types of manure than the farmer used,[147] 'everyone' must know that manure *may* pollute the soil. Second, the court stated that farmers in particular should be aware of these risks. The court identified expert reports and the internet as sources for the proposition that this fact is widely known. Consequently, it may be required of farmers that they familiarize themselves with such facts, which results in a *Garantenstellung* for professional farmers.[148]

It is important to note that facts of common knowledge are not the same as ready knowledge. Few people will be able to name the capital of Guinea-Bissau or the density of zinc off the cuff, but both facts can easily be looked up in an encyclopedia or on the internet. Therefore, they are facts of common knowledge.

In general, courts are not obliged to discuss facts of common knowledge with the parties during the proceedings. However, when the court is not sure whether a particular fact is of common knowledge, it must discuss the fact with the parties. This creates a dichotomy: there are facts that are patently of common knowledge and facts that are, in the court's view, *presumably* of common knowledge. In such cases, the Supreme Court ruled, the court must discuss such facts with the accused and the prosecutor.[149] One wonders how facts of common knowledge can be

---

143 Bijzondere Raad van Cassatie, 5 December 1945, *NOR* 3.

144 In the case mentioned above, the court of appeal stated that manure may cause environmental problems. This is a (general) fact of common knowledge and, addressing the farmer in particular, a well-known fact within the profession of the accused. Consequently, on farmers rests a special duty to avoid soil pollution by manure. Gerechtshof 's-Hertogenbosch, 28 September 2010, *ECLI*:NL:GHSHE:2010:BN8480 para B.2.

145 Violation of Article 13 of the Soil Protection Act and Article 1a of the Economic Offences Act.

146 To substantiate his claim, the farmer relied on a ruling by the Supreme Court in which the Supreme Court held that it is not common knowledge that 16 m3 horse manure can result in soil pollution. Gerechtshof 's-Hertogenbosch, 28 September 2010, *ECLI*:NL:GHSHE:2010:BN8480. HR 6 June 2000, *ECLI*:NL:HR:2000:AA6088.

147 Environmental problems arise in respect to pig, cow and poultry manure. The farmer used horse and mushroom manure.

148 Gerechtshof 's-Hertogenbosch, 28 September 2010 LJN: BN8480. In a similar way: Gerechtshof 's-Hertogenbosch, 1 October 2007 LJN: BB4570. Another example is presented by Kelk, who discussed the *Garantenstellung* for air travellers regarding drugs smuggling. Kelk 2013, p. 271.

149 HR 11 January 2011, *ECLI*:NL:HR:2011:BP0291m. nt. Mevis.

subject to debate: if there is doubt about the notoriety of a particular fact, it is, by definition, *not* notorious. Nevertheless, in such cases, the adversarial character of the proceedings is upheld in that the parties can comment on the fact in question.

The Supreme Court held that when a party disputes that such a fact is of common knowledge, the court must respond and explain why it concluded that the fact is of common knowledge.[150]

3.3.2.3 Contextual Facts

The following pages will present an overview of Dutch case law concerning crimes that have been committed in the context of an armed conflict or war.[151] In such cases, the contextual fact of the existence of an armed conflict or a state of war has to be proven. The acts committed by the accused have to be placed within the context of such an armed conflict or state of war. In order to prove these contextual facts, use has been made of facts of common knowledge. These cases are of particular relevance because they demonstrate how facts of common knowledge can be used as a shortcut to proof.

Crimes Committed in the Context of an Armed Conflict or a State of War

Dutch courts have not often dealt with cases concerning crimes that were committed in the context of an armed conflict or war. Two periods can be discerned: the first post-World War II years when Dutch collaborators were prosecuted before so-called extraordinary courts and the more recent prosecutions (2005–2013) of asylum seekers that, allegedly, committed war crimes in their countries of origin. In this period, two Dutch nationals also stood trial for having committed war crimes in Iraq and Liberia, respectively. These two cases will also be discussed under the heading 'recent prosecutions'.

3.3.2.4 The First Post-WWII Years

The Dutch government-in-exile approved the Extraordinary Criminal Law Decree (ECLD) in December 1943 which, despite the absence of parliamentary approval, functioned next to the provisions of the Dutch Criminal Code as the basis for the

---

[150] HR 12 July 2011, *ECLI*:NL:HR:2011:BQ6555 para 2.5.; HR 11 January 2011, *ECLI*:NL:HR:2011:BP0291 m. nt. Mevis. para 3.2.2.

[151] 'War' refers to the situation in which a formal declaration of war precedes the hostilities. The component 'war' is incorporated in Article 101 (joining foreign armed forces) and Article 102 CC (aiding the enemy during a state of war). Article 107a CC states that Articles 101 and 102 CC are also applicable in case of an armed conflict in which The Netherlands are involved.

post-war prosecutions.[152] Temporary extraordinary courts were set up consisting of both civil and military judges. Five extraordinary courts were set up that heard cases as a first-instance court.[153] No appeal was possible against the judgments of the extraordinary courts; the accused could, however, lodge cassation proceedings at the Extraordinary Court of Cassation in The Hague. Similar to ordinary cassation proceedings, the Extraordinary Court of Cassation could quash the judgment of an extraordinary court due to errors on questions of law. The extraordinary courts had to grant leave to the accused to initiate cassation proceedings against their judgments. The factual conclusions of the extraordinary court could not be challenged during the cassation proceedings because the admissibility of evidence and the weighing of the evidence were the prerogatives of the extraordinary court. However, because facts of common knowledge do not require proof, the Extraordinary Court of Cassation could determine whether a fact was indeed of common knowledge.

The ECLD stipulated that the extraordinary courts could impose the death penalty in cases concerning crimes that, according to the provisions of the Criminal Code, were punishable by 15 years' imprisonment or more.[154] Most accused faced charges of joining the German armed forces (punishable under Article 101 CC with a maximum sentence of 15 years' imprisonment) and aiding the German occupying forces (punishable under Article 102 CC with a maximum sentence of 15 years' imprisonment). The case law concerning these two crimes will be discussed separately.

Joining the German Armed Forces

Article 101 CC (old) states in translation:

> The Dutchman who, out of his own free will, joins the armed forces of a foreign power, knowing that this power is at war with The Netherlands, or in the anticipation of war with The Netherlands, will be punished with imprisonment of fifteen years. Joining the armed forces of a foreign power in the anticipation of war is only punishable if the war breaks out.[155]

---

[152] For a detailed account of the drafting process and the constitutional implications, see: Belinfante 1978, pp. 17–52. Besluit van 22 december 1943, houdende vaststelling van het Besluit Buitengewoon Strafrecht. See also: Rüter 1973, pp. 111–115.

[153] The extraordinary courts are called 'Bijzonder Gerechtshof' in Dutch. In the Dutch criminal justice system, 'gerechtshof' normally refers to a court of appeal. To avoid confusion, the term extraordinary court will be used to refer to such a 'Bijzonder gerechtshof', instead of the misleading term 'extraordinary court of appeal'. The extraordinary courts were set up in Amsterdam, The Hague, Den Bosch, Arnhem and Leeuwarden. Cf. Belinfante 1978, pp. 95–96.

[154] Belinfante 1978, pp. 27–28.

[155] In Dutch: 'De Nederlander die vrijwillig in krijgsdienst treedt bij eene buitenlandsche mogendheid, wetende dat deze met Nederland in oorlog is, of in het vooruitzicht van een oorlog met Nederland, wordt, in het laatste geval indien de oorlog uitbreekt, gestraft met gevangenisstraf van ten hoogste vijftien jaren' (oud). The phrase 'knowing that this power is at war with The Netherlands' was omitted by the Criminal Law in Wartime Act, 10 July 1952, *Stb.* 1952, 408 (*Wet Oorlogsstrafrecht*).

The contextual component of Article 101 CC is the state of war: when the war does not break out, joining the armed forces of a foreign power does not come within the article's reach. In order to convict an accused, the state of war has to be proven.

The existence of a state of war, including the duration of the war, was regarded as a fact of common knowledge by the extraordinary courts. For example, in a case concerning a Dutchman who worked as a driver for the German *Luftwaffe*, the Amsterdam extraordinary court held that it was a fact of common knowledge that The Netherlands were in a state of war since 10 May, 1940.[156]

In several cases the existence of the state of war was used as a line of defence: accused argued that the war had ended with the cessation of hostilities and the Dutch capitulation on 15 May, 1940. Consequently, they argued, joining the German armed forces after 15 May, 1940 was not a crime under Article 101 CC because their acts were not committed during a state of war. The extraordinary courts and the Extraordinary Court of Cassation uniformly rejected this view: they held that it was common knowledge that The Netherlands were at war with Germany between 10 May, 1940 and 5 May, 1945.[157] Noach was somewhat less precise and stated that the war ended in May 1945, while Van Eck argued that the war started as early as April 1939 and ended with the German general capitulation on 9 May 1945.[158] The state of war applied to the whole territory of The Netherlands.[159] The liberation of the southern part of The Netherlands in 1944 did not result in the cessation of the state of war in that part of the country. Theoretically, one could commit the crime of Article 101 CC in the liberated, southern part of The Netherlands until 5 May 1945 or, if one adhered to the view that the state of war ended with the general capitulation of Germany, until 9 May 1945.

From a fair trial perspective, the use of facts of common knowledge to 'prove' a contextual fact is problematic. The fairness of the proceedings may be infringed upon when the accused is confronted with facts of common knowledge for the first time in the court's final judgment. This can take the accused by surprise: he is confronted with facts he did not, and by definition, cannot dispute. This infringes upon the adversarial nature of proceedings, especially when it concerns components that are included in the *probandum* and are an important component of the

[156] Bijzonder Gerechtshof Amsterdam, 1 December 1945, *NOR* 37.

[157] Bijzonder Gerechtshof 's-Gravenhage, 25 September 1945, *NOR* 2; Bijzonder Gerechtshof Amsterdam, 1 December 1945, *NOR* 37; Bijzonder Gerechtshof Amsterdam, 1 December 1945, *NOR* 41; Bijzonder Gerechtshof Arnhem, 27 February 1946, *NOR* 49; Bijzonder Gerechtshof Amsterdam, 22 December 1945, *NOR* 50; Bijzonder Gerechtshof 's-Gravenhage, 4 September 1945, *NOR* 155; Bijzondere Raad van Cassatie, 4 March 1946, *NOR* 302; Bijzonder Gerechtshof 's-Hertogenbosch, 26 February 1947, *NOR* 781.

[158] Noach 1948, p. 155; Van Eck 1945, pp. 190–191, 204.

[159] That is, the European part of the kingdom.

statutory definition of the crime.[160] Moreover, the public character of the proceedings and the principle of immediacy may be infringed upon.[161] Dreissen observed that in German criminal proceedings, the court is obliged to discuss facts of common knowledge during the trial proceedings.[162] According to the Dutch law of criminal procedure, however, the court is not under an obligation to identify facts of common knowledge in the judgment. Facts of common knowledge do not have to be proven and, therefore, do not have to be supported by reference to specific means of proof or to be discussed during the trial proceedings.[163] If one of the parties argues that a particular fact is not of common knowledge, then the court must specifically respond to that argument. This presupposes that the parties are able to 'predict' which facts are likely to be regarded as common knowledge by the court.

By considering the state of war as a fact of common knowledge, the extraordinary courts took notice of the contextual component of Article 101 CC. This is similar to the manner in which contextual facts (or *chapeau* elements) are proven by the international criminal tribunals, regarding war crimes, crimes against humanity and genocide.[164] In Chap. 4, this will be discussed in more detail.

In order to convict the accused it was not sufficient to determine that a state of war existed. In the old definition of the crime of joining the enemy, it had to be proven that the accused knew that he had joined the enemy during a state of war. With the implementation of the Criminal Law in Wartime Act in 1952 this phrase was deleted. The extraordinary courts had to determine whether the accused knew that a state of was existed.

According to the extraordinary courts, the knowledge of the state of war could also be based on common knowledge. In a case before the Amsterdam extraordinary court, it was concluded that the accused knew The Netherlands were at war with Germany: the existence of a state of war had to be regarded as a fact of common knowledge and was *therefore* also known to the accused.[165] In a case before the extraordinary court in The Hague, the connection between contextual and subjective components was made more explicit, when the court concluded that it was common knowledge that units of the Dutch navy and army, under the command of the Dutch government, fought against the German army and that persons of the

---

160 Cf. Dreissen 2007, p. 57. Reijntjes referred to Röling, who stated that it is the accused's right to know in detail the factual grounds upon which he is convicted. Remmelink, on the other hand, was of the opposite view: facts of common knowledge do not need to be explicitly mentioned in the judgment. HR 26 August 1958, *NJ* 1959, 95; HR 7 January 1975, *NJ* 1975, 197; Reijntjes 2006, p. 57.

161 Cf. Nijboer 2011, pp. 208–209.

162 Dreissen 2007, pp. 288–290.

163 Cf. HR, 11 January 2011, *ECLI*:NL:HR:2011:BP0291 para 3.2.2.

164 E.g. the widespread and systematic character of an attack in the articles on crimes against humanity. Cf. Article 7 ICC Statute, Article 3 ICTR Statute.

165 Bijzonder Gerechtshof Amsterdam, 1 December 1945, *NOR* 37. See also: Bijzonder Gerechtshof Amsterdam, 1 December 1945, *NOR* 41; Bijzonder Gerechtshof Arnhem, 27 February 1946, *NOR* 49; Bijzonder Gerechtshof Amsterdam, 22 December 1946, *NOR* 50.

age and maturity of the accused were aware of this fact. Therefore, the accused had knowledge of the state of war.[166]

The difference in reasoning between these two rulings is subtle, but significant. The Amsterdam extraordinary court based the conclusion that the accused had knowledge of the state of war solely on a fact of common knowledge, whereas the extraordinary court in The Hague based its finding only in part (although a significant part) on common knowledge. The accused's knowledge of the state of war was derived from his age and maturity.

The Extraordinary Court of Cassation approved this line of reasoning. In a similar case concerning Article 101 CC, counsel for the accused argued that the intent of the accused could not be derived solely from facts of common knowledge. In his advisory opinion, the Advocate-Fiscal agreed to this proposition, but stated that in this case the argument was without merit because the extraordinary court had based its conclusion of the accused's intent only in part on a fact of common knowledge. The Court of Cassation agreed that the extraordinary court was right in finding that the state of war was common knowledge for persons of the accused's age and intellectual capacities, which the extraordinary court had observed during the trial proceedings.[167]

In a case before the extraordinary court in The Hague, the state of war was regarded as common knowledge but was, nevertheless, unknown to the accused, resulting in an acquittal. The court concluded that the accused was unaware of the state of war when he joined the German navy: he was mentally incapable to grasp the meaning of the state of war.[168]

Aiding the Enemy During a State of War

Article 102 CC (old) states in translation:

> Imprisonment with a maximum of fifteen years shall be imposed on him who, intentionally, during a state of war, aides the enemy or damages the interests of the state to the benefit of the enemy.[169]

Article 11 ECLD, as quoted by Van Eck, stipulates that the extraordinary courts can impose the death penalty, life imprisonment or temporary imprisonment with a maximum of 20 years.[170] Similar to Article 101 CC, which contains a contextual and subjective component (the state of war and the knowledge thereof),

---

[166] Bijzonder Gerechtshof's-Gravenhage, 4 September 1945, *NOR* 155.

[167] Bijzondere Raad van Cassatie, 4 March 1946, *NOR* 302.

[168] Bijzonder Gerechtshof's-Gravenhage, 29 July 1946, *NOR* 445.

[169] Cf. Van Eck 1945, p. 143. In Dutch: 'Met gevangenisstraf van ten hoogste vijftien jaren wordt gestraft hij, die opzettelijk, in tijd van oorlog, den vijand hulp verleent of den staat tegenover den vijand benadeelt.'.

[170] Van Eck 1945, p. 368.

Article 102 CC requires that the accused intentionally aided the enemy during a state of war. The contextual component 'war' falls within the scope of the accused's intent: the intent must include aiding the enemy *during the war*.[171] In several cases, the existence of a state of war and the proof of the intent of the accused were based on facts of common knowledge.

In the case against Max Blokzijl, notorious for his pro-German radio propaganda, the extraordinary court in The Hague held that the state of war was a fact of common knowledge. The accused's defence that he believed the war had ended with the capitulation of the Dutch armed forces in May 1940 was rejected on the basis that it was common knowledge that persons with the intellectual capacity of the accused knew that the state of war had not ended before May 1945.[172] Moreover, the court deemed it of common knowledge that national socialists in The Netherlands (of which the accused was a prominent member) aided the enemy to the detriment of the Allies between 1941 and May 1945.[173] Compared with the legal definition of the crime of aiding the enemy during times of war, the accused was, to a significant extent, convicted on the basis of facts of common knowledge. The state of war, his knowledge thereof and the fact that national socialists aided the enemy during the war, were all considered common knowledge. The evidence that the accused acted intentionally, necessary for a conviction based on Article 102 CC, derived from testimony the accused gave during the trial proceedings, in particular when the accused testified that he made propaganda for the German New Order in his radio speeches. He denied, however, that he did so during a state of war.[174] The court combined the statement of the accused that he had intentionally delivered his radio speeches with the facts of common knowledge and imposed the death penalty.[175]

Before the Extraordinary Court of Cassation, Blokzijl specifically challenged the reasoning of the extraordinary court regarding the use of facts of common knowledge. The Extraordinary Court of Cassation approved the reasoning of the extraordinary court, however, and endorsed the finding of the extraordinary court that the knowledge of the accused, based on common knowledge, could be inferred from his profession as a journalist.[176]

---

171 Cf. Van Eck 1945, p. 272. Cf. Langemeijer 1952, p. 491.

172 Bijzonder Gerechtshof Den Haag, 25 September 1945, *NOR* 2. CABR, BRC 10/45 inv. nr. 74349 (*M. Blokzijl*) Proces-verbaal Politieke Opsporingsdienst 's-Gravenhage No. 976 C.B. (22 augustus 1945). For a similar line of reasoning, see: Bijzonder Gerechtshof Amsterdam, 29 November 1945, *NOR* 40; Bijzonder Gerechtshof 's-Gravenhage, 19 March 1946, *NOR* 80; Bijzondere Raad van Cassatie, 17 June 1946, *NOR* 395.

173 Bijzonder Gerechtshof 's-Gravenhage, 25 September 1945, *NOR* 2. Bijzondere Raad van Cassatie, 5 December 1945, *NOR* 3, sub IV.

174 Bijzonder Gerechtshof's-Gravenhage, 25 September 1945, *NOR* 2.

175 Bijzonder Gerechtshof's-Gravenhage, 25 September 1945, *NOR* 2. For a similar case in which the accused's intent was based to a large extent on facts of common knowledge, see: Bijzonder Gerechtshof Amsterdam, 11 April 1946, *NOR* 321.

176 Bijzondere Raad van Cassatie, 5 December 1945, *NOR* 3, sub IV.

In response to an argument raised in Blokzijl's defence, the Extraordinary Court of Cassation held that Articles 338 and 339 CCP must be regarded as complementary and of the same standing. It is within the discretion of the courts to make inferences from the means of proof of Article 338 CCP. According to the Court, this discretion to select the evidence presented during trial also extends to Article 339 (2) CCP.[177] Consequently, courts may rely on either Article 338 or Article 339(2) to prove a crime.

A final observation on the post-WWII case law concerns the adversarial character of the trial proceedings. It follows from Articles 338 and 339 CCP that facts of common knowledge cannot be disputed. This means that the adversarial character of proceedings, when it comes to those notorious facts, is absent. If applied properly, this should not be of any concern because those facts cannot be part of the *probandum* and, therefore, are not detrimental to the accused. In a judgment of the extraordinary court in The Hague, the court tried to uphold the adversarial character of proceedings. In the early case against the national socialist Van Genechten, installed by the occupying German forces as Procurator-General of the so-called 'Peace Court of Appeal' in The Hague, the extraordinary court considered the existence of a state of war common knowledge. It further stated that this fact had not been challenged by the accused during the proceedings.[178] One could argue that it is immaterial whether the accused acknowledges or denies that a fact is notorious, as Article 339(2) CCP instructs the court not to require evidence of notorious facts, which renders the opinion of the accused irrelevant. It remains solely within the competence of the court to determine whether a particular fact is of common knowledge.

A similar reasoning can be found in a judgment of the extraordinary court in Den Bosch. As many others, the accused denied that he knew Germany and The Netherlands were at war during 1943 and 1944. In its judgment, the court reiterated that the state of war was of common knowledge and that no special circumstance had been put forward to substantiate the argument of the accused.[179]

The manner in which the extraordinary courts dealt with the contextual fact of the state of war shows how problematic it can be to conclude that a state of war existed on the basis of facts of common knowledge. The adversarial character of

---

[177] Bijzondere Raad van Cassatie, 5 December 1945, *NOR* 3, sub IV.

[178] However, Van Genechten had challenged his knowledge of the state of war. His dossier contains a statement he made before a police officer. In this statement, which Van Genechten authorized, he stated that he believed the war was over when the Dutch armed forces surrendered to the German armed forces. Bijzonder Gerechtshof's-Gravenhage, 17 October 1945, *NOR* 7. CABR, BRC 27/45 inv. nr. 74376 (*R. van Genechten*) Proces-verbaal Politieke Opsporingsdienst 's-Gravenhage No. 979 C.B. (27 augustus 1945) p. 3.

[179] Bijzonder Gerechtshof's-Hertogenbosch, 26 February 1947, *NOR* 781.

the trial proceedings is infringed, in particular when the accused denies that he had knowledge of the state of war. It is one thing to regard the contextual fact of the state of war as a fact of common knowledge, but it is quite something different to use facts of common knowledge to prove the accused's intent. In such cases it is better, from the perspective of adversarial and fair proceedings, to base such findings on legal means of proof that have been discussed during the trial proceedings. This way, the adversarial character of the proceedings is guaranteed.

3.3.2.5 More Recent Cases Regarding International Crimes

Besides the post-WWII cases, Dutch courts have dealt with international crimes in the recent past. The previous paragraph revealed how problematic the use of fact of common knowledge regarding contextual facts can be from the perspective of a fair and adversarial procedure. The question then arises how Dutch courts have handled the more recent cases in which contextual facts also played a pivotal role. Similar to the post-WWII cases, the acts of the accused have to be placed within the context of an armed conflict.

The recent prosecutions were conducted on the basis of the Criminal Law in Wartime Act (*Wet Oorlogsstrafrecht*), the International Crimes Act (*Wet Internationale Misdrijven*), the Convention against Torture Implementation Act (*Uitvoeringswet Folteringverdrag*) and the Convention against Genocide Implementation Act (*Uitvoeringswet genocideverdrag*). They have resulted in a small number of judgments, which are primarily concerned with war crimes. Due to a lack of jurisdiction between 15 May 1945 and the implementation of the International Crimes Act on 1 October 2003, no charges of crimes against humanity could be brought before Dutch courts during this period.[180] Charges of genocide were brought in the case against a Rwandan asylum seeker, but these charges were dismissed due to a lack of jurisdiction.[181]

Therefore, the analysis will be focused on the contextual component of war crimes: the existence and nature, either international or non-international, of an armed conflict. First, two cases will be discussed involving Rwandans who were prosecuted for their role in the Rwandan genocide of 1994. This discussion will be followed by the cases against members of the Afghan military who were prosecuted for their role during the armed conflict in Afghanistan between 1978 and 1992. Finally, two cases against Dutch nationals will be discussed. One case concerns the supply of components of chemical weapons to the Iraqi regime of

---

[180] Jofriet 2009, pp. 14–15. Cf. *Kamerstukken II*, 2000/01, 26262, 9, p. 5.

[181] Rechtbank Den Haag, 24 June 2007, *ECLI*:NL:RBSGR:2007:BB0494; Gerechtshof Den Haag, 17 December 2007, *ECLI*:NL:GHSGR:2007:BC0287; HR 21 October 2008, *ECLI*:NL:HR:2008:BD6568.

Saddam Hussein, while the other concerns war crimes and the supply of weapons to the regime of Charles Taylor in Liberia.

The Case Against Joseph M.

The case against the Rwandan asylum seeker Joseph M. was brought before the district court of The Hague in the fall of 2008. The accused faced charges of war crimes based on Article 8 of the Criminal Law in Wartime Act and, in the alternative, torture under Article 2(b) of the Convention against Torture Implementation Act.[182] The charges of genocide were dismissed, due to a lack of jurisdiction.[183] The district court concluded that sufficient evidence had been presented to convict the accused on the torture charges.[184] The accused was acquitted, however, of the charges of war crimes under the Criminal Law in Wartime Act. The district court concluded that insufficient evidence had been presented for the nexus between the acts of the accused and the armed conflict. On the question of whether an armed conflict existed during the relevant period, the district court observed:

> With reference to established case law of the ICTR, the Court concludes that during the period described in the charges (from 6 April up to and including 17 July 1994) a non-international armed conflict took place between the FAR and the RPF. The FAR was the government army. The RPF was a structured and disciplined army under responsible command, which had partial control over Rwandan territory and which was able to execute military operations in a coordinated manner and to meet the obligations of humanitarian laws of war.[185]

The district court relied on case law of the ICTR to conclude that an armed conflict existed during the relevant period. During the parliamentary debates on the International Crimes Act, the Minister of Justice stated that Dutch courts, when hearing a case concerning international crimes, must take into account the international standards on the correct interpretation of the elements of crimes.[186] It was

---

[182] Uitvoeringswet Folteringverdrag. Wet van 29 september 1988, tot uitvoering van het Verdrag tegen foltering en andere wrede, onmenselijke of onterende behandeling of bestraffing, *Stb.* 1988, 478. Repealed by the implementation of the International Crimes Act (Article 20).

[183] Rechtbank Den Haag, 24 July 2007, *ECLI*:NL:RBSGR:2007:BB0494; Gerechtshof Den Haag, 17 December 2007, *ECLI*:NL:GHSGR:2007:BC0287; HR, 21 October 2008, *ECLI*:NL:HR:2008:BD6568.

[184] Rechtbank Den Haag, 23 March 2009, *ECLI*:NL:RBSGR:2009:BI2444 Chapter 15, paras 54–66.

[185] Rechtbank Den Haag, 23 March 2009, *ECLI*:NL:RBSGR:2009:BK0520 Chapter 15, para 26 (court provided English translation of Rechtbank Den Haag, 23 March 2009, *ECLI*:NL:RBSGR:2009:BI2444).

[186] *Kamerstukken II*, 2001/02, 28337, 3, p. 5.

emphasized that this was already common practice in the interpretation of the Criminal Law in Wartime Act, in particular in relation to the element 'laws and customs of war' contained in Article 8 of the Criminal Law in Wartime Act.[187]

However, a distinction must be made between the *interpretation* of an element and the legal means of proof that are used to *prove* that element. When the court interprets, for example, the element 'armed conflict', it should take into account the manner in which the international criminal tribunals have interpreted this element. Subsequently, the court must determine whether sufficient and reliable evidence has been presented to conclude that an armed conflict occurred during the relevant period.

In its conclusion that an armed conflict existed, the court, next to the reference to 'established case law', referred to one decision of the ICTR Appeals Chamber. In this interlocutory decision in *Karemera*, the Appeals Chamber held that the existence of a non-international armed conflict in Rwanda between 1 January and 17 July 1994 was a notorious fact, not subject to reasonable dispute.[188] The Appeals Chamber held that the existence of an armed conflict has to be regarded as a fact of common knowledge.

The ICTR Trial Chamber *in the same case* had ruled, however, that the existence of an armed conflict must be proven by the prosecutor by other means than by judicially noticing it as a fact of common knowledge. The existence of an armed conflict must be determined on a case by case basis, after evidence has been presented by the parties.[189] The Appeals Chamber, nevertheless, took judicial notice of this fact under Rule 94(A) of the ICTR Rules of Procedure and Evidence. This entails that the fact is regarded as a fact of common knowledge, which means that Trial Chambers are obliged to take judicial notice of this fact. The fact becomes indisputable, allowing no evidence in rebuttal to be presented.[190]

The manner in which the district court in The Hague relied on the finding of the ICTR Appeals Chamber regarding the existence of an armed conflict raises some questions. First, it is remarkable that the ICTR Trial Chamber refused to regard the existence of an armed conflict as a fact of common knowledge. The Trial Chamber argued that such a legal finding must be based on the presentation of evidence (which can be challenged by the defence) and not on common knowledge. The

---

187 *Kamerstukken II*, 2001/02, 28337, 3 p. 6. Cf. Gerechtshof Den Haag, 7 July 2011, *ECLI*:NL:GHSGR:2011:BR0686 p. 48.

188 ICTR, Decision on Prosecutor's Interlocutory Appeal of Decision on Judicial Notice, *Prosecutor v. Karemera et al.*, Case No.: ICTR-98-44-AR73(C), A. Ch., 16 June 2006, para 29. With reference to a decision by the Appeals Chamber in *Prosecutor v. Semanza.*

189 ICTR, Decision on Motion for Judicial Notice, *Prosecutor v. Karemera*, Case No.: ICTR-98-44-R94, T. Ch. III, 9 November 2005, para 11.

190 Rule 94(A) reads in full: 'A Trial Chamber shall not require proof of facts of common knowledge but shall take judicial notice thereof.' The legal effects of Rule 94(A), in terms of probative value, are established in the case law.

ICTR has a hierarchical structure in which decisions of the Trial Chamber regarding both factual and legal questions can be reversed by the Appeals Chamber. However, when two chambers differ with regard to the notoriety of a particular fact, the preferred way to proceed should be to require the presentation of legal means of proof.

Second, from the perspective of a fair and adversarial trial it is troublesome that elements of the legal definition of a crime are proven by reference to a fact of common knowledge, as the adversarial character of the proceedings may be harmed. It is imperative that the adversarial character of the proceedings ('une procédure contradictoire') is upheld.

The reasoning of the district court in The Hague with respect to the existence and character of the armed conflict is, therefore, unsatisfactory. The court relied on an interlocutory decision of the ICTR Appeals Chamber in which the Appeals Chamber relied on a fact of common knowledge to prove the existence of an armed conflict. Chapter 4 will present a more detailed analysis of the use of facts of common knowledge by the international criminal tribunals, but it is noted here that facts of common knowledge cannot be challenged before the international criminal tribunals. This means that the Chambers are not under an obligation to allow the defence to present evidence in rebuttal in order to challenge the notoriety of such a fact. This has detrimental consequences for the adversarial character of the trial proceedings.

The judgment the district court relied on did not allow for an adversarial dispute on the existence and nature of the armed conflict. This entails that an important contextual component of the crimes alleged is proven, although indirectly, on the basis of an indisputable fact of common knowledge. Although the finding of the district court was not detrimental to the accused in the end (the nexus between his acts and the armed conflict could not be proven, resulting in an acquittal), when the court would have found a nexus, the finding of guilt would have relied in part on common knowledge. The presentation of legal means of proof on the armed conflict in Rwanda, such as an expert statement or documentary evidence, would have been preferable. Besides providing the district court the possibility to determine itself whether an armed conflict existed (rather than relying on the findings by the ICTR Chambers), it would enable the parties to comment and, if necessary, dispute the evidence presented.

The district court convicted Joseph M. for the torture charges and sentenced him to 20 years' imprisonment. He was acquitted for the war crime charges. Both the accused and the prosecutor appealed the decision by the district court.

Appeal Proceedings

The court of appeal in The Hague considered, *inter alia*, whether a nexus existed between the armed conflict and the acts of the accused regarding the war crimes charges. The court of appeal first summed up the relevant case law of the *ad hoc* Tribunals to determine the appropriate legal interpretation of an armed conflict, just as the Minister of Justice had envisaged during the parliamentary debates on the International Crimes Act.[191] The same holds true for the nexus-element and the status as a protected person under Common Article 3 of the Geneva Conventions. The court of appeal concluded that, during the period of 6 April and 17 July 1994, an armed conflict existed in Rwanda which was not of international character. The court of appeal referred to the judgment of the ICTR Trial Chamber in *Kayishema and Ruzindana*.[192]

The ICTR Trial Chamber in this case delivered its judgment before the *Semanza* appeal judgment and the Appeals Chamber decision in *Karemera*, in which the existence of an armed conflict was considered a fact of common knowledge.[193] This means that the court of appeal, unlike the district court, did not rely on facts of common knowledge to prove the contextual fact of the existence of an armed conflict. The ICTR Trial Chamber in *Kayishema and Ruzindana* based its finding on the existence of an armed conflict on legal means of proof, instead of on a fact of common knowledge.

The court of appeal concluded that the acts of the accused were committed in the furtherance of, or under the guise of, the armed conflict (the nexus-standard which was applied before the *ad hoc* Tribunals) against protected persons and, therefore, constituted war crimes.[194] Joseph M. was convicted to life imprisonment. The Supreme Court rejected the arguments raised by the accused during the cassation proceedings and confirmed the judgment of the court of appeal.[195]

The Case Against Yvonne B.

In another case concerning the Rwandan genocide, the accused faced charges of genocide and war crimes. Yvonne B. was accused of genocide, attempted genocide, murder, conspiracy to commit genocide, incitement to commit genocide and war crimes (unlawful assault and threat).[196] Ultimately, she was convicted only of incitement to commit genocide. She was acquitted of the other genocide charges and the war crimes charges.

---

191 The Government referred to the fact that international case law already took a prominent place in the interpretation of certain aspects of the Criminal Law in Wartime Act. Gerechtshof Den Haag, 7 July 2011, *ECLI*:NL:GHSGR:2011:BR0686, para 16.3.1.

192 Gerechtshof Den Haag, 7 July 2011, *ECLI*:NL:GHSGR:2011:BR0686, para 17.2. (The Court referred to para 173 of the ICTR trial judgment. This is, in fact, para 172.). ICTR, Judgment, *Prosecutor v. Kayishema and Ruzindana*, ICTR-95-1-T, T. Ch. II, 21 May 1999, para 172.

193 ICTR, Judgment, *Prosecutor v. Semanza*, ICTR-97-20-A, A. Ch., 20 May 2005; ICTR, Decision on Prosecutor's Interlocutory Appeal of Decision on Judicial Notice, *Prosecutor v. Karemera*, ICTR-98-44-AR73(C), A. Ch., 16 June 2006.

194 Gerechtshof Den Haag, 7 July 2011, *ECLI*:NL:GHSGR:2011:BR0686, para 17.5.

195 HR, 26 November 2013, *ECLI*:NL:HR:2013:1420.

196 Rechtbank Den Haag, 1 March 2013, *ECLI*:NL:RBDHA:2013:8710, Chapter 1.

Regarding the genocide charges, the district court referred to the famous interlocutory decision of the ICTR Appeals Chamber in *Karemera*, in which the Appeals Chamber held:

> The fact of the Rwandan genocide is part of world history, a fact as certain as any other, a classic instance of a 'fact of common knowledge'.[197]

The evidence against the accused regarding the charge of incitement to commit genocide consisted mainly of witness statements. Witnesses testified that the accused participated in public meetings in which she incited the public to sing genocidal songs.[198] The district court had to determine whether the accused acted with the required special intent to destroy, in whole or in part, a protected group. The district court, referring to the *Van Anraat* case, took the following general factors into consideration:

- the general framework in which the criminal offence took place;
- the circumstance that the protected group systematically became the victim of other unlawful acts;
- the extent in which the crimes were committed;
- hitting systematically on victims because of belonging to a certain group;
- the repetition of destructive and discriminative acts;
- the number of victims;
- the way in which the crimes were committed;
- the area where the perpetrator was active;
- the evidence aim of the perpetrator to take the life of the victims;
- the seriousness of the genocidal acts which were committed;
- the frequency of the genocidal acts in a certain area;
- the general political framework in which the crimes were committed;
- expressions made by the perpetrator regarding the position and/or fate of the protected group.[199]

The district court derived the accused's genocidal intent from the following specific factors:

- the general as well as political framework in which the defendant's remarks were made;
- the circumstance that the Tutsis at that time systematically became the victim of violence merely based on their ethnicity;
- the manner in which and the specific context in which the defendant made her remarks;
- the fact that the defendant made her remarks repeatedly;
- the defendant's social position as CDR-member and prominent local resident, as well as her authority over the public.[200]

---

197 Rechtbank Den Haag, 1 March 2013, *ECLI*:NL:RBDHA:2013:BZ4292, para 5.31.

198 Rechtbank Den Haag, 1 March 2013, *ECLI*:NL:RBDHA:2013:BZ4292, Chapter 12.

199 Rechtbank Den Haag, 1 March 2013, *ECLI*:NL:RBDHA:2013:8710, Chapter 12.11.

200 Rechtbank Den Haag, 1 March 2013, *ECLI*:NL:RBDHA:2013:8710, para 12.20.

In this paragraph the district court placed the specific acts of the accused in the context of the general and political framework (or context) of Rwanda in the early summer of 1994. The acts of the accused were placed in the genocidal context that existed during this period. The court provided a detailed and comprehensive framework in which the acts of the accused were placed, without simply referring to the fact that the Rwandan genocide was a 'classic instance of a fact of common knowledge'. This way of reasoning allows for a detailed examination of the conclusions of the court and enabled the accused to specifically challenge those aspects of the general framework and personal factors with which she disagreed. By providing such a detailed and transparent approach to the question of whether the accused acted with genocidal intent, the court enabled the accused to challenge the evidence effectively.

Regarding the war crimes charges, the district court held:

> The RPF was a structured and disciplined army under the supervision of a responsible commander, which partially dominated Rwandan territory, that was capable of executing military operations in a coordinated manner and satisfying the requirements of the humanitarian laws of war.[201]

The court concluded that a non-international armed conflict existed in Rwanda between 1 October 1990 and 17 July 1994. The court based this finding on the interlocutory decision of the ICTR Appeals Chamber in *Karemera* and the judgment of the Trial Chamber in *Akayesu*. Similar to *Joseph M.*, the court referred to *Karemera* in which the existence of a non-international armed conflict was regarded as a fact of common knowledge.[202] In the trial judgment in *Akayesu*, the ICTR Trial Chamber I concluded that an armed conflict not of an international character existed during the period described in the indictment.[203] The Trial Chamber based this finding on documentary evidence presented during the trial proceedings.

The district court concluded that no nexus existed between the acts of the accused and the armed conflict and acquitted the accused on the war crimes charges. She was, however, convicted of incitement to commit genocide and punished to imprisonment for 6 years and 8 months.

The Cases Against Afghan Asylum Seekers

In 2005 and 2007, several cases were brought before the district court in The Hague involving Afghan asylum seekers who had served in the Afghan military.

---

[201] Rechtbank Den Haag, 1 March 2013, *ECLI*:NL:RBDHA:2013:8710, para 19.9. (court-provided English translation of Rechtbank Den Haag, 1 March 2013, *ECLI*: NL:RBDHA:2013:BZ4292).

[202] ICTR, Decision on Prosecutor's Interlocutory Appeal of Decision on Judicial Notice, *Prosecutor v. Karemera et al.*, A. Ch., ICTR-98-44-AR73(C), 16 June 2006, para 29.

[203] ICTR, Judgment, *Prosecutor v. Akayesu*, T. Ch. I, ICTR96-4-T, 2 September 1998, para 627.

The 2005 cases concerned two former members of the Afghan military intelligence service who were accused of torture and of having committed war crimes during the armed conflict in Afghanistan, which lasted from 1978 until 1992. They were prosecuted under the Criminal Law in Wartime Act and the Convention against Torture Implementation Act.

The district court concluded in both cases that an armed conflict existed in Afghanistan between 1978 and 1992. The conflict was qualified as non-international.[204] In both cases, the court paid extensive attention to the evidence of both the existence and the nature of the conflict. The evidence consisted of the testimony of an expert, the result of documentary research conducted by the police, several witness statements and the testimony the accused gave during the trial proceedings.[205] On the basis of these legal means of proof, the district court concluded that the contextual element of the existence of an armed conflict was proven. In both cases, the accused were convicted of having committed war crimes.

In the case from 2007 against a former officer of the Afghan military intelligence service, the district court held with respect to the existence and nature of an armed conflict:

> In this respect it needs to be pointed out that the District Court, following the District Court and the Court of Appeal in the cases mentioned above,[206] agrees with the Public Prosecution Service and the defense, that the armed conflict in Afghanistan in the eighties of the last century, was mainly a non-international conflict between the regime in Kabul and the "Mujahedeen", that revolted against this regime – also using arms. It's true that this regime was partly supported by Russian advisors and army divisions and participated in the armed conflict, yet this was not a conflict between two sovereign states.[207]

Apart from the reference to the judgments of the district court and court of appeal, no other legal means of proof were identified by the court.[208] The court of appeal endorsed this finding of the district court:

---

[204] Rechtbank Den Haag, 14 October 2005, *ECLI*:NL:RBSGR:2005:AU4347, pp. 6–9; Rechtbank Den Haag, 14 October 2005, *ECLI*:NL:RBSGR:2005:AU4373, para 11.

[205] Rechtbank Den Haag, 14 October 2005, *ECLI*:NL:RBSGR:2005:AU4347, p. 9; Rechtbank Den Haag, 14 October 2005, *ECLI*:NL:RBSGR:2005:AU4373, pp. 6–8.

[206] Rechtbank Den Haag, 14 October 2005, *ECLI*:NL:RBSGR:2005:AU4373; Rechtbank Den Haag, 14 October 2005, *ECLI*:NL:RBSGR:2005:AU4347; Gerechtshof Den Haag, 29 January 2007, *ECLI*:NL:GHSGR:2007:AZ7147; Gerechtshof Den Haag, 29 January 2007, *ECLI*:NL:GHSGR:2007:AZ7143.

[207] Rechtbank Den Haag, 25 June 2007, *ECLI*:NL:RBSGR:2007:BA9575, p. 3. court-provided translation of *ECLI*:NL:RBSGR:2007:BA7877.

[208] Judgments and decisions of courts are a distinct category of documentary evidence, according to Article 344(1)(1) CCP.

> There is no dispute regarding the nature of the conflict in this case, which was primarily a non-international conflict.[209]

The court of appeal did not explicitly refer to particular means of proof that supported this conclusion.

The manner in which both the district court and the court of appeal concluded that an armed conflict existed in the relevant period, is an example of courts that rely on the factual findings of another court (or, another bench within the same court). In this case, both the prosecutor and the defence agreed with the factual conclusions of the district court. This entails that the existence and character of an armed conflict were discussed during the proceedings; as such, the adversarial character of the proceedings was respected. However, courts should be careful when they 'import' the factual conclusions of other courts. The parties must be allowed to comment upon such conclusions and have the opportunity to effectively challenge the conclusions when they wish to do so. In the international context a rather detailed framework has been developed in order to safeguard the accused from the import of facts that have been established by other courts (or by another chamber of the same tribunal). This will be discussed extensively in Chap. 4. It is noted here that, when courts act in such a way, it is imperative that the accused is able to effectively challenge these facts.

The Cases Against Dutch Nationals: Van Anraat

The Dutch businessman Van Anraat was accused of having supplied components for chemical weapons that were used against the Kurds by the Iraqi-regime under Saddam Hussein in the 1980s. Van Anraat faced charges of aiding and abetting genocide and aiding and abetting war crimes. He was acquitted for the genocide charge, but convicted for being an aider and abettor to war crimes committed by the Hussein regime.

Considering the war crimes charges, the district court had to determine whether an armed conflict existed in the relevant period. The court was presented with the following means of proof: a report by an investigating officer on the history of the Kurds in Iraq, a report written by two employees of the prosecution service and the testimony of a witness who had helped write Human Rights Watch reports on

[209] Gerechtshof Den Haag, 16 July 2009, *ECLI*:NL:GHSGR:2009:BK8758. Court-provided translation of *LJN*: BJ2796. The Court of Appeal stated in para 68: 'The Court of Appeal would begin by noting that it is not in the dispute that the present case concerns a non-international armed conflict in the period referred to in the indictment, that the defendant had knowledge of this conflict, and that there is a close relationship between this conflict and the criminal offence of which the defendant is accused (the 'nexus requirement'). In this sense, the general criteria for crimes covered by common Article 3 are fulfilled.' The Supreme Court dismissed the cassation appeal lodged by the prosecution. It did not comment on the cited passage of the District Court and Court of Appeal. HR 8 November 2011, *ECLI*:NL:HR:2011:BR6598.

Iraq.[210] The reports were mainly based on historical studies and non-governmental organizations reports.[211]

On the basis of these legal means of proof, the court concluded:

a. that in the period from 22 September 1980 to 20 August 1988, an international armed conflict took place between Iran and Iraq as defined in armed conflict law;
b. that a non-international armed conflict took place as defined in armed conflict law on the territory of Iraq between Iraqi government troops on one side and armed (Kurdish) resistance groups on the other side. This non-international armed conflict had already started long before the period mentioned in the charges and lasted even thereafter.[212]

The manner in which the district court considered whether an armed conflict existed is an example of how, ideally, such contextual facts should be proven. The legal means of proof are clearly identified and, more importantly, it is clear on which sources the reports are based. Although one might argue that the underlying sources should be presented during the trial proceedings (for instance, by appointing an expert who could summarize and explain the main findings of the historical studies), it is completely clear how the district court came to the conclusion that an armed conflict existed. Under Dutch evidence law, no strict 'best evidence' rule exists: the summary and analysis of the investigators suffice (except, of course, when the court deems it necessary to be presented with the original sources of such reports. There is, however, no statutory obligation to do so).[213] Van Anraat was convicted to 15 years' imprisonment.

---

210 Rechtbank Den Haag, 23 December 2005, *ECLI*:NL:RBSGR:2005:AX6406, paras 10.1–10.3.

211 The report by the investigation officer was mainly based on the following sources: 'A modern history of the Kurds', third revised edition, 2004, by David McDowell; 'Report on the situation on human rights in Iraq,' 19-2-1993, Mr. Max van der Stoel, E/CN.4/1993/45; 'Report on the situation on human rights in Iraq', 25-2-1994, Mr. Max van der Stoel, E/CN.4/1994/58; 'Genocide in Iraq, The Anfal Campaign against the Kurds', New York, 1993, Middle East Watch/Human Rights Watch; 'Bureaucracy of Repression; the Iraqi Government in its own words', New York, 1994, Middle East Watch/Human Rights Watch; the decrees, orders, reports, etc. confiscated by the Kurds in 1991 in Northern Iraq; Chemical weapons use in Kurdistan, Washington 1988 and a written testimony in a Belgian file. The anonymous source study was mainly based on: general review of the Stockholm International Peace Research Institute (SIPRI) and the Harvard Sussex Program, that includes all kinds of resolutions and newspaper articles; 'Genocide in Iraq: The Anfal Campaign against the Kurds', New York, 1993, Middle East Watch/Human Rights Watch; a report by the American Department of Navy, 10 December 1990, Stephen Pelletière and Douglas Johnson; several historical-political studies, especially: 'The longest war: The Iran-Iraq war', Westview Press Boulder Co 1990; 'The lessons of modern war vol II, The Iran-Iraq war', Westview Press Boulder Co 1990; 'A modern history of the Kurds', third revised edition, IB Taurus & Co, New York 2004; 'The Kurds between Iran and Iraq' in Middle East report, Vol 16, no. 4 July August 1986.

212 Rechtbank Den Haag, 23 December 2005, *ECLI*:NL:RBSGR:2005:AX6406, para 10.4.

213 Cf. the observation by Stein: 'The traditional 'best evidence rule' that prefers original documents over their duplicates is one of the many manifestations of the best evidence principle.' Stein 2005, p. 39.

Appeal Proceedings

Both the prosecutor and Van Anraat initiated appeal proceedings against the judgment of the district court. On the existence and nature of the armed conflict, the court of appeal held:

> Regarding the attacks that took place in the proven period on the places in Iraq mentioned in the proven charges under count 1. alternatively, the Court considers it a proven fact that these were carried out within the framework of an international and/or non-international armed conflict (as also proven by the court of first instance). [...] For proof of the nature of the armed conflict, the Court's opinion is particularly founded on the official report dated 19 May 2005 drawn up by an investigating officer, which includes the report on an investigation that had been conducted regarding certain sources, as well as on a report drawn up by (employee PPS 1 [Public Prosecution Service, KV]) and (employee PPS 2), included in the case file under reference number F61. Furthermore, the Court's judgment rests partly on the statement made by the (co-author of the Human Rights Watch reports) at the hearing at the first instance court on 30 November 2005.[214]

Similar to the judgment of the district court, it is clear on which sources the court of appeal based its finding on the existence and nature of the armed conflict. The contextual component was, therefore, proven by legal means of proof that were presented during the trial proceedings. The Supreme Court rejected the complaints by the accused against the judgment of the court of appeal. Due to a violation of the right to be tried within a reasonable time, the sentence imposed by the court of appeal (17 years' imprisonment) was reduced to 16 years and 6 months.[215]

The Cases Against Dutch Nationals: Kouwenhoven

The other case in which a Dutch national stood trial involved the businessman Kouwenhoven. He faced charges of war crimes and economic crimes under the Criminal Law in Wartime Act and the Economic Offences Act in conjunction with the Liberian Sanctions Regulations 2001. Kouwenhoven was accused of being involved in war crimes that were committed by the armed forces of Liberia between 2000 and 2002. He was also accused of supplying weapons to the Liberian regime of Charles Taylor.

The district court in The Hague acquitted the accused of the charges of war crimes under Articles 8 and 9 of the Criminal Law in Wartime Act, because the personal involvement of the accused could not be proven.[216]

---

214 Gerechtshof Den Haag, 9 May 2007, *ECLI*:NL:GHSGR:2007:BA6734 (court provided translation of *ECLI*:NL:GHSGR:2007:BA4676) para 11.2.

215 HR, 30 June 2009, *ECLI*:NL:HR:2009:BG4822.

216 Rechtbank Den Haag 7 June 2006, *ECLI*:NL:RBSGR:2006:AY5160, para 6 (court provided translation of *ECLI*:NL:RBSGR:2006:AX7098).

Kouwenhoven was convicted for two violations of the Liberian Sanctions Regulations 2001 in conjunction with the Economic Offences Act.[217] Although the district court acquitted the accused of the war crimes charges, it did conclude that a non-international armed conflict existed in Guinea and Liberia at the relevant time and places.[218] The district court did not specify on which means of proof this conclusion was based. Kouwenhoven was sentenced to 8 years' imprisonment; both the prosecutor and the accused appealed the judgment of the district court.

Appeal Proceedings

The court of appeal in The Hague acquitted the accused of all charges, stating that insufficient evidence had been presented for the involvement of the accused with the war crimes. Regarding the weapon supplies, the court of appeal held that the witness statements on which the district court relied were inconsistent. Therefore, the court of appeal concluded, insufficient evidence was presented for the charges concerning the supply of weapons.

Although the court of appeal acquitted the accused, the court concluded that an armed conflict existed during the relevant period. Unlike the district court, the court of appeal identified the sources on which this conclusion was based:

> That there was an armed conflict (whether international or not) – at least when considering the circumstances – in and around the second Liberian civil war, the Court of Appeal gleans from general reports, such as of the International Crisis Group, the Global IDP (Internal Displaced Persons) Database and consecutive official country reports from the Netherlands Ministry of Foreign Affairs.[219]

Similar to the reasoning in *Van Anraat*, it is clear on which means of proof the court relied.

The case is currently pending before the court of appeal in Den Bosch after a referral from the Supreme Court. The Supreme Court referred the case due to the fact that the court of appeal in The Hague refused to hear two witnesses for the

---

217 Rechtbank Den Haag, 7 June 2006, *ECLI*:NL:RBSGR:2006:AY5160 (court provided translation of *ECLI*:NL:RBSGR:2006:AX7098).

218 'The court is of the opinion that the present evidence has demonstrated sufficiently that in February 2001 in Gueckedou in Guinea, in the year 2002 in Voinjama in Liberia and in the period from 1 December 2001 through 30 June 2002 in Kolahun, at least in the neighborhood of Kolahun, in Liberia during of a [sic] non-international conflict, contrary to international common law (in particular the common law [the court meant customary law, KV] ban on attacks carried out without making any distinctions between soldiers or civilians, torture, inhuman treatment, rape, looting and acts of violence against civilians) and the stipulations set out in the common Article 3 of the Geneva Conventions dated August 12, 1949, members of one of the combating parties acted as described in the charges of the indictment.' Rechtbank Den Haag, 7 June 2006, *LJN*: AY5160 para 6 (court provided translation of *LJN*: AX7098).

219 Gerechtshof Den Haag, 10 March 2008, LJN: BC7373 para 9.3 (court provided translation of *LJN*: BC6068).

prosecution. The court provided insufficient reasons for this decision. The Supreme Court did not comment on the reasoning of the court of appeal regarding the existence of an armed conflict.[220]

3.3.2.6 Conclusion

The manner in which contextual components of war crimes have been proven in the cases discussed above, varies considerably. In the post-WWII cases, the existence and duration of the war were considered to be facts of common knowledge; in the most recent cases, legal means of proof were required to prove the context in which the accused committed his crimes. The fair trial implications of using facts of common knowledge to prove contextual components will be discussed in detail in Chap. 5. It will be shown that the court must ensure that the accused can challenge any factual conclusion, including facts that others may regard as indisputable. The procedural context in which facts are presented and evidence is weighed requires that the accused is given the opportunity to participate effectively in his own trial.

3.3.3 Chain Evidence

3.3.3.1 Legal Framework

When an accused faces several charges that are similar to each other (e.g. an accused is suspected of three rapes), the court can use chain evidence to convict the accused. The court may do so when it concludes that the charges are strikingly similar to each other; in other words, the same *modus operandi* can be discerned regarding each particular charge. When chain evidence is used, the charges are not proven by legal means of proof but by analogy: the evidence that the accused committed an offence is partially based on the conclusion that he has committed another offence. The requirements for the use of chain evidence will be discussed in detail below.

Chain evidence has been developed in the case law of the Dutch courts: the Code of Criminal Procedure does not, as such, provide guidance on the use of such evidence. One of the first cases in which the Supreme Court ruled on the use of chain evidence stems from 1930. In this case, the accused faced four charges of sexual assault on four boys. The assaults were committed over a period of four months; and the assaults, as such, were unrelated to each other. The evidence consisted mainly of the statements of the victims. The accused was acquitted of one charge, but convicted for the other three charges. The Supreme Court upheld the

[220] HR 20 April 2010, *ECLI*:NL:HR:2010:BK8132.

reasoning of the court of appeal: specifically, the court of appeal, confirming the findings of the district court, held that the statements of the victims had probative value regarding their own assault, but also for the other two assaults.[221] The statements were used back and forth, so to say.[222] The Supreme Court held that such an approach was allowed, because the assaults were similar to each other.[223]

The defining characteristic of chain evidence is this similarity between the charges; that is, the *modus operandi* regarding the different charges is similar. The question then arises how one determines whether there are sufficient similarities between the charges to consider the use of chain evidence. In an instructive advisory opinion to the Supreme Court, the Advocate General argued that one should distinguish clearly between inter-individual variation and intra-individual variation in human behavior. The first notion refers to the criterion that the variation of human behavior between different people should be great: the behaviour of a particular person must be really typical. The latter notion refers to the idea that the variation of behaviour of a particular person should be small.[224]

When a court considers the use of chain evidence, the court has to determine whether the charges are similar: is the *modus operandi* essentially the same regarding each charge? Then the court must determine whether it is convinced that all charges, with the similar *modus operandi*, are committed by one particular person. The final question then is whether the accused is this particular person. Chain evidence can be used to prove any part of the *probandum*, including the *mens rea* of the accused. The Supreme Court rejected the argument that a conviction for a particular charge cannot be based to a significant degree on chain evidence.[225] Chain evidence can also be used to corroborate other evidence, in order to meet the evidentiary threshold of, for example, the *unus testis, nullus testis*-rule.[226]

---

[221] HR 24 November 1930, *NJ* 1931, pp. 118–119. Reference is often made to HR 5 November 1928, *NJ* 1929, 333–334 in which, at first sight, chain evidence was used. The case concerned an accused that faced a charge of performing an abortion. The evidence consisted of the statement of the woman who requested the abortion of her foetus and the statements of two witnesses. These two witnesses stated that the accused had also performed abortions a few years earlier (for which the accused was never charged). Although this resembles chain evidence, a closer look reveals it is not. The court ruled that the two witness statements had probative value regarding the charge. This differs, however, fundamentally from HR 24 November 1930, *NJ* 1931: in the latter case the accused faced several charges. The statements of the victims were used back and forth to prove the charges. In HR 5 November 1928 the accused faced one charge and the court held that the witness statements had probative value. Consequently, there is no 'chain' here: chain evidence is used to prove *several* charges, not a single charge.

[222] This type of chain evidence is defined as quasi chain evidence. The different types of chain evidence will be discussed in the following pages.

[223] 'gelijksoortige handelingen'. HR, 24 November 1930, *NJ* 1931, p. 119.

[224] Advisory Opinion, para 5.3.1., HR, 15 November 2011, *NJ* 2012, 279, m. nt. Reijntjes.

[225] HR 14 March 2006, *NJ* 2007/345, m. nt. Mevis, para 6.4.

[226] Cf. Advisory Opinion of Advocate General Knigge, HR 20 March 2012, *LJN*: BV9339, para 5.7.

Chain evidence is predominantly used when there are insufficient means of proof for each particular charge: by using chain evidence the evidence for charge 1 can be used for the evidentiary basis of charge 2 and vice versa. Chain evidence is often used in cases concerning sexual assault and fraud offences; in such cases, the collected evidence is often insufficient to meet the standard of proof for each particular charge.

3.3.3.2 Different Concepts of Chain Evidence[227]

The fact that chain evidence has been developed in case law might explain why several concepts of chain evidence can be discerned. Three different concepts of chain evidence can be discerned in the judgments of the district courts and courts of appeal. The following sections will present explanations of each concept and show that, in fact, only one concept can properly be considered as chain evidence.

'Quasi Chain Evidence'

The first category of chain evidence, called 'quasi chain evidence', entails the following. The court hears a case in which the accused faces several, similar charges. The court concludes that the *modus operandi* is similar in relation to each charge and uses the means of proof regarding one particular charge to prove the other charges and vice versa. Such means of proof, for example a witness statement, are then used to prove each particular charge. The witness statements have, in other words, probative value for each particular charge.

This line of reasoning has been considered as a proper use of chain evidence.[228]. It has, however, nothing to do with chain evidence. Such reasoning resembles what in English law of criminal evidence is called cross-admissibility:

> In technical parlance, this scenario presents issues of 'cross-admissibility', that is to say, is the evidence pertaining to one count on the indictment also admissible in relation to the other count(s) on the indictment and vice versa? So, [...] could evidence specifically relating to robbery #1 also be used as partial proof of robberies #2-#4; and evidence specifically relating to robbery #2 also be used to prove robberies #1, #3, and #4; and so on?[229]

---

[227] The different concepts have been discussed earlier in Vriend 2013, pp. 131–134.

[228] Gerechtshof Den Haag, 18 June 2004, *ECLI*:NL:GHSGR:2004:AP2846, para 5.41; Rechtbank Den Haag, 10 May 2005, *ECLI*:NL:RBSGR:2005:AT5317; Rechtbank Den Haag, 9 October 2006, *ECLI*:NL:RBSGR:2006:AY9763; Rechtbank Den Haag, 11 December 2006, *ECLI*:NL:RBSGR:2006:AZ4197; Gerechtshof Amsterdam, 13 September 2010, *ECLI*:NL:GHAMS:2010:BN7812; Rechtbank Haarlem, 22 March 2011,*ECLI*:NL:RBHAA:2011:BR1528; Gerechtshof Arnhem, 26 June 2012, *ECLI*:NL:GHARN:2012:BW9404

[229] Roberts and Zuckerman 2010, pp. 607–608.

To use the same means of proof for several charges is legitimate when such means of proof do have probative value regarding each particular charge. In this case, the court has to explain why a means of proof that seems to have probative value for a particular charge also has probative value for the other charges. Such 'cross-admissibility' requires solid reasoning from the court; it is, however, not to be considered chain evidence.

'Superfluous Chain Evidence'

The second category of cases in which the courts referred to the concept of chain evidence consists of cases in which the use of chain evidence was superfluous. In this category, the courts reason along the following lines. The court hears a case involving several charges and, similar to the first category, concludes that the *modus operandi* is similar in relation to each charge. The court then concludes that there is sufficient evidence to prove each charge separately, but, referring to the similarity between the charges, also takes chain evidence into account to convict the accused.[230]

It is, in this category of cases, simply superfluous to use chain evidence for a conviction. When there is sufficient evidence regarding each particular charge, it is no longer necessary to consider whether chain evidence can be used.

'Real Chain Evidence'

The last category of cases consists of proper chain evidence: this is the category in which the distinct character of chain evidence comes to the fore. When a court considers the use of real chain evidence, the reasoning unfolds as follows. Again, the court is confronted with an accused who faces several, similar charges. The court concludes that a similar *modus operandi* can be discerned regarding the different charges. The court concludes that there is sufficient evidence to prove one or more charges. This conclusion can then be used to prove other, similar charges for which insufficient evidence has been presented. The Rotterdam district court held in 2010 that 'real' chain evidence entails that the conclusion that the accused has committed a particular offence is used, together with other evidence, to prove that the accused has committed another, similar offence.[231]

---

[230] Gerechtshof Amsterdam, 8 September 2010, *ECLI*:NL:GHAMS:2010:BN6408; Rechtbank Amsterdam, 7 October 2010, *ECLI*:NL:RBAMS:2010:BN9737; Gerechtshof Amsterdam, 19 March 2012, *ECLI*:NL:GHAMS:2012:BV9608; Rechtbank Utrecht, 6 June 2012, *ECLI*:NL:RBUTR:2012:BW7647, para 4.3.2.

[231] Rechtbank Rotterdam, 12 April 2010, *ECLI*:NL:RBROT:2010:BM0727, para 3.2.4.

The use of chain evidence in Dutch criminal proceedings is controversial. Chain evidence is normally used when the case file contains insufficient evidence regarding each particular charge (the category of superfluous chain evidence is the obvious exception).[232] The standard of proof is then met by using chain evidence: the resemblance between the different charges results in sufficient evidence for a conviction. The risks of using chain evidence have been highlighted by the case of Lucia de B., a nurse who was wrongfully convicted for seven murders and three attempted murders.[233],[234]The court of appeal in this case relied predominantly on chain evidence.[235] De B. was accused of having killed infants and elderly people in three hospitals in The Hague. The court of appeal concluded that De B. had administered a (potentially) lethal doses of medications to two patients. One of them died, while the other survived. The court concluded that sufficient evidence had been presented to convict De B. for murder and attempted murder regarding these two patients. The other six murders and two attempted murders were proven with the help of chain evidence: the court concluded that the other charges showed a striking similarity with the proven murder and attempted murder. The latter two were regarded as the strongest links, so to say, to which the other cases were connected. The similarities the court of appeal identified were as follows:

- the patients died suddenly and unexpectedly or suffered from a life-threatening incident;
- no medical cause could be found that could explain the death or incident; and
- the accused was present at the medical unit of the patient at the time of the death or incident.

These similarities, combined with evidence regarding each particular patient, were sufficient for the court of appeal to convict De B. for seven murders and three attempted murders. She was sentenced to life imprisonment and compulsory psychiatric treatment, which was later reversed to life imprisonment without compulsory psychiatric treatment.[236]

The manner in which the court of appeal used chain evidence is a prime example of the potential dangers of chain evidence: the conviction is to a significant

---

[232] Cf. De Wilde 2009, p. 563; Demeersseman 2009; Dreissen 2007, pp. 206–212; Dreissen 2011, pp. 213–223; Röttgering 2006, pp. 36–42; Derksen 2006; Gerechtshof Arnhem, 14 April 2010, m. nt. Mevis *LJN*: BM0876.

[233] Gerechtshof Den Haag, 18 June 2006, *ECLI*:NL:GHSGR:2006:AP2846.

[234] The district court convicted De B. to life imprisonment for four murders and three attempted murders. The district court did not use chain evidence. Rechtbank Den Haag 24 March 2003, *LJN*:AF6172.

[235] Mevis observed that the court of appeal seemed to have used quasi chain evidence. However, he argued, it is likely that the fact that two counts could be proven without using chain evidence made it easier for the court of appeal to consider the use of chain evidence in the first place. It can be argued that this means that although quasi chain evidence was used, the two strong cases functioned *de facto* as real chain evidence. HR, 14 March 2006, *LJN*:AU5496, m.nt. P.A.M. Mevis (para 19).

[236] Gerechtshof Amsterdam, 13 July 2006, *ECLI*:NL:GHAMS:2006:AY3864.

degree based on the two charges that could be proven. The other charges are proven by analogy and not by legal means of proof that meet, without more, the standard of proof. It is obvious that such reasoning depends on how strong the two strongest links in the chain actually are: one must be sure that the murder and attempted murder meet the standard of proof on the basis of legal means of proof. Only then can the other charges be chained to them. In the case of De B., those two links were not as strong as the court of appeal thought they were. In revision proceedings, serious doubts were raised regarding the incidents and deaths of the patients. The court of appeal held that there was simply not enough evidence to conclude that the incidents and deaths were caused by a factor other than a medical one.[237] The fact that no medical causes could be identified, does not mean that external factors (including any interventions by De B.) were the cause for these incidents and deaths, according to the court of appeal. The court of appeal in the revision proceedings found insufficient evidence for a conviction and acquitted De B. of all charges of murder and attempted murder.[238] This case shows that courts should use chain evidence very carefully and provide the accused with sufficient procedural safeguards.

The use of chain evidence, in particular the category of real chain evidence, is an example of a shortcut to proof. When real chain evidence is used, the court does not rely on legal means of proof to convict the accused for a particular charge. Rather, the accused is convicted by analogy: the fact that the accused committed another, similar offence has probative value regarding the other charge. Chapter 5 will present a discussion of the fair trial implications of the use of chain evidence. The possibility for the accused to effectively challenge the use of chain evidence will be of particular interest.

3.3.4 Confessions

The archetypical way of avoiding a full criminal trial is to confess to the charges. Criminal proceedings are either avoided altogether (the guilty plea procedure) or they are significantly shortened when the accused confesses (the confession as the *regina probationis*). The accused does not challenge the charges, which means that there is no longer any need for adversarial proceedings: there is no contested issue left for the court to decide.

Depending on the particular characteristics of the criminal justice system, the confession results in either out of court procedure in which the court has no (or a very limited) role, or it is regarded as a means of proof. The Dutch criminal justice

[237] Gerechtshof Arnhem, 14 April 2010, *ECLI*:NL:GHARN:2010:BM0876, para 3.

[238] Gerechtshof Arnhem, 14 April 2010, *ECLI*:NL:GHARN:2010:BM0876.

system is an example of the latter category, whereas in international criminal proceedings the confession has to be regarded as a procedural fact which obviates the need for trial proceedings altogether. In the following pages the place and legal character of the confession in Dutch criminal proceedings will be discussed. The part on the confession as such is the introduction to the legal concept of the *ad informandum* cases. In such cases, the confession of the accused is essential.

3.3.4.1 Legal Framework

In the articles in the Code of Criminal Procedure on the means of proof, no reference is made to the confession as such; instead, Article 339 and Article 341 CCP refer to the 'statement of the accused'.[239] According to the CCP, the confession (for reasons of consistent terminology, this term will be used) is just one of the legal means of proof. The CCP does not make a procedural distinction between cases in which the accused confesses or denies the charges.[240] In practice, however, trial proceedings will differ significantly when the accused confesses: the court still has to determine whether sufficient other evidence has been presented (due to the *nuda confessio* rule), but trial proceedings will be more concentrated on sentencing issues.

When we discuss confessions in Dutch criminal proceedings, it is necessary to distinguish between confessions that result in an out of court settlement, pre-trial confessions that are submitted to the case file and confessions uttered during trial proceedings. The two latter categories may overlap: confessions made during pre-trial investigations are often repeated or confirmed during the trial proceedings. The following pages are concerned with confessions related to the *nulla poena sine iudicio* principle as discussed in Chap. 1. This means that the accused has confessed during the trial proceedings.

3.3.4.2 The Confession and the Legal Character of Dutch Criminal Proceedings

The essentially inquisitorial Dutch criminal procedure, the dominant position of the judge and the emphasis on impartial and accurate fact-finding help to explain why confessions do not have a similar procedural effect as in adversarial systems: the moment the case has been called by the court, the prosecutor and the accused

[239] This has not always been the case: Article 428 of the 1838 CCP referred to the confession of the accused as a means of proof.

[240] It is noted that the court is not obliged to provide a fully reasoned judgment when the accused confesses (Article 359(3) CCP).

have no material say anymore regarding the type of proceedings.[241] This fits well within the inquisitorial type of criminal proceedings in which the court has been entrusted, *inter alia*, with the task of accurate fact-finding. It would be antithetical to such systems to allow the parties to withdraw the case from the court when they deem this in their interest. A confession does not, in other words, set aside the principle of *nulla poena sine processu*. The court must decide autonomously whether sufficient evidence has been presented. The proceedings will come to an end only when the court determines it has been sufficiently informed to render a final verdict. The CCP mirrors this court-dominated procedure.[242] In adversarial systems, the confession obviates the need for presenting more evidence: the contest between the two parties has ended, and the trial moves to the sentencing stage. Because the contest is terminated, the fact-finder has no need to require more evidence, even if this would be in the interest of accurate fact-finding, enhancing the public character of proceedings or any other interest extraneous to respecting the autonomy of the parties. An outcome that has been agreed between the parties, which is not in conformity with the material truth, is acceptable: the contest model of proceedings is regarded as superior to the official inquiry model. The manner in which criminal justice systems consider confessions can be regarded as a distinctive feature which has its roots in the old dichotomy between inquisitorial and adversarial procedures.

In present inquisitorial procedures, the confession is regarded as a means of proof which helps the court to reach an accurate factual conclusion. A confession is by no means required to declare the charges proven, and the confession is, as such, insufficient proof to convict.[243] In this regard, current inquisitorial procedures differ significantly from the archetypical inquisitorial procedures, in which the confession was regarded as necessary (the *regina probationis*) to declare the charges proven and, consequently, to punish. Formally, in present-day proceedings, the confession is nothing more than just a means of proof. The effect in terms of probative value of a confession is, however, much more significant: although confessions must be regarded with some suspicion to filter out the false ones, confessions will facilitate the court's ability to conduct fact-finding.

[241] This does not imply that the manner in which both parties conduct their cases does not influence the proceedings. However, this is within the court-controlled setting of trial proceedings ('onderzoek ter terechtzitting'). The CCP does not contain a mechanism similar to common law systems where a confession during trial proceedings results in a different procedure altogether. Cf. Boek and Nijboer 1994, p. 56 'De haast ideologische verbinding tussen het zoeken naar de 'materiële waarheid' met een inquisitoire stijl van procederen' in de typisch Nederlandse situatie laat weinig ruimte voor een eigen processuele inbreng van de verdachte.' Cf. Damaška 1972–1973, pp. 511–512.

[242] Article 270 CCP states that the investigation by the court starts with the president of the court calling the case. Article 272(1) states that the president is in charge of the proceedings. The proceedings will come to an end when the court deems this appropriate, according to Article 345 CCP. Cf. Damaška 1972–1973, p. 564.

[243] Article 341(4) CCP.

After the close of proceedings, the court can just list the means of proof in case of a confession, instead of presenting a fully reasoned judgment.[244] During the 2003 parliamentary debates, the rationale for the introduction of abbreviated reasoning in the judgment was found in the input of the parties during the proceedings. This entails that criminal proceedings should be more responsive to the arguments presented by the parties (cf. the appeal procedures discussed above): when the accused does not bring forward any objections against the charges, there is no need, the Minister of Justice argued, to provide him with a fully-reasoned judgment.[245] A contested trial should in fact be concentrated on those issues that remain in dispute between the parties.[246] The responsibility of the court to conduct accurate fact-finding and to explain the reasons for a particular decision, however, are left intact: the possibility of rendering an abbreviated judgment is discretionary. This way, the court is always able to provide a fully reasoned judgment if it deems this necessary.

3.3.4.3 Plea Bargaining in Dutch Criminal Proceedings?

There were debates in the 1990s on the introduction of a separate procedure for accused who confess to the charges. Such a separate procedure has not been incorporated into the CCP, though. Commenting on the findings and recommendations of the Moons-committee, the Minister of Justice underlined the advantages of a separate procedure for accused who confess to the charges. Besides increased efficiency of the proceedings, the Minister favoured a more adversarial approach in criminal proceedings. He stated that criminal proceedings should concentrate on those issues that are in dispute.[247] Accused who confess to the charges limit the dispute to sentencing, whereas those who deny the charges request the court to fully investigate all factual and legal claims made by the prosecution. The Minister of Justice stated that a confession in this regard should be understood as a statement that has been delivered before the court, in which the accused confesses to the charges. The proceedings then move to the sentencing stage, in which the accused may present any mitigating circumstances.[248]

---

[244] Article 359(3) CCP.

[245] *Kamerstukken II*, 2003/04, 29255, 3, p. 6.

[246] '(…) de concentratie van de motiveringsverplichtingen op daadwerkelijke geschilpunten die in het voorgaande besloten ligt, een uitvloeisel is van een meer algemene ontwikkeling, de behandeling van de strafzaak door de rechter vooral te richten op geschilpunten.' *Kamerstukken II*, 2003/04, 29255, 3, p. 7.

[247] 'In de eerste plaats is kenmerkend voor een kwalitatief hoogwaardig procesrecht dat het is gericht op de inzet van het geding.' Corstens 1993, p. 187.

[248] Memorie van Toelichting, as quoted in: Corstens 1993, p. 189.

According to the Minister of Justice, a separate procedure should not be regarded as a *corpus alienum* in Dutch criminal procedure: the CCP does already provide for different procedures, for example depending on the age of the accused or on the severity of the crime. The possibility to avoid public proceedings by complying with a transaction and the use of *ad informandum* cases are other examples in which the confession of the accused results in a differentiated procedure.[249] The Minister of Justice argued that, when the accused confesses before the district court, the appeal proceedings will be limited to sentencing.[250] Similar to the transaction and *ad informandum* procedures, the accused may freely determine whether he wants to rely on his procedural rights or waive them. In this regard, the Minister argued, a differentiated procedure is nothing extraordinary. The rules of evidence contained in the CCP apply without reservations to this procedure: the *nuda confessio* rule still applies.[251]

The objections against a separate procedure for accused who confess were numerous. Hildebrandt emphasized that a distinction should be made between two notions of the confession. First, the confession can be regarded as a means of proof: combined with other evidence (or in its own right, when no *nuda confessio*-rule applies), it helps to reach the applicable standard of proof and, ideally, contributes to accurate fact-finding. The second notion of the confession regards the confession as a procedural fact. This resembles the manner in which guilty pleas are regarded in international criminal proceedings and in typical adversarial, common law procedures. An accused may, provided he is sufficiently informed of his rights, waive the right to full criminal proceedings by confessing to the charges. Such a waiver has often been the result of a bargaining process. It is easy to see that the latter notion fits well within the adversarial system, where the fact-finder relies heavily on the procedural choices of the parties.[252]

One of the major objections to the separate procedure concerned the shift from the inquisitorial procedure to a party-driven procedure.[253] In the latter procedure, the confession is regarded as a procedural fact. This, it was argued, would result in less emphasis on accurate fact-finding and would introduce 'formal truth' in the criminal justice system.[254] The public character of the proceedings would diminish: the bargaining process that normally precedes the confession leads to a negotiated truth which is at odds with the public, impartial discussion and determination

[249] The transaction, however, does not require a confession: it requires the consent of the accused to the conditions proposed by the prosecutor.

[250] Memorie van Toelichting, as quoted in: Corstens 1993, pp. 187–188.

[251] Memorie van Toelichting, as quoted in: Corstens 1993, p. 189.

[252] Hildebrandt 1993, pp. 123–136.

[253] Jörg 1993, p. 204; De Doelder and't Hart 1992, p .629. Cf. Boek and Nijboer 1994, pp. 41–58.

[254] Cf. Jörg, who argued that party autonomy and conflict resolution become more important, to the detriment of accurate fact-finding. Jörg 1993, p. 205.

of the facts. Related to the criticism on the increased role of the parties is the concern that, in inquisitorial procedures in general, parties do not have a determinative say in the manner in which the procedure is conducted. Parties are able to influence the outcome of the procedure (by calling witness, challenging the evidence etc.), but the procedure as such is determined by the CCP and the court itself. Considering that the court in Dutch criminal proceedings has the exclusive competence to call and close a case, a separate procedure for the parties would not be in line with this principle.

It is noted that an agreement between the parties, including a confession, does not inevitably lead to diverting the case from the court altogether. In common law systems, the court has to ensure that the plea, as the result of the bargaining process, was informed, unequivocal and based on the free will of the accused before it can be accepted by the court. Criminal justice systems in which the procedure is predominantly for the parties to choose can thus be combined with judicial control on the outcome of the procedure. It is instructive to refer to Rule 62bis of the ICTY RPE, which states that the Trial Chamber may only enter a finding of guilt when the guilty plea is, *inter alia*, based on a 'sufficient factual basis for the crime'.[255] This means that values extraneous to respecting party autonomy (accurate fact-finding) may set the plea aside. At the ICC, the Trial Chamber must be satisfied that 'the admission of guilt is supported by the facts'.[256] It may also refuse to accept an admission of guilt when acceptance is not in the interests of justice, in particular the interests of the victims.[257] This means that the public character of a contested trial may set aside an agreement reached by the parties.

The revision of the Dutch Code of Criminal Procedure, which will be implemented in the coming years, does not change the effect and probative value of the confession in Dutch criminal proceedings. The confession remains, as such, insufficient evidence to meet the standard of proof (the *nuda confessio* rule still applies). No special procedure will be introduced for accused who confess. The possibility to deliver an abbreviated judgment when the accused confesses will remain.

3.3.5 Cases Ad Informandum

The confession does not, in the context of Dutch criminal proceedings, result in a diversion of the case from the court: it is not a procedural fact which diverges the case from regular trial proceedings. The confession is regarded as an important

---

255 Cf. Article 65 ICC Statute, which requires also that the Trial Chamber is satisfied that 'the admission of guilt is supported by the facts'.

256 Article 65(1)(c) ICC Statute.

257 Article 65(4) ICC Statute.

means of proof, and the proceedings will be concentrated on other issues that are contested. However, the confession of the accused does play a pivotal role in a particular type of cases: the *ad informandum* cases.[258]

Ad informandum cases resemble the English concept of 'offences taken into consideration', often referred to as 'TIC'. Zander gave the following description of TIC's:

> A different form of 'confession' is the admission by someone who either pleads guilty or is found guilty that he committed *other* offences. If this happens before the court case, they are mentioned in court and 'taken into consideration' for the purpose of sentencing. (Hence they are called TICs). The advantage for the accused is that they cannot be brought up against him. The advantage for the police is that they can 'clear the books' – the success rate of cleared up crime in that force area improves.[259]

In case of a habitual offender, the use of *ad informandum* cases increases efficiency: the accused is formally charged with, for example, one charge of shop-lifting. If he confesses to certain other instances of shop-lifting, the court may take those latter confessions into consideration regarding the sentence. The cases are then finally disposed of: the prosecutor may not bring the *ad informandum* cases to court again. The *ad informandum* cases are similar to the formal charge(s). Corstens and Borgers stated that the quality of the crimes (i.e. the crime's legal definition) is included in the charges. The *ad informandum* cases are useful to indicate the quantity of the crimes.[260] Thus, a charge of burglary can be combined with several *ad informandum* cases regarding burglaries: to include an *ad informandum* case regarding assault, for example, is not allowed. The Supreme Court held in 2014 that the practice of *ad informandum* cases can be very helpful in cases of large-scale possession of child pornography. The charges in such cases can be limited to a maximum of five pictures, the Supreme Court held.[261] When the court concludes that these pictures consist of child pornography, the element of large-scale possession can be 'proven' by the confession of the accused that he possesses, for example, thousands of such pictures. This obviates the need to charge the accused with the possession of each picture separately.

3.3.5.1 Legal Framework

Processing cases *ad informandum* has been developed in case law; no statutory basis exists for this practice. This is remarkable, considering the fact that criminal cases are finally disposed of without an explicit legal basis. Considering the

[258] According to CBS Statistics Netherlands, 2130 cases were processed *ad informandum* in 2013. http://statline.cbs.nl/StatWeb/publication/?DM=SLNL&PA=81534NED (last visit: 1 January 2016).

[259] Zander 2007, p. 336 (emphasis in original); Cf. Brants and Stapert 2004, p. 20.

[260] Corstens and Borgers 2014, p. 872.

[261] HR 24 June 2014, *ECLI*:NL:HR:2014:1497.

legality principle of Article 1 CCP, a statutory basis for this practice is needed. The current practice has been approved by the Supreme Court.[262] In the near future, the practice of handling cases *ad informandum* will be codified, though: the Minister of Security and Justice has stated that the *ad informandum* practice will be included in the revision of the Code of Criminal Procedure.[263] Until the CCP has been revised, the requirements that have been developed in the case law remain relevant.

Processing cases *ad informandum* occurs mostly, and preferably, when the accused is present during the proceedings. In front of the court, the accused confesses to the cases that are presented *ad informandum* by the prosecutor. In the indictment, the prosecutor will inform the accused of the *ad informandum* cases. In order to take these cases into consideration, the accused has to confess during the proceedings and the prosecutor has to indicate that no new charges will be filed for these cases. When the court concludes that the accused has committed these crimes, the court may take them into consideration regarding the sentence.[264]

The Supreme Court held that when the accused is not present during the proceedings, the case may still be taken into consideration. The following requirements apply:

(1) the accused must be informed in the indictment, or at least before the start of the proceedings, that the prosecutor intends to present several cases *ad informandum*;
(2) it must be probable, on the basis of an out of court confession, that the accused committed the cases that are to be taken into consideration; and the prosecutor must indicate that no charges will be filed for the cases that are taken into consideration by the court.[265]

The fact that *ad informandum* cases are not formal charges has two important consequences. First, the requirements contained in Article 261 CCP on the formulation of the charges are not, as such, applicable: it suffices for the prosecutor to notify the accused that certain cases will be brought to the attention of the court *ad informandum*. The prosecutor provides a summary description of these cases in the indictment, including the place and date of each particular case.[266] Considering the fact that the accused is not formally charged, the question arises how this relates to the right to be informed in detail of the nature and cause of the accusation, as formulated in Article 6(3)(a) ECHR. Similar to the requirements for a formal charge, the description of the *ad informandum* case must be such as to

[262] HR 13 February 1979, *NJ* 1979, 269, m.nt. ThWvV.

[263] Ministry of Security and Justice, 'Kamerbrief over modernisering Wetboek van Strafvordering', 30 September 2015, pp. 110–111.

[264] E.g. HR 11 November 2008, *ECLI*:NL:HR:2008:BE9634, para 2.3.

[265] HR 8 December 2009, *ECLI*:NL:HR:2009:BK0949, para 3.3.

[266] Corstens and Borgers 2014, p. 872.

provide the accused 'with sufficient information as is necessary to understand fully the extent of the charges against him with a view to preparing an adequate defence.'[267] The Court emphasized the connection with the right to be provided with adequate time and facilities to prepare a defence, protected under Article 6(3)(b) ECHR.[268] The notification of the prosecutor to present cases *ad informandum* should be sufficiently detailed and done in a timely manner in order to enable the accused to make an informed choice regarding these cases.

Second, the rules of evidence are not applicable to *ad informandum* cases: Articles 338–344a CCP apply only to formal charges. Consequently, the *nuda confessio* rule does not apply; that is, the confession of the accused suffices for the court to take the case into consideration (although the court is not obliged to do so). Franken argued that although the rules of evidence are not applicable to *ad informandum* cases, the same standard of proof should apply as for normal charges. In other words, the court must be convinced beyond reasonable doubt that the accused committed the *ad informandum* case. Any other conclusion, according to Franken, would result in circumventing the rules of evidence.[269]

3.3.5.2 Ad Informandum Cases as Shortcuts

The principle of *nulla poena sine iudicio* is fully adhered to: the court may process a case *ad informandum* when the accused confesses (during the proceedings itself or out of court) and the prosecutor states that no separate charges will be filed.[270] The court may then take this case into consideration in sentencing. The prosecutor is barred from prosecuting the accused for the same case. This follows from due process considerations: if the prosecutor has brought a case *ad informandum* before the court and the court takes it into consideration regarding the sentence, the prosecutor cannot instigate new proceedings.[271]

The fact that the prosecutor is barred from filing formal charges regarding the *ad informandum* case when the court has taken it into consideration, means that the case is finally disposed of. The derogation from the ideal type described in the Introduction (in which every part of the charges has to be proven by legal means of proof that are discussed during the proceedings) entails that the practice of *ad informandum* cases is a shortcut: full criminal proceedings are avoided.

---

[267] ECtHR, 25 July 2000, App. No.: 23969/94, (*Mattoccia v. Italy*), para 60.

[268] ECtHR, 25 July 2000, App. No.: 23969/94, (*Mattoccia v. Italy*), para 60.

[269] Franken 1993, p. 143.

[270] HR 8 December 2009, *ECLI*:NL:HR:2009:BK0949, para 3.3.

[271] HR 13 February 1996, *ECLI*:NL:HR:1996:ZC9529, para 6.2. Regarding the *ne bis in idem*-principle and *ad informandum* cases, see: Franken 1993, pp. 27–33.

Considerations of efficiency, including the benefits for the accused ('clearing the books'), are legitimate, and this practice certainly helps to process a greater number of cases. Similar to the other shortcuts and diversions that were discussed, the question arises of how the accused can participate effectively regarding the *ad informandum* cases. Avoiding a full criminal trial comes at a price: the accused must be enabled to effectively invoke his fair trial rights. In Chap. 5, the practice of *ad informandum* cases will be evaluated with the participatory model of proof as the normative framework.

3.3.6 Appeal Proceedings

Appeal proceedings provide another example of a shortcut in criminal proceedings. As has been described in the Introduction, shortcuts are mechanisms that deviate from the ideal type of conducting criminal proceedings: charges are proven on the basis of legal means of proof that are discussed during the proceedings. Appeal proceedings deviate from this ideal type because the proceedings before the court of appeal are narrowed: the proceedings are concentrated on the objections that the prosecutor or the accused has formulated against the judgment of the district court. Despite the fact that the court of appeal remains responsible for accurate fact-finding and for providing the accused a fair trial, appeal proceedings differ from trial proceedings. In this section the legal framework of the appeal proceedings will be discussed. Moreover, attention will be paid to the manner in which appeal proceedings are actually conducted in practice. The focus will be on the position of the accused: how can he effectively participate during the appeal stage?

3.3.6.1 Legal Framework

When appeal proceedings are discussed, a distinction must be made between cases concerning crimes ('misdrijven') and infractions ('overtredingen'). One must also distinguish between the position of the prosecutor and the accused.

When the case concerns a crime, the prosecutor can appeal the judgment of the district court. The accused can also appeal the judgment, unless he has been acquitted of all the charges.[272] This is an example of *point d'intérêt, point d'action*: if the accused has been acquitted, he has nothing to gain from the appeal proceedings. Therefore, his notice of appeal will be declared inadmissible. When the accused has been convicted of a crime, he can appeal the judgment. There is,

[272] Article 404(1) CCP.

however, one exception to this rule. The accused must initiate leave to appeal proceedings when:

- he has been convicted for a crime with a maximum sentence of 4 years' imprisonment; and
- the sentence that the district court imposed did not exceed 500 €.

When both criteria are met, the presiding judge of the court of appeal must determine whether granting leave to appeal is in the interest of justice.[273] According to the Minister of Justice, granting leave to appeal in such minor cases may be in the interest of justice when the presiding judge has doubts about whether sufficient and reliable evidence was presented during the first-instance proceedings or when the sentence that was imposed seems to be too high.[274]

The leave to appeal procedure has an uncertain future, though: the Human Rights Committee of the UN held in *Mennen v. The Netherlands* that Article 14, para 5 of the ICCPR requires a review by a higher tribunal of both conviction and sentence:

> Such review, in the frame of a decision regarding a leave to appeal, must be examined on its merits, taking into consideration on the one hand the evidence presented before the first instance judge, and on the other hand the conduct of the trial on the basis of the legal provisions applicable to the case in question.[275]

Van Kempen and Pesselse concluded that the current leave to appeal procedure is not in conformity with the standards set by the Human Rights Committee.[276] In *Lalmohamed v. The Netherlands*, the ECtHR held that the grounds of appeal of the accused require a 'full and thorough evaluation of the relevant factors.'[277] Considering the limited review that is conducted in leave to appeal procedures, it can be questioned whether this is in conformity with the requirements of Article 6. The Minister of Justice stated that the leave to appeal procedure will be abolished in the near future: besides the criticism of the HRC and the ECtHR, the procedure appeared to be less effective than envisaged.[278]

In case of infractions, appeals can be lodged by both the prosecutor and the accused unless the sentence consists of no more than 50 €, or when the court has not imposed a sentence, according to Article 9a CC.[279] Similar to the possibility of lodging an appeal for crimes, the accused cannot appeal a judgment in which he was acquitted of all charges.

---

[273] 'belang van een goede rechtsbedeling', Article 410a(1) CCP.

[274] *Kamerstukken II*, 2005/06, 30320, 3, p. 24.

[275] HRC, 24 August 2010, Communication No. 1797/2008, U.N. Doc. CCPR/C/99/D/1797/2008 (2010), (*Mennen v. The Netherlands*).

[276] Van Kempen and Pesselse 2014, p. 93.

[277] ECtHR, 22 February 2011, App. No.: 26036/08, (*Lalmahomed v. The Netherlands*), para 37.

[278] Ministry of Security and Justice, 'Kamerbrief over modernisering Wetboek van Strafvordering', 30 September 2015, p. 116.

[279] Article 404(2) CCP.

One of the aims of the appeal proceedings is accurate fact-finding: the case is reviewed by a court that has both the case file and the judgment of the district court at its disposal.[280] Although appeal proceedings are normally concentrated on the objections of the parties, the court of appeal has to ensure that its judgment is based on an accurate factual basis. Article 415(1) CCP states that the provisions on trial proceedings, evidence and the contents of the judgment are applicable to appeal proceedings as well. This allows the court of appeal to conduct accurate fact-finding itself.

The responsibility for the court of appeal to conduct accurate fact-finding *proprio motu* can also be derived from the provisions on the admissibility of new evidence during the appeal proceedings.[281] The fact that new evidence can be presented during the appeal means that the appeal proceedings are not a marginal review of the conclusions of the district court.

Article 410 CCP states that the prosecutor must file his objections against the judgment of the district court within fourteen days after he has lodged the appeal. The accused may also file his objections, although he is not obliged to do so.[282] At the beginning of the appeal proceedings, the prosecutor is requested to formulate his objections against the judgment: when the prosecutor has not filed his objections, the court of appeal may declare the appeal inadmissible.[283] When the accused does not file his objections before the beginning of the appeal proceedings, and does not formulate his objections at the beginning of the appeal proceedings, the court of appeal may declare the appeal inadmissible.[284] It is within the discretion of the court of appeal to declare the appeal inadmissible: if the court wants to hear the case, although no objections have been formulated, the court is free to do so. This will normally only occur when the court of appeal concludes that the district court has made a significant legal or factual error.

The fact that both the prosecutor and the accused are requested to file their objections against the judgment of the district court when they lodge an appeal, is a defining characteristic of Dutch appeal proceedings. According to the Minister of Justice, appeal proceedings require an 'active attitude' from the parties: when the prosecutor or accused lodges an appeal, the objections against the judgment of the district court must be presented to the court of appeal.[285] According to the

---

280 Article 422(2) CCP states that the court of appeal may use the transcript of the first-instance proceedings in its deliberations.

281 Article 414 CCP. Article 412(3) CCP states that the accused must be informed of the possibility to present new evidence before the court of appeal.

282 Article 410(1) CCP. In case of leave to appeal proceedings the accused is obliged to file his objections, according to article 410(4) CCP. Article 410a(2) CCP provides for an exception to this obligation.

283 Article 416(3) CCP.

284 Article 416(2) CCP.

285 *Kamerstukken II*, 2005/06, 30320, 3, p. 11.

Supreme Court, however, the objections do not need to be very detailed, especially when the objections are formulated by the accused.[286]

3.3.6.2 The Scope of the Appeal Proceedings

Article 415(2) CCP states that the court of appeal shall concentrate the appeal proceedings on the objections that are formulated by the parties and on every other matter the court of appeal deems relevant:

> The court of appeal shall concentrate the proceedings on the objections put forward by the accused and the public prosecutor against the first instance judgment. The court of appeal shall deliberate on any other matter it deems necessary.

This entails that appeal proceedings are not trials de novo, but a second stage in the proceedings in which the parties present their objections against the judgment of the district court. The court of appeal is responsible for accurate fact-finding and must ensure that the accused receives a fair trial.[287] Traditionally, appeal proceedings provide for a full rehearing of the case, in which every factual and legal aspect of the case can be discussed. Although in practice the appeal proceedings will be concentrated on contested issues, this does not alter the character of the appeal proceedings. It does, however, require an active attitude from the parties, especially from the accused. From a fair trial perspective, it is vital that he is properly informed of the character of the appeal proceedings and the manner in which he can effectively challenge the evidence against him.

The trial proceedings are relevant for the appeal stage as well: Article 417 CCP states that, unless the accused requests to do so, documentary evidence which has been read out during the trial proceedings does not have to be read out again during the appeal proceedings. Moreover, the court of appeal takes into consideration the transcript of the trial proceedings during its deliberations.[288]

3.3.6.3 The Character of Appeal Proceedings

Appeal proceedings have a hybrid character: although the proceedings are concentrated on the objections of the parties, the court remains responsible for accurate fact-finding. Moreover, the court has to ensure that the accused receives a fair trial.

---

[286] HR 19 June 2007, *NJ* 2007, 629, m.nt. P.A.M. Mevis, para 3.5.

[287] The character of the appeal proceedings has not changed profoundly: the court of appeal has always been responsible for a fair and accurate outcome of the appeal proceedings. The focus, however, of the appeal proceedings has shifted towards the parties. On the history of appeal proceedings and the legal character of appeal proceedings, see: De Hullu 1989, pp. 183–214.

[288] Article 422(2) CCP.

This means that the court of appeal must act *proprio motu* when it deems a certain aspect of the case important, even if the parties have not raised it in their objections.

The hybrid character of Dutch appeal proceedings can be illustrated by referring to the distinction made by Damaška between proceedings conducted in hierarchical and coordinate justice systems.[289] The hierarchical system consists of several layers of officials conducting fact-finding in a hierarchical, authoritative system. The findings of lower courts are subject to review and may be quashed by the superior court, whose members are in general more experienced judges than the first-instance judges. In the coordinate system there is no hierarchy between fact-finders, which means that the fact-finding process is limited to one stage of proceedings. Typically, appeal proceedings in coordinate systems are limited to questions of law, not of fact. The hierarchical system presupposes a succession of stages, in which each stage contributes to the final outcome. In coordinate systems, there is a tendency to concentrate the proceedings, in particular when lay decision-makers enter the stage. The culmination of such proceedings is the famous 'day in court'.[290] In this regard, the concept of 'trial' is associated with coordinate justice systems with lay participation, whereas the concept of 'proceedings' is more characteristic for hierarchical justice systems with professional fact-finders. Damaška observed that appeal proceedings are not something extraordinary in hierarchical systems, but an important part of the proceedings as a whole. On the accuracy of the findings of the first-instance court, he observed:

> The great significance attributed to 'quality control' by superiors in a hierarchical organization inevitably detracts from the importance of original decision making: the latter acquires an aura of provisionality [sic].[291]

This observation underlines the importance of appeal proceedings in a criminal justice system that consists of multiple layers of proceedings. Although the idea that judgments by first-instance courts are 'provisional' can be criticized, Damaška revealed from a systemic perspective the importance of appeal proceedings in hierarchical legal systems. Considering the prominent position of appeal proceedings in hierarchical criminal justice systems, it is vital that appeal proceedings can indeed contribute to accurate fact-finding. This depends to a significant extent on the manner in which the accused is able to participate effectively during the appeal proceedings.

3.3.6.4 Law in Action: Interviews with Judges

The observations above illustrate the hybrid character of appeal proceedings: the court of appeal is responsible for providing a fair trial and conducting accurate fact-finding, but the proceedings will be focused on the input of the parties.

289 Damaška 1986, pp. 47–70.

290 Damaška 1986, p. 62.

291 Damaška 1986, p. 49.

This interplay during the appeal proceedings between the court, the prosecutor and the accused is of interest here because it helps to provide an answer to the question of how the accused can participate effectively during the proceedings. Therefore, it is essential to know how appeal proceedings are actually conducted. In order to analyse the practice of appeal proceedings, interviews have been held with judges working in the courts of appeal. Considering that Article 415(2) CCP allows the court of appeal to direct the proceedings to any matter it deems relevant, input from practitioners is essential to understand the workings of appeal proceedings.

Interviews have been held with nine judges from different courts of appeal. The aim of these interviews was to analyse how appeal proceedings are conducted, with regard to the different roles of the court and the parties.[292] The interviews were conducted under the promise of anonymity.[293] Because a limited number of judges were interviewed, no general conclusions can be drawn. The interviews do, however, give an indication of how appeal proceedings are conducted in practice.

Judges who worked in the courts of appeal prior to the 2006 amendment, did not notice a great difference after the introduction of Article 415(2) CCP.[294] Prior to the introduction, the CCP already required the court of appeal to ask the accused and the prosecutor (that is, if he had filed an appeal himself) to bring forward their objections against the judgment of the district court. This focused the appeal proceedings to particular objections against the judgment, such as the length or kind of sentence that the district court imposed.

The manner in which the presiding judge presided over the appeal proceedings was of great importance: it was within the court's discretion to discuss the case thoroughly, but the Code of Criminal Procedure did not preclude the court of appeal to focus on the objections that were raised by the parties. In this regard, some judges noted, Article 415(2) CCP merely codified the manner in which most judges presided over the appeal proceedings already. Several judges observed that, since the introduction of Article 415(2) CCP, defence counsel put forward more specific objections against the judgment of the district court. This is also greatly enhanced by Article 416(2) CCP, which states that the court of appeal can declare the appeal inadmissible if no objections have been filed nor brought forward during the appeal proceedings itself.[295]

---

[292] Five of the judges were senior judges ('senior raadsheer'), while the other four were ordinary judges ('raadsheer').

[293] The transcripts of the interviews are kept in the author's archive.

[294] One senior judge did notice a great difference after the implementation of Article 415(2) CCP. He observed that appellate proceedings, prior to the implementation, were often trials de novo. This has changed profoundly since the 2006 amendment.

[295] For examples in which the court of appeal declared the appeal admissible, although no objections were presented, see *inter alia*: Gerechtshof Den Bosch, 29 November 2010, *ECLI*:NL:GHSHE:2010:BO9735; Gerechtshof Arnhem, 27 August 2009, *ECLI*:NL:GHARN:BJ6248; Gerechtshof Amsterdam, 22 July 2010, *ECLI*:NL:GHAMS:BN3122. Cf. Keulen 2012, pp. 3–14.

The Minister of Justice envisaged that the focus on the objections of the parties would enhance the efficiency of the appeal proceedings.[296] Most judges stated that the objections filed by the prosecutor are concise and of a decent quality. The quality of objections filed by defence counsel varies tremendously. Some judges stated that it was the strategy of the defence to see what the district court would make of the evidence presented. On appeal, objections were raised that could have been put forward during the trial proceedings. One experienced judge commented that this practice seems to be coming to an end: objections are normally brought before the district court. Considering the quality of the objections raised by defence counsel, two judges favoured a more stringent approach. They argued that objections should be clear, precise and not repetitive. They further asserted that one should not simply repeat the arguments that have been presented before the district court.

One senior judge favoured appeal proceedings in which uncontested matters are not reviewed by the court of appeal. When the accused files objections against a certain charge or the sentence, the appeal proceedings will be strictly limited to those objections. The court will not consider the facts *proprio motu* even if the court of appeal disagrees with the findings of the district court. An important safeguard in this respect is the manner in which the accused files his appeal: if he is informed about the consequences of a 'partial' appeal, the court may ignore matters that are not brought forward by him.

Related to the quality of the objections is the question of how leading these objections are during the appeal proceedings. The interplay between the prosecutor, the accused, his defence counsel and the court of appeal is influenced by the quality of the objections. The observations of the judges varied here: some stated that the objections were leading for the proceedings, where others found that they were not. The latter group regarded objections merely as points that need to be discussed. Most judges emphasized the particular responsibility of the court of appeal with regard to accurate fact-finding. However, most of them also stated that focusing on a particular matter *proprio motu*, is not done frequently. They reported that the court of appeal discusses the matter only when the judges find something extraordinary during the preparation of the case which has gone unnoticed by the parties (a sentence that diverges from standard sentencing guidelines, for example).

During the parliamentary debates on the introduction of the new Article 415(2) CCP, the issue was raised whether the appeal proceedings could be limited to the sentence that the district court imposed.[297] When, for example, an accused has confessed during the trial proceedings and appeals the judgment, because of the sentence, should it be possible to limit the appeal to the imposed sentence? The Minister of Justice argued that a 'sentence appeal' would infringe on the fact-finding task of the court of appeal. Because the court of appeal is responsible for accurate fact-finding, it would be undesirable to limit the role of the court of appeal to

---

[296] *Kamerstukken II*, 2005/06, 30aan320, 3, p. 9.

[297] *Kamerstukken II*, 2005/06, 30320, 3, pp. 14–15.

sentencing.[298] Sentencing appeals restrict the appeal proceedings: the factual conclusions of the district court could bind the court of appeal in this respect.

In practice, however, accused regularly limit their objections to the sentence by arguing that the sentence is too high or the sentence should be conditional, for example. In other cases, the accused merely wishes to postpone the enforcement of the sentence. At first sight, this would favour separate appeal procedures for accused who limit their appeal to the sentence. Several judges stated that objections regarding the sentence are often factual appeals in disguise. Regularly, the accused states during the appeal proceedings that he filed an objection against the sentence because his contribution to the crime was negligible (the accused, for example, argued that he was an aider and abettor instead of a co-perpetrator). In such cases, the court of appeal must still discuss the facts on which the sentence was based. Some judges stated that even when the accused limits the appeal to the sentence, it may still be necessary to distil from the facts which are the aggravating and mitigating circumstances regarding the sentence. Therefore, it would be rather artificial to introduce a distinction in the CCP between factual and sentencing appeals.

Another issue that was discussed with the judges was whether appeal proceedings differ depending on the type of cases. The articles on appeal proceedings in the CCP do not make any distinction between different types of cases (for example between shoplifting and murder cases). Practice appears to be very diverse, which makes any generalization difficult: a murder trial might be very simple when it comes to the evidence, whereas a case concerning public disorder might be very complicated. Cases in which the accused confessed to the charges are normally quite straightforward. The proceedings on appeal will then concentrate on the personal circumstances of the accused regarding the appropriate sentence.

Appeal proceedings can differ from ordinary appeal proceedings, though, when the case is voluminous and complicated, such as cases concerning the International Crimes Act or fraud cases. Several judges who have handled these types of cases emphasized that the proceedings differ from ordinary proceedings. This is not due to a different attitude of the court of appeal; instead, the difference can be explained by the quality and experience of the prosecutor and defence counsel. The prosecution has specialized branches for international crimes and large-scale fraud cases. On the side of the defence, counsel too is often experienced and specialized in such cases. This has consequences for the proceedings on appeal: frivolous objections are seldom made, time-schedules are adhered to and both prosecution and defence counsel tend to focus on the complicated and controversial issues in the first-instance judgment. In this regard, the appeal proceedings are streamlined and focused on the most controversial issues of the case.

---

[298] *Kamerstukken II*, 2005/06, 30320, 3, pp. 14–15.

3.3.6.5 The Future of Appeal Proceedings in Criminal Cases

Currently, the Code of Criminal Procedure is being revised. The Minister of Security and Justice has informed parliament that over the next years, several amendments of the CCP will be presented in parliament. It is envisaged that the last revisions will take effect in 2018.[299] Regarding appeal proceedings, the Minister stated that the appeal should be focused even more on the objections against the judgment of the district court (although the court of appeal can still direct the proceedings to any matter it deems relevant). This is already the case, as was discussed above. However, the Minister emphasized that the main stage of criminal proceedings should be the trial stage. Because appeal proceedings should be focused more on the objections against the judgment of the district court, those objections must be duly reasoned. As a result, the Minister proposed to oblige the parties to file well-reasoned objections.[300] The amendment regarding appeal proceedings is expected in May 2016. It is premature to speculate on the consequences for the appeal proceedings. However, it seems that a more active attitude is required from the parties to have the case reviewed before the court of appeal. The ability to participate effectively in the proceedings, including the appeal stage, is of paramount importance regarding the fair trial rights of the accused. Chapter 5 will present an answer to the question of how the accused can participate effectively during the appeal proceedings.

References

Ashworth A, Redmayne M (2010) The criminal process. Oxford University Press, Oxford

Belinfante AD (1978) In plaats van bijltjesdag. De geschiedenis van de bijzondere rechtspleging na de Tweede Wereldoorlog. Van Gorcum, Assen

Bleichrodt FW (1996) Onder voorwaarde: een onderzoek naar de voorwaardelijke veroordeling en andere voorwaardelijke modaliteiten. Gouda Quint, Deventer

Bleichrodt FW (2011) Bewijsmimima: een nieuwe invulling?. In: Kempen van PHPHMC, Machielse AJ, Sackers HJB, Vegter PC (eds) Levend strafrecht: strafrechtelijke vernieuwingen in een maatschappelijke context. Kluwer, Deventer

Blok AJ, Besier LCh (1925) Het Nederlandsche strafproces, Deel II. H.D. Tjeenk Willink en Zoon, Haarlem

Boek JLM, Nijboer JF (1994) De bekentenis als de koningin van het bewijs. Delikt en Delinkwent 1:41–58

Borgers MJ (2012) De toepassing van de bewijsminimumregel. Delikt en Delinkwent 10:873–893

Brants C, Stapert B (2004) Voor wat hoort wat: plea bargaining in het strafrecht. Boom Juridische Uitgevers, The Hague

[299] Ministry of Security and Justice, 'Kamerbrief over modernisering Wetboek van Strafvordering', 30 September 2015, p. 31.

[300] Ministry of Security and Justice, 'Kamerbrief over modernisering Wetboek van Strafvordering', 30 September 2015, pp. 115–116.

Cleiren CPM (2010) De rechterlijke overtuiging: een sprong met hindernissen. RM Themis 5(6):259–267
Clermont KM (2009) Standards of proof revisited. Vermont Law Rev 33:469–487
Corstens GJM (ed) (1993) Rapporten herijking strafvordering 1989–1992. Gouda Quint, Arnhem
Corstens GJM, Borgers MJ (2014) Het Nederlands strafprocesrecht. Kluwer, Deventer
Crijns JH (2004) Het wetsvoorstel OM-afdoening: een wolf in schaapskledij. Sancties 4:225–236
Crijns JH (2006) Rationaliteiten achter de Wet OM-afdoening. In: Cleiren CPM (ed) Op zoek naar samenhang: het Algemeen kader herziening strafvordering nader beschouwd. Kluwer, Deventer, pp 51–70
Crijns JH (2010) De strafrechtelijke overeenkomst. De rechtsbetrekking met het Openbaar Ministerie op het grensvlak van publiek—en privaatrecht. Kluwer, Deventer
Crijns JH (2014) Op zoek naar consistentie: bestraffing buiten de rechter om in strafrecht en bestuursrecht. RM Themis 6:263–274
Crijns JH (2015) Artikel 257f. In: T&C Strafvordering
De Doelder H, ’t Hart AC (1992) Aparte procedure voor bekennende verdachten? Nederlands Juristenblad 20:629–630
De Hullu J (1989) Over rechtsmiddelen in strafzaken. Gouda Quint, Arnhem
Demeersseman B (2009) Mogelijkheden voor gebruik van schakelbewijs. Trema 4:149–156
De Wilde B (2009) Schakelconstructies in bewijsmotiveringen. Delikt en Delinkwent 6:563–588
Damaška MR (1972–1973) Evidentiary barriers to conviction and two models of criminal procedure: a comparative study. Univ Pennsylvania Law Rev 121:507–589
Damaška MR (1986) The faces of justice and state authority: a comparative approach to the legal process. Yale University Press, New Haven, London
Damaška MR (1990) Atomistic and holistic evaluation of evidence: a comparative view. In: Clark DS (ed) Comparative and private international law: essays in honour of John Merryman. Duncken and Humblot, Berlin
Damaška MR (1992) Of hearsay and its analogues. Minn Law Rev 76:425–458
Damaška MR (1995) Free proof and its detractors. Am J Comp Law 43(3):343–357
Damaška MR (1997) Evidence law adrift. Yale University Press, New Haven, London
Derksen T (2006) Lucia de B. Reconstructie van een gerechtelijke dwaling. Veen Magazines, Diemen
Dreissen WHB (2007) Bewijsmotivering in strafzaken. Boom Juridische Uitgevers, The Hague
Dreissen WHB (2011) Schakelbewijs in Nederland en de Verenigde Staten. In: Koenraadt F, Wolleswinkel R (eds) Homo ludens en humaan strafrecht. Boom Juridische Uitgeverij, The Hague
Dreissen WHB (2014) Van A naar Beter via Duitsland. Strafblad 6:432–438
Dubelaar MJ (2015) Inleidende opmerkingen bij Tweede Boek, Titel VI, Derde Afdeling. In: T&C Strafvordering
Duker MJA (2012) De verkorte bewijsmotivering bij bekennende verdachten: is er nog een toekomst? Delikt en Delinkwent 6:550–567
Enschedé ChJ (1966) Bewijzen in het strafrecht. RM Themis pp 488–518
Embregts MCD (2003) Uitsluitsel over bewijsuitsluiting; een onderzoek naar de toelaatbaarheid van onrechtmatig verkregen bewijs in het strafrecht, het civiele recht en bestuursrecht. Kluwer, Deventer
Franken AA (1993) Voeging in strafzaken. Gouda Quint, Arnhem
Franken AA (2002) para 66.3.6. In: Handboek strafzaken
Garé DMHR (1994) Het onmiddellijkheidsbeginsel in het Nederlandse strafproces. Gouda Quint, Arnhem
Groenhuijsen MS, Simmelink JBHM (2005) Het wetsvoorstel OM-afdoening op het grensvlak van juridische techniek en strafprocessuele uitgangspunten. In: Jordaans AHEC, Mevis PAM, Wöretshofer J, Praktisch strafrecht (liber amicorum J.M. Reijntjes). Wolf Legal Publishers, Nijmegen, pp 171–197

Hartmann AR (2004) Buitengerechtelijke afdoening II. In: Groenhuijsen MS, Knigge G (eds) Dwangmiddelen en Rechtsmiddelen. Derde interimrapport onderzoeksproject Strafvordering 2001. Kluwer, Deventer

Hartmann AR (2005) Strafbeschikking en bestuurlijke boete: wildgroei in de handhaving? Justitiële verkenningen 31(6):84–96

Hildebrandt M (1993) Een buitensporige procedure. In: Hildebrandt M, Van Kampen PTC, Nijboer JF, Wiersinga H (eds) Een afzonderlijke procedure voor de bekennende verdachte?. Gouda Quint, Arnhem, pp 123–136

Jackson JD, Summers SJ (2012) The internationalisation of criminal evidence: beyond the common law and civil law traditions. Cambridge University Press, Cambridge

Jofriet JRG (2009) De Wet Internationale Misdrijven. Kluwer, Deventer

Jörg N (1993) Een vereenvoudigde procedure in strafzaken. Nederlands Juristenblad 6:199–205

Kelk C (2013) Studieboek materieel strafrecht. Kluwer, Deventer

Keulen BF, Knigge G (2010) Strafprocesrecht. Kluwer, Deventer

Keulen BF (2012) Naar een appèl met appeal. Over bezwaar en (hoger) beroep in strafzaken. RM Themis 1:3–14

Kooijmans T (2011) Dat is mijn zaak!. Tilburg University, Tilburg

Krikke A (1983) De rechtsgrond van bewijsuitsluiting in strafzaken. In: Melai AL, André de la Porte E, Bremmer WMA (eds) Bij deze stand van zaken: bundel opstellen aangeboden aan A.L. Melai. Gouda Quint, Arnhem

Langemeijer GE (1952) De wetgever tegenover opzet en schuld. Nederlands Juristenblad 24:485–496

Lens KME, Pemberton A, Cleven I (2015) Tussenrapportage onderzoek pilots herstelbemiddeling: een eerste evaluatie. Tilburg University/Intervict, Tilburg

Melai AL (1975) Fouillering en onrechtmatig verkregen bewijs. In: Praesidium Libertatis: Opstellen over het thema vrijheid en recht, uitgegeven ter gelegenheid van het 400-jarig bestaan der Rijksuniversiteit Leiden. Kluwer, Deventer

Melai AL (1992) Het strafgeding: polariteit en tegenspraak. In: Polariteit en tegenspraak: een selectie uit het werk van A.L. Melai. Gouda Quint, Arnhem

Mevis PAM (2004) Strafbeschikking openbaar ministerie, WAHV en 'kleine ergernissen'. Delikt en Delinkwent 4:353–367

Murphy P (2003) Evidence, proof, and facts: an introductory essay. In: Murphy P (ed) Evidence, proof, and facts: a book of sources. Oxford University Press, Oxford, pp 2–6

Nijboer JF (1982) Algemene grondslagen van de bewijsbeslissing in het Nederlandse strafprocesrecht. Gouda Quint, Arnhem

Nijboer JF (1987) De doolhof van de Nederlandse strafwetgeving: de systematische grondslag van het algemeen deel van het W.v.Sr. Wolters Noordhoff, Groningen

Nijboer JF (2011) Strafrechtelijk bewijsrecht. Ars Aequi Libri, Nijmegen

Noach WME (1948) De bijzondere rechtspleging. Straf- en tuchtrechtelijk optreden tegen onvaderlandslievend gedrag uit de bezettingsjaren. Martinus Nijhoff, The Hague

Osinga P (1992) Transactie in strafzaken: een onderzoek naar de positie van de transactie in het strafrechtelijk systeem. Gouda Quint, Arnhem

Peters AAG (1972) Het rechtskarakter van het strafrecht. Kluwer, Deventer

Pompe WPJ (1959) Het bewijs in strafzaken. Paleis der Academiën, Brussel

Reijntjes JM (2006) Eigen wetenschap van de rechter; algemene bekendheid en ervaringsregels. Strafblad 1:46–58

Roberts P, Zuckerman A (2010) Criminal evidence. Oxford University Press, Oxford

Röttgering AEM (2006) Schakelbewijs: een spooktrein in het bewijsrecht. Strafblad, pp 36–42

Rüter CF (1973) Enkele aspecten van de strafrechtelijke reactie op oorlogsmisdrijven en misdrijven tegen de menselijkheid. Amsterdam University Press, Amsterdam

Schoep GK (2015) art. 359 Sv. In: T&C Strafvordering

Sikkema E, Kristen FGH (2013) Strafbeschikking en ZSM: verschuivingen binnen de strafrechtshandhaving. In: De Jong F, Kool RSB (eds) Relaties van gezag en verantwoordelijkheid: strafrechtelijke ontwikkelingen. Boom Juridische Uitgevers, The Hague, pp 179–205

Stein A (2005) Foundations of evidence law. Oxford University Press, Oxford
Stein F (1893) Das private Wissen des Richters. Untersuchungen zum Beweisrecht beider Prozesse. C.L, Hirschfeld, Leipzig
Tapper C (2010) Cross & Tapper on evidence. Oxford University Press, Oxford
Twining W (1990) Rethinking evidence: exploratory essays. Northwestern University Press, Evanston
Valkenburg WECA (2015) Art. 167 Sv. In: T&C Strafvordering
Van Boom WH, Tuil ML, Van der Zalm I (2010) Feiten van algemene bekendheid en ervaringsregels – virtuele werkelijkheid? Nederlands Tijdschrift voor Burgerlijk Recht 7:36–43
Van den Biggelaar GJM (1994) De buitengerechtelijke afdoening van strafbare feiten door het Openbaar Ministerie. Gouda Quint, Arnhem
Van Dorst AJA (2015) Cassatie in strafzaken. Kluwer, Deventer
Van Eck D (1945) Het misdrijf van hulp aan de vijand in verband met de bepalingen van het Besluit Buitengewoon Strafrecht. Dekker en Van de Vegt, Utrecht
Van Kempen PHPHMC, Pesselse G (2014) Het verlofstelsel in hoger beroep in strafzaken. In: Van Kempen PHPHMC et al (eds) Hoger beroep: renovatie en innovatie. Het appel in het burgerlijk, straf-en bestuursprocesrecht. Kluwer, The Hague
Van Woensel AM (1997) Art. 339 Sv. In: Melai/Groenhuijsen et al. Wetboek van Strafvordering
Volk K (2010) Grundkurs StPO. Verlag C.H. Beck, Munich
Vriend KCJ (2013) Inzichtelijk gebruik van schakelbewijs in strafzaken: een Bayesiaans perspectief. Expertise en Recht 4:131–134
Walton D, Macagno F (2005) Common knowledge in legal reasoning about evidence. Int Commentary Evid 3(1):1–42
Zander M (2007) Cases and materials on the english legal system. Cambridge University Press, Cambridge
Zuckerman AAS (1992) The principles of criminal evidence. Oxford University Press, Oxford

Chapter 4
Diversions and Shortcuts in the Law of International Criminal Procedure

Abstract In this chapter diversions and shortcuts in international criminal proceedings are discussed. Two diversions are identified in the proceedings before the ICTY, ICTR, and ICC: the guilty plea and the admission of guilt. Four shortcuts to proof are discerned in international criminal proceedings: agreed facts, judicial notice of facts of common knowledge, judicial notice of adjudicated facts and documentary evidence, and appeal proceedings.

Keywords Diversions · Shortcuts · Guilty plea · Admission of guilt · Agreed facts · Judicial notice · Facts of common knowledge · Adjudicated facts · Appeal proceedings · ICTY · ICTR · ICC

Contents

K. Vriend, *Avoiding a Full Criminal Trial*, International Criminal Justice Series 8, DOI 10.1007/978-94-6265-153-1_4

4.1 Introduction

The previous chapter described what a full criminal trial entails in Dutch criminal proceedings. The main characteristics of the proceedings were discussed, with a focus on three elements: the admissibility of evidence, the weighing of the evidence and the element of a reasoned judgment. The mechanisms were discussed that either diverted the case from the proceedings altogether or provided for a shortcut to proof. Similar to the previous chapter, the characteristics of the full criminal trial in international criminal proceedings will be discussed here with these three elements in mind. The proceedings at the two ad hoc Tribunals, the ICTY and ICTR, will be discussed, as well as the proceedings before the ICC.[1] Subsequently, the diversions and shortcuts that can be discerned in international criminal proceedings will be discussed. First, some preliminary observations are made regarding the terminology that is used in international criminal law regarding basic concepts of evidence law.

4.1.1 Preliminary Observations

In his contribution to *International Criminal Procedure: Principles and Rules*, Klamberg observed that:

> One standard of admissibility is shared by all international criminal courts, namely that they are not bound by any national rules of evidence. However, key terms such as relevance, probative value, reliability and credibility are not used in a coherent way. This becomes an even greater problem during the final evaluation of the evidence. There is arguably a difficulty in clarifying these terms through amendments to the Statutes and/or the RPE's. Instead the judges should, through reasoned opinions, explain or indicate how these terms are to be understood.[2]

It is true that the case law of the international criminal courts concerning these basic concepts of evidence law is far from consistent and clear. Concepts are defined differently (although, mostly, not to a great extent), which leads, in turn, to academic debates on the correct interpretation of these concepts. The aim of the drafters of the Rules of Procedure and Evidence (RPE), to unshackle themselves from the technical, common-law approach to evidence, has, paradoxically, led to ill-defined or ambiguous concepts. Basic notions such as relevance, probative value and weight are used in an inconsistent manner. This has sometimes resulted

[1] For a detailed analysis of the procedural models at the ad hoc Tribunals and the ICC, see: Zappalà 2013, pp. 44–54. Zappalà argued that the proceedings at the ICTY and ICTR are adversarial in nature. However, the judges at these Tribunals have tried to increase judicial control over the proceedings in order to provide for efficient trials. Regarding the ICC, Zappalà observed that the proceedings are a mix of adversarial and inquisitorial elements.

[2] Klamberg 2013b, p. 1043.

in highly technical observations from the judges in their decisions. An example is this excerpt from the Appeal Judgment in *Naletilić & Martinović* on the admission of documentary evidence:

> Pursuant to Rule 89 (C), a Chamber may admit any relevant evidence which it deems to have probative value. The implicit requirement that a piece of evidence be prima facie credible – that it have sufficient indicia of reliability – 'is a factor in the assessment of its relevance and probative value'.[3]

Both relevance and probative value have to be determined by an implicit (!) requirement of *prima facie* credibility, which consists of sufficient indicia of reliability. The wording of decisions on the admissibility of evidence almost seems to imply that the question of whether or not to admit a particular piece of evidence is an exercise in taxonomy: the RPE provide two basic concepts (relevance and probative value), which are then to be sub-divided into concepts reminiscent of the manner in which evidence is processed in common law jury trials. Evidence law in common law countries is often highly technical in order to facilitate the parties to carefully review whether certain evidence may be brought to the attention of the jury. It is doubtful whether such a detailed analysis of evidence during the admissibility stage is anything more than semantics, particularly in trial proceedings conducted before professional judges. One may distinguish theoretically between the concepts of 'credibility' and 'reliability', but it is unlikely that such a distinction is really helpful for determining the admissibility of a piece of evidence. To structure the analysis, it is essential that consistent terminology is used, but the number of terms will be kept to a minimum. For this analysis there is no need for all kinds of technical sub-rules and observations from case law that distinguish between factors that are, for the most part, only relevant within a specific judicial setting: the trial by jury. The most important and basic notions regarding evidence are relevance, probative value and weight.

Relevance, contained in Rule 89 (C) ICTY and ICTR RPE and Article 69(4) ICC Statute, can be defined as the logical relationship between a *factum probans* and a *factum probandum*. In other words, evidence is relevant when it relates to a fact that has to be proven. To identify *which* facts have to be proven in criminal proceedings, one has to take into account the legal framework in which the proceedings are conducted. The charges and the underlying facts have to be proven, and any fact that testifies to the probability of such facts is relevant. Facts that relate to the existence of an alibi or a defence are also relevant: they relate to the facts that have to be proven (in case of an alibi this is an inverse relationship). When it is clear which facts have to be proven, the question of whether a piece of evidence is relevant to the proceedings becomes a matter of common sense.

Probative value, given that the evidence is relevant, refers to the degree of trustworthiness of the particular piece of evidence. In other words, does the evidence

[3] ICTY, Judgment, *Prosecutor v. Naletilić & Martinović*, Case No.: IT-98-34-A, A. Ch., 3 May 2006, para 402 (emphasis in original).

make the existence of a fact more or less likely? The factors that help to determine the probative value of a piece of evidence during the admissibility stage are numerous and vary among different categories of evidence. For example, to determine the probative value of hearsay evidence, Chambers have taken into account whether the statement was given voluntarily and whether it was truthful and trustworthy.[4] Regarding the admissibility of documentary evidence, relevant factors include the origin, source and use of the documents involved.[5] For expert evidence to be admissible, the expert statement or report must be sufficiently reliable:

> there must be sufficient information as to the sources used in support of statements, and these must be clearly indicated in order to allow the other party or the Trial Chamber the basis on which the expert witness reached his or her conclusions.[6]

In *Katanga*, ICC Trial Chamber II stated:

> Once the probative value of a particular item of evidence has been determined, the Chamber must weigh this against the potential prejudice, if any, that its admission might cause.[7]

It is instructive to discuss the relationship between probative value and prejudice regarding the admissibility of evidence. Article 69(4) ICC Statute states that the Court, ruling on admissibility, may take into account any prejudice the evidence may cause to a fair trial or to the fair evaluation of the testimony of a witness. The notion of prejudice is a well-known concept in common law criminal law systems, where the judge has to rule on the prejudicial effect a certain piece of evidence may have on the jury. A classic example is bad character evidence, where the jury is getting acquainted with the criminal record, or its relevant parts, of the accused. Such evidence is normally inadmissible because its probative value is expected to be outweighed by its prejudicial effect.[8] However, such a reading of

---

[4] ICTY, Decision on Prosecutor's Appeal on Admissibility of Evidence, *Prosecutor v. Aleksovski*, Case No.: IT-95-14/1-AR73, A. Ch., 16 February 1999, para 15.

[5] ICTY, Decision to Unseal Confidential Decision on the Admissibility of Certain Challenged Documents and Documents for Identification, *Prosecutor v. Hadžihasanović*, Case No.: IT-01-47-T, T. Ch. II, 2 August 2004, para 56.

[6] ICTY, Decision on Prosecution Motion for Admission of Morten Torkildsen Report and its Associated Exhibits, *Prosecutor v. Hadžić*, Case No.: IT-04-75-T, T. Ch., 15 July 2013, para 9. Cf. Trial Chamber III in *Stanišić & Simatović*: '[...] the expert statement must meet the minimum standards of reliability. There must be sufficient information as to the sources used in support of the statements. The sources must be clearly indicated and accessible in order to allow the other party or the Trial Chamber to test or challenge the basis on which the expert witness reached his or her conclusions. In the absence of clear references or accessible sources, the Trial Chamber will not treat such a statement or report as an expert opinion, but as the personal opinion of the witness, and weigh the evidence accordingly.' ICTY, Decision on Prosecution's Submission of the Expert Report of Nena Tromp and Christian Nielsen pursuant to Rule 94*bis*, *Prosecutor v. Stanišić & Simatović*, Case No.: IT-03-69-PT, T. Ch. III, 18 March 2008, para 9.

[7] ICC, Decision on the Prosecutor's Bar Table Motions, *Prosecutor v. Katanga & Ngudjolo Chui*, Case No.: ICC-01/04-01/07, T. Ch. II, 17 December 2010, para 37.

[8] Roberts and Zuckerman 2010, pp. 586–600.

prejudice in international criminal proceedings would be incorrect: it would require the judges to estimate the prejudicial effect the evidence, when admitted, would have on their final deliberations. Acknowledging its prejudicial effect would, in fact, result in eliminating its prejudicial effect. It seems more plausible to consider 'fair evaluation of testimony' as part of a fair trial. Any prejudice to a fair evaluation of a witness statement would then have to be determined from the perspective of the defence: does the admission of the evidence have a prejudicial effect on the right of the accused to examine and challenge the witness or his statement?[9]

In *Katanga*, the Trial Chamber identified several categories of prejudicial evidence that may infringe upon the rights of the accused. Repetitive and time-consuming evidence, although probative, may be excluded in order to respect the accused's right to be tried without undue delay.[10] Witness statements, although probative, may be excluded when the witness is not available for examination at trial (provided the accused has not waived his right to examine the witness, or had the opportunity to examine the witness when the statement was recorded). To do otherwise would infringe upon the right to examine the witnesses.[11] A statement of a co-accused may be excluded, because the co-accused cannot be compelled to be examined by, or on behalf of, the accused.[12] And, finally, statements made by the accused may be excluded when there are serious concerns that they have been obtained in violation of his right to remain silent and his right not to incriminate himself.[13]

The final basic notion discussed here is the weight of the evidence. As understood here, weight refers to the ultimate probative value the Chamber attaches to a

---

[9] Piragoff argued that this provision is not solely concerned with the interests of the accused: 'Therefore, a fair trial, and prejudice thereto, may also incorporate or be counter-balanced by some aspects of the fair treatment of victims and witnesses, and not merely fair treatment of an accused, provided that these aspects are not "prejudicial to or inconsistent with the right of the accused or a fair and impartial trial.". The fairness of a trial may encompass considerations that are broader than the rights of an accused and other participants, and may require a balancing process of the factors mentioned in Article 64 para 2 which may be inter-related rather than distinct. Alternatively, if some of these rights and interests are not encompassed within the concept of "fair trial", they may find their expression and protection in the concept of "fair evaluation of the testimony of a witness", which is also included in para 4.' Piragoff 2008, p. 1325.

[10] ICC, Decision on the Prosecutor's Bar Table Motions, *Prosecutor v. Katanga & Ngudjolo Chui*, Case No.: ICC-01/04-01/07, T. Ch. II, 17 December 2010, para 41.

[11] ICC, Decision on the Prosecutor's Bar Table Motions, *Prosecutor v. Katanga & Ngudjolo Chui*, Case No.: ICC-01/04-01/07, T. Ch. II17 December 2010, paras 42–51.

[12] ICC, Decision on the Prosecutor's Bar Table Motions, *Prosecutor v. Katanga & Ngudjolo Chui*, Case No.: ICC-01/04-01/07, T. Ch. II, 17 December 2010, paras 52–54.

[13] ICC, Decision on the Prosecutor's Bar Table Motions, *Prosecutor v. Katanga & Ngudjolo Chui*, Case No.: ICC-01/04-01/07, T. Ch. II, 17 December 2010, paras 55–65.

piece of evidence.[14] Determining weight, therefore, is done holistically after the close of proceedings, when all evidence has been presented. Considering that the final determination is conducted by professional judges, statutory rules of weight (such as the rule on corroborative evidence)[15] are virtually absent.[16]

Rules of weight infringe upon the prerogative of the judge to weigh each piece of evidence in the context of the totality of the evidence (which, in fact, results in a hermeneutic process: each piece of evidence is weighed against the totality of the evidence, and the totality of the evidence is, at the same time, influenced by weighing the individual pieces of evidence). Rules of weight do exist, however, in relation to the distinct category of evidence in cases of sexual violence. Rule 70 ICC RPE precludes the Chamber from inferring consent on the part of the victim in certain circumstances (such as the silence of, or lack of resistance by, the victim).[17]

Besides the few statutory rules of weight, the case law of the Tribunals provides for some rules of weight. The Appeals Chamber held in *Martić* that evidence which has not been subjected to cross-examination and goes to the acts or conduct of the accused must, if used for the conviction, be corroborated.[18] However, a general rule of corroboration does not exist:

> The Appeals Chamber recalls that a Trial Chamber is at liberty to rely on the evidence of a single witness when making its findings. The testimony of a single witness may be accepted without the need for corroboration, even if it relates to a material fact.[19]

After the total weight of the evidence has been determined, it is juxtaposed with the standard of proof.[20] In the *Ntagurera et al.* appeals judgment, the Appeals

---

[14] Cf. Trial Chamber II in *Katanga & Ngudjolo Chui*: 'The Chamber wishes to remind the parties that probative value and evidentiary weight are two similar but distinct concepts. Under Article 69(4) of the Statute, probative value is a key criterion in any determination on admissibility. It follows that the Chamber must determine the probative value of an item of evidence *before* it can be admitted into the proceedings. Probative value is determined on the basis of a number of considerations pertaining to the inherent characteristics of the evidence. Evidentiary weight, however, is the relative importance that is attached to an item of evidence in deciding whether a certain issue has been proven or not.' ICC, Decision on the Prosecutor's Bar Table Motions, *Prosecutor v. Katanga & Ngudjolo Chui*, Case No.: ICC-01/04-01/07, T. Ch. II, 17 December 2010, para 13 (emphasis in original).

[15] Cf. Klamberg 2013a, pp. 179–182.

[16] Cf. Rule 63(4) RPE ICC: 'Without prejudice to Article 66, para 3, a Chamber shall not impose a legal requirement that corroboration is required in order to prove any crime within the jurisdiction of the Court, in particular, crimes of sexual violence.'

[17] See also Rule 96 ICTY and ICTR RPE.

[18] ICTY, Decision on the Appeal against the Trial Chamber's Decision on the Evidence of Witness Milan Babić, *Prosecutor v. Milan Martić*, Case No.: IT-95-11-AR73.2, A. Ch., 14 September 2006, para 20.

[19] ICTY, Judgment, *Prosecutor v. Haradinaj et al.*, Case No.: IT-04-84-A, A. Ch., 19 July 2010, para 219.

[20] The rather mechanical terminology used does not imply that fact-finding *in criminalibus* is, in fact, a mechanical or mathematical exercise in which pieces of evidence have a certain weight that can be quantified and added to the total corpus of evidence. These terms are used to describe the judge's task in, at least for lawyers, familiar terminology.

Chamber commented on the process of evaluating the evidence before a Chamber may enter a conviction. According to the Appeals Chamber, this process consists of three stages. First, the Chamber evaluates the credibility of each piece of evidence in light of the total body of evidence presented; second, the Chamber determines whether the alleged facts are proven beyond a reasonable doubt; and finally, the Chamber decides whether all elements of the crime and the mode of liability have been proven.[21]

The proof beyond a reasonable doubt standard is a principle of international criminal law.[22] This common law concept can be equated with the *conviction intime* and *conviction raisonnée* standards that are applicable in continental Europe. As discussed earlier, the main difference between these two standards of proof is not the degree of belief (both standards require, in fact, the same degree of belief in the guilt of the accused), but the obligation for the judge to hand down a reasoned opinion.

With these preliminary observations in mind, we now turn to the rules concerning the admissibility of evidence, the weighing of evidence and the requirement of providing reasons for the final judgment.

4.1.2 Rules of Admissibility in International Criminal Proceedings

The admissibility of evidence in international criminal proceedings is governed exclusively by the Statutes and Rules of Procedure and Evidence of the international courts. The legal instruments of the ICTY, ICTR and the ICC all contain provisions stating that national rules of evidence are not binding upon them.[23]

The general provisions of the international tribunals on the admission of evidence provide for a lenient approach to the admissibility of evidence: all evidence

---

[21] ICTR, Judgment, *Prosecutor v. Ntagurera et al.*, Case No.: ICTR-99-46-A, A. Ch., 7 July 2006, para 174.

[22] Jacobs 2013, p. 1148. Cf. Article 66 ICC Statute. In Čelebići, the Appeals Chamber discussed the use of circumstantial evidence in relation to the standard of proof. The Appeals Chamber held: 'A circumstantial case consists of evidence of a number of different circumstances which, taken in combination, point to the guilt of the accused person because they would usually exist in combination only because the accused did what is alleged against him [...]. Such a conclusion must be established beyond reasonable doubt. It is not sufficient that it is a reasonable conclusion available from that evidence. It must be the *only* reasonable conclusion available. If there is another conclusion which is also reasonably open from that evidence, and which is consistent with the innocence of the accused, he must be acquitted.' ICTY, Judgment, *Prosecutor v. Delalić* et al., Case No.: IT-96-21-A, A. Ch., 20 February 2001, para 458 (emphasis in original).

[23] Rule 89(A) ICTY RPE, Rule 89(A) ICTR RPE, Rule 63(5) ICC RPE.

is to be admitted, unless stated otherwise.[24] Technical rules on admissibility are not included in the legal instruments, which resembles the principle of free proof. Thus, the Statutes and Rules of Procedure and Evidence have an inclusionary character ('no relevant evidence may be excluded, unless stated otherwise'). Evidence is only declared inadmissible when it is irrelevant, does not have any probative value or when its admission would be contrary to values extraneous to accurate fact-finding. When we analyse the exceptions to the inclusionary principle, we are confronted with numerous situations in which evidence is declared inadmissible, however. These exceptions will be discussed. The exceptions to the principle of the free admission of evidence will be categorized according to the *objective* the exclusion strives to achieve. Similar to the discussion in the previous chapter, exclusionary rules (or, rules of non-admissibility)[25] can be divided into intrinsic and extrinsic exclusionary rules. Intrinsic exclusionary rules refer to those rules that exclude evidence to enhance the accuracy of the fact-finding process. Such rules may also be called epistemic exclusionary rules because they aim to exclude evidence that, from a non-legal perspective, does not contribute to accurate fact-finding. Extrinsic exclusionary rules are rules that exclude evidence in order to achieve an aim extraneous to accurate fact-finding. For example, rules excluding illegally obtained evidence exist, *inter alia*, to ensure that the authorities abide by their own laws.

In his analysis of the law of evidence of England and Wales, Andrew Choo distinguished between exclusionary *rules* and exclusionary *discretion*.[26] An exclusionary rule is a rule, which, upon the fulfilment of certain conditions, excludes a piece of evidence categorically: it is an imperative rule. A classic example is the common law hearsay rule. Roberts and Zuckerman observed that:

> the hearsay rule excludes (1) out-of-court statements (2) adduced for their truth, unless a well-established exception to the exclusionary rule applies.[27]

Leaving the numerous exceptions to the rule aside for now, the rule obliges the trial judge to exclude a statement when the conditions enumerated under (1) and (2) have been fulfilled. Rule 96 ICTY RPE and Rule 71 ICC RPE, to be discussed in more detail below, are examples of such exclusionary rules: any evidence that

---

[24] Rule 89(C) ICTY RPE and Rule 89(C) ICTR RPE state: 'A Chamber may admit any relevant evidence which it deems to have probative value.' Article 69(4) ICC Statute provides: 'The Court may rule on the relevance or admissibility of any evidence, taking into account, *inter alia*, the probative value of the evidence and any prejudice that such evidence may cause to a fair trial or to a fair evaluation of the testimony of a witness, in accordance with the Rules of Procedure and Evidence.'

[25] Cf. the definition of exclusionary rules by Roberts and Zuckerman: 'Exclusionary rules of evidence might be conceptualized as evidentiary standards purporting to encapsulate—or at least serve as durable proxies for—good epistemic or normative reasons for ignoring relevant information in criminal adjudication.' Roberts and Zuckerman 2010, p. 98.

[26] Choo 2012, pp. 13–15.

[27] Roberts and Zuckerman 2010, p. 364.

goes, in cases of sexual assault, to the prior sexual conduct of the victim or witness shall not be admissible. In such cases, the Chamber is asked to answer two simple questions: (1) does the sexual assault involve the witness or victim? (2) does the evidence testify to the prior sexual conduct of the witness or victim? If so, the evidence must be excluded.

Exclusionary discretion is a more complex concept because it bestows upon the Chamber a discretionary power to rule on the admissibility of evidence. However, this discretionary power is firmly put in context. For example, Article 69(7)(b) ICC Statute states that evidence that was obtained in violation of the ICC Statute or internationally recognized human rights shall be declared inadmissible *if* the admission would be antithetical to and seriously damage the integrity of the proceedings. It is within the Chamber's discretion to determine whether the admission of the evidence would result in the forbidden effect stated in this article. The exercise of discretion is restricted, or put in context, by the general objective to safeguard the integrity of the proceedings.

The distinction between exclusionary rules and exclusionary discretion may be useful to analysing the different wording of the relevant Rules of Procedure and Evidence: Rule 96(iv) ICTY RPE precludes the admission of evidence relating to prior sexual conduct of the victim categorically ('*shall* not be admitted in evidence'). Rule 89(D) ICTY RPE, on the other hand, is an example of exclusionary discretion: the Chamber *may* exclude evidence if the probative value is substantially outweighed by the need to ensure a fair trial.

When discussing admissibility, one other important distinction must be made. This is the distinction between facts concerning the individual criminal responsibility of the accused and facts that are more peripheral or contextual to the acts of the accused. This distinction can also be discerned in the rules of admissibility. For example, Rule 92*bis* ICTY RPE allows for the admission of written statements or transcripts without the attendance of the witness concerned when the testimony relates to matters *other* than the acts and conduct of the accused. Considering the scope of international criminal proceedings in terms of the charges, the factual basis of the charges and the massive volume of evidence presented, the need to streamline the proceedings is pressing. In terms of admissibility, a two-track system has been put into place. ICC Trial Chambers have held that relevant factors to determine whether prior recorded testimony may replace *viva voce* testimony are:

> (i) that the testimony relates to issues which are not materially in dispute; (ii) that it is *not central to core issues in the case, but rather provides relevant background information*; and (iii) that it is corroborative of other evidence.[28]

[28] ICC, Decision on the Prosecution's Application for the Admission of the Prior Recorded Statements of Two Witnesses, *Prosecutor v. Lubanga Dyilo*, Case No.: ICC-01/04-01/06, T. Ch. I, 15 January 2009, para 24 (emphasis added). ICC, Corrigendum to the Decision on the Prosecution Motion for Admission of Prior Recorded Testimony of Witness P-02 and Accompanying Video Excerpts, *Prosecutor v. Katanga & Ngudjolo Chui*, Case No.: ICC-01/04-01/07, T. Ch. II, 27 August 2010, para 14.

Although these ICC decisions concern the admission of prior recorded written witness statements with the witness present in court for cross-examination, they are relevant to point to the distinction being made between contextual facts and facts that go directly to proof of the individual criminal responsibility of the accused. The difference between core issues and contextual issues does not have an absolute character, but may vary from case to case. In cases concerning low-level perpetrators, the contextual elements, such as the existence of a widespread or systematic attack, are indeed contextual: the accused himself was not able to influence in any way the existence of the context in which he operated. Trial Chambers should be conscious about such distinctions and allow the accused to participate and challenge any evidence that goes to proof of his personal criminal responsibility.

4.1.2.1 Intrinsic Exclusionary Rules

The existence of intrinsic exclusionary rules in international criminal proceedings seems at odds with the fact that the fact-finding process is conducted by professional judges. The ratio for excluding material that is *prima facie* relevant, but subject to an exclusionary rule, is normally found in the mistrust in lay adjudicators, who must be shielded from material that they are most likely not able to weigh appropriately. Professional judges, so the argument goes, are able to identify such prejudicial material and leave it out of their final deliberations.

Intrinsic exclusionary rules are indeed hard to find in international criminal law. The legal frameworks of the ad hoc Tribunals and the ICC both contain only one provision that can be characterized as an (at least partially) intrinsic exclusionary rule. Rule 95 ICTY RPE and ICTR RPE states:

> No evidence shall be admissible if obtained by methods which cast substantial doubt on its reliability or if its admission is antithetical to, and would seriously damage, the integrity of the proceedings.

Article 69(7)(a) ICC Statute:

> Evidence obtained by means of a violation of this Statute or internationally recognized human rights shall not be admissible if: (a) the violation casts substantial doubt on the reliability of the evidence; […].

Both provisions oblige Trial Chambers to exclude unreliable evidence. The first part of Rule 95 ICTY and ICTR RPE can be characterized as an intrinsic exclusionary rule: evidence which, due to the manner in which it was obtained, is unreliable must be excluded. Article 69(7)(a) ICC Statute is more specific regarding the source of the unreliability of the evidence. Evidence that is unreliable must be excluded according to this Article when the unreliability stems from a violation of the Statute or internationally recognized human rights.

The term ‘reliability’ warrants some discussion, particularly in the light of the general admissibility requirement that each piece of evidence must be relevant and have probative value.[29] Klamberg, in his analysis of the case law of the ad hoc Tribunals, shows that the concept of reliability is not easily defined.[30] The ICTY Appeals Chamber held that evidence is reliable when it may prove the truth of its contents. The evidence, a hearsay statement in this particular case, must be voluntary, truthful and trustworthy.[31] In fact, the requirement of voluntariness can easily be subsumed under the general requirements of truthfulness and trustworthiness. These last requirements are, arguably, nothing more than aspects of one of the basic concepts of admissibility: probative value.[32]

Regarding the reliability of documentary evidence during the admissibility stage, the Trial Chamber in *Ngirabatware* held that some factors are taken into account:

> the extent to which their [the documents', KV] content is corroborated by other evidence; their provenance; whether the documents submitted are originals or copies; if copies, whether these were registered or filed with an institutional authority; and whether these are signed, sealed, stamped or certified in any way.[33]

ICC Trial Chamber I in *Lubanga* stated that the following indicia of reliability, regarding several logbooks and notebooks, were taken into account: the absence of any motive for the fabrication of the documents; the fact that the documents were created contemporaneously with the events they described; that the documents are internally consistent; that the documents seem to be corroborated by a witness statement and, finally, that the documents are signed by 'relevant social workers'.[34] The Appeals Chamber in *Kordić & Čerkez* held that:

> a piece of evidence may be so lacking in terms of the indicia of reliability that it is not 'probative' and is therefore inadmissible.[35]

---

[29] Rule 89(C) ICTY RPE and ICTR RPE: 'A Chamber may admit any relevant evidence which it deems to have probative value.'; Article 69(4) ICC Statute: 'The Court may rule on the relevance or admissibility of any evidence, taking into account, *inter alia*, the probative value of the evidence and any prejudice that such evidence may cause to a fair trial or to a fair evaluation of the testimony of a witness, in accordance with the Rules of Procedure and Evidence.'

[30] Klamberg 2013a, pp. 351–355. Cf. Klamberg 2013b, p. 1025.

[31] ICTY, Decision on Prosecutor's Appeal on Admissibility of Evidence, *Prosecutor v. Aleksovski*, Case No.: IT-95-14/1-AR73, A. Ch., 16 February 1999, para 15.

[32] Cf. ICTR, Decision on Joseph Nzirorera's Appeal of Decision on Admission of Evidence Rebutting Adjudicated Facts, *Prosecutor v. Karemera et al.*, ICTR-98-44-AR73.17, A. Ch., 29 May 2009, para 14: 'Only evidence that is reliable and credible may be considered to have probative value.' The other concept of admissibility is relevancy.

[33] ICTR, Decision on Prosecution Motion for Admission of Documentary Evidence, *Prosecutor v. Ngirabatware*, Case No.: ICTR-99-54-T, T. Ch. II, 4 July 2012, para 33.

[34] ICC, Decision on the Admissibility of Four Documents, *Prosecutor v. Lubanga Dyilo,* Case No.: ICC-01/04-01/06, T. Ch. I, 13 June 2008, paras 37–40.

[35] ICTY, Decision on Appeal Regarding Statement of a Deceased Witness, *Prosecutor v. Kordić & Čerkez*, IT-95-14/2-AR73.5, A. Ch., 21 July 2000, para 24.

And, in somewhat circular terms:

> At the stage of the admission of evidence, the implicit requirement of reliability means no more than that there must be sufficient indicia of reliability to make out a prima facie case [for the admission of the evidence, KV].[36]

From this perspective, Rule 95 ICTY and ICTR RPE and Article 69(7)(a) ICC Statute underline the importance of admitting solely evidence that has some probative value and emphasize that evidence obtained by methods that may have jeopardized or minimized its probative value, must be excluded. 'Some' probative value (or *prima facie* probative value) suffices at the admissibility stage: only when all the evidence has been presented, the court will determine the ultimate weight it attaches to particular pieces of evidence, weighed against the other evidence.

When reliability is indeed regarded as synonymous to probative value, it becomes clear why the first part of Rule 95 ICTY and ICTR RPE and Article 69(7)(a) ICC Statute have been categorized under the intrinsic exclusionary rules. The message they convey is that the Chamber has to ensure that relevant evidence that has been collected in a manner that jeopardizes its probative value is excluded from the proceedings. It is noted that this is different from exclusionary rules that exclude evidence obtained by illegal methods but where the particular piece of evidence, nevertheless, has probative value. The question of whether or not to exclude evidence obtained during an illegal search and seizure surely concerns the *method* of obtaining the evidence, but it does not necessarily concern the *probative value* of the evidence. Such evidence is excluded because the methods by which it was obtained violate an extrinsic value, such as the right to privacy or the fact that the investigating authorities must abide by the law. The Rule and Article discussed are concerned with the intrinsic value of accurate fact finding.

4.1.2.2 Extrinsic Exclusionary Rules

The legal frameworks of the ad hoc Tribunals and the ICC contain a wide variety of extrinsic exclusionary rules: rules that exclude relevant (and possibly probative) evidence due to an objective extraneous to accurate fact-finding. Considering that the exclusion of such material potentially undermines the most central goal of any criminal trial (accurate fact-finding), a solid justification must be provided for each rule.[37] First, the extrinsic exclusionary rules of the ad hoc Tribunals will be discussed, followed by the rules that are contained in the legal framework of the ICC.

---

[36] ICTY, Decision on Application of Defendant Zejnil Delalić for Leave to Appeal Against the Decision of the Trial Chamber of 19 January 1998 for the Admissibility of Evidence, *Prosecutor v. Delalić* et al., IT-96-21-AR73.2, A. Ch., 4 March 1998, para 17.

[37] Cf. Laudan's remark: 'It thus seems fair to say that, whatever else it is, a criminal trial is first and foremost an *epistemic* engine, a tool for ferreting out the truth from what will often initially be a confusing array of clues and indicators.' Laudan 2006, p. 2 (emphasis in original).

The Ad Hoc Tribunals

The general rule: Rule 89(D) ICTY RPE

The most general extrinsic rule is Rule 89(D) ICTY RPE: 'A Chamber may exclude evidence if its probative value is substantially outweighed by the need to ensure a fair trial'.[38] Despite its general wording, the provision has not been used often.[39]

In an early decision on interlocutory appeal, the Appeals Chamber held that:

> the threshold standard for the admission of evidence [...] should not be set excessively high, as often documents are sought to be admitted into evidence, not as ultimate proof of guilt or innocence, but to provide a context and complete the picture presented by the evidence gathered.[40]

Examples where Rule 89(D) was applied include disclosure violations that caused prejudice to the defence, 'restrictions on the content and manner of presentation of the testimony of the witness', and the situation in which a statement made by the accused in his capacity as a witness was subsequently included in his own case.[41] Considering the tendency to admit as much relevant evidence as possible, the fact that this particular Rule has not often been applied should not come as a surprise.

Protection against self-incrimination: Rule 90 (E) ICTY and ICTR RPE

Rule 90(E) ICTY and ICTR RPE protects witnesses from giving self-incriminatory testimony. However, the Trial Chamber has the power to compel the witness to answer a particular question, even if the answer would incriminate the witness. This statement may not be used in any subsequent proceedings against the witness (except for the offence of perjury).[42] In *Karemera et al.*, an accused refused to testify in another trial, because he feared his testimony would touch upon matters that were excluded in his own trial. Testifying on these matters could lead, he argued, to a reopening of his case on these matters, despite the protection of Rule 90(E). The Trial Chamber concurred and held that his testimony was not essential for the current proceedings. The motion by the defence to hear the witness was accordingly denied.[43]

---

[38] The Rules of Procedure and Evidence of the ICTR do not contain a similar provision.

[39] Sluiter 2009, p. 316.

[40] ICTY, Decision on Application Of Defendant Zejnil Delalić for Leave to Appeal Against the Decision of the Trial Chamber of 19 January 1998 for the Admissibility of Evidence, *Prosecutor v. Delalić et al.*, Case No.: IT-96-21-AR73.2, A. Ch., 5 March 1998, para 20.

[41] ICTY, Decision on Joint Defence Oral Motion Pursuant to Rule 89(D), *Prosecutor v. Haradinaj et al.*, Case No.: IT-04-84bis-T, T. Ch. II, 28 September 2011, para 7.

[42] E.g. ICTY, Decision on Accused's Motion to Subpoena Svetozar Andrić, *Prosecutor v. Karadžić*, Case No.: IT-95-5/18-T, T. Ch., 28 May 2013, para 16.

[43] ICTR, Decision on Joseph Nzirorera's Motion to Postpone or Compel the Testimony of Augustin Ngirabatware, *Prosecutor v. Karemera et al.*, T. Ch. III, Case No.: ICTR-98-44-T, 3 May 2010.

Such an extrinsic exclusionary rule lies, according to the European Court of Human Rights, at 'the heart of a notion of a fair trial'. Its rationale lies in respect for the will of the accused and the need to prevent compulsion or coercion by the investigating authorities.[44]

Unavailable witnesses: Rule 92quater ICTY RPE and Rule 92bis ICTR RPE

Rule 92*quater* ICTY RPE and Rule 92*bis* ICTR RPE provide for the admission of written testimony or transcript from an unavailable witness. Such evidence may be admitted even if not all the requirements of Rule 92*bis* ICTY RPE and Rule 92*bis* (B) ICTR RPE have been observed. If a witness has given testimony in other proceedings or otherwise and the witness has subsequently died, is untraceable or is unable (either physically or mentally) to testify, the previous statement may be admitted. Rule 92*bis* (D) ICTR RPE states that such evidence may only go to proof of matters other than the acts or conduct of the accused. The corresponding Rule in the ICTY RPE leaves it to the Chamber's discretion whether or not to admit such evidence. Rule 92*quater* (B) states:

> If the evidence goes to proof of acts and conduct of an accused as charged in the indictment, this may be a factor against the admission of such evidence, or that part of it.

This limb of the Rule must be read in conjunction with the general admissibility requirements of Rule 89(C) and Rule 89(D), concerning relevancy, probative value and the question of whether evidence must be excluded due to fair trial considerations.[45] Considering that Rule 92*quater* (B) has to be read in conjunction with the general admissibility rules, a question may arise as to why it is not categorized under the intrinsic exclusionary rules: Rule 89(C) states that evidence must be declared inadmissible when it has no probative value. Rule 92*quater* (B) is categorized under the extrinsic exclusionary rules, because if the Chamber had found that the statement was unreliable it would have already excluded it under Rule 92*quater* (A).[46] According to Rule 92*quater* (B), a factor against the admis-

---

[44] ECtHR (GC), 17 December 1996, App. No.: 19187/91, (*Saunders v. United Kingdom*), para 68.

[45] ICTY, Decision on Second Prosecution Motion for Admission of Evidence Pursuant to Rule 92*quater*, *Prosecutor v. Milutinović et al.*, Case No.: IT-05-87-T, T. Ch., 5 March 2007, para 6: 'Thus, Rule 92*quater* requires that two conditions be satisfied, namely the unavailability of a person whose written statement or transcript is sought to be admitted, and the reliability of the evidence therein. In addition, the Trial Chamber must ensure that the general requirements of admissibility of evidence as set out in Rule 89 are satisfied, namely that the proffered evidence is relevant and has probative value as provided in Rule 89(C). The Trial Chamber must also consider whether the probative value of the evidence is substantially outweighed by the need to ensure a fair trial under Rule 89(D) and thereby not unduly prejudicial.'

[46] Rule 92(A): 'The evidence of a person on the form of a written statement or transcript who has subsequently died, or who can no longer with reasonable diligence be traced, or who is by reason of bodily or mental condition unable to testify orally may be admitted, whether or not the written statement is in the form prescribed by Rule 92*bis*, if the Trial Chamber: (i) is satisfied of the person's unavailability as set out above; and (ii) find from the circumstances in which the statement was made and recorded that it is reliable.'

sion of the witness statement is when the statement relates to the acts and conduct of the accused. To admit such evidence could infringe upon the right of the accused to challenge any incriminating evidence against him.

Protecting the integrity of the proceedings: Rule 95 ICTY and ICTR RPE

The first part of Rule 95 ICTY and ICTR RPE has been discussed as an intrinsic exclusionary rule. The second part of the rule has an extrinsic exclusionary character: evidence shall not be admissible if its admission would be antithetical to and seriously damage the integrity of the proceedings. The rule is mandatory and provides for a high threshold: violations of domestic criminal procedural law are normally insufficient and the use of terms such as 'antithetical' and 'seriously damage' indicates that the violation must be substantial.[47] In *Brđanin*, the Trial Chamber held that:

> in applying the provisions of Rule 95, this Tribunal considers all the relevant circumstances and will only exclude evidence if the integrity of the proceedings would indeed otherwise be seriously damaged.[48]

> and:

> before this Tribunal evidence obtained illegally is not, a priori, inadmissible, but rather that the manner and surrounding circumstances in which evidence is obtained, as well as its reliability and effect on the integrity of the proceedings, will determine its admissibility.[49]

It is not the Tribunal's task to deter and punish criminal investigators for obtaining evidence illegally.[50] Involuntary statements of witnesses, obtained by way of oppressive conduct may be excluded under Rule 95.[51] The same holds true for witness testimony that has been tampered with by one of the parties.[52] In the Tribunals' case law, evidence has not often been declared inadmissible under Rule 95. The fact that the Tribunals do not regard themselves as judicial bodies that should monitor the activities of the (domestic) investigating authorities may

---

[47] CTY, Decision on the Defence "Objection to Intercept Evidence", *Prosecutor v. Brđanin*, Case No.: IT-99-36-T, T. Ch. II, 3 October 2003, para 63; ICTR, Decision on Exclusion of Testimony and Admission of Exhibit, *Prosecutor v. Renzaho*, Case No.: ICTR-97-31-T., T. Ch. I, 20 March 2007, para 16. Cf. Klamberg 2013a, pp. 400–401.

[48] ICTY, Decision on the Defence "Objection to Intercept Evidence", *Prosecutor v. Brđanin*, Case No.: IT-99-36-T, T. Ch. II, 3 October 2003, para 61 (emphasis in original).

[49] ICTY, Decision on the Defence "Objection to Intercept Evidence", *Prosecutor v. Brđanin*, Case No.: IT-99-36-T, T. Ch. II, 3 October 2003, para 55.

[50] ICTY, Decision on the Defence "Objection to Intercept Evidence", *Prosecutor v. Brđanin*, Case No.: IT-99-36-T, T. Ch. II, 3 October 2003, para 63.

[51] ICTY, Order for Guidelines on the Admission and Presentation of Evidence and Conduct of Counsel in Court, *Prosecutor v. Perišić*, Case No.: IT-04-81-T, T. Ch. I, 29 October 2008, para 38; ICTY, Order Setting Out the Guidelines for the Presentation of Evidence and the Conduct of the Parties during the Trial, *Prosecutor v. Šešelj*, Case No.: IT-03-67-T, T. Ch. III, 15 November 2007, para 13.

[52] ICTR, Decision on Interlocutory Appeal Regarding Witness Proofing, *Prosecutor v. Karemera et al.*, Case No.: ICTR-98-44-AR73.8, A. Ch., 11 May 2007, para 13.

explain the reluctance of the Tribunals to exclude relevant and probative evidence under this provision.[53]

Prior sexual conduct of the victim: Rule 96(iv) ICTY and ICTR RPE

Rule 96(iv) ICTY and ICTR RPE states that evidence relating to the prior sexual conduct of the victim shall not be admissible. The ICTR version of the rule adds that prior sexual conduct may not be raised as a defence. In an early decision in the history of the Tribunals, the *Delalić* Trial Chamber observed that the exclusion of such evidence was to protect the victims from 'harassment, embarrassment and humiliation'.[54] The protection the rule provides cannot be waived by the witness giving testimony: it is an imperative exclusionary rule.[55] It is noteworthy that the rationale for this rule is found solely in the emotional well-being of the witness and not in any prejudicial effect such testimony may have on the judges. The fact that a witness may not testify on this matter under any circumstances, *even if* the testimony has probative value and the witness gives testimony voluntarily, infringes upon the fact-finding capacities of the Trial Chamber. This is not to say that a vulnerable witness should be exposed to aggressive cross-examination regarding their sexual history. However, in a court setting where professional judges direct the proceedings and can influence the way the parties conduct their questioning (both on the content of their questions and the manner in which they phrase their questions), the rule seems superfluous.

The International Criminal Court

Fair trial considerations: Article 69(4) ICC Statute

According to Article 69(4) ICC Statute, the court must, when ruling on the relevancy or admissibility of the evidence, take into account the prejudicial effect the evidence may cause to the fair trial rights of the accused or to a fair evaluation of the testimony of a witness.[56] The Appeals Chamber has held that this provision is

---

[53] The Trial Chamber in *Brđanin* held: 'By excluding what would appear to be on a *prima facie* basis relevant and important evidence, it would only be denying itself the possibility of having available evidence which would be otherwise difficult, if not impossible, to obtain. The function of this Tribunal is not to deter and punish illegal conduct by domestic law enforcement authorities by excluding illegally obtained evidence.' ICTY, Decision on the Defense "Objection to Intercept Evidence"', *Prosecutor v. Brđanin*, Case No.: IT-99-36-T, T. Ch II, 3 October 2003, para 63.

[54] ICTY, Decision on the Prosecution's Motion for the Redaction of the Public Record, *Prosecutor v. Delalić et al.*, Case No.: IT-96-21-T, T. Ch., 5 June 1997, para 48.

[55] ICTY, Decision on the Prosecution's Motion for the Redaction of the Public Record, *Prosecutor v. Delalić* et al., Case No.: IT-96-21-T, T. Ch., 5 June 1997, para 58.

[56] The Article specifically states that the court must take into account the prejudicial effect the evidence may cause to the fair evaluation of the testimony of a witness. The fair evaluation of witness testimony is, however, part of the right to a fair trial.

mandatory, in the sense that the Trial Chamber must consider relevance, probative value and any prejudicial effect at some point during the proceedings. This may be done when the evidence is submitted, during the trial or at the end of the trial.[57]

Prejudice, a concept derived from common law, can best be described here as evidence which is pejorative to the need to ensure a fair trial. Evidence that, if admitted, may raise a fair trial issue (such as admitting witness testimony without the possibility of witness examination) can be excluded at the admissibility stage. Piragoff, commenting on Article 69, wrote that:

> evidence may possess prejudicial value that tends to obscure the true degree of probative value of an item of evidence or tends to offend or prejudice other values that the trial is supposed to protect, such as a fair trial or the fair trial evaluation or protection of a witness.[58]

The first part of this quote is problematic and seems to be based on a common law approach to the possible prejudicial effect of evidence. In a bifurcated court setting, it is indeed possible to consider the prejudicial effect certain evidence (for example, character evidence) may have when it is presented to the jury. This is, however, impossible in international criminal proceedings. It would require the judges to deliberate on any prejudicial effect the admission of the evidence would have on their own determination of the correct probative value of the evidence. To undertake this would, in fact, result in the elimination of any prejudicial effect: once a judge is aware of any prejudicial effect, he should be able to correctly assess the evidence. An example of a Trial Chamber deliberating on the possible prejudicial effect of evidence can be found in *Bagosora*, where the ICTR Appeals Chamber commented on the Trial Chamber's findings:

> The Trial Chamber correctly stated that evidence of prior criminal acts of the Accused is inadmissible for the purpose of demonstrating 'a general propensity or disposition' to commit the crimes charged. The Trial Chamber emphasized that 'this does not preclude the introduction of such evidence for other valid purposes'. The Trial Chamber found that the Prosecutor failed to show that the proposed testimony had any relevance beyond showing that the Accused committed crimes on previous occasions, which was not directly relevant to the crimes charged in the Indictments. Thus, the Trial Chamber correctly excluded the evidence because it had a low probative value but a substantial prejudicial effect.[59]

This quote is an example of the difficult position a Chamber finds itself in when evidence is presented that is not directly relevant to the case, but which might very well influence the manner in which other evidence is weighed. The example

---

[57] ICC, Judgment on the Appeals from Mr Jean-Pierre Bemba Gombo and the Prosecutor Against the Decision of Trial Chamber III entitled "Decision on the Admission into Evidence of Materials Contained in the Prosecution's List of Evidence", *Prosecutor v. Bemba*, Case No.: ICC-01/05-01/08 OA 5 OA 6, A. Ch., 3 May 2011, para 37.

[58] Piragoff 2008, p. 1324.

[59] ICTR, Decision on Prosecutor's Interlocutory Appeals Regarding Exclusion of Evidence, *Prosecutor v. Bagosora et al.*, Case No.: ICTR-98-41-AR73 and ICTR-98-41-AR93.2, A. Ch., 19 December 2003, para 14.

concerns the possible prejudicial effect on the fair assessment of the evidence and not the possible prejudicial effect on the fair trial rights of the accused. An example of evidence that might negatively impact on these rights would be the admission of a substantial number of anonymous witness statements or witness statements from unavailable persons.[60]

Considering the flexible admissibility regime at the ICC, it is unlikely that this Article will result in the exclusion of a considerable amount of pieces of evidence due to the negative impact on the fair trial rights of the accused.

Protecting the integrity of the proceedings: Article 69(7)(b) ICC Statute

The Chamber must declare evidence inadmissible when the evidence has been obtained by a violation of the Statute or internationally recognized human rights and where the admission of such evidence would be antithetical to and seriously damage the integrity of the proceedings. The violation as such is insufficient: the admission of the evidence must be antithetical to and seriously damaging to the integrity of the proceedings.[61] A non-serious violation may lead to the inadmissibility of the evidence, as long as the criteria of Article 69(7)(b) are met.[62] However, similar to the ad hoc Tribunals, the ICC is hesitant to exclude evidence. The Trial Chamber in *Lubanga* held that:

> the Chamber endorses the human rights and ICTY jurisprudence which focuses on the balance to be achieved between the seriousness of the violation and the fairness of the trial as a whole.[63]

Trial Chamber I held that violations of domestic procedural norms (including those that aim to protect human rights) are, as such, insufficient to meet the criteria of Article 69(7)(b).[64] Ambos argued convincingly, however, that evidence obtained by torture must be declared inadmissible (either under Article 69(7)(a) or (b) ICC Statute).[65]

The fact that the ICC exclusively hears cases involving serious violations of international criminal law is not a factor that is taken into account in decisions on the admissibility of evidence.[66] In other words, the focus is on the violation and its

---

[60] Rule 68 ICC RPE allows for prior recorded testimony to be admitted, provided that the prosecutor and defence have had the opportunity to examine the witness during the recording or when the witness is available in court and does not oppose the submission of the recorded testimony.

[61] Piragoff 2008, pp. 1334–1335.

[62] ICC, Decision on the Admission of Material from the "Bar Table", *Prosecutor v. Lubanga Dyilo*, Case No.: ICC-01/04-01/06, T. Ch. I., 24 June 2009, para 35.

[63] ICC, Decision on the Confirmation of Charges, *Prosecutor v. Lubanga Dyilo*, Case No.: ICC-01/04-01/06, Pre-T. Ch. I, 29 January 2007, para 89.

[64] ICC, Decision on the Admission of Material from the "Bar Table", *Prosecutor v. Lubanga Dyilo*, Case No.: ICC-01/04-01/06, T. Ch. I., 24 June 2009, para 36.

[65] Ambos 2009.

[66] ICC, Decision on the Admission of Material from the "Bar Table", *Prosecutor v. Lubanga Dyilo*, Case No.: ICC-01/04-01/06, T. Ch. I., 24 June 2009, para 44.

effect on the proceedings: the Chamber will not balance the violation against the seriousness of the case.

Prior sexual conduct of the victim: Rule 71 ICC RPE

The rationale for the exclusion of evidence relating to the prior or subsequent sexual conduct of a witness or victim has been discussed above regarding the ad hoc Tribunals and corresponds with the rationale behind Rule 71 ICC RPE. In addition to the corresponding rules at the ad hoc Tribunals, the ICC Rule also precludes admission of the subsequent sexual conduct of a victim or witness. The Rule is 'subject to Article 69, para 4' (the general admissibility standard of evidence), which means that exceptions to the Rule are possible.[67]

Admissibility during pre-trial proceedings

In *Katanga* the question was raised whether different admissibility standards apply during the confirmation hearing and the trial proceedings. The Single Judge held that:

> the admission of evidence at [the pre-trial] stage is without prejudice to the Trial Chamber's exercise of its functions and powers to make a final determination as to the admissibility and probative value.[68]

The Trial Chamber in *Lubanga* held that evidence admitted during the pre-trial proceedings is not automatically admitted during the trial proceedings.[69]

The ultimate weight to be attached to the evidence is of course a matter for the Trial Chamber. During the confirmation hearing, the prosecutor must support the charges with sufficient evidence to establish reasonable grounds to believe the person committed the crime.[70] The Single Judge held that this criterion of Article 61(5) ICC Statute is a *lex specialis* in relation to the general admissibility standard of Article 69 ICC Statute. However, the prosecution is not allowed to rely upon witnesses during the confirmation hearing, upon which it cannot rely during the trial proceedings. The Single Judge emphasized that the question of admissibility is left to the Trial Chamber. Although the purpose and legal framework of the confirmation hearing and trial proceedings are indeed different, it seems that patently inadmissible evidence (either due to a lack of relevance or probative value) should

---

67 Klamberg 2013b, p. 1035.

68 ICC, Decision on the Admissibility for the Confirmation Hearing of the Transcripts of Interview of Deceased Witness 12, *Prosecutor v. Katanga & Ngudjolo Chui*, Case No.: ICC-01/04-01/07, Pre-T.Ch. I, 18 April 2008, p. 5.

69 ICC, Decision on the Status Before the Trial Chamber of the Evidence Heard by the Pre-Trial Chamber and the Decisions of the Pre-Trial Chamber in Trial Proceedings, and the Manner in Which Evidence Shall Be Submitted, *Prosecutor v. Lubanga Dyilo*, T. Ch. I, Case No.: ICC-01/04-01/06, 13 December 2007, para 8.

70 Article 61(5) ICC Statute.

be excluded by the Single Judge. Here, the Single Judge must anticipate the final decision of the Trial Chamber regarding admissibility.

4.1.3 Weighing the Evidence

Article 74(2) ICC Statute states that the Trial Chamber's final decision can be based solely on evidence that has been submitted and discussed before the Chamber during trial proceedings. The Appeals Chamber in *Bemba* reiterated that evidence which has not been submitted and discussed during the trial proceedings may not be relied on.[71] A similar provision is absent in the legal instruments of the ad hoc Tribunals. However, to base a finding on evidence that has not been presented or discussed properly would violate the right to an adversarial trial. Respecting the principle of immediacy is vital in order to ensure that the accused can effectively participate and challenge the evidence against him.

In the *Lubanga* judgment, ICC Trial Chamber I held that evidence submitted and discussed at trial encompassed both oral testimony as well as any written statements tendered into evidence.[72] Accordingly, the judgment can only be based on admissible evidence that has been discussed (that is, evidence that is part of the trial record).[73] The applicable standard of proof before the ad hoc Tribunals and the ICC is similar: proof beyond reasonable doubt.[74] This standard applies to each element of the crimes charged and must be applied to the entire body of evidence, instead of being applied to isolated pieces of evidence.[75] This means that a holistic approach must be taken regarding the standard of proof. An atomistic evaluation of the pieces of evidence is reserved for the admissibility stage. When the evidence allows for any other reasonable explanation than the guilt of the accused, the accused must be acquitted.[76]

---

[71] ICC, Judgment on the Appeals of Mr Jean-Pierre Bemba Gombo and the Prosecutor Against the Decision of Trial Chamber III entitled: "Decision on the Admission into Evidence of Materials contained in the Prosecution's List of Evidence", *Prosecutor v. Bemba Gombo*, Case No.: ICC-01/05-01/08 OA 5 OA 6, 3 May 2011, para 45.

[72] ICC, Judgment pursuant to Article 74 of the Statute, *Prosecutor v. Lubanga Dyilo*, Case No.: ICC-01/04-01/06, T. Ch. I, 14 March 2012, para 98.

[73] ICC, Judgment pursuant to Article 74 of the Statute, *Prosecutor v. Lubanga Dyilo*, Case No.: ICC-01/04-01/06, T. Ch. I, 14 March 2012, para 101.

[74] Article 66 ICC Statute; Rule 87(A) ICTY and ICTR RPE;

[75] ICC, Judgment pursuant to Article 74 of the Statute, *Prosecutor v. Lubanga Dyilo*, Case No.: ICC-01/04-01/06, T. Ch. I, 14 March 2012, para 92; ICTY, Judgment, *Prosecutor v. Stanišić & Simatović*, Case No.: IT-03-69-T, T. Ch. I, 30 May 2013, para 7. ICTY, Judgment, *Prosecutor v. Halilović*, Case No.: IT-01-48-A, A. Ch., 16 October 2007, para 119.

[76] ICTR, Judgment and Sentence, *Prosecutor v. Karemera & Ngirumpatse*, Case No.: ICTR-98-44-T, T. Ch. III, 2 February 2012, para 100. Cf. the Mrkšić Appeal Judgment, referring to the Tadić Appeal Judgment: 'the proof must be such as to exclude not every hypothesis or possibility of innocence, but every fair or rational hypothesis which may be derived from the evidence, except that of guilt.' ICTY, Judgment, *Prosecutor v. Mrkšić & Šljivančanin*, Case No.: IT-95-12/1-A, A. Ch., 5 May 2009, para 220.

Numerous attempts have been made to define the concept of proof beyond reasonable doubt. References are made to famous common law definitions of the concept, as well as their civil law counterparts (*conviction intime*, *conviction raisonnée*).[77] Defining and re-defining this concept is, in my view, not very helpful. Each definition boils down to the observation that proof beyond reasonable doubt requires a high degree of probability that the accused is in fact guilty of the crimes charged. Such degree of probability is sometimes expressed as a percentage (where proof beyond reasonable doubt is somewhere in the 85–100 % range). The *in dubio pro reo* principle gives the accused the benefit of the doubt, which underlines the high level of certainty required for a conviction. The definition of beyond reasonable doubt is, for all practical purposes, that of a high degree of probability or certainty of the guilt of the accused.

Weighing the totality of the evidence instead of determining the weight of each piece of evidence in isolation can be discerned in all international courts.[78] This approach to the massive volume of evidence presented during international criminal proceedings seems, at first sight, to be a proper and epistemologically sound method for determining the guilt or innocence of the accused. However, upon closer scrutiny some conceptual problems arise. A holistic approach to weighing the evidence seems to be possible only when the volume of evidence is limited: a holistic approach can be undertaken in cases in which the evidence consists of only a small number of different pieces of evidence, for example witness statements. Any deficiencies or inconsistencies in each particular witness statement can be repaired or compensated by taking into account the other evidence. Thus, deficient witness statements still have probative value since they are not weighed in isolation. It would be contrary to the aim of accurate fact-finding to do otherwise. However, in international criminal proceedings it is not unusual for the judges to hear dozens or even hundreds of witnesses testifying on a variety of matters over an extended period of time. Besides oral and written testimony, hundreds or thousands of exhibits are admitted into evidence.[79]

---

[77] Cf. Rohan 2010, pp. 650–670; Klamberg 2013a, pp. 128–144; Jacobs 2013, pp. 1128–1149. For a historical overview of the origins of the standard of proof beyond reasonable doubt in the Anglo-American law of evidence: Shapiro 1991, pp. 1–42.

[78] Klamberg 2013a, p. 157.

[79] Cf. the Trial Chamber in Stanišić and Župljanin: 'The Trial Chamber admitted a large body of evidence during the trial. The Prosecution called 80 witnesses to give evidence *viva voce*, and the Defence called 12 witnesses. The Trial Chamber admitted the evidence of 30 witnesses tendered by the Prosecution and seven witnesses tendered by the Defence pursuant to Rule 92 *bis*; 45 witnesses tendered by the Prosecution and three by the Defence pursuant to Rule 92 *ter*; nine witnesses tendered by the Prosecution and four witnesses by the Defence pursuant to Rule 92 *quater*; and six witnesses tendered by the Prosecution and three witnesses by the Defence pursuant to Rule 94 *bis*. The Trial Chamber admitted into evidence 3028 exhibits tendered by the Prosecution and 1349 exhibits tendered by the Defence. The Trial Chamber took judicial notice of 1042 adjudicated facts, and the parties agreed to 113 facts.' ICTY, Judgment, *Prosecutor v. Stanišić & Župljanin*, Case No.: IT-08-91-T, T. Ch. II, 27 March 2013, para 17.

The ICTR Appeals Chamber in *Musema*, referring to *Tadić*, held that:

> a tribunal of fact must never look at the evidence of each witness as if it existed in a hermetically sealed compartment; it is the accumulation of *all* the evidence in the case which must be considered. The evidence of one witness, when considered by itself, may appear to be of poor quality, but it may gain strength from other evidence of the case.[80]

In *Ntagerura et al.*, discussed earlier, the Appeals Chamber discerned three stages in the fact-finding process of Trial Chambers. First, the credibility of the relevant evidence must be assessed. This must be done by evaluating individual pieces of evidence against the background of the entire body of evidence. The second step is to determine whether the evidence presented by the prosecution is sufficient to establish the existence of an alleged fact. It is here that the standard of proof beyond a reasonable doubt must be applied. During the final deliberations, the Trial Chamber has to determine whether all elements of the crimes alleged and the mode of liability have been proven.[81]

In the *Lubanga* trial judgment, the Trial Chamber followed a similar approach, when it stated that individual pieces of evidence had been weighed in the context of 'any other admissible and probative material.'[82] The Chamber also held that the 'parties and participants were responsible for identifying the evidence that is relevant to the Article 74 Decision in their final submissions.'[83] This emphasis on the role of the parties and participants in providing the evidentiary framework for the Chamber's ultimate decision is at odds with Article 69(3) ICC Statute, which specifically gives the Chamber the authority to request the submission of all evidence it deems relevant for the determination of the truth. This provision underlines the autonomous position of the Chamber in fact-finding: it should not depend on the submissions from the parties.

4.1.3.1 Combining Evidence in International Criminal Proceedings

Considering the massive volume of evidence presented in international criminal proceedings, the question arises as to how evidence can be properly combined in such complex proceedings. Evidence scholars Anderson, Schum and Twining have formulated five questions regarding the evaluation of evidence. Although they have not specifically addressed the evaluation or weighing of evidence in

---

80 ICTR, Judgment, *Prosecutor v. Musema*, Case No.: ICTR-96-13-A, A. Ch., 16 November 2001, para 134 (emphasis in original).

81 This final step is reminiscent of the civil law concept of qualifying or categorizing the facts that have been proven. ICTR, Judgment, *Prosecutor v. Ntagerura et al.*, Case No.: ICTR-99-46-A, A. Ch., 7 July 2006, para 174.

82 ICC, Judgment, *Prosecutor v. Lubanga Dyilo*, Case No.: ICC-01/04-01/06, T. Ch. I., 14 March 2012, para 94.

83 ICC, Judgment, *Prosecutor v. Lubanga Dyilo*, Case No.: ICC-01/04-01/06, T. Ch. I., 14 March 2012, para 95.

international criminal proceedings, their observations are a good starting point for an analysis of how international tribunals deal with this matter.

These authors compared the evaluation of evidence with the grading of exams: they argued that every trier of fact or grader wants his decision to be as accurate and rational as possible. At the same time, however, they realize that there remains an 'inescapable personal element' in the evaluation or grading process. These are the questions they ask themselves:

1. How can we express assessments of weight (the *vocabulary* of evaluation, analogous to a marking scheme)?
2. What are the standards for decision of factual issues (cf. the pass mark)?
3. How can judgments of weight and probative force be *combined*?
4. What are the *criteria for evaluating* the probative force of individual items of evidence or the weight of a "mass" of evidence in a given case (cf. *reasons* for awarding or debiting marks or awarding a particular overall grade)?
5. To what extent *could* the law of evidence prescribe *rules of weight or evaluation* (cf. marking rules)?[84]

The first question is addressed in the majority of the judgments delivered by the ad hoc Tribunals. Similarly, ICC Trial Chambers have devoted chapters to the evaluation of evidence in their final judgments.[85] In the judgments, the findings of facts are normally preceded by an overview of factors that were taken into account in relation to the distinct categories of evidence. For example, relevant factors regarding the evaluation of testimony of *viva voce* witnesses include the witness' demeanour during his testimony, the internal consistency of the testimony, the lapse of time between the event and the testimony and the possible impact the event had on the witness.[86] Factors relevant for the evaluation of documentary evidence include the source of the document and the chain of custody.[87] Regarding the evaluation of expert evidence, Chambers have taken into account the competence of the expert and the methodologies that were used.[88]

---

[84] Anderson et al. 2005, p. 228 (emphasis in original). The fifth question will not be discussed here: this touches upon whether it is desirable at all to formulate rules of weight.

[85] ICC, Judgment pursuant to Article 74 of the Statute, *Prosecutor v. Lubanga Dyilo*, Case No.: ICC-01/04-01/06, T. Ch. I, 14 March 2012, paras 92–123; ICC, Judgment pursuant to Article 74 of the Statute, *Prosecutor v. Ngudjolo*, Case No.: ICC-01/04-02/12, T. Ch. II, 18 December 2012, pp. 17–28; ICC, Judgment pursuant to Article 74 of the Statute, *Prosecutor v. Katanga*, Case No.: ICC-01/04-01/07, T. Ch. II, 7 March 2014, pp. 39–51.

[86] ICTY, Judgment, *Prosecutor v. Tolimir*, Case No.: IT-05-88/2-T, T. Ch. II, 12 December 2012, para 36; ICTY, Judgment, *Prosecutor v. Perišić*, Case No.: IT-04-81-T, 6 September 2011, T. Ch. I, para 26; ICTR, Judgment and Sentence, *Prosecutor v. Muvunyi*, Case No.: ICTR-2000-55A-T, T. Ch. II, 12 September 2006, para 14.

[87] ICTY, Judgment, *Prosecutor v. Perišić*, Case No.: IT-04-81-T, 6 September 2011, T. Ch. I, para 31; ICTY, Judgment, *Prosecutor v. Gotovina et al.*, Case No.: IT-06-90-T, T. Ch. I, 15 April 2011, para 31.

[88] ICC, Judgment pursuant to Article 74 of the Statute, *Prosecutor v. Lubanga Dyilo*, Case No.: ICC-01/04-01/06, T. Ch. I, 14 March 2012, para 112; ICTY, Judgment, *Prosecutor v. Tolimir*, Case No.: IT-05-88/2-T, T. Ch. II, 12 December 2012, para 39; ICTR, Judgment, *Prosecutor v. Zigiranyirazo*, 18 December 2008, T. Ch. III, para 93.

The second and fourth question combined are concerned with the question of how reliable or trustworthy the evidence in fact is: what is the weight or probative value of each particular piece of evidence? Statements from, for example, witnesses who have committed atrocities themselves may be regarded as less reliable and therefore carry less weight.

The third question is, for present purposes, the most interesting one: how do judges combine the findings in a case with a massive amount of evidence? Convictions for international crimes require the prosecution to present evidence regarding, *inter alia*, the mode of liability of the accused, the contextual elements of the crime and the factual basis of the underlying crimes. The structure of the judgments mirrors this approach. The table of contents of the *Tolimir* judgment, for example, consists of four parts describing the Chamber's factual findings on the structure of the military and police of the Republika Srpska and the events in Žepa and Srebrenica. These factual parts are followed by two parts on the legal findings and the individual criminal responsibility of the accused.[89]

In weighing the evidence, Chambers have consistently held that they evaluate each piece of evidence in light of the entire body of evidence. However, the judges fail to explain what they actually mean by this. To evaluate a random witness statement in light of the entire body of evidence seems, from an epistemological point of view, simply wrong: to do so would take into account irrelevant evidence in the evaluation of the witness statement. If witnesses A1 and A2 testify on events in village A, why should their statements be evaluated in light of the testimony of witness B on events in village B, witness C on village C and so on? What would make sense is to evaluate the statement of witness A1 in light of the statement of witness A2. At this point, we could conclude that evaluating a piece of evidence in light of the other evidence is simply wrong: the judges have lost sight of a basic concept of evidence law, namely, to consider solely *relevant* evidence. However, in such complex proceedings as the ones conducted before the international tribunals, things get more complicated. In these proceedings the evidence of events in village A does have some relevancy considering the evidence on similar events in village B. The fact that, for example, extermination as a crime against humanity can only be proven when the extermination is part of a widespread or systematic attack results in a complex interdependency of the individual pieces of evidence. Seemingly isolated events may then be construed as a widespread or systematic attack. Evaluating each piece of evidence in light of the entire body of evidence then becomes much more complex: it in fact describes a process in which pieces of evidence are evaluated back and forth. In order to determine the probability of the occurrence of a particular fact, the evidence is juxtaposed against the other evidence. This also occurs the other way around: to determine the probability of the occurrence of contextual elements, one has to look at the isolated events. This resembles a hermeneutic circle: the larger part (e.g. a widespread attack) can only

[89] ICTY, Judgment, *Prosecutor v. Tolimir*, Case No.: IT-05-88/2-T, T. Ch. II, 12 December 2012.

be understood or construed by looking at several isolated events (e.g. atrocities committed in several villages in a certain area) and vice versa. The isolated events, in turn, may then be regarded as part of the bigger picture.[90] In *Stanišić and Simatović*, ICTY Trial Chamber I held that:

> In making factual findings, the Trial Chamber generally considered the alleged crimes separately and by incident. When the circumstances so allowed, the Trial Chamber considered the evidence on certain crimes together. The Trial Chamber remained mindful of events occurring in temporal and geographical proximity of an incident and considered whether relevant inferences could be drawn from such events.[91]

The Chamber started with stating that evidence has been evaluated separately to make factual findings on a specific point. It continued by stating that such evidence may also be combined to form the evidentiary basis for other crimes. This reflects the interdependency of the individual pieces of evidence referred to above.

Here, some final remarks on the evaluation of evidence in international criminal proceedings. In most judgments, the Chambers of the ad hoc Tribunals and the ICC devote several pages to the general framework of the evaluation of specific categories of evidence. For example, the manner in which the testimony of traumatized witnesses is weighed indicates that Chambers are well aware of the possible pitfalls of such testimony. The same holds true for the authenticity and reliability of documents that were collected many years ago during an armed conflict and of which the chain of custody is not always clear. Findings of expert witness are evaluated with the (academic) qualifications of the expert in mind, including the methodology used in the expert's report. However, despite the efforts to evaluate different types of evidence in an epistemologically sound manner, the reasoning of the Chambers is unsatisfactory. What is missing is a clear and concise explanation of how the Chambers cope with the massive volume of evidence that is presented over several years. The magnitude of the evidentiary basis presented and the often prolonged proceedings must have consequences for the evaluation of evidence. Klamberg concluded on the evaluation of evidence by the ad hoc Tribunals, that they:

> have adopted 'the exclusion of every reasonable hypothesis of innocence method' whereby alternative hypothesis are eliminated.[92]

This is a useful insight. However, the question of how fact-finders cope or should cope with the quantities of evidence in international criminal proceedings

---

[90] Cf. C.K. Hall on Article 7 ICC Statute: 'The Statute and the Elements of Crimes both make clear that the acts must occur as *part* of an attack. However, the acts could constitute the attack itself. For example, the mass murder of civilians may suffice as an attack against the civilian population. There is no requirement that a separate attack against the same civilians, within which the murders were committed, should be proven.' Hall 2008, pp. 174–175 (emphasis in original).

[91] ICTY, Judgment, *Prosecutor v. Stanišić & Simatović*, Case No.: IT-03-69-T, T. Ch. I, 30 May 2013, para 35. Similar: ICTY, Judgment, *Prosecutor v. Gotovina et al.*, Case No.: IT-06-90-T, T. Ch. I, 15 April 2011, para 60.

[92] Klamberg 2013a, p. 195.

is left unanswered in both the literature and the Tribunals' case law. This question is more pertinent if we take into account that the tribunals' process cases that are often concerned with the same factual basis. Add to this the existence of a considerable number of undisputed or undisputable facts that have emerged from years of litigation and the *sui generis* character of the international evidentiary context becomes clear. There is no ready answer to the question raised, but how fact-finders process evidence is of great importance for understanding the process of weighing evidence.[93]

4.1.4 Reasoned Judgments

The Statutes and Rules of Procedure and Evidence of all international courts oblige the Chamber to provide reasons for its decision on the guilt or innocence of the accused.[94] The obligation to hand down a reasoned judgment is a principle of the law of international criminal procedure.[95] A reasoned judgment is necessary to provide for a fair trial. A reasoned judgment allows the accused to consider whether or not to file an appeal, and it also enables the parties to verify whether the Chamber has taken their arguments into account. From the perspective of the Chamber, the obligation to hand down a reasoned judgment obliges the judges to make sure that the weighing or evaluation process is accounted for. This, in turn, ensures that the parties, the Appeals Chamber (provided an appeal is filed) and the public in general can get acquainted with the reasoning of the Chamber.[96] According to the 2009 ICTY Manual on Developed Practices, the drafting process of the final judgment should start well before all the evidence is heard. Considering the size and complexity of the cases, the timing of the final judgment would be unreasonably delayed if the judgment would be drafted from scratch

---

[93] Klamberg concluded that judges in international criminal proceedings evaluate the evidence in a Baconian way. Klamberg 2013a, p. 161. Anderson et al.: "What Bacon argued was that we would be far better off performing evidential tests designed to eliminate any hypothesis we are considering. The hypothesis that best resists our most concerted efforts to eliminate it, as well as any other hypotheses, is the one in which we should have increasing confidence. This strategy has become known as *induction by elimination*.' Anderson et al. 2005, p. 257 (emphasis in original).

[94] Article 23(2) ICTY Statute; Article 22(2) ICTR Statute; Article 74(5) ICC Statute.

[95] Jørgensen and Zahar 2013, p. 1199.

[96] Cf. The Grand Chamber of the ECtHR in *Taxquet v. Belgium*: '[…] for the requirements of a fair trial to be satisfied, the accused, and indeed the public, must be able to understand the verdict that has been given; this is a vital safeguard against arbitrariness. As the court has often noted, the rule of law and the avoidance of arbitrary power are principles underlying the Convention. […] In the judicial sphere, those principles serve to foster public confidence in an objective and transparent justice system, one of the foundations of a democratic society.' ECtHR (GC), 16 November 2010, App. No.: 926/05, (*Taxquet v. Belgium*), para 90.

after the close of proceedings.[97] ICTY Chambers have held that it is not required that each and every detail is accounted for in the final judgment: the fact that a certain piece of evidence is not explicitly mentioned in the judgment does not mean it has not been taken into account by the Chamber.[98]

The judgments of the international courts are lengthy: describing factual findings regarding multiple crime sites, contextual elements and the individual criminal responsibility of the accused result in hundreds of pages of legal and factual findings. For present purposes, the manner in which Chambers have evaluated the evidence on a particular charge is not of primary interest. What are of interest are the 'preliminary' observations by the Chambers, in which the Chambers account for the weighing of various categories of evidence. Although this approach makes clear whether the judges are aware of the epistemological issues that may arise in respect to each category, this approach does not *as such* provide for a thorough analysis of the process of evaluating the evidence. The judgments are for the most part narratives summing up the factual findings of the Chamber. The footnotes, referring to witness testimony or exhibits, allow for verification of the Chamber's findings, but in a rather implicit manner. The Chamber apparently believed a certain witness or found that a certain exhibit had sufficient probative value. Only when specific evidence or charges have been challenged does the Chamber provide a more detailed account of its findings. This manner of drafting judgments means that, unless evidence is challenged specifically, the Chamber will start with outlining in a general way the manner in which categories of evidence are evaluated and proceed by presenting factual findings without explicitly discussing the probative value of each piece of evidence.

4.1.5 Conclusion

In international criminal proceedings, the full criminal trial can be defined as follows. The *nulla poena sine iudicio* principle can be regarded as the cornerstone of the legal framework in which the international courts operate. At the ad hoc Tribunals, the original Statutes and Rules of Procedure and Evidence did not provide for abbreviated proceedings after the parties had entered into plea negotiations. At the ICC, however, the original Statute already provided for proceedings on an admission of guilt.

Full trial proceedings before the Chamber are regarded, both at the ad hoc Tribunals and the ICC, as the forum in which fact-finding is conducted and in which the fair trial rights of the accused can be effectively respected. Ideally,

[97] ICTY/UNICRI, *ICTY Manual on Developed Practices*, UNICRI Publisher 2009, p. 109.

[98] ICTY, Judgment, *Prosecutor v. Stanišić & Simatović*, Case No.:IT-03-69-T, T. Ch. I, 30 May 2013, para 34; ICTY, Judgment, *Prosecutor v. Gotovina & Markač*, Case No.: IT-06-90-A, A. Ch., 16 November 2012, para 132.

evidence is presented and discussed in an adversarial setting in which the parties can participate effectively.

In order to facilitate the fact-finding mission of the Chamber, rules of admissibility regarding evidence are not very prominent: the Chamber is entrusted to rule on the relevance and probative value of the evidence presented. Technical rules of admissibility, important evidentiary gatekeepers in common law systems, are kept to a minimum in international criminal proceedings. Similarly, the Chamber is left considerable discretion regarding the weighing of evidence: the total amount of evidence is weighed holistically after the close of the proceedings. Subject to the standard of proof beyond reasonable doubt, the Chamber must determine whether the evidence that was presented regarding the elements of the charges meets this standard. This considerable freedom regarding the evaluation of evidence must be accounted for, however: the Chamber is obliged to hand down a reasoned judgment in which it accounts for the factual and legal conclusions it draws.

4.2 Diversions in the Law of International Criminal Procedure

4.2.1 Introduction

In the following pages, the diversions and shortcuts that are used in international criminal proceedings are discussed. The guilty plea and admission of guilt are discussed first, as diversions from the full criminal trial. Subsequently, the various shortcuts in the legal frameworks of the ad hoc Tribunals and ICC are presented.[99]

---

[99] At the ICTY and ICTR, the defence can request the Trial Chamber to deliver a judgment of acquittal after the close of the prosecutor's case ('no case to answer'-motion). Such motions, filed pursuant to Rule 98 *bis* ICTY/ICTR RPE, will not be included in the analysis: a judgment of acquittal is not an avoidance mechanism. A motion for a judgment of acquittal invites the Trial Chamber to acquit the accused after the prosecution has closed its case and before the commencement of the case of the defence. This by no means implies that the defence waives the right to challenge the evidence: the defence only argues that there is no (sufficient) evidence to challenge in the first place. Cf. the remark by the Trial Chamber in *Kordić and Čerkez*: 'The test that the Chamber has enunciated—evidence on which a reasonable Chamber could convict—proceeds on the basis that generally the Chamber would not consider questions of credibility and reliability in dealing with a motion under Rule 98*bis*, leaving those matters to the end of the case. However, there is one situation in which the Chamber is obliged to consider such matters: it is where the Prosecution's case has completely broken down, either on its own presentation, or as a result of such fundamental questions being raised through cross examination as to the reliability and credibility of witnesses that the Prosecution is left without a case.' ICTY, Decision on Defence Motions for Judgment of Acquittal', *Prosecutor v. Kordić and Čerkez*, Case No.: IT-95-14/2-T, T. Ch., 6 April 2000, para 28. See also ICTY, Decision on Motion for Judgment of Acquittal, *Prosecutor v. Milošević*, Case No.: IT-02-54-T, T. Ch., 16 June 2004, para 13.

4.2.2 Guilty Pleas

The archetypical diversion from the full criminal trial is the guilty plea: by confessing to the charges, the accused acknowledges his criminal responsibility. This obviates the need to have his guilt determined by the court after full criminal proceedings. In an adversarial context, there is no need to determine the guilt of the accused when there is no contested issue left: when the parties agree not to bring the case before the trier of fact, the autonomy of the parties to determine the course of the proceedings has to be respected.

Although the ad hoc Tribunals have accepted a significant number of plea agreements, the use of this diversion in international criminal proceedings is still controversial. Is it appropriate to negotiate on the criminal responsibility of an accused that faces charges of genocide? Are guilty pleas desirable in the context of complex international crimes with regard to the aims of accurate fact-finding and the creation of an accurate historical record? Such questions are legitimate and explain in part why this diversion is often criticized. For present purposes, however, the guilty plea and the admission of guilt (the ICC functional equivalent of the guilty plea) will be regarded as a given: the legal framework of the ad hoc Tribunals and the ICC provide for this diversion, and a rather detailed framework has emerged regarding guilty pleas and admissions of guilt. The chapter will refrain from discussing whether negotiations in the international context are desirable or appropriate: it will give a detailed overview of the working of this diversion instead.[100] First, guilty pleas at the ad hoc Tribunals are discussed, followed by admissions of guilt at the ICC.

4.2.3 Legal Framework of Guilty Pleas Before the Ad Hoc Tribunals

The guilty plea criteria of the ad hoc Tribunals originate from their early case law: the original Rules of Procedure and Evidence did not provide for a detailed legal framework regarding the criteria for a valid guilty plea. In the original RPE, the accused was called upon to enter a plea of guilty or not guilty at his initial appearance before the Trial Chamber.[101] The practice of plea bargaining, however, made it necessary to amend the Rules of Procedure and Evidence to provide for an

---

[100] Cf the sentencing judgment in *Nikolić*, in which the Trial Chamber elaborated on the question whether plea agreements are appropriate in international criminal proceedings. ICTY, Sentencing Judgment, *Prosecutor v. Nikolić*, Case No.: IT-02-60/1-S, T. Ch. I, 2 December 2003, paras 57–73.

[101] Rule 62(iii) ICTY RPE (original version of 11 February 1994); Rule 62(iii) ICTR RPE (version of 29 June 1995).

accurate framework. The amendment followed the seminal ruling of the ICTY Appeals Chamber in *Erdemović*, in which the criteria for a valid guilty plea were discussed in detail. Currently, Rule 62*bis* ICTY RPE and Rule 62(B) ICTR RPE contain four criteria that will be discussed below.

4.2.3.1 Voluntariness

The criterion of voluntariness was first formulated in October 1997 by Judges McDonald and Vohrah, in their separate opinion to the Appeals Chamber judgment in *Erdemović*. They divided voluntariness into two components. First, the accused must be mentally competent to understand the consequences of pleading guilty.[102] Second, the plea must have been entered into without threats or inducements other than the expectation of a sentence reduction.[103] This second component is closely related to the right not to incriminate oneself. It follows from ICTR case law that the criteria 'freely' and 'informed', as incorporated in the ICTR RPE, can be equated with the two components of the requirement of voluntariness.[104] To determine whether a guilty plea was entered into voluntarily, the Trial Chamber may consider the conditions under which the agreement was reached.[105] In practice, the Trial Chamber verifies whether the plea was entered into freely and voluntarily by asking the accused during the plea hearing whether he was threatened or induced to enter a guilty plea.[106] No plea agreements have been refused by the Chamber on the ground that they were entered into involuntary.

The criterion of voluntariness resembles the criteria for a valid waiver of procedural rights. One of the criteria for a valid waiver is whether the accused has waived his rights out of his own free will, without being threatened or induced to do so. The European Court of Human Rights held that a plea bargain may only be accepted when the bargain was accepted in a 'genuinely voluntary manner'.[107]

---

[102] ICTY, Joint Separate Opinion of Judge McDonald and Judge Vohrah, *Prosecutor v. Erdemović*, Case No.: IT-96-22-A, A. Ch., 7 October 1997, para 10.

[103] ICTY, Joint Separate Opinion of Judge McDonald and Judge Vohrah, *Prosecutor v. Erdemović*, Case No.: IT-96-22-A, A. Ch., 7 October 1997, para 10.

[104] ICTR, Judgment and Sentence, *Prosecutor v. Ruggiu*, Case No.: ICTR-97-32-I, T. Ch. I, 1 June 2000, para 11; ICTR, Judgment and Sentence, *Prosecutor v. Rutaganira*, Case No.: ICTR-95-1C-T, T. Ch. III, 14 March 2005, para 28; ICTR, Joint Motion for Consideration of Plea Agreement between Omar Serushago and the Office of the Prosecutor, *Prosecutor v. Serushago*, Case No.: ICTR-97-39, T. Ch. I, 4 December 1998, para 3.

[105] ICTY, Sentencing Judgment, *Prosecutor v. Nikolić*, Case No.: IT-02-60/1-S, T. Ch. I, 2 December 2003, para 52.

[106] For example, ICTR, Judgment and Sentence, *Prosecutor v. Serugendo*, Case No.: ICTR-2005-84-I, T. Ch. I, 12 June 2006, para 11.

[107] ECtHR, 29 April 2014, App. No.: 9043/05, (*Natsvlishvili and Togonidze v. Georgia*), para 92. See also ECtHR, 27 February 1980, App. No.: 6903/75, (*Deweer v. Belgium*), para 49.

4.2.3.2 Informed

In their separate opinion to the Appeals Chamber judgment in *Erdemović*, Judges McDonald and Vohrah commented on the informed-criterion and stated that 'informed' consists of two components.[108] First, the accused must understand the nature of the charges and the consequences of pleading guilty in general. This relates to the first sub-criterion of voluntariness. Second, the accused must be aware of the nature and distinction between any alternative charges, such as, in *Erdemović*, the distinction between murder as a crime against humanity and murder as a war crime.[109]

When Chambers determine whether the accused was sufficiently informed to enter a guilty plea, they focus on the nature of the charges and the consequences of pleading guilty in terms of waiving a number of rights.[110] These elements are indeed vital for any valid plea: the accused must be sufficiently informed on the procedural consequences of pleading guilty and the fact that his case will not be brought before an independent and impartial tribunal. Moreover, the accused must be informed of the fact that the Trial Chamber is not bound in any way by the sentencing recommendations of the parties. Regarding the evidence, the accused is unable to challenge the evidence during regular trial proceedings. Weigend and

---

108 The judges argued for the insertion in the RPE of the common law criteria on guilty pleas: 'This common law institution of the guilty plea should, in our view, find a ready place in an international criminal forum such as the International Tribunal confronted by cases which, by their inherent nature, are very complex and necessarily require lengthy hearings if they go to trial under stringent financial constraints arising from allocations made by the United Nations itself dependent upon the contributions of States.' ICTY, Joint Separate Opinion of Judge McDonald and Judge Vohrah, *Prosecutor v. Erdemović*, Case No.: IT-96-22-A 7 October 1997 para 2.

109 Idem, para 14. In the plea hearing on the original guilty plea, Presiding Judge Jorda tried to ensure that the accused was aware of the alternative charges. However, the questioning of the accused consisted of *indicating* that the accused was charged with alternative charges. No substantive interrogation took place to ensure that the accused grasped the difference between murder as a crime against humanity and murder as a war crime. After the Appeals Chamber remitted the case to another Trial Chamber, the accused was asked again if he understood the charges against him. Presiding Judge Mumba explained, albeit very briefly, the difference between the two murder charges and asked whether the accused understood the charges and had discussed them with his lawyer. After the accused answered in the affirmative, the accused was asked to enter pleas to the charges. ICTY, Transcript of proceedings 31 May 1996, *Prosecutor v. Erdemović*, Case No.: IT-96-22-D, p. 7; ICTY, Transcript of proceedings, *Prosecutor v. Erdemović*, 14 January 1998, Case No. IT-96-22-Tbis, pp. 17–18.

110 For example, in *Deronjić*, the accused waived: '(a) the right to plead not guilty and require the Prosecution to prove the charges in the Indictment beyond a reasonable doubt at a public trial; (b) the right to prepare and put forward a defence to the charges at such public trial; (c) the right to be tried without undue delay; (d) the right to be tried in his presence, and to defend himself in person at trial or through legal assistance of his own choosing at trial; (e) the right to examine at trial, or have examined, the witnesses against him and to obtain the attendance and examination of witnesses on his behalf at a trial under the same conditions as witnesses against him; and (f) the right not to be compelled to testify against himself.' ICTY, Plea Agreement, *Prosecutor v. Deronjić*, Case No.: IT-02-61-PT, 29 September 2003, para 13.

Turner argued that, considering the disclosure obligations in the legal framework of the ad hoc Tribunals, the prosecutor should disclose any exculpatory evidence to the accused in order to comply with the informed-criterion.[111] In Chap. 5, it will be argued that this obligation should also include the incriminating evidence or at least a summary thereof: only in this way can the accused be considered to be truly informed regarding his plea. The Chamber can only accept a guilty plea when there is a sufficient factual basis for the charges to which the accused pleads guilty. The sufficient factual basis, discussed in more detail below, can be derived from either objective indicia or the lack of any disagreement between the prosecutor and accused. This implies that, in general, the accused will have knowledge on the facts of the case (and, ideally, of the evidence supporting these facts). However, Chambers do not determine whether the accused was sufficiently informed regarding the evidence against him when he pleaded guilty.

In *Erdemović*, the Appeals Chamber held that the plea was not informed because the accused and his counsel did not fully grasp the difference between murder as a crime against humanity (to which the accused pleaded guilty) and murder as a war crime.[112] The transcript of proceedings before the Trial Chamber revealed that the presiding judge did not explicitly explain the difference between the two charges and relied on the assumption that counsel had properly instructed the accused.[113] As noted by Judges McDonald and Vohrah, the counsel for the accused did not possess sufficient knowledge of international humanitarian law to understand the distinction between the different charges.[114]

Normally, the presiding judge will ask the accused whether he has made an informed choice. In the *Todorović* plea hearing, the presiding judge asked the accused:

> Have you discussed the matter fully with your counsel, and has he informed you of the nature of the charges against you and of the consequences of pleading guilty to a crime against humanity?[115]

Upon the response of the accused ('Yes'), the informed-criterion was complied with. The plea hearings in other cases follow a similar pattern, whereby the Chamber is satisfied when the accused affirms that he has made an informed decision. When it appears that the accused is not fully aware of the nature of his plea

---

[111] Weigend and Turner 2013, p. 1381.

[112] ICTY, Judgment, *Prosecutor v. Erdemović*, Case No. IT-96-22-D, A. Ch., para 20.

[113] ICTY, Transcript of proceedings, *Prosecutor v. Erdemović*, Case No.: IT-96-22, T. Ch., 31 May 1996, p. 7.

[114] ICTY, Joint Separate Opinion of Judge McDonald and Judge Vohrah, *Prosecutor v. Erdemović*, Case No. IT-96-22-A, A. Ch.,7 October 1997, p. 13.

[115] ICTY, Transcript of proceedings of 19 January 2001, *Prosecutor v. Todorović*, Case No.: IT-95-9/1, T. Ch., p. 802. The plea hearing in *Sikirica* et al. was held in a similar matter. ICTY, Transcript of proceedings of 19 September 2001, *Prosecutor v. Sikirica* et al., Case No.: IT-95-8, T.Ch. III, p. 5647.

or the consequences of pleading guilty, a more detailed discussion between the Chamber and the accused is necessary.

4.2.3.3 Not Equivocal

A valid guilty plea must not be equivocal: the plea must be unqualified, clear and unconditional.[116] McDonald and Vohrah observed that this resembles the guilty plea practice in most common law jurisdictions[117]:

> This requirement imposes upon the court in a situation where the accused pleads guilty but persists with an explanation of his actions which in law amounts to a defence, to reject the plea and have the defence tested at trial.[118]

In *Erdemović* the accused stated that he acted under duress, which provided a reason for Judge Cassese to conclude in his dissenting opinion that the plea of the accused was equivocal. Pleading guilty *and* invoking the defence of duress renders the plea equivocal.[119] In *Momir Nikolić*, the Trial Chamber stated that in order to determine whether the plea was unequivocal, the Trial Chamber considered whether the accused intended to raise any defence.[120] Apart from *Erdemović*, this criterion has never been a contested matter in proceedings before the ad hoc Tribunals.

4.2.3.4 Sufficient Factual Basis

The Trial Chamber can only accept a guilty plea when there is a sufficient factual basis for the crimes to which the accused pleaded guilty. This entails that it is not for the prosecutor and accused to divert the case from the Trial Chamber. Even when the accused has reached an agreement with the prosecutor regarding his criminal responsibility, it is for the Chamber to approve the diversion from the full

---

116 The ECtHR also held that a waiver of rights must be unequivocal. ECtHR, 21 February 1990, App. No.: 11855/85, (*Håkansson and Sturesson v. Sweden*), para 66.

117 With the notable exception of the United States. McDonald and Vohrah argued: 'It would appear that in the United States the constitutional right to plead as one chooses outweighs any requirement that a defence be tested on the merits at trial.' ICTY, Joint Separate Opinion of Judge McDonald and Judge Vohrah *Prosecutor v. Erdemović*, Case No.: IT-96-22-A, A. Ch., 7 October 1997, para 29.

118 Idem, para 29.

119 ICTY, Separate and Dissenting Opinion of Judge Cassese, *Prosecutor v. Erdemović*, Case No.: IT-96-22-A, A. Ch., 7 October 1997, para 50. Judges McDonald and Vohrah did not find the plea to be equivocal, but opted for remittal on the ground that the plea was uninformed. ICTY, Joint Separate Opinion of Judge McDonald and Judge Vohrah, *Prosecutor v. Erdemović*, Case No.: IT-96-22-A, A. Ch., 7 October 1997, paras 88–91.

120 ICTY, Sentencing Judgment, *Prosecutor v. Nikolić*, Case No.: IT-02-60/1-S, T. Ch. I., 2 December 2003, para 52.

trial proceedings. The factual basis for the guilty plea, which can be derived either from 'independent indicia' or from the 'lack of any material disagreement between the parties'.[121]

Although it is for the Trial Chamber to accept the guilty plea, the guilty plea is regarded as a diversion and not as a shortcut to proof. One could argue that, considering this requirement of judicial approval, the guilty plea is a shortcut to proof: the *nulla poena sine iudicio* principle is respected, and the Trial Chamber conducts fact-finding itself. This would, however, be a misrepresentation of the manner in which guilty pleas are regarded in the practice of the ad hoc Tribunals. In general, Chambers have not conducted in-depth fact-finding themselves. Clarifications or the presentation of some additional evidence have been required, but the absence of any material disagreement regarding the facts is normally sufficient to meet the standard of a sufficient factual basis. This entails that the factual basis for the guilty plea is provided by the parties themselves, with only marginal judicial supervision.[122]

Trial Chambers rely predominantly on the absence of disagreement between the parties and base the sentencing judgment on the facts that are agreed upon in the plea agreement. Although the plain wording of Rule 62*bis* ICTY RPE and Rule 62(B) ICTR RPE allows the Chamber to rely on facts that are not included in the plea agreement, the Trial Chamber in *Dragan Nikolić* stated:

> Having accepted a guilty plea on the basis of a plea agreement, a Trial Chamber operating in a party-driven system such as the ICTY is thereafter limited to what is specifically contained in, or annexed to, the plea agreement. Simply put, the Trial Chamber cannot go beyond what is contained in a plea agreement with regard to facts of the case and the legal assessment of these facts.[123]

---

[121] Rule 62*bis* (iv) ICTY RPE; Rule 62(B)(iv) ICTR RPE.

[122] At the ICTY, 15 out of 21 guilty plea cases relied exclusively on agreements between the prosecutor and the accused; in 2 cases material presented at trial was included in the plea agreement. In only 4 cases did the Chamber rely on independent indicia (*Mrđa*, *Jokić*, Češić and *Milan Babić*). At the ICTR, all guilty plea cases derive the factual basis underlying the conviction from the absence of disagreement between the prosecutor and the accused. No independent indicia were presented in guilty plea cases at the ICTR (ICTR, Judgment and Sentence, *Prosecutor v. Kambanda*, Case No.: ICTR 97-23-S, 4 September 1998, para 7; ICTR, Sentence, *Prosecutor v. Serushago*, Case No.: ICTR 98-39-S, 5 February 1999, para 8; ICTR, Judgment and Sentence, *Prosecutor v. Ruggiu*, Case No.: ICTR-97-32-I, 1 June 2000, para 23; ICTR, Sentencing Judgment, *Prosecutor v. Nzabirinda*, Case No.: ICTR-2001-77-T, 23 February 2007, para 14; ICTR, Judgment and Sentence, *Prosecutor v. Rutaganira*, Case No.: ICTR-95-1C-T, 14 March 2005, para 29; ICTR, Judgment and Sentence, *Prosecutor v. Bisengimana*, Case No.: ICTR-00-60-T, 13 April 2006, para 25.; ICTR, Judgment and Sentence, *Prosecutor v. Serugendo*, Case No.: ICTR-2005-84-I, 12 June 2006, para 11; ICTR, Sentencing Judgment, *Prosecutor v. Rugambarara*, Case No.: ICTR-00-59-T, 16 November 2007, para 8; ICTR, Judgment and Sentence, *Prosecutor v. Gaa*, Case No.: ICTR-07-90-R77-I 4 December 2007, para 4; ICTR, Sentencing Judgment, *Prosecutor v. Bagaragaza*, Case No.: ICTR-05-86-S, 17 November 2009, para 16.

[123] ICTY, Sentencing Judgment, *Prosecutor v. Dragan Nikolić*, Case No.: IT-94-2-S, T. Ch. II, 18 December 2003, para 48. The same line of reasoning can be found in *Deronjić*, with the same judge, Schomburg, presiding. ICTY, Sentencing Judgment, *Prosecutor v. Deronjić*, Case No.: IT-02-61-S, T. Ch. II, 30 March 2004 para 41.

The Trial Chamber further acknowledged the problematic nature of plea agreements in international criminal proceedings, when it stated that plea agreements might create a gap between historical accuracy and the parties' version of the crimes.[124] The ability to provide an accurate historical record of events may be undermined by relying solely or to a decisive extent on a partisan presentation of the relevant facts.

In *Mrđa*, *Jokić*, *Češić* and *Milan Babić*, the Trial Chamber took independent indicia into account, next to the agreed facts that were included in the plea agreements. In *Mrđa* and *Jokić*, witness statements delivered in the pre-trial phase were used to establish the required factual basis.[125] Although the Chamber did not examine these statements thoroughly (in fact they were only referred to), the Chamber was not satisfied with the absence of disagreement between the parties in order to accept the plea. In *Milan Babić*, supplementary material was filed next to the plea agreement and the statement of facts.[126] In *Češić*, independent indicia included witness statements and documentary evidence. Unlike *Mrđa* and *Jokić*, the Trial Chamber in *Češić* derived the independent indicia from the submissions of the parties. During the plea hearing, the prosecution and defence were asked whether any independent indicia existed to establish the sufficient factual basis. When both parties answered in the affirmative, the Chamber concluded that a sufficient factual basis therefore existed for the guilty plea.[127]

In *Simić*, where the accused entered into a plea agreement 51 months after his initial appearance and where the prosecution had been presenting evidence for 83 days, the Trial Chamber relied on the facts in the plea agreement.[128] Although the plea agreement refers to evidence presented at trial, it is unclear why the Trial Chamber did not include independent indicia in determining the factual basis and the validity of the guilty plea.

In *Plavšić*, the accused, co-president of the Serbian Republic of Bosnia and Herzegovina, pleaded guilty to persecutions as a crime against humanity and was sentenced to 11 years imprisonment. The factual basis was derived solely from the so-called 'Factual Basis for Plea of Guilt' filed jointly by the prosecution and defence.[129]

---

[124] ICTY, Sentencing Judgment, *Prosecutor v. Dragan Nikolić*, Case No.: IT-94-2-S, T. Ch. II, 18 December 2003, para 122.

[125] ICTY, Transcript of proceedings, *Prosecutor v. Mrđa*, Case No.: IT-02-59-PT, T. Ch. I, 24 July 2003, p. 88. ICTY, Transcript of proceedings, *Prosecutor v. Jokić*, Case No.: IT-01-42-PT, T. Ch. I, 27 August 2003, p. 149.

[126] Consisting of an expert report on propaganda and material that related to public speeches made by the accused. ICTY, Sentencing Judgment, *Prosecutor v. Milan Babić*, Case No.: IT-03-72-S, T. Ch. I, 29 June 2004, para 11.

[127] ICTY, Transcript of proceedings, *Prosecutor v. Češić*, Case No.: IT-95-10-PT, T. Ch. I, 8 October 2003, pp. 91–92.

[128] ICTY, Sentencing Judgment, *Prosecutor v. Simić*, Case No.: IT-95-9/2-S, T. Ch. II, 17 October 2002 para 21.

[129] ICTY, Sentencing Judgment, *Prosecutor v. Plavšić*, Case No.: IT-00-39&40/1-S, T. Ch., 27 February 2003, para 9. ICTY, Factual Basis for Plea of Guilt, *Prosecutor v. Plavšić*, Case No.: IT-00-39&40-PT, 30 September 2003.

In *Kambanda*, where the Rwandan prime minister of the 1994 interim government stood trial, the Trial Chamber accepted the plea agreement and stated on the factual basis underlying the charges of genocide, conspiracy to commit genocide, direct and public incitement to commit genocide, complicity in genocide and murder and extermination as crimes against humanity:

> Considering the factual and legal issues contained in the agreement concluded between you [the accused, KV] and the Office of the Prosecutor and that you have acknowledged that both you and your counsel have signed, the Tribunal finds you guilty on the six counts brought against you.[130]

Kambanda was sentenced to life imprisonment, a verdict upheld on appeal. He not only faced the most severe charges the Tribunal's mandate provided for, he was also one of the first accused to be convicted by the ICTR. The factual basis was derived from the absence of disagreement between the parties; the sentencing judgment of the Trial Chamber contained no reference to independent indicia. In addition to facts concerning specific acts of the accused, such as his personal involvement in inciting low-level officials to kill civilians, contextual facts or *chapeau* elements were also included in the plea agreement:

> Jean Kambanda admits that there was in Rwanda in 1994 a widespread and systematic attack against the civilian population of Tutsi, the purpose of which was to exterminate them.[131]

To include contextual elements and legal characterizations in the plea agreement is, as such, not problematic: the accused acknowledges that he committed his crimes within the context of genocide or an armed conflict. It transpires from the sentencing judgment that the factual basis for these contextual elements was found in the agreement between the accused and the prosecutor.

4.2.3.5 Discretionary Powers of the Trial Chamber?

The wording of Rule 62*bis* ICTY RPE and Rule 62(B) ICTR RPE implies that the Trial Chamber may refuse to accept a guilty plea, even when all the requirements have been met: the Trial Chamber *may* enter a finding of guilt. Is there any discretion left for the Trial Chamber to reject the agreement between the prosecutor and accused? Vasiliev observed that Trial Chambers will accept a guilty plea when the formal criteria have been fulfilled. He referred to the Trial Chamber in *Momir Nikolić*, in which the Chamber held that it could refuse to accept a guilty plea if it is in the interests of justice to do so.[132] In *Obrenović*, the Trial Chamber observed:

---

130 ICTR, Judgment and Sentence, *Prosecutor v. Kambanda*, Case No.: ICTR-97-23-S, T. Ch., 4 September 1998, para 7.

131 ICTR, Judgment and Sentence, *Prosecutor v. Kambanda*, Case No.: ICTR-97-23-S, T. Ch., 4 September 1998, para 39.

132 Vasiliev 2014, p. 422.

> the acceptance of a guilty plea pursuant to a plea agreement must follow careful consideration by a trial chamber of numerous factors including inter alia whether the remaining charges reflect the totality of an accused's conduct, whether an accurate historical record will be created, whether the terms of the agreement fully respect the rights of the accused, and whether due regard is accorded to the interests of victims.[133]

Such remarks by Trial Chambers are rare: only in *Momir Nikolić* and *Obrenović* did the Trial Chamber refer to any discretion regarding the judicial approval of guilty pleas. A related question is how Chambers should approach guilty pleas that are the result of fact and charge bargaining. A factual bargain entails the prosecutor and accused negotiating on the factual basis underlying the charges; a charge bargain entails negotiations on the charges (and legal qualifications) of the conduct of the accused. In his dissenting opinion to the Trial Chamber's sentencing judgment in *Deronjić*, Judge Schomburg vehemently opposed such bargains. He argued that the prosecutor must ensure that the 'entire picture' of the crimes is presented to the Chamber.[134] Although he acknowledged that the prosecutor is responsible for the drafting of the charges, this may not lead to an 'arbitrary selection of charges or facts'.[135]

4.2.4 Admissions of Guilt at the ICC

4.2.4.1 Introduction

The ICC Statute provides for proceedings on an admission of guilt. This resembles the guilty plea practice of the ad hoc Tribunals, although the wording of the relevant article differs. Guariglia and Hochmayr argue that this difference was the result of the drafting process of the Rome Statute, in which delegations from both common law countries and civil law countries had to agree on this diversion.[136] From a common law perspective, the archetypical guilty plea obviates the need for a contested trial altogether, whereas from a civil law perspective a confession is merely a means of proof that the court has to take into account. This has resulted in a somewhat hybrid formulation, which is both reminiscent of the guilty plea and

133 ICTY, Sentencing Judgment, *Prosecutor v. Obrenović*, Case No.: IT-02-60/2-S, T. Ch. I, 10 December 2003, para 19.

134 ICTY, Dissenting Opinion of Judge Wolfgang Schomburg, *Prosecutor v. Deronjić*, Case No.: IT-02-61-S, T. Ch. II, 30 March 2004, para 7.

135 ICTY, Dissenting Opinion of Judge Wolfgang Schomburg, *Prosecutor v. Deronjić*, Case No.: IT-02-61-S, T. Ch. II, 30 March 2004, para 10. The Trial Chamber in *Dragan Nikolić*, presided over by Judge Schomburg, observed in its sentencing judgment that 'the admitted facts are limited to those in the agreement, which might not always reflect the entire available factual and legal basis.' ICTY, Sentencing Judgment, *Prosecutor v. Dragan Nikolić*, Case No.: IT-94-2-S, T. Ch. II, 18 December 2003, para 122.

136 Guariglia and Hochmayr 2008, pp. 1220–1223.

the confession. Weigend and Turner concluded that, despite the different wording, negotiations between the prosecutor and accused are allowed under this provision.[137] This, in fact, introduces plea-bargaining in the procedural framework of the ICC.

4.2.4.2 Legal Framework

Article 65 ICC Statute contains the criteria for the proceedings after an admission of guilt has been filed. First, the admission of guilt must be informed: the accused must understand the nature and consequences of the admission of guilt (Article 65(1)(a)). Second, the accused must have made the admission voluntarily after consultation with defence counsel (Article 65(1)(b)). Finally, the admission must be supported by the facts of the case, which can be derived from the charges, agreed facts or any other evidence that was presented by the prosecutor or the accused (Article 65(1)(c)).

Understanding the nature and consequences of the admission of guilt

This criterion resembles the informed-criterion of the ad hoc Tribunals. In order for an admission of guilt to be accepted, the accused must be aware of the nature of the charges (i.e. the differences between the charges, the modes of liability etc.) and of the procedural consequences of an admission of guilt. This refers to the waiver of procedural rights that the accused would enjoy during regular trial proceedings. In this respect, it also vital that the accused is aware of the fact that sentencing is ultimately a matter for the Trial Chamber to decide upon: sentencing recommendations are, similar to the ad hoc Tribunals, not binding upon the Chamber.[138] Unlike the ad hoc Tribunals, the criterion of non-equivocation is not mentioned explicitly. Guariglia and Hochmayr argued convincingly, however, that this criterion is included in the informed-criterion of Article 65(1)(a) ICC Statute.[139]

Voluntariness

In order for the Chamber to accept the admission of guilt, the Chamber must determine whether the admission has been made voluntarily. The accused must have admitted his guilt in the absence of any coercion, threats or promises other than the conditions contained in the admission. An important difference in the legal frameworks of the ad hoc Tribunals is the fact that the ICC Statute explicitly requires that the accused has had sufficient consultation with his defence counsel regarding his admission of guilt. This enables the accused to make a well-informed and voluntary decision.

[137] Weigend and Turner 2013, p. 1389.

[138] Article 65(5) ICC Statute.

[139] Guariglia and Hochmayr 2008, p. 1228.

Factual basis of the admission of guilt

Any admission of guilt must be supported by the facts of the case: diverting from the full criminal proceedings is not permitted without a solid factual basis for the criminal responsibility of the accused. Unlike the ad hoc Tribunals, the ICC's legal framework refers to three categories of evidence from which the factual basis of the admission of guilt can be derived:

> (i) The charges brought by the Prosecutor and admitted by the accused; (ii) Any materials presented by the Prosecutor which supplement the charges and which the accused accepts; and (iii) Any other evidence, such as the testimony of witnesses, presented by the Prosecutor or the accused.[140]

The mere absence of disagreement between the prosecutor and accused does not suffice for the establishment of a sufficient factual basis: the Chamber is required to conduct more substantial fact-finding in this regard. Article 65(2) ICC Statute states that when the Chamber is satisfied that the criteria of para 1 have been complied with, it shall determine whether all the 'essential facts that are required to prove the crime' have been established. If this is the case, the Chamber may convict the accused.

The Chamber may require a more complete presentation of the facts if this is in the interests of justice. In particular, the interest of the victims has to be taken into account when the Chamber is presented with an admission of guilt. Thus, the agreement between the prosecutor and accused on diverting the case from full criminal proceedings is, as such, not decisive: the Chamber has to determine whether a more complete presentation of the case would be in the interests of justice. Weigend and Turner concluded that the ICC Trial Chambers have a more significant role regarding the acceptance of admission of guilt than the ad hoc Tribunals.[141] When the admission of guilt is not accepted by the Trial Chamber, the admission will be regarded as not having been made. The case will then be remitted to another Trial Chamber in order to provide for a full contested trial. So far, no admissions of guilt have been filed: it remains to be seen how the Trial Chambers will proceed when an admission of guilt is filed.

4.3 Shortcuts in the Law of International Criminal Procedure

4.3.1 Introduction

In the following pages, the shortcuts to proof that can be discerned in international criminal proceedings are discussed. As stated in the Introduction, shortcuts are

---

140 Article 65(1)(c) ICC Statute.

141 Weigend and Turner 2013, p. 1396.

mechanisms that allow for an abbreviated presentation and discussion of the evidence before the trier of fact. The principle of immediacy is infringed upon: the evidence is not fully presented and discussed during the proceedings. The shortcuts that are discussed include agreed facts, facts of common knowledge, judicial notice of adjudicated facts and appeal proceedings.

4.3.2 Agreed Facts

The prosecutor and the accused can agree that particular facts are not in dispute between them. Such uncontested facts can be brought to the attention of the Chamber. When the Chamber notes the agreement on the uncontested facts, no evidence has to be presented to prove the particular facts. This shortcut to proof enables the parties and the Chamber to focus on the issues that remain contested between them (provided that the Chamber, acting *proprio motu*, does not require the presentation of additional evidence or submissions regarding the agreed facts). First, the practice at the ad hoc Tribunals is discussed, followed by the ICC.

4.3.2.1 The Ad Hoc Tribunals

Rule 65*ter* (H) ICTY RPE and Rule 73*bis* (B)(ii) ICTR RPE stipulate that the parties may record uncontested matters, including facts that are not in dispute between them.[142] The parties can even be ordered to make an effort to submit a list of agreed facts to the pre-trial Judge or the Trial Chamber.[143] Both provisions are related to the pre-trial phase, but their scope is broader: Chambers can also note agreed facts during the trial phase.[144]

The consequences of agreed facts are in the first place a matter for the parties themselves: the Chamber merely notes that certain facts are uncontested between the prosecutor and accused. This explains why the general admissibility criteria of Rule 89 ICTY/ICTR RPE are not consistently applied by the Chambers when they note the agreement between the parties. The Chamber has not conducted a

[142] According to Rule 65*ter* (E)(i) ICTY RPE the prosecutor must indicate in its pre-trial brief which matters are uncontested. Rule 73*bis* (B)(ii) ICTR RPE contains a similar provision.

[143] E.g. ICTY, Second Order on Agreed Facts, *Prosecutor v. Milutinović et al.*, Case No.: IT-05-87-T, T. Ch., 15 February 2007, para 4.

[144] E.g. ICTY, Decision on Agreed Facts, *Prosecutor v. Karadžić*, Case No.: IT-95-5/18-T, T. Ch., 14 February 2013, para 3. Rule 65*ter* (M) ICTY RPE states that the Trial Chamber may exercise any function of the pre-trial Judge. Rule 73*bis* ICTR RPE concerns the pre-trial conference, presided over by the Trial Chamber. The Rule does not contain a similar provision as Rule 65*ter* (M) ICTY RPE.

thorough analysis of the facts and the supporting evidence itself.[145] However, the legal effect is more substantial than simply recording an *inter partes* agreement. The Trial Chamber in *Karadžić* held:

> it is the view of the Chamber that where the parties do agree on matters of fact and this agreement is recorded by the Chamber, it does not render those facts evidence, but rather simply makes them facts in support of which no evidence needs be brought and upon which the Chamber may rely, should it so choose, in its final judgment.[146]

Consequently, facts that are uncontested and agreed upon by the parties can be included in the Chamber's final judgment. For instance, the Trial Chamber in *Perišić* held that when the Chamber refers in the judgment to an agreed fact, the fact is regarded as 'accurate'.[147] Such facts are normally referred to in a footnote, without discussing the particular relevance and probative value of the facts: the Chamber apparently considered them to be relevant and probative.[148]

---

145 In *Perišić*, the Trial Chamber did take Rule 89(C) ICTY RPE into account, regarding the relevance and probative value of the agreed facts. The Trial Chamber in *Karadžić*, however, observed: 'The Prosecution asserts that the Chamber "must" accept such recorded agreed facts as evidence under Rule 89(C), requiring a finding of relevance and probative value. However, while some other Trial Chambers have previously noted that the effect of recording points of agreement between the parties at trial is to accept those points of agreement as evidence pursuant to Rule 89, this Chamber respectfully differs from that proposition. It considers that the admission of evidence, or indeed the taking of judicial notice of adjudicated facts or facts of common knowledge pursuant to Rule 94(B), is an entirely different process from a simple recording that the parties have agreed on certain facts. In the former case, it is clearly necessary for a Chamber to be satisfied as to relevance before admitting testimony or a piece of documentary evidence, or before taking judicial notice. However, agreement between the parties is primarily a matter for the parties themselves, and they may choose to agree on any number of matters which the Chamber may, ultimately, consider have no bearing on the case.' ICTY, Decision on "Prosecution Response to Karadžić's Submission of Agreed Facts and Motion for Reconsideration, *Prosecutor v. Karadžić*, Case No.: IT-95-5/18-T, T. Ch., 26 August 2010, para 9; ICTY, Second Decision in Respect of Srebrenica Agreed Facts, *Prosecutor v. Perišić*, Case No.: IT-04-81-T, T. Ch. I, 30 September 2009, p. 1.

146 E.g. ICTY, Decision on Agreed Facts, *Prosecutor v. Karadžić*, Case No.: IT-95-5/18-T, T. Ch., 14 February 2013, para 5. In *Stanišić & Simatović*, the Chamber observed that 'the Chamber may rely on these facts for the truth of their content without additional evidence, but is not bound by them'. ICTY, Decision on Motion for Admission of Agreed Facts, *Prosecutor v. Stanišić & Simatović*, Case No.: IT-03-69-T, T. Ch. I, 12 January 2011, p. 1.

147 ICTY, Judgment, *Prosecutor v. Perišić*, Case No.: IT-04-81-T, T. Ch. I, 6 September 2011, para 62. In *Haradinaj*, the Trial Chamber held that is considered the agreed facts with all the other evidence in the case. This again shows the holistic approach to weighing the evidence. ICTY, Judgment, *Prosecutor v. Haradinaj et al.*, Case No.: IT-04-84-T, T. Ch. I., 3 April 2008, para 17.

148 E.g. ICTY, Judgment, *Prosecutor v. Halilović*, Case No.: IT-01-48-T, T.Ch. I, 16 November 2005, fn. 516, 527, 530. ICTY, Judgment, *Prosecutor v. Dragomir Milošević*, Case No.: IT-98-29/1-T, T. Ch. III, 12 December 2007, fn. 1–5.

Agreed facts may refer to (detailed) factual situations,[149] but also to the *chapeau* elements of the crimes alleged. In *Stanišić & Simatović*, the Trial Chamber held:

> The parties agreed as to the existence of an armed conflict in Croatia and Bosnia-Herzegovina at all times relevant to the crimes alleged in the Indictment. The Trial Chamber has considered the parties' agreement in the light of a number of Adjudicated Facts and evidence with regard to the outbreak of the armed conflict in Croatia and Bosnia-Herzegovina. Accordingly, the Trial Chamber finds that there was an armed conflict in the territory of Croatia and Bosnia-Herzegovina that extended throughout the period relevant to the crimes charged in the Indictment.[150]

Unlike the criteria for taking judicial notice of adjudicated facts, agreed facts may go to the acts and conduct of the accused. In *Blagojević & Jokić*, the Trial Chamber held in this regard:

> An accused may agree to a prejudicial or incriminating fact. In such cases, particularly where the fact may have direct impact on establishing the guilt of an accused, the Trial Chamber as guarantor of the rights of the accused, may find it necessary to enquire whether the accused has made such an admission voluntarily and understands the possible consequences of such an admission.[151]

This is reminiscent of the manner in which Trial Chambers determine whether a guilty plea has been entered according to the criteria of Rule 62*bis*. It stands to reason that when the accused agrees to particular facts relating to his criminal responsibility, the same guarantees apply when the accused waives his right to trial proceedings altogether and pleads guilty to the charges.

Apart from the fact that agreement between the parties is required before the Chamber can note an agreed fact, the main difference with adjudicated facts concerns the probative value of such facts. Agreed facts can be relied upon in the final judgment when the particular fact is relevant, has probative value and is reliable.[152] The Chamber determines this in a holistic manner: the agreed fact is weighed against the background of all the other evidence admitted. When the Chamber decides to judicially notice an adjudicated fact, it considers the fact as a 'well-founded presumption for the accuracy of that fact'.

---

[149] E.g., the prosecution and defence counsel in *Delić* agreed that 'On 8 June 1993, the RBiH Presidency issued a decision on the restructuring of the ABiH Supreme Command Headquarters to include establishing the post of Commander of the Main Staff.' ICTY, Judgment, *Prosecutor v. Delić*, Case No.: IT-04-83-T, T. Ch. I, 15 September 2008, para 5.

[150] ICTY, Judgment, *Prosecutor v. Stanišić & Simatović*, Case No.: IT-03-69-T, T. Ch. I, 30 May 2013, para 958.

[151] ICTY, Decision on Prosecution's Motion for Judicial Notice of Adjudicated Facts and Documentary Evidence, *Prosecutor v. Blagojević & Jokić*, Case No.: IT-02-60-T, T. Ch. I, 19 December 2003, para 14.

[152] Although not all Chambers consider the agreed fact in light of the general admissibility criteria of Rule 89(C) when an agreement is noted, when the agreed fact is included in the final judgment the Chamber must consider whether the fact is relevant and reliable. Seen this way, Chambers differ only regarding the moment when the criteria have to be considered: when the agreed facts are noted or after the close of the proceedings.

The use of agreed facts at the ICTY and ICTR is rather limited, compared to the practice of judicially noticing facts under Rule 94(A) and (B). At the ICTY, Trial Chambers have noted agreements of fact only in ten cases, whereas the practice at the ICTR seems to be absent.[153]

4.3.2.2 The International Criminal Court

Rule 69 ICC RPE stipulates that the prosecutor and defence may agree on factual issues. Such an agreement is submitted to the Chamber, which may consider that no further evidence has to be presented regarding these facts.[154] Similar to the provisions on admissions of guilt, the Chamber may order that a more complete presentation of the facts is in the interests of justice, particularly in the interests of the victims. For example, the legal representatives of the victims in *Nourain & Jerbo Jamus* opposed the 'drastic truncation of the facts', which would result from the joint submission of the prosecutor and accused. They argued that evidence has to be presented in order to do justice to the full criminal responsibility of the accused.[155]

The prosecutor and accused are often encouraged by the Chamber to reach agreement on as many factual issues as possible, which hopefully will result in expedited proceedings focused on the contested issues of the case.[156] In *Nourain & Jerbo Jamus* the prosecution and defence not only reached agreement on particular facts, they even indicated which issues would be contested during the proceedings. In this way, they proposed to narrow the trial proceedings to a significant extent.[157] The Chamber concurred and held that the proceedings would

153 At the ICTY, agreements of fact were noticed in *Halilović*, *Stanišić & Simatović*, *Milutinović et al.*, *Boškoski & Tarčulovski*, *Haradinaj et al.*, *Dragomir Milošević*, *Rasim Delić*, *Hadzić*, *Karadžić*, *Mladić*, and *Perišić*.

154 E.g. ICC, Decision on Agreements as to Evidence, *Prosecutor v. Katanga & Ngudjolo Chui*, Case No.: ICC-01/04-01/07, T. Ch. II, 3 February 2011, para 5.

155 ICC, Decision on the Joint Submission regarding the Contested Issues and the Agreed Facts, *Prosecutor v. Abdallah Banda Abakaer Nourain & Saleh Mohammed Jerbo Jamus*, Case No.: ICC-02/05-03/09, T. Ch. IV, 28 September 2011, para 12.

156 The Trial Chamber in *Bosco Ntaganda* encouraged the parties to reach agreements on factual issues. ICC, Decision on Prosecution and Defence Joint Submission on Agreed Facts, *Prosecutor v. Bosco Ntaganda*, Case No.: ICC-01/04-02/06, T. Ch. VI, 22 June 2015. Regulation 54 stipulates that the Trial Chamber, at a status conference, may issue an order regarding any evidence on which the prosecution and defence agree under Rule 69.

157 In their Joint Submission, the prosecution and defence agreed that only three issues remained contested: '(i) Whether the attack on the MGS Haskanita on 29 September 2007 was unlawful; (ii) If the attack is deemed unlawful, whether the Accused persons were aware of the factual circumstances that established the unlawful nature of the attack; and (iii) Whether AMIS was a peacekeeping mission in accordance with the Charter of the United Nations.' ICC, Decision on the Joint Submission regarding the Contested Issues and the Agreed Facts, *Prosecutor v. Abdallah Banda Abakaer Nourain & Saleh Mohammed Jerbo Jamus*, Case No.: ICC-02/05-03/09, T. Ch. IV, 28 September 2011, para 3.

be focused on the contested issues identified in the agreement between the prosecutor and defence. It also held that additional evidence or submissions could be required at a later stage, if required by the interests of justice.[158] This entails that the Chamber remains fully responsible for accurate fact-finding: when necessary, the Chamber can require a more complete presentation of the facts and supporting evidence.

The striking difference with the provisions at the ad hoc Tribunals concerning agreed facts is that ICC Chambers have to take into account the interests of justice when an agreement on factual issues is submitted. The Chamber may order that evidence will be presented in order to allow the victims to participate effectively. In *Katanga*, the Chamber included a limited number of agreed facts in the final judgment.[159] This means that the uncontested facts were considered conclusively proven, based on the agreement between the prosecutor and Katanga's defence. Similarly, the Trial Chamber in *Ngudjolo* took the agreed facts into account in its final judgment.[160] So far, not much use has been made of agreed facts before the ICC. The number of cases in which an agreement on factual issues was reached is small and the number of agreed facts in those cases is limited. Although agreed facts are a shortcut to proof, in practice they will only contribute marginally to an expeditious trial that is focused on the contested issues of the case.

4.3.3 Judicial Notice of Facts of Common Knowledge

4.3.3.1 Introduction

Facts of common knowledge in international criminal proceedings provide for an interesting shortcut to proof: facts of common knowledge are conclusively proven. This entails that the prosecutor is not required to present evidence to establish the particular fact and that evidence in rebuttal is inadmissible. In international criminal proceedings, the practice of taking judicial notice of facts of common knowledge is of particular relevance because such facts have been used to prove parts of the charges.

158 ICC, Decision on the Joint Submission regarding the Contested Issues and the Agreed Facts, *Prosecutor v. Abdallah Banda Abakaer Nourain & Saleh Mohammed Jerbo Jamus*, Case No.: ICC-02/05-03/09, T. Ch. IV, 28 September 2011, paras 44–46.

159 ICC, Judgment Pursuant to Article 74 of the Statute, *Prosecutor v. Katanga*, Case No.: ICC-01/04-01/07, T. Ch. II, 7 March 2014, para 73.

160 ICC, Judgment Pursuant to Article 74 of the Statute, *Prosecutor v. Ngudjolo*, Case No.: ICC-01/04-02/12, T. Ch. II, 18 December 2012, para 39.

4.3.3.2 Legal Framework

The Rules of Procedure and Evidence of the ad hoc Tribunals contain a similar provision on facts of common knowledge: 'A Trial Chamber shall not require proof of facts of common knowledge but shall take judicial notice thereof.'[161]

A noticeable difference between the legal framework of the ad hoc Tribunals and the ICC is the fact that the ICC Statute seems to leave the Chamber discretion to judicially notice facts of common knowledge. The ICC Statute states that: 'The Court shall not require proof of facts of common knowledge but *may* take judicial notice of them'.[162] Piragoff argued that the different wording can be explained by the aim of the ICC to provide an accurate historical record and to provide the victims with as much reliable evidence as possible. Therefore, judicial notice may be taken in one case, whereas it is denied in the other, because it is in the interest of the victims to do so. The Chamber will instead hear the complete presentation of evidence.[163] The aim of providing an accurate historical record is also often heard at the ad hoc Tribunals. The *Karemera* decision on the Rwandan genocide serves as a prime example. By concluding authoritatively on a solid evidentiary basis that atrocities were committed and declaring such findings to be established beyond any doubt, judicial notice serves the very aim of providing victims a complete and incontestable narrative. Moreover, when facts reach the standard of indisputability, no evidence in rebuttal is admissible. This effectively silences deniers and may be an antidote for politically motivated accused that want to present a revisionist version of history. On the other hand, extensive use of judicial notice, in particular in relation to historical facts, may result in an imposed narrative, whereby the tribunal's narrative can be perceived as politically motivated.

For the analysis of the practice of facts of common knowledge, the case law of the ad hoc Tribunals will be discussed; those Tribunals have produced the most extensive and relevant case law on this shortcut to proof.

4.3.3.3 Rationale for Judicial Notice of Facts of Common Knowledge

Chambers take judicial notice of facts of common knowledge for several reasons. Most prominent is the enhancement of judicial economy, resulting in a trial without undue delay: if indisputable, and mostly undisputed, facts must be proven by the regular means of proof the result will be protracted and inefficient trials.[164]

---

161 Rule 94(A) ICTY/R RPE.

162 Article 69(6) ICC Statute. Emphasis added.

163 Piragoff 2008, p. 1308.

164 This was already acknowledged in an early case: ICTY, Decision on the Pre-Trial Motion by the Prosecution requesting the Trial Chamber to take Judicial Notice of the International Character of the Conflict in Bosnia-Herzegovina, *Prosecutor v. Simić et al.*, ICTY-IT95-9-PT, T. Ch., 25 March 1999, p. 4. Cf. Jørgensen 2013, p. 720.

In order to avoid this, the Chamber may deem facts to be of common knowledge and concentrate on those facts that are in dispute and require formal proof. In his Separate Opinion to an Appeals Chamber interlocutory decision at the SCSL, Judge Robertson stated on the expediency argument:

> In my view, expedition and judicial economy do not accurately reflect the real purpose of this Rule [Rule 94, KV], and the 'balance' sets up a false dichotomy between the assumed purpose of economy and the rights of the defendant. Expedition and economy may be the *result* of judicial notice, but the purpose of the Rule is rather to promote a fair trial for all parties both by relieving them of the burden of proving facts that have been established convincingly elsewhere and by enabling the tribunal to take into account in its decision the full panoply of relevant facts currently available in the world. […] Judicial notice is not, most emphatically, a prosecution tool that must be 'balanced' or 'weighed' against countervailing rights to a fair trial: it is a procedure that can and also should be used by defendants to simplify a task which might otherwise be beyond their resources. They benefit, as much as the Prosecution and the Court, from any expedition that results. Facts that can be judicially noticed must be judicially noticed – Rule 94(A) is mandatory.[165]

Another reason in favour of judicial notice is the desire to deliver consistent and uniform judgments on factual issues: it is undesirable when Chambers of the same Tribunal arrive at different factual conclusions concerning the same crime base.[166] This also relates to the aim of creating an accurate historical record of mass atrocities: from that perspective, which should not hold too prominent of a place in criminal proceedings concerning the determination of guilt or innocence of individuals, diverging judgments are indeed undesirable.[167] Nevertheless, if a Chamber concludes, on the basis of new evidence or on a different interpretation of existing evidence, that a particular factual situation existed, it should feel free to conclude accordingly, even if it contradicts the findings of other Chambers.

---

[165] SCSL, Separate Opinion of Justice Robertson to Fofana-Decision on Appeal against "Decision on Prosecution's Motion for Judicial Notice and Admission of Evidence"', *Prosecutor v. Norman et al.*, SCSL-2004-14-AR73, A. Ch., 16 May 2005, para 15 (emphasis in original). The RPE of the SCSL are similar to the RPE of the ICTR, including the Rule on judicial notice of facts of common knowledge.

[166] ICTR, Decision on the Prosecutor's Motion for Judicial Notice and Presumptions of Facts pursuant to Rules 94 and 54, *Prosecutor v. Semanza*, ICTR-97-20-I, T. Ch. III, 3 November 2000, para 20; SCSL, Fofana-Decision on Appeal against "Decision on Prosecution's Motion for Judicial Notice and Admission of Evidence"', *Prosecutor v. Norman et al.*, SCSL-2004-14-AR73, A. Ch., 16 May 2005, para 22. ICTY, Decision on Motion for Judicial Notice of ICTY Convictions, *Prosecutor v. Perišić*, ICTY-IT-04-81-PT, T. Ch. I, 25 September 2008, para 7. Tapper 2010, p. 84.

[167] On the relationship of history writing and international criminal tribunals, see: Wilson 2011. Commenting on the 1961 Eichmann trial, philosopher Hannah Arendt stated: 'The purpose of a trial is to render justice, and nothing else; even the noblest of ulterior purposes—"the making of a record of the Hitler regime which would withstand the test of history," as Robert G. Storey, executive trial counsel at Nuremberg, formulated the supposed higher aims of the Nuremberg Trials—can only detract from the law's main business: to weigh the charges brought against the accused, to render judgment, and to mete out due punishment.' Arendt 1963, p. 232.

4.3.3.4 Probative Value of Facts of Common Knowledge

When a Chamber concludes that a fact is of common knowledge, the fact is established conclusively.[168] Facts of common knowledge cannot be challenged further during the proceedings: evidence in rebuttal is inadmissible.[169]

The ICTR Appeals Chamber in *Karemera* emphasized that taking judicial notice of facts of common knowledge is not discretionary but mandatory, which follows from the plain wording of Rule 94(A) ICTR RPE. When a Trial Chamber identifies a fact of common knowledge, that is relevant to the case, it must take judicial notice of that fact. Moreover, and more importantly, when the Appeals Chamber has determined that a fact is of common knowledge, Trial Chambers must take judicial notice if the particular fact is relevant to the case.[170] Consequently, facts of common knowledge do not only prevent the parties to the current proceedings from presenting evidence in rebuttal; this also extends to future cases when the fact is relevant to the proceedings. Trial Chambers are bound by decisions of the Appeals Chamber, but not by other Trial Chambers in this respect.[171]

---

[168] ICTR, Decision on Prosecutor's Motion for Judicial Notice and Presumptions of Facts pursuant to Rules 94 and 54, *Prosecutor v. Semanza*, ICTR-97-20-I, T. Ch. III, 3 November 2000, para 41.; ICTR, Decision on Prosecutor's Interlocutory Appeal of Decision on Judicial Notice, *Prosecutor v. Karemera* et al., ICTR-98-44-AR73(C), A. Ch., 16 June 2006, para 42.

[169] ICTY, Decision on Prosecution Motions for Judicial Notice of Adjudicated Facts and for Admission of Written Statements of Witnesses pursuant to Rule 92bis, *Prosecutor v. Krajišnik*, ICTY-IT-00-39-PT, T. Ch. I, 28 February 2003, para 16.

[170] ICTR, Decision on Prosecutor's Interlocutory Appeal of Decision on Judicial Notice, *Prosecutor v. Karemera et al.*, ICTR-98-44-AR73(C), A. Ch., para 29; ICTR, Decision on Prosecutor's Motion for Judicial Notice of Facts of Common Knowledge, *Prosecutor v. Nizeyimana*, ICTR-2001-55C-PT, T. Ch. III, 3 March 2010, para 5; ICTR, Decision on the Prosecution's Motion for Judicial Notice, *Prosecutor v. Ndahimana*, ICTR-2001-68-PT, T. Ch. III, 7 April 2010, para 4. ICTR, Decision on Prosecutor's Motion for Judicial Notice, *Prosecutor v. Bizimungu*, ICTR-99-50-T, T. Ch. II, 22 September 2006, para 7.

[171] ICTY, Decision on the Pre-Trial Motion by the Prosecution Requesting the Trial Chamber to take Judicial Notice of the International Character of the Conflict in Bosnia-Herzegovina, *Prosecutor v. Simić* et al., ICTY-IT-95-9-PT, T. Ch., 25 March 1999, p. 4; ICTY, Decision Granting in Part Prosecution's Motions for Judicial Notice of Adjudicated Facts pursuant to Rule 94(B), *Prosecutor v. Stanišić and Župljanin*, ICTY-IT-08-91-T, T. Ch. II, 1 April 2010, para 26: 'no principle of *stare decisis* applies between Trial Chambers of the Tribunal.' 'The Appeals Chamber considers that decisions of Trial Chambers, which are bodies with coordinate jurisdiction, have no binding force on each other, although a Trial Chamber is free to follow the decision of another Trial Chamber if it finds that decision persuasive.' ICTY, Judgment, *Prosecutor v. Aleksovski*, ICTY-IT-95-14/1-a, A. Ch., 24 March 2000, para 114. ICTR, Decision on Motion for Judicial Notice, *Prosecutor v. Karemera et al.*, ICTR-98-44-R94, T. Ch. III, 9 November 2005, para 6.

4.3.3.5 Identifying Facts of Common Knowledge

Before discussing the specific requirements for judicial notice under Rule 94(A), it is important to note that proposed facts must still meet the Rule 89(C) criteria of relevancy and probative value.[172] The ICTR Appeals Chamber has held that 'Rule 94 of the Rules is not a mechanism that may be employed to circumvent the ordinary requirement of relevance and thereby clutter the record with matters that would not otherwise be admitted.'[173]

How can one discern a fact of common knowledge? According to the Trial Chamber in *Semanza*:

> The term 'common knowledge' is generally accepted as encompassing '...those facts which are not subject to reasonable dispute including, common or universally known facts, such as general facts of history, generally known geographical facts and the laws of nature.' A common example of a fact of common knowledge are the days of the week. In addition, and perhaps more importantly for the present purposes, 'common knowledge' also encompasses those facts that are generally known within a tribunal's territorial jurisdiction.[174]

The Trial Chamber then undertook a two-pronged test: first, it determined whether a fact is common knowledge, and second, whether this matter is reasonably indisputable. A fact is indisputable 'if it is either universally known within the territorial jurisdiction of a court or capable of accurate and ready determination by resort to sources whose accuracy cannot be reasonably be called into question.'[175] In part, this is circular reasoning: in order to determine whether a fact is of common knowledge, the Chamber determines whether it is universally known within the jurisdiction of the Tribunal. A more convincing approach would be when facts of common knowledge must have some factual basis in trustworthy sources such as an encyclopedia or scientific literature. It is possible that a certain belief is universally known within the jurisdiction of a court, but lacks any (scientific) credibility. It would be unjust to consider this as common knowledge and take judicial notice of it. It is not necessary that a matter is universally known, as long as it is

---

[172] E.g. ICTY, Decision on Motion for Judicial Notice of ICTY Convictions, *Prosecutor v. Perišić*, ICTY-IT-04-81-PT, T. Ch. I, 25 September 2008, para 10.

[173] ICTR, Judgment, *Prosecutor v. Semanza*, ICTR-97-20-A, A. Ch., 20 May 2005, para 189; ICTY, Decision on Appellant's Motion for Judicial Notice, *Prosecutor v. Nikolić*, ICTY-IT-02-60/i-A, A. Ch., 5 April 2005, para 17.

[174] ICTR, Decision on the Prosecutor's Motion for Judicial Notice and Presumptions of Facts pursuant to Rules 94 and 54, *Prosecutor v. Semanza*, ICTR-97-20-I, T. Ch. III, 3 November 2000, para 23. References omitted.

[175] ICTR, Decision on the Prosecutor's Motion for Judicial Notice and Presumptions of Facts pursuant to Rules 94 and 54, *Prosecutor v. Semanza*, ICTR-97-20-I, T. Ch. III, 3 November 2000, para 24. Similar: ICTY, Decision on Appellant's Motion for Judicial Notice, *Prosecutor v. Nikolić*, ICTY-IT-02-60/1-A, A. Ch., 1 April 2005, para 10. ICTY, Decision on Blagoje Simić's Motion for Admission of Additional Evidence, Alternatively for Taking of Judicial Notice, *Prosecutor v. Simić*, ICTY-IT-95-9-A, A. Ch., 1 June 2006, para 25.

known within the Tribunal's jurisdiction.[176] That the facts must have some public character appears to be undisputed.[177]

A contested issue is whether judicial notice can be taken of legal characterizations. One could argue that only facts can be judicially noticed. On the basis of these facts, the Chamber can then draw legal conclusions. This is not, however, how judicial notice of facts of common knowledge has been interpreted by the ad hoc Tribunals. The Appeals Chamber has consistently held that:

> The question is not whether a proposition is put in legal or layman's terms (so long as the terms are sufficiently well defined such that the accuracy of their application to the described situation is not reasonably in doubt). The question is whether the proposition can reasonably be disputed.[178]

Accordingly, the Appeals Chamber took judicial notice under Rule 94(A) of terms as 'widespread or systematic attacks against a civilian population'[179] and of the existence of 'an armed conflict not of an international character in Rwanda between 1 January 1994 and 17 July 1994'.[180] Most prominently and controversially, the Appeals Chamber in *Karemera* took judicial notice of the Rwandan genocide as a fact of common knowledge: 'The fact of the Rwandan genocide is a part of world history, a fact as certain as any other, a classic instance of a "fact of common knowledge."'[181]

---

176 ICTR, Decision on the Prosecutor's Motion for Judicial Notice and Presumptions of Facts pursuant to Rules 94 and 54, *Prosecutor v. Semanza*, ICTR-97-20-I, T. Ch. III, 3 November 2000, para 31.

177 ICTY, Decision on Appellant's Motion for Judicial Notice, *Prosecutor v. Nikolić*, ICTY-IT-02-60/1-A, A. Ch., 1 April 2005, para 34. The Appeals Chamber held, quite obviously, that military secrets of material labelled 'strictly confidential' are not facts of common knowledge.

178 ICTR, Decision on Prosecutor's Interlocutory Appeal of Decision on Judicial Notice, *Prosecutor v. Karemera*, ICTR-98-44-AR73(C), A. Ch., 16 June 2006, para 29; ICTY, Decision on Interlocutory Appeals against Trial Chamber's Decision on Prosecution's Motion for Judicial Notice of Adjudicated Facts and Prosecution's Catalogue of Agreed Facts, *Prosecutor v. Milošević*, ICTY-IT-98-29/1-AR73.1, A. Ch., 26 June 2007, para 21.

179 ICTR, Judgment, *Prosecutor v. Semanza*, ICTR-97-20-A, A. Ch., 20 May 2005, para 192.

180 ICTR, Judgment, *Prosecutor v. Semanza*, ICTR-97-20-A, A. Ch., 20 May 2005, para 192. In December 2007, ICTY Trial Chamber II declined to take judicial notice of these proposed facts of common knowledge: 'During the period from at least April to 31 December 1992, a state of armed conflict existed on the territory of Bosnia and Herzegovina', and, 'During the period from at least April to 31 December 1992, there was an ongoing widespread or systematic attack against the Bosnian Muslim and Bosnian Croat civilian population on the territory of the Serbian Republic of Bosnia Herzegovina, later known as *Republika Srpska*'. ICTY, Decision on Judicial Notice, *Prosecutor v. Stanišić*, ICTY-IT-04-79-PT, T. Ch. II, 14 December 2007.

181 ICTR, Decision on Prosecutor's Interlocutory Appeal of Decision on Judicial Notice, *Prosecutor v. Karemera*, ICTR-98-44-AR73(C), A. Ch., 16 June 2006, para 35. For a critical discussion of this decision: Mamiya 2007. Cf. the Trial Chamber in *Semanza*, which stated: 'A fundamental question in this case is whether "genocide" took place in Rwanda. Notwithstanding the over-abundance of official reports, including United Nations reports confirming the occurrence of genocide, this Chamber believes that the question is so fundamental, that formal proofs should be submitted bearing out the existence of this jurisdictional elemental crime.' ICTR, Decision on the Prosecutor's Motion for Judicial Notice and Presumptions of Facts pursuant to Rules 94 and 54, *Prosecutor v. Semanza*, ICTR-97-20-I, T. Ch. III, 3 November 2000, para 36.

Unlike the criteria for judicial notice under Rule 94(B), Chambers cannot even consider whether the proposed fact is (or contains) a legal characterization: Chambers do not enjoy any discretion and must judicially notice the fact when the Appeals Chamber has held that the fact is of common knowledge and not reasonably disputable.[182]

In order to assess whether the fact is of common knowledge and not subject to reasonable dispute, the purported fact must be well defined: a conviction as such is not sufficiently well defined to be taken judicial notice of.[183] This also holds true for 'documents' contained in the United Nations Blue Book Series: without a proper identification of the documents judicial notice is requested for, judicial notice will be denied.[184] Chambers have categorically refused to take notice of documents pursuant to Rule 94(A) and have held that only facts are eligible for judicial notice under this rule.[185] Chambers differ in respect to facts that are contained in documents generated by a (non-judicial) body of the United Nations. The ICTY Trial Chamber in *Prlic* declined to take judicial notice, because facts contained in such documents did not become facts of common knowledge, where the ICTR Trial Chamber in *Ngirabatware* seemed to base the finding of notoriety of the fact on its origins, namely an organ of the United Nations.[186] ICTR Trial Chambers have held that:

> legislative, executive, and administrative and organizational laws of Rwanda properly qualify for judicial notice and that the legislation and documents relating to the administrative organization of a geographic area and the legislative law of a country fall within matters of common knowledge, which may fairly be judicially noticed.[187]

---

182 ICTY, Decision on Interlocutory Appeals against Trial Chamber's Decision on Prosecution's Motion for Judicial Notice of Adjudicated Facts and Prosecution's Catalogue of Agreed Facts, *Prosecutor v. Milošević*, ICTY-IT-9829/1-AR73.1, A. Ch., 26 June 2007, para 21. Under Rule 94(B), proposed facts may not include findings or characterizations that are of an essentially legal nature. ICTY, Decision on Motion for Judicial Notice of ICTY Convictions, *Prosecutor v. Perišić*, ICTY-IT-04-81-PT, T. Ch. I, 25 September 2008, para 12; ICTY, Decision on Third and Fourth Prosecution Motions for Judicial Notice of Adjudicated Facts, *Prosecutor v. Krajišnik*, ICTY-IT-00-39-T, T. Ch. I, 24 March 2005, para 15.

183 ICTY, Decision on Motion for Judicial Notice of ICTY Convictions, *Prosecutor v. Perišić*, ICTY-IT-04-81-PT, T. Ch. I, 25 September 2008, para 16.

184 ICTR, Decision on the Prosecutor's Motion for Judicial Notice pursuant to Rules 73, 89 and 94, *Prosecutor v. Bagosora* et al., ICTR-98-41-T, T. Ch. III, 11 April 2003, para 57.

185 ICTY, Decision on Prosecution Motion to Admit Documentary Evidence, *Prosecutor v. Milutinović et al.*, ICTY-IT-05-87-T, T. Ch., 10 October 2006, para 20; ICTR, Decision on Prosecution's Motion for Judicial Notice Pursuant to Rules 73, 89 and 94, *Prosecutor v. Bizimungu et al.*, ICTR-99-50-I, T. Ch. II, 2 December 2003, para 26.

186 ICTY, Decision on "Prosecution Motion for Judicial Notice of Facts of Common Knowledge and Admission of Documentary Evidence pursuant to Rules 94(A) and 89(C)"', *Prosecutor v. Prlić* et al., ICTY-IT-04-74-PT, T. Ch. II, 3 February 2006, p. 6; ICTR, Decision on Prosecutor's Motion for Judicial Notice of Facts of Common Knowledge, *Prosecutor v. Ngirabatware*, ICTR-99-54-T, T. Ch. II, 15 July 2010, paras 10–11.

187 ICTR, Decision on the Prosecution's Motion for Judicial Notice, *Prosecutor v. Ndahimana*, ICTR-2001-68-PT, T. Ch. III, 7 April 2010, para 5. With references to other case law.

The adoption of a Resolution by the General Assembly of the United Nations is regarded as common knowledge.[188] Under the old Rules of Procedure and Evidence, which did not include Rule 94 (B), an ICTR Trial Chamber took judicial notice of the 'contents of resolutions of the Security Council because it is an organ of the United Nations which established the Tribunal.'[189] This is remarkable because Chambers normally take judicial notice of the adoption, existence or authenticity of documents, without judicially noticing their contents. The Trial Chamber in *Nyiramasuhuko* took judicial notice under Rule 94(A) of the existence and authenticity of documents (certain Rwandan laws) but refused to take judicial notice of the facts contained therein.[190] A similar approach was followed by the Trial Chamber in *Bizimungu*.[191] The Trial Chamber in *Karemera* however, took judicial notice of the existence, authenticity *and* contents of the Rwandan constitution, several domestic laws and the Arusha Accords. It declined to take judicial notice of the interpretation of these legal documents, though.[192]

Since the adoption of Rule 94(B), Chambers can easily judicially notice documents without putting them in the indisputable category of facts of common knowledge.[193]

---

188 ICTY, Judgment, *Prosecutor v. Brđanin*, ICTY-IT-99-36-T, T. Ch. II, 1 September 2004, para 152.

189 ICTR, Decision on the Prosecutor's Motion for Judicial Notice and Presumptions of Fact pursuant to Rules 94 and 54, *Prosecutor v. Semanza*, ICTR-97-20-I, T. Ch. III, 3 November 2000, para 38.

190 ICTR, Decision on the Prosecutor's Motion for Judicial Notice and Admission of Evidence, *Prosecutor v. Nyiramasuhuko*, ICTR-97-21-T, T. Ch. II, 15 May 2002, para 133. Another Chamber declined to take judicial notice of the interpretation of the application of laws. ICTR, Decision on the Prosecutor's Motion for Judicial Notice and Admission of Evidence, *Prosecutor v. Nyiramasuhuko et al.*, ICTR-97-21-T, T. Ch. II, 15 May 2002, para 121.

191 ICTR, Decision on the Prosecutor's Motion for Judicial notice pursuant to Rules 73(A), 94(A) and 89 of the Rules and Article 7 of the Statute, *Prosecutor v. Bizimungu* et al., ICTR-00-56-T, T. Ch. II, 6 December 2005, para 15. Cf. ICTR, Decision on the Prosecutor's Motion for Judicial Notice, *Prosecutor v. Seromba*, ICTR-2001-66-T, T. Ch. III, 14 July 2005, para 18.

192 ICTR, Decision on the Prosecutor's Motion for Judicial Notice, *Prosecutor v. Karemera* et al, ICTR-98-44-T, T. Ch. III, 30 April 2004, para 33. In *Bizimungu*, the Chamber stated that judicially noticing documents under Rule 94(A) is, by definition, impossible because it only applies to facts, not documents. This line of reasoning has not been followed by other Chambers, however. ICTR, Decision on Prosecution's Motion for Judicial Notice pursuant to Rules 73, 89 and 94, *Prosecutor v. Bizimungu*, ICTR-99-50-I, T. Ch. II, 2 December 2003, para 26. In his Dissenting Opinion, Justice Robertson emphasized the different nature of facts of common knowledge and propositions of law. Judicial notice of this latter category may not be taken, because it is for the court to interpret the evidence according to general principles of legal interpretation. SCSL, Fofana – Decision on Appeal Against "Decision on Prosecution's Motion for Judicial Notice and Admission of Evidence", *Prosecutor v. Norman et al.*, SCSL-2004-14-AR73, A. Ch., 16 May 2005, Dissenting Opinion Robertson, p. 6.

193 Rule 94(B) was included in the ICTR RPE on 3 November 2000.

4.3.3.6 Facts of Common Knowledge and the Probandum

In international criminal proceedings, facts of common knowledge have been used to prove significant parts of the *probandum*. Contextual elements of crimes have been established by referring to common knowledge. The most notorious example is found in *Karemera*, in which the prosecution requested the Trial Chamber to take judicial notice of six facts as facts of common knowledge. The most contentious ones were:

> Between 6 April 1994 and 17 July 1994, there was a genocide in Rwanda against the Tutsi ethnic group,
>
> and,
>
> The following state of affairs existed in Rwanda between 6 April 1994 to 17 July 1994: There were throughout Rwanda widespread or systematic attacks against a civilian population based on Tutsi ethnic identification. During the attacks, some Rwandan citizens killed or caused serious bodily or mental harm to person[s] perceived to be Tutsi. As a result of the attacks, there were a large number of deaths of persons of Tutsi ethnic identity.[194]

The Trial Chamber, as other Trial Chambers and the Appeals Chamber had done before, refused to take judicial notice of these facts.[195] The Trial Chamber in *Semanza* held on the request of the prosecutor to judicially notice the Rwandan genocide as common knowledge:

> A fundamental question in this case is whether 'genocide' took place in Rwanda. Notwithstanding the over-abundance of official reports, including United Nations reports confirming the occurrence of genocide, this Chamber believes that the question is so fundamental, that formal proofs should be submitted bearing out the existence of this jurisdictional elemental crime.[196]

---

[194] As cited in: ICTR, Decision on Interlocutory Appeal of Decision on Judicial Notice, *Prosecutor v. Karemera et al.*, ICTR-98-44-AR73(C), A. Ch., 16 June 2006, para 33. The other facts are: 'Between 6 April 1994 and 17 July 1994, citizens native to Rwanda were severally identified according to the following ethnic classifications: Tutsi, Hutu and Twa.'; 'In 1994, Rwanda was a State party to the Genocide Convention of 1948, to the Geneva Convention of 1949, and to the Additional Protocol II of 1977 of the Geneva Conventions.'; 'Between 1 January 1994 and 17 July 1994 in Rwanda there was an armed conflict not of an international character.'

[195] ICTR, Decision on the Prosecutor's Motion for Judicial Notice of Adjudicated Facts, *Prosecutor v. Ntakirutimana and Ntakirutimana*, ICTR-96-10-T and ICTR96-17-T, T. Ch. I, 22 November 2001; ICTR, Decision on the Prosecutor's Motion for Judicial Notice pursuant to Rule 94 of the Rules, *Prosecutor v. Kajelijeli*, ICTR-98-44A-T, T. Ch. II, 16 April 2002; ICTR, Decision on the Prosecutor's Motion for Judicial Notice and Admission of Evidence, *Prosecutor v. Nyiramasuhoko* et al, ICTR-98-42-T, T. Ch. II, 15 May 2002; ICTR, Decision on the Prosecutor's Motion for Judicial Notice pursuant to Rules 73, 89 and 94, *Prosecutor v. Bagosora et al.*, ICTR-98-41-T, T. Ch. III, 11 April 2003.

[196] ICTR, Decision on the Prosecutor's Motion for Judicial Notice and Presumptions of Facts pursuant to Rules 94 and 54, *Prosecutor v. Semanza*, ICTR-97-20-I, T. Ch. III, 3 November 2000, para 36. The Chamber did however take judicial notice of the 'existence of the enumerated acts comprising the crime of genocide as provided in Article 2 and recited in para 3(a) of Appendix A, including killing or causing serious bodily harm to members of a group.'

The Appeals Chamber endorsed this finding.[197] However, the Appeals Chamber in *Karemera*, deciding upon an interlocutory appeal from the prosecution against the Trial Chamber's refusal to take judicial notice of the Rwandan genocide, did take judicial notice of the Rwandan genocide as a 'classic' fact of common knowledge. Notice was also taken of the existence of widespread or systematic attacks on the Tutsi civilian population and of the fact that a non-international armed conflict existed in Rwanda between 1 January 1994 and 17 July 1994. The Appeals Chamber commented on the relationship between facts of common knowledge and components of crimes (the *probandum*). It stated that even if facts of common knowledge are components of crimes, Chambers are obliged to judicially notice them. The ICTR Appeals Chamber held that instead of submitting formal proof to prove the components of the crime, facts of common knowledge may provide for an alternative way to meet the burden of proof:

> Of course the Rule 94(A) mechanism sometimes will alleviate the Prosecution's burden to introduce evidence proving certain aspects of the case. As the Appeals Chamber explained in Semanza, however, it does not change the burden of proof, but simply provides another way for that burden to be met.[198]

In *Semanza*, the Appeals Chamber made a distinction between contextual facts and facts that relate to the criminal responsibility of the accused. Facts that do not touch upon the individual criminal responsibility of the accused can be proven by facts of common knowledge.[199] We may take, for example, an accused facing a charge of murder as a crime against humanity allegedly committed during the genocidal campaign of 1994. The relevant provision in the ICTR Statute reads:

> The International Tribunal for Rwanda shall have the power to prosecute persons responsible for the following crimes when committed as part of a widespread or systematic attack against any civilian population on national, political, ethnic, racial or religious grounds, (a) murder, [...].[200]

Various Chambers, including the Appeals Chamber, took judicial notice of the following facts of common knowledge: 'widespread or systematic attacks based on Tutsi ethnic identification occurred' and 'Rwandan citizens were classified by ethnic group between April 1994 and July 1994'.[201] The *Twa*, *Hutu* and *Tutsi* are

---

197 ICTR, Judgment, *Prosecutor v. Semanza*, ICTR-97-20-A, A. Ch., 20 May 2005, para 192. The Appeals Chamber did also endorse the Trial Chambers' finding that it was common knowledge that widespread and systematic attacks against a Tutsi civilian population occurred and that an armed conflict not of an international character existed.

198 ICTR, Decision on Prosecutor's Interlocutory Appeal of Decision on Judicial Notice, *Prosecutor v. Karemera et al.*, ICTR-98-44-AR73(C), A. Ch., 16 June 2006, para 30. Emphasis added.

199 ICTR, Decision on Motions for Reconsideration, *Prosecutor v. Karemera et al.*, ICTYR-98-44-AR73(C), A. Ch., 1 December 2006, para 16.

200 Article 3 ICTR Statute. Similar provisions are included in the Statutes of the other tribunals.

201 ICTR, Judgment, *Prosecutor v. Semanza*, ICTR-97-20-A, A. Ch., 20 May 2005, para 192.

protected groups under the Genocide Convention, which means that they also constitute a protected group under the ICTR Statute.[202]

What are the consequences of these decisions? First, all the above facts of common knowledge have been identified or endorsed by the Appeals Chamber under Rule 94(A). This means that Trial Chambers are obliged to take judicial notice of them. Second, the *probandum* is proven to a significant extent by facts of common knowledge. The context is regarded as common knowledge, which means that the only components the prosecution has to formally prove are the charge of murder and that the murder is *part* of a widespread or systematic attack; the attack as such has been judicially noticed already. This reduces the burden of proof for the prosecutor and results in indisputable findings: the judicially noticed facts cannot be challenged by the accused.

The same approach was taken in cases concerning genocide and war crimes. As stated earlier, the Appeals Chamber judicially noticed the Rwandan genocide in *Karemera* as a fact of common knowledge. Previously, the Trial Chamber had declined to take judicial notice of this fact, and its reasons for doing so deserve close attention. The Chamber stated:

> As a result, it does not matter whether genocide occurred in Rwanda or not, the Prosecutor must still prove the criminal responsibility of the Accused for the counts he has charged in the Indictment. Taking judicial notice of such a fact as common knowledge does not have any impact on the Prosecution's case against the Accused, because it is not a fact to be proved.[203]

On appeal, the Appeals Chamber stated that whether or not genocide had occurred in Rwanda was of obvious relevance to the prosecutor's case: it is a *necessary*, although not sufficient element that has to be proven.[204] By judicially noticing the Rwandan genocide, relevant context is provided for a better understanding of the accused's individual actions. This 'genocidal context' is not only relevant for accused facing charges of genocide: the nationwide genocidal campaign can also be used to establish the context of other crimes, such as extermination or persecutions as crimes against humanity.[205] It follows that formal proof is only required for the genocidal acts under Article 2 ICTR Statute, including the special intent (*dolus specialis*) necessary for a conviction for genocide. Heller, commenting on the relationship between common knowledge and special intent,

---

[202] The 1948 Genocide Convention protects national, ethnical, racial and religious groups. These correspond with Article 3 ICTR Statute. ICTR, Decision on Prosecution Motion for Judicial Notice, *Prosecutor v. Karemera*, ICTR-98-44-R94, T. Ch. III, 9 November 2005, para 8; ICTR, Decision on Prosecutor's Interlocutory Appeal of Decision on Judicial Notice, *Prosecutor v. Karemera et al.*, ICTR-98-44-AR73(C), A. Ch., 16 June 2006, para 25.

[203] ICTR, Decision on Prosecution Motion for Judicial Notice, *Prosecutor v. Karemera*, ICTR-98-44-R94, T. Ch. III, 9 November 2005, para 7.

[204] ICTR, Decision on Prosecutor's Interlocutory Appeal of Decision on Judicial Notice, *Prosecutor v. Karemera et al.*, ICTR-98-44-AR73(C), A. Ch., 16 June 2006, para 36.

[205] ICTR, Decision on Prosecutor's Interlocutory Appeal of Decision on Judicial Notice, *Prosecutor v. Karemera et al.*, ICTR-98-44-AR73(C), A. Ch., 16 June 2006, para 36.

argued that the *Karemera* decision and the Trial Chamber's judgment in *Akayesu* form a 'potentially lethal pair'. In *Akayesu*, the Trial Chamber held that in the absence of a confession, the accused's intent can be inferred from presumptions of fact. In other words, the special intent can be inferred from the context in which the accused has committed his actions. It is this (genocidal) context of which *Karemera* took judicial notice under Rule 94(A), and this would then result in proving the genocidal intent by inferring it from an indisputable fact of common knowledge.[206] According to Heller, this would amount to 'an unacceptable prejudicial result.'[207] In the *Gatete* judgment, the Trial Chamber reiterated established case law when it stated that:

> In the absence of direct evidence, a perpetrator's intent to commit genocide may be inferred from relevant facts and circumstances that can lead beyond any reasonable doubt to the existence of the intent. Factors that may establish the specific intent include the general context, the perpetration of other culpable acts systematically directed against the same group, the scale of atrocities committed, the systematic targeting of victims on account of their membership in a particular group, or the repetition of destructive and discriminatory acts.[208]

In cases concerning war crimes charges, the existence and nature of the armed conflict is regarded as common knowledge. The ICTR held that a non-international armed conflict existed in Rwanda between 1 January 1994 and 17 July 1994.[209]

In proceedings before the ICTY, the Trial Chamber in *Simić et al.* referred to the Appeals Chamber interlocutory decision in *Tadić* in which the Appeals Chamber held that it would be for each Chamber to determine the existence and character of an armed conflict in the territory of the former Yugoslavia.[210] This does not mean, however, that the Chamber declined to take judicial notice of the existence of an armed conflict in a certain area: judicial notice under Rule 94(B)

---

206 Heller 2007. ICTR, Judgment, *Prosecutor v. Akayesu*, ICTR-96-4-T, T. Ch. I, 2 September 1998, para 523.

207 Heller 2007, p. 162.

208 ICTR, Judgment and Sentence, *Prosecutor v. Gatete*, ICTR-2000-61-T, T. Ch. III, 31 March 2011, para 583. Emphasis added. Similar: ICTR, Judgment and Sentence, *Prosecutor v. Kanyarukiga*, ICTR-2002-78-T, T. Ch. II, 1 November 2002, para 636; ICTR, Judgment and Sentence, *Prosecutor v. Ntawukulilyayo*, ICTR-05-82-T, T. Ch. III, 3 August 2010, para 451. ICTR, Judgment, *Prosecutor v. Seromba*, ICTR-2001-66-A, A. Ch., 12 March 2008, para 176; ICTY, Judgment, *Prosecutor v. Jelisić*, ICTY-IT-95-10-A, A. Ch., 5 July 2001, para 47.

209 ICTR, Judgment, *Prosecutor v. Semanza*, ICTR-97-20-A, A. Ch., 20 May 2005, para 192.

210 ICTY, Decision on the Defence Motion for Interlocutory Appeal on Jurisdiction, *Prosecutor v. Tadić*, ICTY-IT-94-1-AR72, A. Ch., 2 October 1995; ICTY, Decision on the Pre-Trial Motion by the Prosecution Requesting the Trial Chamber to take Judicial Notice of the International Character of the Conflict in Bosnia-Herzegovina, *Prosecutor v. Simić et al.*, ICTY-95-9-PT, T. Ch., 25 March 1999, p. 4.

has been taken of the existence of an armed conflict in a specific area or town.[211] Thus, accused before the ICTY may still present evidence in rebuttal, but accused before the ICTR may not.

4.3.3.7 Submission by the Parties or Proprio Motu?

The provisions on facts of common knowledge state that Chambers do not enjoy discretion when deciding on judicial notice of facts of common knowledge: when a fact is considered common knowledge, judicial notice must be taken. The provisions are silent on the question of whether the Chamber may only take judicial notice at the request of the parties or whether it must take judicial notice *proprio motu*.[212] This differs from Rule 94(B) of the ad hoc Tribunals, according to which judicial notice of adjudicated facts and documentary evidence may be taken either at the request of the parties or by the Chamber itself after hearing the parties. When judicial notice under Rule 94(A) must be taken *proprio motu*, decisions of the Appeals Chamber on common knowledge must, when the facts are relevant for the case, be judicially noticed in future proceedings. The major difference is that judicial notice *proprio motu* under Rule 94(B) requires the Chamber to hear the parties, whereas Rule 94(A) does not. In *Simić et al.*, the Trial Chamber did not take judicial notice of the international character of the armed conflict in Bosnia and Herzegovina, but it did take judicial notice *proprio motu* under Rule 94(A) of the date of independence of Bosnia and Herzegovina and its recognition by the European Community.[213] The prosecution had not requested the Trial Chamber to do so, which means that the defence in its response did not comment on these facts but concentrated on the character of the armed conflict.[214] The facts of common knowledge, therefore, were not discussed in court.[215]

---

[211] E.g.: ICTY, Decision on Prosecution Motion for Judicial Notice of Adjudicated Facts and for Admission of Written Statements of Witnesses pursuant to Rule 92bis, *Prosecutor v. Krajišnik*, ICTY-IT-00-39-PT, T. Ch. I., 28 February 2003; ICTY, Prosecution's Motion for Judicial Notice of Adjudicated Facts, *Prosecutor v. Krajišnik*, ICTY-IT-00-39-PT, T. Ch. I., 7 November 2002, fact 150. Judicial notice was taken of: 'On 8 April 1992, an armed conflict broke out in Foca town, mirroring events unfolding in other municipalities.'

[212] In the majority of cases, it is the prosecution that files a motion for judicial notice. A rare example of a defence motion regarding judicial notice under Rule 94(A): ICTR, Decision on Defence Motion for the Trial Chamber to take Judicial Notice of the Value of the Rwandan Currency, *Prosecutor v. Nshogoza*, ICTR-07-91-T, T. Ch. III, 16 April 2009.

[213] ICTY, Decision on the Pre-trial Motion by the Prosecution requesting the Trial Chamber to take Judicial Notice of the International Character of the Conflict in Bosnia-Herzegovina, *Prosecutor v. Simić* et al., ICTY-IT-95-9-PT, T. Ch., 25 March 1999, p. 5.

[214] ICTY, Defense Response to pre-Trial Motion by the Prosecution requesting the Trial Chamber to take Judicial Notice of the International Character of the Conflict in Bosnia-Herzegovina, *Prosecutor v. Simić et al.*, ICTY-IT-95-9-PT, T. Ch., 3 February 1999; ICTY, Pre-Trial Motion by the Prosecution requesting the Trial Chamber to take Judicial Notice of the International Character of the Conflict in Bosnia-Herzegovina, *Prosecutor v. Simić et al.*, ICTY-IT-95-9-PT, T. Ch., 16 December 1998.

[215] Cf. Morgan 1943–1944, p. 294.

In earlier decisions in *Stanišić*, *Prlić et al.* and in the Dissenting Opinion of Judge Hunt in *Milošević*, it was held that the onus rests upon the prosecution to establish that a proposed fact of common knowledge is not subject to reasonable dispute.[216] This has the advantage that when the prosecution provides reasons for its request, it gives the defence the opportunity to respond. In *Dragomir Milošević*, the Trial Chamber first determined whether any of the proposed facts should be judicially noticed under Rule 94(A), although no request towards that end was made.[217] Thus, Chambers have the authority to judicially notice facts of common knowledge *proprio motu*, notwithstanding a Rule 94(B) motion.

Article 69(6) ICC Statute allows the Court to take judicial notice of facts of common knowledge. The wording suggests that a Chamber may take judicial notice *proprio motu*, without hearing the parties. In practice, however, it seems that parties are invited to submit proposed facts of common knowledge to the Chamber, which are, preferably, also agreed upon by the prosecution and defence.[218] Although the wording of Article 69(6) is a bit ambiguous ('The Chamber *shall* not require proof of facts of common knowledge but *may* take judicial notice of them.'), the ICC Chambers will not require proof of such facts.

4.3.3.8 Judicial Notice and Appeal Proceedings

Unlike motions on appeal concerning the admissibility of evidence in general, interlocutory motions concerning facts of common knowledge are subject to de novo review at the ad hoc Tribunals.[219] Determining whether a fact is of common knowledge is a legal question. This means that the Appeals Chamber can fully review the Trial Chamber's decision.[220] When the Appeals Chamber has decided

[216] ICTY, Decision on Judicial Notice, *Prosecutor v. Stanišić*, ICTY-IT-04-79-PT, T. Ch. II, 14 December 2007, para 12; ICTY, Decision on "Prosecution motion for Judicial Notice of Facts of Common Knowledge and Admission of Documentary Evidence pursuant to Rules 94(A) and 89(C)", *Prosecutor v. Prlić* et al., ICTY-IT-04-74-PT, T. Ch. II, 3 February 2006, p. 6; ICTY, Dissenting Opinion of Judge Hunt to Decision on the Prosecution's Interlocutory Appeal Against the Trial Chamber's 10 April 2003 Decision on Prosecution Motion for Judicial Notice of Adjudicated Facts, *Prosecutor v. Milošević*, ICTY-IT-02-54-AR73.5, A. Ch., 28 October 2003, para 11.

[217] ICTY, Decision on Prosecution's Motion for Judicial Notice of Adjudicated Facts and Prosecution's Catalogue of Agreed Facts with Dissenting Opinion of Judge Harhoff, *Prosecutor v. Milošević*, ICTY-IT-98-29/1-T, T. Ch. III, 10 April 2007, para 25.

[218] ICC, Order Instructing the Participants and the Registry to Respond to Questions of Trial Chamber II for the Purpose of the Status Conference (Article 64(3)(a) of the Statute), *Prosecutor v. Katanga and Ngudjolo*, ICC-01/04-01/07, T. Ch. II, 13 November 2008, p. 9.

[219] Interlocutory appeals are subject to leave by the Trial Chamber (Rule 72(B) ICTY RPE; Rule 73(B) ICTR RPE; Article 82(1)(d) ICC Statute). No interlocutory appeals have been lodged at the ICC regarding facts of common knowledge.

[220] ICTR, Decision on Prosecutor's Interlocutory Appeal of Decision on Judicial Notice, *Prosecutor v. Karemera et al.*, ICTR-98-44-AR73(C), A. Ch., 16 June 2006, para 23.

that a particular fact is of common knowledge, Trial Chambers are bound by this decision, provided the fact is relevant for the proceedings.

4.3.4 Judicial Notice of Adjudicated Facts and Documentary Evidence

4.3.4.1 Introduction

Taking judicial notice of adjudicated facts and documentary evidence has become an important mechanism in international criminal proceedings to speed up trials. Although the concept is rooted in domestic practice, the manner in which the ad hoc Tribunals have relied upon this shortcut to proof is without precedent. The ICTR Trial Chamber in *Ntakirutimana* held that 'facts of common knowledge and adjudicated facts constitute different, albeit possibly overlapping, categories: a fact of common knowledge is not necessarily an adjudicated fact, and vice versa.'[221] Although these categories are indeed related, it will be shown that judicial notice of adjudicated facts and documentary evidence has distinctive features that must be clearly distinguished from facts of common knowledge.

When a Chamber takes judicial notice of an adjudicated fact or documentary evidence, it 'imports' the factual conclusions of another Chamber into the proceedings: the judicially noticed facts are presumed to be correct, and no evidence has to be presented to establish these facts. Although evidence in rebuttal is admissible, judicial notice provides for an important shortcut to proof: when no evidence in rebuttal is presented, the judicially noticed fact is normally conclusively established.

4.3.4.2 Legal Framework

The Rules of Procedure and Evidence of the ad hoc Tribunals allow Chambers to judicially notice both adjudicated facts and documentary evidence.[222] Rule 94(B) ICTY RPE explicitly states that judicial notice can only be taken of the authenticity of the documents.[223] Besides documentary evidence, judicial notice can be

---

[221] ICTR, Decision on the Prosecutor's Motion for Judicial Notice of Adjudicated Facts, *Prosecutor v. Ntakirutimana and Ntakirutimana*, ICTR-96-10-T and ICTR-96-17-T, T. Ch. I, 22 November 2001, para 25.

[222] Rule 94(B) ICTY RPE; Rule 94(B) ICTR RPE. Sub-rule 94 (B) was adopted by the ICTY judges in the revised Rules of Procedure and Evidence of 9 and 10 July 1998. Not surprisingly, it was envisaged by the judges that this rule would expedite proceedings. Cf. 1998 Annual report by the President of the ICTY submitted to the UN Security Council and General Assembly, A/53/219, S/1998/317, 10 August 1998, pp. 28–29. Kwon 2007, pp. 360–376. Sub-rule 94 (B) was adopted by the ICTR judges on 3 November 2000.

[223] Rule 94(B) ICTY RPE.

taken of adjudicated facts from other proceedings before the ad hoc Tribunals. The legal framework of the ICC does not provide for taking judicial notice of adjudicated facts and documentary evidence. The following analysis is therefore based on the case law of the ad hoc Tribunals.

4.3.4.3 Rationale for Judicial Notice of Adjudicated Facts and Documentary Evidence

The most prominent reason to take judicial notice is to enhance judicial economy and to deliver uniform judgments.[224] Stewart observed that 'the scope of judicial notice is much broader in a specialist jurisdiction specifically established to try a small range or offences within a limited geographical and temporal sphere.'[225] This holds true for the ad hoc Tribunals, which have a limited temporal and geographical jurisdiction. This may explain why the Statute and Rules of Procedure and Evidence of the ICC provide solely for judicial notice of facts of common knowledge: it is unlikely that large numbers of accused will face charges concerning the same crime base.

The objective of providing an authoritative and just historical record favours taking judicial notice of large numbers of adjudicated facts. The Appeals Chamber in *Karemera* has ruled, however, that the aim of creating uniform case law cannot weigh against the right of the accused to present evidence in rebuttal on judicially noticed facts.[226]

Closely related to the aim of promoting judicial economy is the concentration on the contested issues of the case: the Chamber should not be concerned with those matters that are either indisputable, previously adjudicated or agreed upon by the parties: the sooner the Chamber can concentrate on the disputed issues of the case, the better. From the perspective of the victims, judicial notice prevents witnesses from re-traumatization by avoiding the need for them to give testimony over and over again regarding traumatic events.[227]

---

224 E.g. ICTY, Decision on Appellant's Motion for Judicial Notice, *Prosecutor v. Nikolić*, ICTY-IT-02-60/1-A, A. Ch., 1 April 2005, para 12. ICTR, Decision on Prosecutor's Interlocutory Appeal of Decision on Judicial Notice, *Prosecutor v. Karemera* et al., ICTR-98-44-AR73(C), A. Ch., 16 June 2006, para 39. SCSL, Decision on Defence Application for Judicial Notice of Adjudicated Facts from the RUF Trial Judgment Pursuant to Rule 94(B) and Prosecution Motion for Judicial Notice of Adjudicated Facts from the RUF Judgment', *Prosecutor v. Taylor*, SCSL-03-1-T, T. Ch. II, 17 June 2010, para 26.

225 Stewart 2003, p. 246.

226 ICTR, Decision on Joseph Nzirorera's Appeal of Decision on Admission of Evidence Rebutting Adjudicated Facts, *Prosecutor v. Karemera* et al., ICTR-98-44-AR73.17, A. Ch., 29 May 2009, para 21.

227 ICTY, Decision on the Prosecution's Motion for Judicial Notice of Adjudicated Facts and Prosecution's Catalogue of Agreed Facts with Dissenting Opinion of Judge Harhoff, *Prosecutor v. Milošević*, ICTY-IT-98-29/1-T, T. Ch. III, 10 April 2007, Dissenting Opinion Harhoff, para 5.

4.3.4.4 Probative Value of Adjudicated Facts and Documentary Evidence

Before turning to the probative value of facts under Rule 94(B), it is important to first refer to consistent case law on the admission and probative value of evidence in general. All evidence must comply with the admissibility criteria of Rule 89(C): the evidence must be relevant to the case and have some probative value. The Appeals Chamber held that the doctrine of judicial notice may not be used to circumvent the criteria of Rule 89(C).[228]

Since the 2003 judicial notice decision by the Appeals Chamber in *Milošević*, Chambers have consistently held that the probative value of judicially noticed facts is the establishment of 'a well-founded presumption for the accuracy of this fact, which therefore does not have to be proven again at trial, but which, subject to that presumption, may be challenged at that trial.'[229] Judicially noticed facts are presumed to be correct: it is not necessary that they are undisputed by the parties. The status of judicially noticed facts, as far as their probative value is concerned, deviates from the general evidentiary regime, where it remains entirely within the Chamber's discretion to determine the probative value of each piece of evidence after the close of proceedings. In his Dissenting Opinion to an interlocutory decision in *Milošević*, Judge Hunt advocated a concept of judicial notice of adjudicated facts that is similar to the concept of judicial notice of facts of common knowledge:

> When Rule 94(B) was added, it used the same expression 'judicial notice' as Rule 94(A) had used. Judicial notice was therefore clearly intended to mean the same thing in both paragraphs, that the fact in question is not the subject of reasonable dispute, and thus evidence to establish it is unnecessary.[230]

It follows that evidence to rebut the judicially noticed fact must be declared inadmissible. In his Separate Opinion to the same Appeals Chamber decision, Judge Shahabuddeen argued in favour of a right of presenting evidence in rebuttal: if such a right would not exist, it would infringe upon the presumption of innocence. This infringement would be the result of the impossibility of the parties to

---

[228] ICTR, Judgment, *Prosecutor v. Semanza*, ICTR-97-20-A, A. Ch., 20 May 2005, para 189.

[229] ICTY, Decision on the Prosecution's Interlocutory Appeal Against the Trial Chamber's 10 April 2003 Decision on prosecution Motion for Judicial Notice of Adjudicated Facts, *Prosecutor v. Milošević*, ICTY-IT-02-54-AR73.5, A. Ch., 28 October 2003, p. 4.; ICTR, Decision on Prosecutor's Interlocutory Appeal of Decision on Judicial Notice, *Prosecutor v. Karemera* et al., ICTR-98-44-AR73(C), A. Ch., 16 June 2006, para 42.

[230] ICTY, Dissenting Opinion of Judge David Hunt to the Decision on the Prosecution's Interlocutory Appeal against the Trial Chamber's 10 April 2003 Decision on Prosecution Motion for Judicial Notice of Adjudicated Facts, *Prosecutor v. Milošević*, ICTY-IT-02-54-AR73.5, A. Ch., 28 October 2003, para 8.

dispute evidence that has been conclusively established in another case.[231] According to Shahabuddeen, the ultimate probative value of a fact judicially noticed under Rule 94(B) depends on whether one of the parties wishes to present evidence in rebuttal:

> it appears that the taking of judicial notice of an adjudicated fact creates, if not a presumption, something like a presumption, in that the court must draw an inference that the adjudicated fact judicially noticed is accurate – but only unless and until rebutted.[232]

Judicial notice as envisaged by Hunt has the major advantage that as soon as the court has taken judicial notice of a proposed fact, the probative value of the particular fact is clear: conclusive and not open to evidence in rebuttal. Shahabuddeen more or less leaves it to the non-moving party to rebut the judicially noticed fact. This party-driven approach entails that when evidence in rebuttal is not presented, the fact that was presumed accurate during proceedings *becomes* conclusive evidence after the close of proceedings. In the Trial Chamber's judgment in *Krajišnik*, for example, it remained unclear whether the Chamber regarded the hundreds of judicially noticed facts as conclusive evidence because the defence did not rebut these facts, or because the Chamber assessed their probative value in the context of all the evidence received and made a determination of the probative value itself.[233]

However, the Trial Chamber in *Popović et al.*, recalling the probative value of facts under Rule 94(B), did state that after the close of proceedings, judicially noticed facts are still to be assessed in the light of all the evidence, particularly evidence in rebuttal brought by the non-moving party.[234] When such evidence in rebuttal is absent, the Chamber must still assess the weight of the well-founded presumption. If the Chamber concludes that the judicially noticed fact, 'taking into consideration the totality of the trial record', has probative value the fact is regarded as conclusive evidence. It transpires from the reasoning of the Trial Chamber in *Hadzihasanovic* that facts relating to the historical, political or

---

[231] ICTY, Separate Opinion of Judge Shahabuddeen Appended to the Appeals Chamber's Decision Dated 28 October 2003 on the Prosecution's Interlocutory Appeal Against the Trial Chamber's 10 April 2003 Decision on Prosecution Motion for Judicial Notice of Adjudicated Facts, *Prosecutor v. Milošević*, ICTY-IT-02-54-AR73.5, A. Ch., 31 October 2003, paras 13–14.

[232] ICTY, Separate Opinion of Judge Shahabuddeen Appended to the Appeals Chamber's Decision Dated 28 October 2003 on the Prosecution's Interlocutory Appeal Against the Trial Chamber's 10 April 2003 Decision on Prosecution Motion for Judicial Notice of Adjudicated Facts, *Prosecutor v. Milošević*, ICTY-IT-02-54-AR73.5, A. Ch., 31 October 2003, para 21.

[233] ICTY, Judgment, *Prosecutor v. Krajišnik,*ICTY-IT-00-39-T, T. Ch. I, 27 September 2006, para 1197: 'The Chamber took judicial notice of a number of adjudicated facts pursuant to Rule 94(B). Adjudicated facts admitted into evidence are presumed to be accurate and do not need to be proven again at trial. However, the opposing party may bring evidence to disprove them. Thus, the Chamber has carefully evaluated adjudicated facts in this case in light of all the evidence received.'

[234] ICTY, Judgment, *Prosecutor v. Popović* et al., ICTY-IT-0588-T, T. Ch. II, 10 June 2010, para 71.

military context are fairly easily admitted under Rule 94(B), but the probative value the Chamber adheres to such facts remains within the Chamber's discretion.[235] This results in a system of free admission of evidence, whereby the probative value of the admitted evidence is assessed after the close of proceedings.[236] This seems inconsistent with the specific probative value the Appeals Chamber attaches to facts judicially noticed under Rule 94(B). Assessing the ultimate probative value of the judicially noticed facts against the background of the entire evidentiary record is, however, consistent with the holistic approach to the weighing of evidence of the Chambers. Particular pieces of evidence will be weighed against the backdrop of the entire record.

4.3.4.5 Documentary Evidence

The probative value of judicially noticed documentary evidence deserves some distinct attention. The Trial Chamber in *Milošević*, referring to *Milutinović*, stated that 'the legal effect of judicially noticing documentary evidence is to admit the documents into evidence and to use them for their contents and not merely for their existence and authenticity'.[237] Moreover, the Trial Chamber attached the same probative value to judicially noticed documents as to judicially noticed facts.[238]

In December 2010, the judges of the ICTY amended Rule 94(B): judicial notice of documentary evidence entails that judicial notice of the *authenticity* of the document is taken and not of its contents.[239] Prior to the amendment, judicial notice was sometimes taken of both the authenticity and reliability of the document.[240] Reliability, however, must be discerned from the probative value the Chamber

[235] ICTY, Final Decision on Judicial Notice of Adjudicated Facts, *Prosecutor v. Hadžihasanović and Kubura*, ICTY-IT-01-47-T, T. Ch. II, 20 April 2004; ICTY, Judgment, *Prosecutor v. Hadžihasanović and Kubura*, ICTY-IT-01-47-T, T. Ch. II, para 288.

[236] Cf. ICTY, Judgment, *Prosecutor v. Orić*, ICTY-IT-03-68-T, T. Ch. II, 30 June 2006, para 14. Nerenberg and Timmermann 2011, pp. 450–451.

[237] ICTY, Decision on Prosecution's Motion for Admission of Documentary Evidence Pursuant to Rule 89(C) and Rule 94(B) of the Rules, *Prosecutor v. Milošević*, ICTY-IT-98-29/1-T, T. Ch. III, 24 January 2007, p. 3.

[238] ICTY, Decision on Prosecution's Motion for Admission of Documentary Evidence Pursuant to Rule 89(C) and Rule 94(B) of the Rules, *Prosecutor v. Milošević*, ICTY-IT-98-29/1-T, T. Ch. III, 24 January 2007, p. 3. ICTY, Decision on Prosecution Motion to admit Documentary Evidence, *Prosecutor v. Milutinović* et al., ICTY-IT-05-87-T, T. Ch., 10 October 2006, para 31.

[239] Amendment of 8 December 2010. Article 15 of the ICTY Statute states that the judges shall adopt rules of procedure and evidence.

[240] ICTY, Decision on the Prosecution's First motion for Judicial Notice of Documentary Evidence Related to the Sarajevo Component, *Prosecutor v. Karadžić*, ICTY-IT-95-5/18-T, T. Ch., 31 March 2010, para 11.

ultimately attaches to the document. It seems that this criterion does not add anything substantial to the general requirements of relevance and probative value of Rule 89(C).[241]

At the ICTR, no amendment to Rule 94(B) has been made, but it is established case law that judicial notice of documentary evidence only involves the authenticity and existence of the document, unless specifically stated otherwise.[242] The existence and authenticity of documents stemming from organs of the United Nations, for example, do not require proof.[243] The authenticity of documents is assessed by verifying the source and chain of custody of the document: in whose possession was the document before it was tendered into evidence?[244]

4.3.4.6 Identifying Adjudicated Facts

Over the years, Trial Chambers have formulated requirements that must be fulfilled before a Chamber may take judicial notice. In *Karadžić* the Trial Chamber listed the requirements for adjudicated facts:

(a) The fact must be relevant to the current proceedings;
(b) The fact must be distinct, concrete, and identifiable;
(c) The fact, as formulated by the moving party, must not differ in any substantial way from the formulation of the original judgment;
(d) The fact must not be unclear or misleading in the context in which it is placed in the moving party's motion. In addition, the fact must be denied judicial notice "if it will become unclear or misleading because one or more of the surrounding pur-ported facts will be denied judicial notice";
(e) The fact must be identified with adequate precision by the moving party;
(f) The fact must not contain characterizations of findings of an essentially legal nature;
(g) The fact must not be based on an agreement between the parties to the original proceedings;
(h) The fact must not relate to the acts, conduct, or mental state of the accused; and
(i) The fact must clearly not be subject to pending appeal or review.[245]

---

241 ICTY, Decision on Prosecution Motions for Judicial Notice of Documents Pursuant to Rule 94(B), *Prosecutor v. Šešelj*, ICTY-IT-03-67-T, T. Ch. III, 16 June 2008, para 27.

242 E.g., ICTR, Decision on Prosecution's Motion for Judicial Notice Pursuant to Rules 73, 89 and 94, *Prosecutor v. Bizimungu* et al., ICTR-99-50-I, T. Ch. II, 2 December 2003, paras 32–44. ICTR, Decision on the Prosecutor's Motion for Judicial Notice and Presumptions of Facts pursuant to Rules 94 and 54, *Prosecutor v. Semanza*, ICTR-97-20-I, T. Ch. III, 3 November 2000, para 38. The Trial Chamber stated that besides judicially noticing the existence and authenticity of the documents (Security Council Resolutions and statements by the President of that council) it also took judicial notice of its contents, because the Security Council is a UN organ that established the Tribunal.

243 ICTR, Decision on Prosecution's Motion for Judicial Notice pursuant to Rules 73, 89 and 94, *Prosecutor v. Bizimungu* et al., ICTR-99-50-I, T. Ch. II, 2 December 2003, para 39.

244 ICTY, Judgment, *Prosecutor v. Blagojević and Jokić*, ICTY-IT-02-60-T, T. Ch. I., 17 January 2005, para 29.

245 ICTY, Decision on Accused's Motion for Judicial Notice of Adjudicated Facts Related to Count One, *Prosecutor v. Karadžić*, Case No.: IT-95-5/18-T, T. Ch., 21 January 2014, para 6.

Judicial notice may still be denied, however, when taking judicial notice would not be in the interest of justice. When discussing judicial notice of adjudicated facts, it is useful to distinguish between admissibility requirements and the discretionary power of the Chamber. The requirements summed up above are concerned with admissibility: is the proposed fact truly adjudicated and does it not relate to the individual criminal responsibility of the accused? If all these criteria have been met, it still remains within the Chamber's discretion to deny judicial notice.[246] The criteria emphasize that every proposed fact must have been contested during the previous proceedings, which is the reason why facts contained in plea agreements or agreements of fact cannot be judicially noticed under Rule 94(B). A fact is considered an agreed fact:

> where the structure of the relevant footnote in the original judgment cites the agreed facts between the parties as a primary source of authority. If a Trial Chamber cannot readily determine, by examining the citations in the original judgment, that the fact was not based on an agreement between the parties, it must refrain from taking judicial notice of the fact.[247]

Chambers have to make sure that facts contained in judgments are indeed adjudicated facts and not the summing up of witness statements: it needs to be considered whether the Chamber accepted the fact as evidence and 'made its findings in accordance with it.'[248]

It follows that proposed facts may not be under appeal or review because only facts that have been settled conclusively are eligible for judicial notice. Although facts must have been contested at least once, problems may arise when an accused in the original proceedings only marginally contested a fact because it was of minor relevance for his case. When the fact is of great relevance for the case of another accused in later proceedings, it is questionable whether the fact was really contested during the original proceedings and eligible for judicial notice.[249]

---

[246] This includes both the Trial and Appeals Chamber. Rule 107 of the ICTY RPE: 'The rules of procedure and evidence that govern proceedings in the Trial Chambers shall apply *mutatis mutandis* to proceedings in the Appeals Chamber.' Cf. ICTY, Decision on the Motions of Drago Josipovic, Zoran Kupreškić and Vlatko Kupreškić to Admit Additional Evidence Pursuant to Rule 115 and for Judicial Notice to be Taken Pursuant to Rule 94(B), *Prosecutor v. Kupreškić et al.*, ICTY-IT-95-16-A, A. Ch., 8 May 2001, para 6. The Appeals Chamber did, however, limit the scope of Rule 94(B) in this decision. It stated that, before taking judicial notice, it must have received a request from a party. This seems to contradict the plain wording of Rule 94(B) that allows Chambers to take judicial notice *proprio motu*.

[247] ICTY, Decision Granting in Part Prosecution's Motions for Judicial Notice of Adjudicated Facts Pursuant to Rule 94(B), *Prosecutor v. Stanišić and Župljanin*, ICTY-IT-08-91-T, T. Ch. II, 1 April 2010, para 38.

[248] ICTY, Decision Partially Granting Motion of Mićo Stanišić for Judicial Notice of Adjudicated Facts, *Prosecutor v. Stanišić and Župljanin*, ICTY-IT-08-91-T, T. Ch. II, 29 June 2011, para 5.

[249] As the Appeals Chamber stated in *Karemera*: 'there is reason to be particularly skeptical of facts adjudicated in other cases when they bear specifically on the on the actions, omissions, or mental state of an individual not on trial in those cases as the defendants in those other cases would have had significantly less incentive to contest those facts than they would facts related to their own actions; indeed, in some cases such defendants might affirmatively choose to allow blame to fall on another.' ICTR, Decision on Prosecutor's Interlocutory Appeal of Decision on Judicial Notice, *Prosecutor v. Karemera*, ICTR-98-44-AR73(C), A. Ch., 16 June 2006, para 51.

Judicially noticed facts may not go to the acts, conduct or mental state of the accused, which diminishes the danger of infecting the evidentiary record with matters that were only marginally contested. Within the context of Rule 92*bis*, the Trial Chamber in *Slobodan Milošević* held that acts and conduct of the accused is a 'plain expression and should be given its ordinary meaning: deeds and behavior of the accused.'[250] The Appeals Chamber in *Galić* distinguished, also within the context of Rule 92*bis*, between:

> (a) the acts and conduct of those others who commit the crimes for which the indictment alleges that the accused is individually responsible, and (b) the acts and conduct of the accused as charged in the indictment which establish his responsibility for the acts and conduct of those others.[251]

The latter category concerns the 'real' acts and conduct of the accused of which no judicial notice can be taken. The above decisions concern Rule 92*bis*, but they are applicable to Rule 94(B) as well: both Rules aim to tender into evidence those facts that provide the background for the accused's actions. Neither Rule was intended to facilitate the prosecutor in proving the individual criminal responsibility of the accused.

Facts contained in judgments under appeal may still be eligible if the appeal does not touch upon the accuracy of those particular facts. When the appeal is solely concerned with sentencing, for example, the factual basis is not subject to appeal. The Trial Chamber in *Delić*, however, declined to take judicial notice of any fact deriving from the trial judgment in *Hadžihasanović* (delivered by another Chamber) because the defence of the accused Hadžihasanović had filed an appeal challenging the 'methodology of the conduct of the trial.'[252] The defence argued that by systematically questioning witnesses, the Trial Chamber had erred in law and gave the impression of partiality. Without commenting on the merits of this argument, the *Delič* Trial Chamber concluded that if the Appeals Chamber would find merit in the submissions of the defence, it would render the whole trial judgment unsafe, including any factual conclusion. Therefore, no judicial notice of any fact from the *Hadžihasanović* judgment could be taken.[253]

---

[250] ICTY, Decision on Prosecution Motion for the Admission of Transcripts in Lieu of *viva voce* Testimony pursuant to Rule 92*bis*(D)—Foča Transcripts, *Prosecutor v. Slobodan Milošević*, ICTY-IT-02-54-T, T. Ch., 30 June 2003, para 11.

[251] ICTY, Decision on Interlocutory Appeal Concerning Rule 92*bis* (C), *Prosecutor v. Galić*, ICTY-IT-98-29-AR73.2, A. Ch., 7 June 2002, para 9.

[252] ICTY, Decision on Prosecution's Motion for Judicial Notice of Adjudicated Facts and Joint Motion Concerning Agreed Facts, *Prosecutor v. Delić*, ICTY-IT-04-83-PT, T. Ch. I, 9 July 2007, para 13.

[253] ICTY, Decision on Prosecution's Motion for Judicial Notice of Adjudicated Facts and Joint Motion Concerning Agreed Facts, *Prosecutor v. Delić*, ICTY-IT-04-83-PT, T. Ch. I, 9 July 2007, para 14.

According to *Karemera*, adjudicated facts do not have to be beyond reasonable dispute.[254] This enhances the adversarial character of proceedings: the judicially noticed fact remains rebuttable during proceedings, even if the fact was conclusive evidence in the original proceedings.[255]

An important question is whether judicial notice can be taken of facts that are disputed by the non-moving party. Chambers are obliged to hear parties on motions requesting judicial notice. It is not necessary that the parties agree on the proposed fact, and if one party objects, the Chamber may still take judicial notice.[256] The fact that agreement is not necessary also follows from the possibility to present evidence in rebuttal. Unlike other Trial Chambers, the Chamber in Šešelj stated that judicial notice may only be taken when the proposed fact cannot reasonably be contested by the opposing party.[257] This runs counter to the principle that facts judicially noticed under Rule 94(B) are rebuttable. If the Trial Chamber finds, a priori, that a judicially noticed fact cannot be contested, then judicial notice under Rule 94(B) would result in the same probative value as judicial notice under Rule 94(A): conclusive, instead of rebuttable evidence. Considering the consistent case law on the requirements of Rule 94(B), it is not a prerequisite for judicial notice that the non-moving party cannot reasonably contest the judicially noticed fact. The Trial Chamber in Šešelj erred in this respect.

4.3.4.7 Discretionary Power

When the admissibility requirements are met, Chambers still enjoy discretion to deny judicial notice. It will be denied if it is in the interests of justice to do so, in particular when taking judicial notice would not comply with the rights of the accused to a fair and expeditious trial.[258] The Trial Chamber in *Popović et al.*

---

[254] ICTR, Decision on Prosecutor's Interlocutory Appeal of Decision on Judicial Notice, *Prosecutor v. Karemera*, ICTR-98-44-AR73(C), A. Ch., 16 June 2006, para 40.

[255] Cf. ICTY, Decision on Prosecution Motion for Judicial Notice Pursuant to Rule 94(B), *Prosecutor v. Mejakić et al.*, ICTY-IT-02-65-PT, T. Ch., 1 April 2004. The Trial Chamber stated explicitly that the facts judicially noticed pursuant to Rule 94(B) are subject to evidence in rebuttal.

[256] ICTY, Decision on Prosecution's Motion for Judicial Notice of Adjudicated Facts and Documentary Evidence, *Prosecutor v. Blagojević and Jokić*, ICTY-IT-02-60-T, T. Ch. I, 19 December 2003 para 15.

[257] Cf. ICTY, Decision on Fourth Prosecution Motion for Judicial Notice of Adjudicated Facts, *Prosecutor v. Karadžić*, ICTY-IT-95-5/18-T, T. Ch., 14 June 2010, para 16; ICTY, Decision on Prosecution Motion for Judicial Notice of Adjudicated Facts Pursuant to Rule 94(B), *Prosecutor v. Tolimir*, ICTY-IT-05-898/2-PT, T. Ch. III, 17 December 2009, para 8; ICTY, Decision on Third and Fourth Prosecution Motions for Judicial Notice of Adjudicated Facts, *Prosecutor v. Krajišnik*, ICTY-IT-00-39-T, T. Ch. I, 24 March 2005, para 14; ICTY, Decision on Prosecution's Motion for Judicial Notice of Adjudicated Facts, *Prosecutor v. Stanišić and Simatović*, ICTY-IT-03-69-T, T. Ch. I., 25 November 2009, para 27.

[258] E.g., ICTR, Decision on the Prosecutor's Motion for Judicial Notice of Adjudicated Facts, *Prosecutor v. Ntakirutimana and Ntakirutimana*, ICTR-96-10-T and ICTR-96-17-T, T. Ch. I, 22 November 2001, para 28.

refused to take judicial notice of a number of facts on the basis of its discretionary power. The overarching consideration of the Chamber was whether taking judicial notice would indeed enhance judicial economy while preserving the fair trial rights of the accused. Attention must be paid to the volume and type of evidence the accused is expected to produce if he wishes to challenge a judicially noticed fact: if it is likely that an accused will challenge a judicially noticed fact, judicial economy will not be served.[259] On the contrary, it might even take more time to present evidence in rebuttal. It is then in the interest of justice to deny judicial notice, despite the fact that all admissibility requirements are fulfilled. Trial Chambers have taken judicial notice of thousands of facts, resulting in a significant burden for the accused to present evidence in rebuttal if he wishes to do so.[260] In *Krajišnik*, the Trial Chamber warned the prosecution that large numbers of facts that refer to 'highly detailed descriptions of minor incidents' might result in a unmanageable quantity of judicially noticed facts.[261]

If an accused objects to judicial notice and announces to present evidence in rebuttal, the Chamber may decide to refuse judicial notice: presenting evidence in rebuttal will take considerable time, thereby nullifying the aim of promoting judicial economy.[262] In *Mejakić*, the Chamber, in its discretion, denied judicial notice of facts that are 'too broad, too tendentious, not sufficiently significant, too detailed, too numerous, repetitive of other evidence already admitted by the Chamber or not sufficiently relevant to the case.'[263] Some of these categories (relevance, too broad, too tendentious) are reminiscent of the admissibility criteria,

259 ICTY, Decision on Prosecution Motion for Judicial Notice of Adjudicated Facts with Annex, *Prosecutor v. Popović et al.*, ICTY-IT-05-88-T, T. Ch. II, 26 September 2006, para 16.

260 E.g. ICTY, Decision on Prosecution Motion for Judicial Notice of Adjudicated Facts Pursuant to Rule 94(B), *Prosecutor v. Tolimir*, Case No. IT-05-88/2-PT, 17 December 2009 (judicial notice was taken of over 500 facts); ICTY, Decision Granting in Part Prosecution's Motions for Judicial Notice of Adjudicated Facts Pursuant to Rule 94(B), *Prosecutor v. Stanišić and Župljanin*, Case No. IT-08-91-T, T. Ch. II, 1 April 2010 (judicial notice was taken of over 1000 facts); ICTY, Decision on First Prosecution Motion for Judicial Notice of Adjudicated Facts, 5 June 2009; Decision on Second Motion for Judicial Notice of Adjudicated Facts, 9 October 2009; Decision on Third Prosecution Motion for Judicial Notice of Adjudicated Facts, 9 July 2009; Decision on Fourth Prosecution Motion for Judicial Notice of Adjudicated Facts, 14 June 2009; Decision on Fifth Prosecution Motion for Judicial Notice of Adjudicated Facts, *Prosecutor v. Karadžić*, Case No. IT-95-5-/18-T, T. Ch. III, 14 June 2010. In these five decisions, the Trial Chamber took judicial notice of over 2400 facts.

261 ICTY, Decision on Third and Fourth Prosecution Motions for Judicial Notice of Adjudicated Facts, *Prosecutor v. Krajišnik*, ICTY-IT-00-39-T, T. Ch. I, 24 March 2005, para 22.

262 ICTY, Decision on Prosecution's Motion for Judicial Notice of Adjudicated Facts Pursuant to Rule 94(B), *Prosecutor v. Tolimir*, ICTY-IT-05-88/2-PT, T. Ch. II, 17 December 2009, para 32.

263 ICTY, Decision on Prosecution Motion for Judicial Notice Pursuant to Rule 94(B), *Prosecutor v. Mejakić et al.*, ICTY-IT02-65-PT, T. Ch., 1 April 2004, p. 5; ICTY, Final Decision on Prosecution Motion for Judicial Notice of Adjudicated Facts, *Prosecutor v. Milošević*, ICTY-IT-02-54-T, T. Ch., 16 December 2003.

discussed above. When there is a significant difference between the factual findings of two judgments, Chambers will most likely deny judicial notice.[264]

4.3.4.8 Documentary Evidence

Rule 94(B) concerns both adjudicated facts and documentary evidence. However, the requirements for adjudicated facts and documentary evidence are not the same.[265] Documentary evidence 'consists of documents produced as evidence for evaluation by the Tribunal'.[266] It includes 'not only documents in writing, but also maps, sketches, plans, calendars, graphs, drawings, computerized records, mechanical records, electro-magnetic records, digital records, databases, sound tracks, audio-tapes, videotapes, photographs, slides and negatives.'[267] Documentary evidence does not need to be adjudicated: the only requirements are that the documents were admitted into evidence into previous proceedings and are relevant to the case.[268] Since the amendment of Rule 94(B) in the ICTY Rules of Procedure and Evidence, the Chamber has to determine whether the document was authenticated and admitted into evidence in the original proceedings. It is immaterial whether or not the documents are under appeal or review: the only test is whether they are relevant and authentic.[269] This leaves open the possibility that a party challenges the authenticity of the documents on appeal in the original proceedings. What if the Appeals Chamber in the original proceedings finds the document not to be authentic after all? The conclusion must be that the well-founded presumption of the authenticity of the documentary evidence no longer exists and

[264] ICTY, Decision on Prosecution Motion for Judicial Notice of Adjudicated Facts with Annex, *Prosecutor v. Popović* et al., ICTY-05-88-T, T. Ch. II, 26 September 2006, para 17.

[265] Cf., ICTY, Decision on the Prosecution's Motion for Judicial Notice of Intercepts Related to the Sarajevo Component and Request for Leave to Add One Document to the Rule 65 ter Exhibit List, *Prosecutor v. Karadžić*, ICTY-IT-95-5/18-T, T. Ch., 4 February 2011, para 16. Although Khan and Dixon conclude that documentary evidence does not need to be adjudicated, their proposition that the standard for taking judicial notice is the same for adjudicated facts as documentary evidence is questionable. The criteria for adjudicated facts do not apply to documentary evidence. Khan and Dixon 2009, p. 781.

[266] ICTR, Judgment, *Prosecutor v. Musema*, ICTR-96-13-T, 27 January 2000, para 53.

[267] Nerenberg and Timmermann 2011 p. 445.

[268] ICTY, Decision on Appellant's Motion for Judicial Notice, *Prosecutor v. Nikolić*, ICTY-IT-02-60/1-A, A. Ch., 1 April 2005, para 45. Referring to the Trial Chamber in *Bizimungu*. Rule 94(B), as the Appeals Chamber held, may not be used to circumvent the general requirements of relevance and probative value of Rule 89(C). This includes a *prima facie* determination of whether the documents are reliable. The statement by Nerenberg and Timmermann that reliability does not need to be demonstrated when judicial notice is taken of that document is therefore unsound. Nerenberg and Timmermann 2011, p. 457. Cf. Khan and Dixon 2009, p. 723.

[269] ICTY, Decision on the Prosecution's Motion for Judicial Notice of Intercepts Related to the Sarajevo Component and Request for Leave to Add One Document to the Rule 65 ter Exhibit List, *Prosecutor v. Karadžić*, ICTY-IT-95-5/18-T, T. Ch., 4 February 2011, para 16.

that the Chamber in the case at hand must determine the relevance and authenticity of that evidence itself, bearing in mind the Appeals Chamber's decision.

4.3.4.9 Judicial Notice and the Probandum

It is established case law that judicial notice may not go to the acts, conduct or mental state of the accused. In other words, judicial notice of the *actus reus* and *mens rea* is not allowed. Nevertheless, facts must be relevant to the proceedings and must have some (remote) connection to the criminal responsibility of the accused. The Appeals Chamber in *Karemera* held that:

> Facts that are not related, directly or indirectly, to that criminal responsibility are not relevant to the question to be adjudicated at trial, and, as noted above, thus may neither be established by evidence nor through judicial notice. So judicial notice under Rule 94(B) is in fact available only for adjudicated facts that bear, at least in some respect, on the criminal responsibility of the accused.[270]

This balancing exercise between the relevance of the proposed fact and the prohibition to judicially notice acts or the mental state of the accused has, until the present day, caused much controversy. *Dragomir Milošević* provided an instructive example in this regard. The prosecution requested the Trial Chamber to take judicial notice of facts derived from the trial and appeal judgment in *Galić*. The proposed facts concerned the shelling and sniping campaign launched by the Sarajevo Romanija Corps (SRK) against the civilian population of Sarajevo between 1992 and 1994. The SRK stood under the command of Galić until Milošević took over in the summer of 1994. The prosecution alleged that Milošević 'inherited and continued' this campaign and, therefore, had knowledge or was put on notice of the crimes committed under Galić's command. This would go to prove the allegation in the indictment that the accused continued this shelling and sniping campaign and was aware of its existence since May 1992.[271] The Trial Chamber concluded first that none of the facts derived from *Galić* related to the acts, conduct or mental state of the accused. It then stated that the acts committed under the command of the accused's predecessor have a 'strong link' with the crimes the accused is charged with, 'particularly those which may in effect put the Accused on notice.'[272]

---

[270] ICTR, Decision on Prosecutor's Interlocutory Appeal of Decision on Judicial Notice, *Prosecutor v. Karemera*, ICTR-98-44-AR73(C), A. Ch., 16 June 2006, para 48. Similar: ICTY, Decision on Ratko Mladić's Appeal Against the Trial Chamber's Decisions on the Prosecution Motion for Judicial Notice of Adjudicated Facts, *Prosecutor v. Mladić*, Case No.: IT-09-92-AR73.1, A. Ch., 12 November 2013, para 81.

[271] ICTY, Decision on Prosecution's Motion for Judicial Notice of Adjudicated Facts and Prosecution's catalogue of Agreed Facts with Dissenting Opinion of Judge Harhoff, *Prosecutor v. Milošević*, ICTY-IT-98-29/1-T, T. Ch. III, 10 April 2007, para 10.

[272] ICTY, Decision on Prosecution's Motion for Judicial Notice of Adjudicated Facts and Prosecution's catalogue of Agreed Facts with Dissenting Opinion of Judge Harhoff, *Prosecutor v. Milošević*, ICTY-IT-98-29/1-T, T. Ch. III, 10 April 2007, para 32.

Apparently, putting the accused on notice does not relate to the mental state of the accused.[273] The Trial Chamber, in its discretion, denied judicial notice of these facts because to judicially notice them would be inconsistent with the accused's rights, in particular his right to examine witnesses. Judicial notice would result in imposing a burden to produce evidence to rebut those facts. Reference is made to *Karemera*, where the Appeals Chamber held that in exercising their discretion, Chambers must take into account proposed facts that relate to conduct of physical perpetrators for which the accused is held accountable.[274] Both parties appealed the *Milošević* decision. The prosecution appealed on the ground that the Trial Chamber had erroneously exercised its discretion. The Appeals Chamber held that judicial notice may be taken of the *existence* of crimes committed by others for which the accused is held accountable: the *actus reus* and *mens rea*, however, must be proved by other means than judicial notice.[275] Judicially noticing the existence of these crimes does not imply that the accused knew they were committed or was put on notice.[276] Accordingly, the Trial Chamber erred in exercising its discretion: the rights of the accused are fully respected when judicial notice is taken of these facts, as long as no inferences are drawn regarding the mental state of the accused.

In *Kvočka et al.*, the Trial Chamber took judicial notice of 444 facts agreed upon by the parties. The facts were derived from the Trial Chamber judgments in *Tadić* and Čelebići. The Trial Chamber judicially noticed the common elements of Articles 3 and 5 of the Statute (violations of the laws or customs and

---

[273] In his Dissenting Opinion, Judge Harhoff made a rather artificial distinction when he stated that even if judicial notice was taken of these facts, it could be inferred that the accused was put on notice of the campaign, but the prosecution still has to prove beyond a reasonable doubt that the accused was *in fact* put on notice. ICTY, Decision on Prosecution's Motion for Judicial Notice of Adjudicated Facts and Prosecution's catalogue of Agreed Facts with Dissenting Opinion of Judge Harhoff, *Prosecutor v. Milošević*, ICTY-IT-98-29/1-T, T. Ch. III, 10 April 2007, Dissenting Opinion Harhoff, paras 12–13.

[274] ICTY, Decision on Prosecution's Motion for Judicial Notice of Adjudicated Facts and Prosecution's catalogue of Agreed Facts with Dissenting Opinion of Judge Harhoff, *Prosecutor v. Milošević*, ICTY-IT-98-29/1-T, T. Ch. III, 10 April 2007, para 31.

[275] ICTY, Decision on Interlocutory Appeals Against Trial Chamber's Decision on Prosecution's Motion for Judicial Notice of Adjudicated Facts and Prosecution's Catalogue of Agreed Facts, *Prosecutor v. Milošević*, ICTY-IT-98-29/1-AR73.1, A. Ch., para 16. Cf. the *Krajišnik* Trial Chamber: 'In general, findings related to the *actus reus* or *mens rea* of a crime are deemed to be factual findings. As long as they also comply with the other criteria mentioned above [judicial notice criteria, KV], they may be admitted.' How one can judicially notice facts that go to the *actus reus* or *mens rea* without going to the acts, conduct or mental state of the accused is unclear to me. ICTY, Decision on the Third and Fourth Prosecution Motions for Judicial Notice of Adjudicated Facts, *Prosecutor v. Krajišnik*, ICTY-IT-00-39-T, T. Ch. I, 24 March 2005, para 15.

[276] ICTY, Decision on Interlocutory Appeals Against Trial Chamber's Decision on Prosecution's Motion for Judicial Notice of Adjudicated Facts and Prosecution's Catalogue of Agreed Facts, *Prosecutor v. Milošević*, ICTY-IT-98-29/1-AR73.1, A. Ch., para 17.

war and crimes against humanity, respectively).[277] The Trial Chamber considered that at the relevant times and places there existed an armed conflict, which included a widespread and systematic attack against the Muslim and Croat civilian population, and that there was a nexus between the armed conflict and the widespread and systematic attack on the civilian population. It further took judicial notice of the existence of the Omarska, Keraterm and Trnopolje detention camps and the mistreatment of prisoners in those camps.[278] This decision is remarkable for two reasons. First, the Trial Chamber took judicial notice of all the contextual elements of the crimes alleged: a significant part of the *probandum*. Second, it explicitly *decided* that those elements were established.[279] Normally, Trial Chambers merely state that they take judicial notice of certain facts. In this case, the Trial Chamber gave the judicially noticed facts a different status: instead of a well-founded presumption of accuracy, it regarded those facts as proven beyond reasonable doubt. In the judgment, the Trial Chamber reiterated the existence of the contextual elements and referred to its judicial notice decision, thereby explicitly stating that the contextual elements were proven by judicial notice.[280]

4.3.4.10 No Legal Characterisations

Under Rule 94(A) legal characterizations can be judicially noticed: it is immaterial whether or not facts are put in legal terms. If a fact is indisputable, judicial notice has to be taken. This differs from Rule 94(B), which precludes taking judicial notice of legal characterizations.[281]

Factual findings concern questions such as: 'Was witness A in village X at a certain date?', 'Did he see people getting killed?', 'Did he recognize certain

[277] The facts were also agreed upon by the parties. Taking judicial notice of adjudicated facts, however, is the sole prerogative of the Trial Chamber: it is irrelevant whether the parties agree on the facts.

[278] ICTY, Decision on Judicial Notice, *Prosecutor v. Kvočka et al.*, ICTY-IT-98-30/1-T, T. Ch., 8 June 2000, p. 7.

[279] 'Decides that at the times and places alleged in the indictment, there existed an armed conflict; that this conflict included a widespread and systematic attack against notably the Muslim and Croat civilian population; and that there was a nexus between this armed conflict and the widespread and systematic attack on the civilian population and the existence of the Omarska, Keraterm and Trnopolje camps and the mistreatment of the prisoners therein.' ICTY, Decision on Judicial Notice, *Prosecutor v. Kvočka et al.*, Case No.: IT-98-30/1-T, T. Ch., 8 June 2000, p. 7.

[280] ICTY, Judgment, *Prosecutor v. Kvočka et al.*, Case No.: IT-98-30/1-T, T. Ch. 2 November 2001, paras 122, 790.

[281] E.g. the early decision in *Simić*. ICTY, Decision on the Pre-Trial Motion by the Prosecution requesting the Trial Chamber to take Judicial Notice of the International Character of the Conflict in Bosnia-Herzegovina, *Prosecutor v. Simić et al.*, ICTY-IT-95-9-PT, T. Ch., 25 March 1999, p. 3.

persons killing others?'. These are plain, factual questions that do not involve the interpretation of any legal principle. Assume that witness A testified on these questions and that a Trial Chamber concluded that the testimony is reliable and that it is proven beyond reasonable doubt that witness A was present in village X at a certain date and recognized people killing others. This factual finding may then, provided it does not attest to the acts or conduct of the accused, be judicially noticed under Rule 94(B). If, however, the Trial Chamber concluded on the basis of this testimony that the killings constituted murder, judicial notice may not be taken, because this is a legal finding based upon facts provided by the witness.[282]

The conclusion that the accused committed crimes against humanity is the prerogative of the Chamber hearing the case and cannot be judicially noticed as such. In the Tribunals' case law, findings such as 'widespread and systematic attack',[283] 'civilian population'[284] and 'armed conflict'[285] have been judicially noticed. This raises the question of whether legal *components* of crimes may be judicially noticed. A finding is legal, 'when it involves interpretation or application of legal principles.'[286] The Trial Chamber in *Krajišnik* stated that:

> many findings have a legal aspect, if one is to construe this expression broadly. It is therefore necessary to determine on a case-by-case basis whether the proposed fact contains findings or characterizations of an essentially legal nature, and which must, therefore, be excluded.[287]

The Chamber gave no guidance on how to discern an essentially legal characterization. In decisions on judicial notice in *Karadžić*, the objection was raised by the defence that the proposed facts are, or contain, essentially legal characterizations. The Chamber provided little or no reasons why the contested facts were not legal characterizations. It is often stated that:

> the Chamber has carefully assessed each of the disputed facts in determining whether it contains findings or conclusions of an essentially legal nature, and is satisfied that in none

[282] Cf. Dutch criminal procedure, where these questions are clearly separated in Article 350 CCP. The court has to first determine whether the accused committed the acts alleged. Then, the court determines whether the acts constitute the crime alleged.

[283] ICTR, Decision on Prosecutor's Interlocutory Appeal of Decision on Judicial Notice, *Prosecutor v. Karemera et al.*, ICTR-98-44-AR73(C), A. Ch., 16 June 2006, paras 26–32.

[284] ICTY, Decision on Third and Fourth Prosecution Motions for Judicial Notice of Adjudicated Facts, *Prosecutor v. Krajišnik*, ICTY-IT-00-39-T, T. Ch. I, 24 March 2005 fact no. 146, 153, 192.

[285] Decision on Third and Fourth Prosecution Motions for Judicial Notice of Adjudicated Facts, *Prosecutor v. Krajišnik*, ICTY-IT-00-39-T, T. Ch. I, 24 March 2005, fact no. 179.

[286] E.g., ICTY, Decision on First Prosecution Motion for Judicial Notice of Adjudicated Facts, *Prosecutor v. Karadžić*, ICTY-IT-95-5/18-PT, T. Ch., 5 June 2009, para 29.

[287] ICTY, Decision on Third and Fourth Prosecution Motions for Judicial Notice of Adjudicated Facts, *Prosecutor v. Krajišnik*, ICTY-IT-00-39-T, T. Ch. I, 24 March 2005, para 15. Emphasis in original.

> of the proposed facts challenged by the Accused, the abovementioned terms are used in such as a way as to render the facts essentially legal in nature.[288]

For example, Trial Chambers deemed the following facts to be of an essentially legal nature: relating to the charge of deportation, 'the non-Serb population did not leave on their own free will', 'the measure was intended to dissuade the Bosnian Muslims and the Bosnian Croats leaving the territory from returning at a later stage', 'military operations were undertaken with the specific purpose to drive Bosnian Muslim and Bosnian Croat residents away', 'Bosnian Muslim and Bosnian Croat departures were involuntary in nature,'[289] and 'on 12 and 13 July 1995, upon the arrival of Serb forces in Potocari, the Bosnian Muslim refugees taking shelter in and around the compound were subjected to a terror campaign comprised of threats, insults, looting and burning of nearby houses, beatings, rapes and murders.'[290]

Whether a particular fact contains an essentially legal finding is hard to determine, and Chambers have interpreted this criterion in different ways. The conclusion must be that components of international crimes (which are sometimes legal characterizations or of a legal nature themselves) are judicially noticed on a regular basis.

4.3.4.11 Submission by the Parties or Proprio Motu?

The prosecution, defence and the Chamber itself may take the initiative to take judicial notice of adjudicated facts or documentary evidence. Unlike Rule 94(A), it is obligatory to hear both parties before judicial notice can be taken. Mostly, it is the prosecution that files a motion for judicial notice of adjudicated facts or documentary evidence. A Chamber is not obliged to take judicial notice when both parties file a motion to that end. In *Stanišić*, for example, the prosecution did not oppose 18 facts for which the defence requested judicial notice. The Trial Chamber did not consider whether these proposed facts complied with the Rule 94(B) criteria but admitted them under Rule 65*ter* (H) instead.[291] This Rule states

---

288 ICTY, Decision on Second Prosecution Motion for Judicial Notice of Adjudicated Facts, *Prosecutor v. Karadžić*, ICTY-IT-95-5/18-PT, T. Ch., 9 October 2009, para 44. ICTY, Decision on Third Prosecution Motion for Judicial Notice of Adjudicated Facts, *Prosecutor v. Karadžić*, ICTY-IT-95-5/18-PT, T. Ch., 9 July 2009, para 41; ICTY, Decision on Fifth Prosecution Motion for Judicial Notice of Adjudicated Facts, *Prosecutor v. Karadžić*, ICTY-IT-95-5/18-PT, T. Ch., 14 June 2010, para 47.

289 ICTY, Decision on Second Motion for Judicial Notice of Adjudicated Facts, *Prosecutor v. Karadžić*, ICTY-IT-95-5/18-PT, T. Ch., 9 October 2009, para 45. Emphasis omitted.

290 ICTY, Decision on Third Prosecution Motion for Judicial Notice of Adjudicated Facts, *Prosecutor v. Karadžić*, ICTY-IT-95-5/18-PT, T. Ch., 9 July 2009, para 45.

291 ICTY, Decision on Judicial Notice, *Prosecutor v. Stanišić*, ICTY-IT-04-79-PT, T. Ch. II, 14 December 2007, para 31.

that points of agreement on matters of law and fact shall be recorded.[292] Although the proposed facts were admitted into evidence, they lack the specific probative value of Rule 94(B): they are part of the trial record, but are not well-founded presumptions. It is remarkable that the Chamber did not determine whether the criteria of Rule 94(B) had been met. By admitting those facts into evidence pursuant to Rule 65*ter* (H), the Chamber may have interfered with the case strategy of the parties. It would have been better to apply the Rule 94(B) test and, if some proposed facts were denied judicial notice, invite the parties to file separate motions on factual or legal agreements. Interestingly, after *Stanišić* was joined with the case of Stojan Župljanin, the same Trial Chamber (composed of different judges, though) observed that the absence of any objection by the non-moving party does not mean the facts proposed for judicial notice are agreed upon pursuant to Rule 65*ter* (H): 'It is in the interest of justice to consider facts proposed by one party, to which the other party does not object, as adjudicated facts. This allows the other party to challenge the proposed fact at trial.'[293]

4.3.4.12 Judicial Notice and Appeal Proceedings

Decisions on judicial notice of the ad hoc Tribunals are open to interlocutory appeal when the criteria of Rule 72(B) ICTY RPE or Rule 73(B) ICTR RPE are met.[294] The standard of appellate review on Trial Chamber's decisions on judicial notice under Rule 94(B) was described by the Appeals Chamber:

> a Trial Chamber's exercise of discretion will only be overturned if the challenged decision was (1) based on an incorrect interpretation of governing law; (2) based on a patently incorrect conclusion of fact; or (3) so unfair or unreasonable as to constitute an abuse of the Trial Chamber's discretion.[295]

The scope of review for factual findings is rather limited, especially when parties wish to challenge a Trial Chamber's decision that denied judicial notice based on discretionary considerations. Normally, when the Appeals Chamber concludes

---

292 The Rule refers to the pre-trial Judge, but Rule 65 *ter* (M) allows the Trial Chamber to exercise any of the functions of the pre-trial Judge.

293 ICTY, Decision granting in Part Prosecution's Motions for Judicial Notice of Adjudicated Facts pursuant to Rule 94(B), *Prosecutor v. Stanišić and Zupljjanin*, ICTY-IT-08-91-T, T. Ch. II, 1 April 2010, para 27.

294 Interlocutory appeal may be lodged with certification of the Trial Chamber. Certification can be granted when the issue can significantly affect a fair and expeditious trial or the outcome of the trial and for which, according to the Trial Chamber, an immediate resolution by the Appeals Chamber is required.

295 ICTR, Decision on Prosecutor's Interlocutory Appeal of Decision on Judicial Notice, *Prosecutor v. Karemera*, ICTR-98-44-AR73(C), 16 June 2006, para 43; ICTY, Decision on Interlocutory Appeals Against Trial Chamber's Decision on Prosecution's Motion for Judicial Notice of Adjudicated Facts and Prosecution's Catalogue of Agreed Facts, *Prosecutor v. Milošević*, ICTY-98-29/1-AR73.1, A. Ch., 26 June 2007, para 5.

that the Trial Chamber erred in applying Rule 94(B), the decision will be remanded; the Appeals Chamber will not evaluate all the proposed facts itself.[296]

This approach is in line with the manner in which fact-finding is conducted on appeal. The ICTY and ICTR Statutes state that the Appeals Chamber shall hear appeals when an error of fact has resulted in a miscarriage of justice.[297] This indicates that the burden for a party to challenge a factual finding of a Trial Chamber is quite high: a factual error as such is insufficient as a ground for appeal; the error must have resulted in a miscarriage of justice. The Appeals Chamber emphasized that fact-finding is primarily the task of the Trial Chamber; the Appeals Chamber will only substitute its own factual finding if the Trial Chamber's finding is 'wholly erroneous'.[298]

4.3.4.13 Quantitative Analysis of Judicial Notice at the Ad Hoc Tribunals

Judicial notice of adjudicated facts and documentary evidence is a frequently used shortcut to proof in proceedings before the ICTY. In a substantial number of cases, judicial notice has been taken of adjudicated facts and documentary evidence.[299] At the ICTR, judicial notice of adjudicated facts and documentary evidence has been taken in only 6 out of 77 cases. The number of judicially noticed facts is significantly lower than at the ICTY.[300]

---

296 ICTY, Decision on Interlocutory Appeals Against Trial Chamber's Decision on Prosecution's Motion for Judicial Notice of Adjudicated Facts and Prosecution's Catalogue of Agreed Facts, *Prosecutor v. Dragomir Milošević*, ICTY-98-29/1-AR73.1, A. Ch., 26 June 2007; ICTY, Decision on Appeals Chamber Remand of Judicial Notice of Adjudicated Facts with Separate Opinion of Judge Robinson, *Prosecutor v. Dragomir Milošević*, ICTY-98-29/1-T, T. Ch. III, 18 July 2007; ICTY, Decision on the Prosecution's Interlocutory Appeal Against the Trial Chamber's 10 April 2003 Decision on Prosecution Motion for Judicial Notice of Adjudicated Facts, *Prosecutor v. Slobodan Milošević*, ICTY-IT-02-54-AR73.5, A. Ch., 28 October 2003, p. 3. ICTR, Decision on Prosecutor's Interlocutory Appeal of Decision on Judicial Notice, *Prosecutor v. Karemera et al.*, ICTR-98-44-AR73(C), A. Ch., 16 June 2006, para 43.

297 Article 25(1)(b) ICTY Statute; Article 24(1)(b) ICTR Statute.

298 ICTY, Appeal Judgment, *Prosecutor v. Kupreškić et al.*, ICTY-IT-95-16-A, A. Ch., 23 October 2001, paras 29–30; ICTY, Judgment, *Prosecutor v. Blagojević & Jokić*, ICTY-IT-02-50-A, A. Ch., 9 May 2007, para 9; ICTY, Judgment, *Prosecutor v. Boškoski & Tarčulovski*, ICTY-IT-04-82-A, A. Ch., 19 May 2010, paras 13–14; ICTR, Judgment, *Prosecutor v. Gacumbitsi*, ICTR-2001-64-A, A. Ch., para 8.

299 The cases are: *Prosecutor v. Kvočka et al., Prosecutor v. Sikirica* et al., *Prosecutor v. Ljubičić, Prosecutor v. Krajišnik, Prosecutor v. Slobodan Milošević, Prosecutor v. Stanković, Prosecutor v. Mejakić, Prosecutor v. Hadžihasanović, Prosecutor v. Prlić, Prosecutor v. Popović et al., Prosecutor v. Dragomir Milošević, Prosecutor v. Šešelj, Prosecutor v. Stanišić & Župljanin, Prosecutor v. Perišić, Prosecutor v. Lukić & Lukić, Prosecutor v. Karadžić, Prosecutor v. Đorđević, Prosecutor v. Stanišić & Simatović, Prosecutor v. Tolimir, Prosecutor v. Mladić.*

300 The 6 cases are: *Prosecutor v. Semanza, Prosecutor v. Niyitegeka, Prosecutor v. Bizimungu, Prosecutor v. Karemera, Prosecutor v. Seromba, Prosecutor v. Ndahimana.*

In the cases in which judicial notice was taken, on average 551 facts were noticed by ICTY Trial Chambers; ICTR Trial Chambers took judicial notice of 22 facts, on average. The average number of judicially noticed facts provides only an indication of the diverging practices of the ICTY and ICTR, because the differences between individual cases at the respective Tribunals are substantial. In *Sikirica et al.*, for example, ICTY Trial Chamber III took judicial notice of 45 adjudicated facts, whereas ICTY Trial Chamber I in *Stanišić & Simatović* took judicial notice of 1003 facts.[301] The same holds true for the ICTR Trial Chambers: in *Bizimungu et al.* Trial Chamber II took judicial notice of 2 adjudicated facts; Trial Chamber III in *Karemera et al.* took notice of 102 facts.[302]

Table 4.1 (see pages 197–202) gives an overview of the cases before the ICTY and ICTR in which Trial Chambers have taken judicial notice of adjudicated facts and documentary evidence. The first three columns list the case, case number and the date on which a decision on judicial notice has been taken. In some cases only one decision on judicial notice has been taken, whereas in others as many as seven have been taken. In columns four and five the number of adjudicated facts and documentary evidence are listed for each judicial notice decision. Column six lists the sources of the adjudicated facts and documentary evidence: in *Stanković*, for example, the 36 facts of which notice was taken are derived from the Trial Chamber's judgment ('TJ') and Appeal Chamber's judgment ('AJ') in *Kunarac*. Remarks are made in column seven; columns eight and nine list the total number of adjudicated facts and documentary evidence for each case.

It follows from Table 1. that judicial notice of adjudicated facts and documentary evidence is not taken frequently at the ICTR. When it is taken the number of facts is negligible compared to ICTY practice, *Karemera et al.* being a notable exception. The difference between the practice at the ICTY and the ICTR can probably be explained by the appeal judgment in *Semanza* (2005) and the interlocutory decision of the Appeals Chamber in *Karemera et al.* (2006). As was stated before, the Appeals Chamber considered important contextual elements of genocide, crimes against humanity and war crimes to be of common knowledge.[303]

---

301 ICTY, Decision on Prosecution Motion for Judicial Notice of Adjudicated Facts, *Prosecutor v. Sikirica et al.*, ICTY-IT-95-8-PT, T. Ch. III, 27 September 2000. ICTY, Decision on Prosecution's Motion for Judicial Notice of Adjudicated Facts, 25 November 2009; Decision on Taking Judicial Notice of Adjudicated Facts, 16 December 2009; Decision on Second Prosecution Motion for Judicial Notice of Adjudicated Facts, 28 January 2010; Decision on Third Prosecution's Motion for Judicial Notice of Adjudicated Facts, 23 July 2010; Decision on Taking Judicial Notice of Adjudicated Facts and Corrigendum to the Chamber's First, Second and Third Adjudicated Facts Decisions, 16 September 2010, *Prosecutor v. Stanišić & Simatović*, ICTY-IT-03-69-T, T. Ch. I.

302 ICTR, Decision on the Prosecutor's Motion and Notice of Adjudicated Facts, *Prosecutor v. Bizimungu et al.*, ICTR-99-50-T, T. Ch. II, 10 December 2004; ICTR, Decision on Appeals Chamber Remand of Judicial Notice, *Prosecutor v. Karemera et al.*, ICTR-98-44-T, T. Ch. III, 11 December 2006.

303 ICTR, Decision on Prosecutor's Interlocutory Appeal of Decision on Judicial Notice, *Prosecutor v. Karemera et al.*, ICTR-98-44-AR73(C), A. Ch., 16 June 2006; ICTR, Judgment, *Prosecutor v. Semanza*, ICTR-97-20-A, A. Ch., 20 May 2005, para 192.

When contextual elements are proven under Rule 94(A), the need to take notice of those contextual elements as adjudicated facts is superfluous: the elements are considered notorious and therefore proven. The Appeals Chamber's findings in *Semanza* and *Karemera et al.* are unparalleled in ICTY case law on the Yugoslav conflict. The Appeals Chamber has never ruled as categorically on the Yugoslav conflict regarding its legal character as it has done regarding the Rwandan conflict. The Trial Chamber in *Simić*, referring to the Appeals Chamber in *Tadić*, stated:

> it would be for each Trial Chamber, depending on the circumstances of each case, to make its own determination on the nature of the armed conflict upon the specific evidence presented to it.[304]

If the Appeals Chamber had ruled that the existence and character of an armed conflict in a certain region was common knowledge, it is likely that the number of judicially noticed adjudicated facts in ICTY proceedings would have been much lower. Considering that ICTR practice on judicial notice pursuant to Rule 94(B) is negligible, the focus in the following pages will be on ICTY case law.

The first decision on judicial notice was taken in March 1999 in *Kvočka et al.* This decision was taken after trial judgments were handed down in *Tadić* (May 1997) and Čelebići (November 1998), which had resulted in a considerable number of adjudicated facts.[305] The number of judicially noticed facts is on the rise since the end of 2007. There are several reasons for this trend.

First, more and more factual findings have been made by the Trial Chambers, which increased the number of adjudicated facts of which judicial notice could be taken. The sources from which the adjudicated facts or documentary evidence are selected have become more varied over the years, although early judgments such as *Tadić* and Čelebići remain an important source for adjudicated facts.[306]

Second, the completion strategy of the ICTY encouraged Chambers to speed up the proceedings as much as possible.[307] In 2006 for example, the ICTY judges adopted recommendations of the 'Working Group on Speeding Up Trials', which was established to investigate how proceedings could be conducted more efficiently. The Working Group was composed of Judges Bonomy, Hanoteau and Swart.[308] The greater use of judicial notice of adjudicated facts (especially in the pre-trial

---

[304] ICTY, Decision on the Pre-Trial Motion by the Prosecution Requesting the Trial Chamber to take Judicial Notice of the International Character of the Conflict in Bosnia-Herzegovina, *Prosecutor v. Simić et al.*, ICTY-95-9-PT, T. Ch., 25 March 1999, p. 4.

[305] ICTY, Opinion and Judgment, *Prosecutor v. Tadić*, ICTY-IT-94-1-T, T. Ch., 7 May 1997; ICTY, Judgment, *Prosecutor v. Delalić et al.*, ICTY-IT-96-21-T, T. Ch., 16 November 1998.

[306] See column 7 of Table 1.

[307] Cf. the UN Security Council Resolutions that call upon the Tribunals to implement completion strategies. S/RES/1503 (2003); S/RES/1534 (2004).

[308] S/2005/343, Report on completion strategy by the ICTY President, 25 May 2005, para 6.

phase of the proceedings) was one of the recommendations.[309] This recommendation was endorsed by the judges of the Tribunal and brought into practice.[310]

Third, considering the factual findings in other cases, defence counsel might reason that it is useless to object to all proposed facts contained in the prosecution's judicial notice motions, because certain facts have been proven over and over again. This means that the Trial Chamber is confronted with a motion by the prosecution, to which the defence does not object, or only on minor points. The Trial Chamber, provided that the admissibility requirements for judicial notice are fulfilled, might reason that it is of no use to not judicially notice a fact to which both parties agree and which has been proven by other Chambers. It is hard to trace such reasoning in the text of the decisions. When it can be traced, it is still rather anecdotal and easily contradicted by cases in which the accused is uncooperative and opposes all facts proposed for judicial notice. For example, in *Stanišić & Simatović*, the defence did not object to judicial notice of hundreds of facts.[311] In *Karadžić*, on the other hand, the accused opposed every judicial notice motion filed by the prosecution.[312] Nevertheless, if both parties agree on judicial notice of certain facts, Trial Chambers are reluctant to *not* notice such facts.

The primary aim of judicial notice, as has been stated before, is to enhance judicial economy. It follows that when adjudicated facts meet the admissibility requirements for judicial notice, those facts do not have to be proven again during trial proceedings: they are presumed to be correct. Since all evidence must comply with the requirements of Rule 89(C), judicially noticed facts are relevant and have (some) probative value. One would expect that such facts become conclusive evidence unless (1) other evidence of a fact in issue is presented, and that evidence is considered more reliable than taking judicial notice of the particular fact;[313]

---

309 Greater use of judicial notice was already advocated in 1999 by the Expert Group to Conduct a Review of the Effective Operation and Functioning of the ICTY and ICTR. Cf. Report of the Export Group to Conduct a Review of the Effective Operation and Functioning of the International Tribunal for the Former Yugoslavia and the International Criminal Tribunal for Rwanda, UN Doc. A/54/634, 22 November 1999, para 85.

310 S/2006/353, Report on the completion strategy by the ICTY President, 31 May 2006, para 24.

311 ICTY, Decision on Prosecution's Motion for Judicial Notice of Adjudicated Facts, *Prosecutor v. Stanišić & Simatović*, ICTY_IT-03-69-T, T. Ch. I, 25 November 2009, paras 24–25.

312 ICTY, Response to First Prosecution Motion for Judicial Notice of Adjudicated Facts, 30 March 2009; Response to Second Prosecution Motion for Judicial Notice of Adjudicated Facts, 22 July 2009; Response to Third Prosecution Motion for Judicial Notice of Adjudicated Facts and Motion for List of Witnesses to be Eliminated, 29 May 2009; Response to Fourth Prosecution Motion for Judicial Notice of Adjudicated Facts, 30 November 2009; Response to Fifth Prosecution Motion for Judicial Notice of Adjudicated Facts, 5 February 2010, *Prosecutor v. Karadžić*, ICTY-95-05/18-T, T. Ch. III.

313 The evidence can be presented by the party that filed the motion for judicial notice, or by order of the Trial Chamber pursuant to Rule 98 ICTY RPE (production of additional evidence).

(2) the non-moving party[314] has presented successfully evidence in rebuttal; or (3) after the close of proceedings, the judicially noticed fact is found to be irrelevant or unreliable in light of all the evidence presented. One would also expect that the majority of judicially noticed facts will be incorporated in the final judgment: it is inefficient to take judicial notice and not use those facts in the judgment.

In order to test the assumption that judicially noticed facts are normally incorporated in the judgment unless the fact is replaced by better evidence, rebutted or found unreliable or irrelevant after all, four ICTY cases have been analysed in detail: *Krajišnik, Kvočka et al., Dragomir Milošević* and *Popović et al.* In these cases, a substantial number of facts have been judicially noticed. All cases have been finally settled on appeal.

In Tables 4.2 and 4.3 (see pages 203 and 204), the practice of judicial notice in these four cases is shown. In the first column of both tables the sources of the adjudicated facts are listed and in the second column the number of facts derived from a particular source. The third column indicates, as a percentage, the relative size of the facts derived from a particular source. For example, in *Krajišnik*, 252 facts have been judicially noticed that were derived from the Trial Chamber's judgment in *Tadić*. Those 252 facts correspond to 39 % of the total number of adjudicated facts in *Krajišnik*. Both Tables also indicate how many judicially noticed facts have been incorporated in the final judgment. In *Krajišnik*, 488 out of 645 judicially noticed facts have been used in the final judgment, which equals 76 %. From these Tables, the following observations can be made.

First, the number of judicially noticed facts that is incorporated in the Trial Chamber's judgment is remarkably low. Even in *Krajišnik,* which shows the highest percentage of used facts, only three-quarter of the judicially noticed facts are incorporated in the judgment. The percentages in *Popović et al.* (47 %) and *Dragomir Milošević* (28 %) are significantly lower, and in *Kvočka et al.*, only a mere 2 % of previously judicially noticed facts is included in the judgment. Considering the aim of judicial economy and the recommendations by the Working Group on Speeding Up Trials, this begs the question of how judicial notice can speed up trials when, in the end, so little use is made of it.

Second, facts that are judicially noticed are predominantly derived from one single source. In *Krajišnik*, 252 facts are judicially noticed on the basis of one source: the *Tadić* trial judgment. The same holds true for the 199 facts derived from the *Krnojelac* trial judgment. Only 30 facts out of a total of 645 are derived from multiple sources: 26 facts from the trial judgments in both *Tadić* and Čelebići and 4 from *Krnojelac* and *Kunarac*. In *Kvočka et al.*, 50 out of 444 facts are derived from multiple sources and in *Popović et al.* 107 out of 328. In *Dragomir*

---

[314] Non-moving party refers to the party that is invited to comment upon a motion for judicial notice filed by the other party. In the majority of cases, the prosecution (the moving party) files a motion for judicial notice upon which the defence may respond (non-moving party).

Milošević, all facts are derived from a single Trial Chamber's judgment. This means that a substantial number of judicially noticed facts have been scrutinized only once: in the original proceedings, which were held (many) years ago. One could argue that cases which are often used as sources for judicial notice, such as *Tadić* and Čelebići, have been finally settled on appeal, which provides an additional factual check: if the Trial Chamber erred on the facts, the Appeals Chamber is able to rectify the mistake. We have seen, however, that the standard for appellate review on factual issues is relatively high.

If we take a closer look at the facts that were judicially noticed but not incorporated in the judgment, it appears that Trial Chambers rarely explain why certain facts have not been included the judgment.[315] In general, judgments contain an introductory paragraph in which the Chamber indicated how it has evaluated particular types of evidence that were presented during the proceedings.[316] On judicial notice, a general remark is often made that judicially noticed facts are considered against the background of all the evidence available.[317]

Judicially noticed facts can be left out the judgment when better evidence or evidence in rebuttal is presented, or when the Trial Chamber reconsiders its earlier decision on judicial notice. An example of the first category can be found in *Popović et al.*, where the Trial Chamber took judicial notice of the fact that:

> The plan for Krivaja 95 specifically directed the Drina Corps to 'split apart the enclaves of Zepa and Srebrenica and to reduce them to their urban areas.'[318]

This fact had been adjudicated in the *Krstić* trial judgment. In the *Popović et al.* judgment, this fact is incorporated in the Chamber's factual findings, but no reference is made to its earlier decision on judicial notice. Instead, the source for this

---

[315] The difference between the number of judicially noticed facts and the number of those facts that are incorporated in the judgment, cannot be explained by an amendment of the charges. Most judicial notice decisions have been taken after the indictment was confirmed. In *Kvočka et al.*, the judicial decisions were taken after the amended indictment has been filed. It remains remarkable that no explanation was provided why so little judicially noticed facts have been incorporated in the final judgment.

[316] ICTY, Judgment, *Prosecutor v. Popović et al.*, ICTY-IT-05-88-T, T. Ch. II, 10 June 2010, paras 69–71; ICTY, Judgment, *Prosecutor v. Krajišnik*, ICTY-IT-00-39-T, T. Ch. I, 27 September 2006, para 22; ICTY, Judgment, *Prosecutor v. Dragomir Milošević*, ICTY-98—29/1-T, T. Ch. III, 12 December 2007, para 9.

[317] ICTY, Judgment, *Prosecutor v. Popović* et al., ICTY-IT-05-88-T, T. Ch. II, 10 June 2010, para 71; ICTY, Judgment, *Prosecutor v. Krajišnik*, ICTY-IT-00-39-T, T. Ch. I, 27 September 2006, para 22; ICTY, Judgment, *Prosecutor v. Dragomir Milošević*, ICTY-98—29/1-T, T. Ch. III, 12 December 2007, para 9.

[318] ICTY, Decision on Prosecution Motion for Judicial Notice of Adjudicated Facts with Annex, *Prosecutor v. Popović et al.*, ICTY-IT-05-88-T, T. Ch. II, 26 September 2006, p. 22 fact # 71.

fact is an order given by the Drina Corps Command in July 1995.[319] Such an order is a more direct and better piece of evidence. In *Krajišnik*, of the 157 judicially noticed facts that were not used in the judgment, 19 facts were proven by other evidence; in *Kvočka et al.*, of the 435 unused facts only 1 fact was proven by other evidence; in *Dragomir Milošević*, no better evidence was presented; and in *Popović et al.*, 7 of the 173 judicially noticed facts not used in the judgment were proven by other evidence.

The second category, successful presentation of the evidence in rebuttal by the non-moving party, is not easily detected. To determine this, all the evidence must be analysed and contrasted with the judicially noticed facts. It is unlikely, though, that the explanation for the omission of the judicially noticed facts in the judgment is to be found in an effective evidence-in-rebuttal strategy: presenting evidence in rebuttal is a very time-consuming enterprise and requires the defence to conduct extensive research on its own.[320] Moreover, if the defence had been successful, one would have found remarks by the Trial Chamber that a significant number of judicially noticed facts were not incorporated in the judgment, because reliable evidence in rebuttal was presented. As stated before, apart from some general considerations on judicial notice, the Trial Chambers made no such remarks.

Besides the presentation of better evidence and evidence in rebuttal, a third explanation for not using judicially noticed facts may be that Trial Chambers have reconsidered their decision(s) on judicial notice. After all, such decisions have been taken during the proceedings, and it could well be that after the close of the proceedings the facts that were deemed reliable and relevant when the decision on judicial notice was taken are not so relevant and reliable in light of all the evidence presented. Considering the length of proceedings before the Tribunals, it is not unusual that a decision on judicial notice was taken years before the judges delivered their judgment. It is important to note that in *Krajišnik, Dragomir Milošević* and *Popović et al.*, the composition of the Chamber that took the decision(s) on judicial notice is the same as the Chamber delivering the judgment. It is not unusual that the composition of the Chamber varies over the years, which could explain why facts judicially noticed by a particular bench will not be used in the judgment delivered by other judges. In *Kvočka et al.*, the first decision on judicial notice in March 1999 was taken by Judges May,

Bennouna and Robinson, whereas the second decision (June 2000) and the final judgment (November 2001) were delivered by Judges Rodrigues, Riad and Wald. Even in this case, the discrepancy between the number of judicially noticed facts

---

319 ICTY, Judgment, *Prosecutor v. Popović* et al., ICTY-IT-05-88-T, T. Ch. II, 10 June 2010, footnote 755.

320 In the majority of cases, the non-moving party is the defence. This means that it is upon the defence to present evidence in rebuttal.

and facts used in the judgment cannot be explained by a different composition of the Chamber because the majority of the judicially noticed facts were identified by the same judges that delivered the judgment.

A related question is what *kind* of facts are left out the judgment. It may be that during trial, or even pre-trial, certain facts seem relevant to the case, but after the close of proceedings in the final evaluation it turns out that those facts are actually rather peripheral, if not outright irrelevant. In *Kvočka et al.*, over one hundred facts were judicially noticed concerning the historical and geographical background of the conflict, including the process of disintegration of the Socialist Federal Republic of Yugoslavia. Considering that the accused were charged with atrocities committed in the Omarska, Keraterm and Trnopolje camps, it should come as no surprise that only a handful of those facts were incorporated in the judgment. The relevance of this kind of facts in cases concerning low-level perpetrators can indeed by questioned. It remains unclear what the reasons were for the Trial Chamber to not include these facts. This is unsatisfactory: the Trial Chamber should have provided reasons why these facts were not included in the judgment.

4.3.4.14 Concluding Remarks

The quantitative analysis of judicial notice at the ad hoc Tribunals leads to three conclusions. First, the use of judicial notice differs profoundly between the ICTY and ICTR. Whereas the ICTY noticed thousands of facts, the ICTR only reluctantly used Rule 94(B). Reasons have been given to explain the different approaches, the most prominent of which is the use of facts of common knowledge at the ICTR. This obviated the need to take notice of adjudicated facts.

Second, it transpires from the analysis of the four ICTY cases that the percentage of judicially noticed facts that are actually incorporated in the judgment is relatively low and in one case (*Kvočka et al.*) even negligible. Possible explanations have been suggested. A small number of judicially noticed facts were replaced by better evidence, but whether evidence in rebuttal was successfully presented or whether Chambers reconsidered their earlier decisions cannot be concluded from these cases.

Finally, Chambers have not given detailed reasoning in their judgments as to why they made certain choices when evaluating the evidence. Why was a certain fact included in the judgment and others not? This is a more general point of criticism: compared to the extensive reasoning in the judicial notice decisions, the reasoning in the judgments is rather minimal. Considering the large numbers of unused judicially noticed facts, more elaborate reasoning on this point would have been desirable.

Table 4.1 Overview judicial notice ICTY and ICTR March 1999–June 2011

Case	Case Number	Date	Number of Adjudicated Facts	Number of Documentary Evidence	Source of the Adjudicated Facts or Documentary Evidence	Remarks	Total Number of Adjudicated Facts	Total Number of Documentary Evidence
ICTY								
Kvočka, Miroslav et al.	IT-98-30-PT	19-03-99	106		Tadić TJ; Čelebići TJ		444	
		08-06-00	338		Tadić TJ; Čelebići TJ			
Sikirica, Dusko et al.	IT-95-8-PT	27-09-00	45		Tadić TJ (std.)[1]; Čelebići TJ		45	
Ljubičić, Pasko	IT-00-41-PT	23-01-03	78		Furundžija TJ; Aleksovski TJ; Kupreškić TJ		78	
Krajišnik, Momcilo	IT-00-39-PT	28-02-03	627		Tadić TJ/AJ; Čelebići TJ; Kupreškić TJ; Kunarac TJ; Kvočka TJ; krnojelac TJ	Incorporated in March 2005 Decision.	647	
		24-03-05	647		Tadić TJ/AJ; Čelebići TJ; Kupreškić TJ; Kunarac TJ; Kvočka TJ; krnojelac TJ; Vasiljević TJ			
Milošević, Slobodan	IT-02-54-T	10-04-03	130		Tadić TJ/AJ; Čelebići TJ; Kunarac TJ; Kupreškić TJ		271	
		16-12-03	141		Tadić TJ/AJ; Čelebići TJ; Kunarac TJ; Kupreškić TJ (all std.)			
Stanković, Radovan	IT-96-23/2-PT	16-05-03	36		Kunarac TJ/AJ		36	
Mejakić, Zeljko	IT-02-65-PT	01-04-04	114		Tadić TJ; Čelebići TJ		114	
Hadzihasanovic, Enver & Kubura, Amir	IT-01-47-T	20-04-04	4		Kupreškić TJ; Aleksovski TJ		43	
		14-04-05	39		Kupreškić TJ; Blaškić TJ (std.); Kordić TJ (std.)			

(continued)

Table 4.1 (continued)

Case	Case Number	Date	Number of Adjudicated Facts	Number of Documentary Evidence	Source of the Adjudicated Facts or Documentary Evidence	Remarks	Total Number of Adjudicated Facts	Total Number of Documentary Evidence
ICTY								
Prlić, Jadranko et al.	IT-04-74-PT	14-03-06	86		Kordić TJ (std.); Aleksovski TJ (std.); Kupreškić TJ (std.); Naletilić & Martinović TJ;		268	
		07-09-06	182		Naletilić TJ; Blaškić TJ (both std.)			
Popović, Vujadin et al.	IT-05-88-T	26-09-06	280		Krstić TJ/AJ; Blagojević & Jokić TJ		330	
		02-06-08	50		Krajišnik TJ; Orić TJ			
Milošević, Dragomir	IT-98-29/1-T	10-04-07	113		Galić TJ/AJ		116	
		29-08-07	3		Galić TJ/AJ			
Šešelj, Vojislav	IT-03-67-T	10-12-07	215		annex missing		550	
		08-02-10	181		Mrkšić TJ/AJ			
		23-07-10	154		Krajišnik TJ			
Stanšić, Mico	IT-04-79-PT	14-12-07	853		Tadić TJ (std.); Stakić TJ (std.); Brđanin TJ/AJ; Kvočka TJ (std.); Simić TJ (std.); Čelebići TJ (std.); Vasiljević TJ (std.); Galić TJ (std.)	Joined with Župljanin.	853	
Perišić, Momcilo	IT-04-81-PT	26-06-08	262		Galić TJ/AJ		591	129
		01-09-08		30	Popović Decision	Documentary evidence may be derived from decisions. Cf Par. 9.2.5.		

(continued)

Table 4.1 (continued)

Case ICTY	Case Number	Date	Number of Adjudicated Facts	Number of Documentary Evidence	Source of the Adjudicated Facts or Documentary Evidence	Remarks	Total Number of Adjudicated Facts	Total Number of Documentary Evidence
		02-09-08	64	99	Martić TJ			
		17-09-08	24		Galić TJ			
		22-09-08	100		Krstić TJ/AJ; Blagojević & Jokić TJ/AJ			
		12-01-10	112		Dragomir Milošević TJ/AJ			
		04-05-10	29		Krstić TJ; Blagojević & Jokić TJ; Galić TJ; Martić TJ/AJ; Dragomir Milošević TJ/AJ			
Lukić, Milan & Lukić, Sredoje	IT-98-32/1-T	12-11-08	9		Vasiljević TJ			
Karadžić, Radovan	IT-95-5/18-PT	05-06-09	302		Galić TJ/AJ		2482	45
		09-07-09	466		Krstić TJ/AJ; Blagojević & Jokić TJ/AJ			
		09-okt-09	740		Tadić TJ; Čelebići TJ; Stakić TJ; Martić TJ; Mrkšić; Brđanin TJ/AJ; Kvočka TJ; Krnojelac TJ; Kunarac TJ; Vasiljević TJ			
		14-06-10	725		Krajišnik TJ			
		14-06-10	249		Dragomir Milošević TJ/AJ			
		04-02-11		45	Brđanin TJ/AJ; Krajišnik TJ			
Đorđević, Vlastimir	IT-05-87/1-T	24-07-09		1	Milutinović Decision	Documentary evidence may be derived from decisions. Cf Par. 9.2.5.		1

(continued)

Table 4.1 (continued)

Case	Case Number	Date	Number of Adjudicated Facts	Number of Documentary Evidence	Source of the Adjudicated Facts or Documentary Evidence	Remarks	Total Number of Adjudicated Facts	Total Number of Documentary Evidence
ICTY								
Stanišić, Jovica & Simatović, Franko	IT-03-69-T	25-11-09	419		Brđanin TJ/AJ; Čelebići TJ; Krstić TJ/AJ; Kupreškić TJ; Kvočka TJ; Simić TJ/AJ; Stakić TJ; Strugar TJ; Tadić TJ; Blagojević & Jokić TJ		1066	
		16-12-09	7		Brđanin TJ			
		28-01-10	195		Martić TJ			
		23-07-10	365		Krajišnik TJ			
		16-09-10	17		Krajišnik TJ			
		16-02-12	61		Krajišnik TJ/AC; Martić TJ/AJ; Simić TJ/AJ; Gotovina et al. TJ.			
		10-07-12	2		Lukić & Lukić TJ			
Tolimir, Zdravko	IT-05-88/2-PT	17-12-09	523		Krstić TJ/AJ; Blagojević & Jokić TJ/AJ		523	
Stanišić, Mico & Župljanin, Stojan	IT-08-91-T	01-04-10	1086		Tadić TJ (std.); Čelebići TJ (std.); Kvočka TJ (std.); Vasiljević TJ (std.); Stakić TJ (std.); Simić TJ; Galić TJ; Brđanin TJ (std.); Brđanin AJ; Krajišnik TJ (std.)	This includes the 853 facts that were judically noticed when cases were not yet joined.	1134	
		29-06-11	48		Brđanin TJ (std.); Delelic TJ (std.); Simić TJ (std.); Stakić TJ (std.)			

(continued)

Table 4.1 (continued)

Case ICTY	Case Number	Date	Number of Adjudicated Facts	Number of Documentary Evidence	Source of the Adjudicated Facts or Documentary Evidence	Remarks	Total Number of Adjudicated Facts	Total Number of Documentary Evidence
Mladić	IT-09-92	28-02-12	1149		15 Tribunal judgements[2]		1976[3]	
		21-03-12	332					
		13-04-12	495					
		5-06-12	2					
Semanza, Laurent	ICTR-97-20-I	03-11-00		10	Akayesu TJ			10
Niyitegeka, Eliezer	ICTR-96-14-T	04-09-02	1		Kayishema & Ruzindana TJ; Musema TJ		1	
Bizimungu, Casimir et al.	ICTR-99-50-I	02-12-03		15	Akyezu Decision; Semanza Decision; Bagosora Decision	Documentary evidence may be derived. Cf Par. 9.2.5.	2	15
		10-12-04	2		Kajelijeli TJ; Semanza TJ			
Karemera, Edouard et al.	ICTR-98-44-T	30-04-04		5	Akayesu TJ (extracts); Kayisheme & Ruzindana TJ (extracts); Ruzindana TJ (extracts)		102	5
		11-02-06	102		Akayesu TJ; Semanza TJ; Kajelijeli TJ; Rutaganda TJ; Niyitegeka TJ; Musema TJ; Kayisheme & Ruzindana TJ; Ntakirutimana TJ; Nahimana et al. TJ			

(continued)

Table 4.1 (continued)

Case ICTY	Case Number	Date	Number of Adjudicated Facts	Number of Documentary Evidence	Source of the Adjudicated Facts or Documentary Evidence	Remarks	Total Number of Adjudicated Facts	Total Number of Documentary Evidence
Seromba, Athanase	ICTR-2001-66-T	14-07-05	4		Akayesu TJ; Kayisheme & Ruzindana TJ; Rutaganda TJ; Kajelijeli TJ; Karemera Decision		4	
Ndahimana, Gregoire	ICTR-2001-68-PT	07-04-10	4		Seromba TJ/AJ			

[1] Std. means settled on appeal
[2] ICTY, Decision on Ratko Mladić's Appeal Against the Trial Chamber's Decisions on the Prosecution Motion for Judicial Notice of Adjudicated Facts, Prosecutor v. Mladić, Case No.: IT-09-92-AR73.1, A. Ch. 12 November 2013, par. 2
[3] The Appeals Chamber, in an interlocutory decision, removed 61 facts from the list of judicially noticed facts. According to the Appeals Chamber, the Trial Chamber exceeded its discretion in noticing these facts. ICTZ, Decision on Ratko Mladić's Appeal Against the Trial Chamber's Decisions on the Prosecution Motion for Judicial Notice of Adjudicated Facts, Prosecutor v. Mladić, Case No.: IT-09-92-AR73.1, A. Ch. 12 November 2013

Table 4.2 Judicial notice in *Krajišnik* and *Kvočka et al.*

Krajišnik		
Source	#	%
Tadić TJ	252	39.07
Čelebići TJ	4	0.62
Kupreškić TJ	1	0.16
Kunarac TJ	73	11.32
Kvočka TJ	38	5.89
Krnojelac TJ	199	30.85
Vasiljević TJ	44	6.82
Tadić TJ/AJ	1	0.16
Tadić AJ	3	0.47
Tadić TJ/Čelebići TJ	26	4.03
Krnojelac TJ/Kunarac TJ	4	0.62
Total	**645**	**100.00**
Total # judicially noticed facts in decisions		645
Total # judicially noticed facts in judgement		488
% facts used in judgement		75.7
Kvočka et al.		
Source	#	%
Tadić TJ	389	87.81
Čelebići TJ	4	0.90
Tadić TJ/Čelebići TJ	50	11.29
Total	**443**	**100.00**
Total # judicially noticed facts in decisions		444
Total # judicially noticed facts in judgement		9
% facts used in judgement		2.0

Table 4.3 Judicial notice in *Popovič et al.* and *Dragomir Miloševič*

Popović et al.		
Source	#	%
Krstić TJ	122	37.20
Krstić AJ	3	0.91
Blagojević & Jokić TJ	42	12.80
Krstić TJ/Blagojević & Jokić TJ	97	29.57
Krstić TJ/Krstić AJ	4	1.22
Krstić TJ/Krstić AJ/Blagojević & Jokić TJ	9	2.74
Krstić AJ/Blagojević & Jokić TJ	1	0.30
Krajišnik TJ	17	5.18
Orić TJ	33	10.06
Total	**328**	**100.00**

(continued)

Table 4.3 (continued)

Popović et al.		
Source	#	%
Total # judicially noticed facts in decisions		328
Total # judicially noticed facts in judgement		155
% facts used in judgement		47.3
Dragomir Milošević		
Source	#	%
Galić TJ	116	100.00
Total # judicially noticed facts in decisions		116
Total # judicially noticed facts in judgement		33
% facts used in judgement		28.5

4.3.5 Appeal Proceedings

4.3.5.1 Introduction

The appeal stage in international criminal proceedings allows for a second stage in the proceedings, in which both the conviction and the sentence can be challenged. The possibility for the accused to appeal both conviction and sentence aims, *inter alia*, to enhance accurate fact-finding, to verify whether fair trial rights have been observed during the trial proceedings and to enable the accused (or the prosecutor) to formulate objections against the trial judgment. The right to appeal does not imply that a *quasi*-retrial is held in which all the evidence is presented a second time. On the contrary: mostly, the applicants are requested to limit themselves to those parts of the trial judgment they disagree with. This enables, for example, the accused to limit his appeal to the sentence, without challenging the factual conclusions of the Trial Chamber.

Appeal proceedings in international criminal law are conducted in a hierarchical structure, in which the Appeals Chamber has the final say in both legal and factual matters. Damaška argued that appeal proceedings in a hierarchical structure result in 'provisional' judgments of the lower courts:

> The great significance attributed to 'quality control' by superiors in a hierarchical organization inevitably detracts from the importance of original decision making: the latter acquires an aura of provisionality [sic].[321]

The character of appeal proceedings in international criminal proceedings differs, however, from Damaška's characterization. The Appeals Chamber of the ICTY and ICTR has consistently held that appeal proceedings are not trials de novo: evidence will not be re-evaluated, nor will new evidence be admitted on

[321] Damaška 1986, p. 49.

appeal unless there is a pressing need to do so.[322] Both the accused and the prosecutor are required to put forward their objections to well-defined legal or factual matters. For present purposes, the manner in which errors of law are handled in appeal proceedings is not relevant; this section is solely concerned with the manner in which evidence is processed in appeal proceedings. The manner in which factual errors are addressed by the Appeals Chamber in international criminal proceedings is of interest here.

4.3.5.2 Legal Framework

Article 25 ICTY Statute and Article 24 ICTR Statute allow for two distinct grounds of appeal. First, both the prosecutor and the accused may appeal on the ground that the Trial Chamber made an error of law that has invalidated the judgment. Second, both parties may appeal when the Trial Chamber made an error of fact that has resulted in a miscarriage of justice. The Appeals Chamber has the same powers as the Trial Chamber: the Rules of Procedure and Evidence apply *mutatis mutandis* to the appeal proceedings.[323]

The ICC Statute makes a distinction between the prosecutor and the convicted person, regarding the grounds of appeal. According to Article 81(1)(a) ICC Statute, the prosecutor may appeal on the grounds that the Trial Chamber has made a procedural error, an error of fact or an error of law. The convicted person, or the prosecutor on that person's behalf, may also appeal on these grounds and may, additionally, appeal on 'any other ground that affects the fairness or reliability of the proceedings or decision' (Article 81(1)(b) ICC Statute). Rule 149 ICC RPE states that the rules governing the proceedings before the Pre-Trial Chamber and the Trial Chamber apply *mutatis mutandis* to the appeal proceedings. This includes the provisions on the submission of evidence.[324]

The provisions of the Statutes of the ad hoc Tribunals contain a rather high threshold for a successful appeal: the alleged error must have resulted in either an invalid decision (in case of an error of law) or a miscarriage of justice (in case of an error of fact). The ICC Appeals Chamber may reverse or amend the decision or sentence or order a new trial on two grounds: unfairness of the trial proceedings that has affected the reliability of the Trial Chamber's decision; or, when one of the errors enumerated in Article 81(1) ICC Statute has materially affected the Trial Chamber's decision.[325]

322 Cf. the remarks of Mohamed Shahabuddeen, former judge in the ICTY/ICTR Appeals Chamber: 'A court of rehearing does not appear to exemplify the ICTY appeal procedures; the Appeals Chamber of the ICTY seems to bear a closer affinity to a court of review.' Shahabuddeen 2012, p. 100.

323 Rule 107 ICTY RPE; Rule 107 ICTR RPE.

324 See also Article 83(1) ICC Statute, which states: 'For the purposes of proceedings under Article 81 and this article, the Appeals Chamber shall have all the powers of the Trial Chamber.'

325 Article 83(2) ICC Statute.

The parties have a decisive say regarding the scope of the appeal proceedings: the Appeals Chamber will concentrate the appeal proceedings primarily on the grounds brought forward by the applicants. As the Appeals Chamber held in *Kunarac et al.*:

> As set out in Article 25 of the Statute, the Appeals Chamber's mandate cannot be effectively and efficiently carried out without focused contributions by the parties. In a primarily adversarial system, like that of the International Tribunal, the deciding body considers its case on the basis of the arguments advanced by the parties. It thus falls to the parties appearing before the Appeals Chamber to present their case clearly, logically and exhaustively so that the Appeals Chamber may fulfill its mandate in an efficient and expeditious manner.[326]

The ICC Appeals Chamber held that when the accused alleges that the Trial Chamber committed a factual error, the accused must provide the Appeals Chamber with detailed submissions regarding the interpretation of the evidence. Merely repeating arguments that were presented during the trial proceedings does not suffice: the accused must make clear that the Trial Chamber acted unreasonably in weighing the evidence.[327]

Although the Statutes and Rules of Procedure and Evidence do not specifically address the question, it is highly unlikely that the Appeals Chamber will address factual issues *proprio motu*, i.e. without a specific ground of appeal submitted by the applicants. The Appeals Chambers of the ad hoc Tribunals and the ICC are, however, not barred from conducting such a *proprio motu* fact-finding exercise: Rule 98 ICTY RPE and ICTR RPE allows the Appeals Chamber to order the production of additional evidence during the appeal proceedings.[328] Similar provisions can be found in the ICC Statute.[329] Appeal proceedings are, for all practical purposes, limited to the alleged errors identified by the prosecutor or accused. This means that the accused must act diligently in order to bring factual errors to the attention of the Appeals Chamber.

The Appeals Chamber of the ICTY and ICTR consistently held that appeal proceedings are corrective and not trials de novo: the primary responsibility for

---

[326] ICTY, Judgment, *Prosecutor v. Kunarac et al.*, Case No.: IT-96-23 & IT-96-23-A, A. Ch., 12 June 2002, para 43.

[327] ICC, Judgment on the Appeal of Mr Thomas Lubanga Dyilo Against his Conviction, *Prosecutor v. Lubanga Dyilo*, Case No.: ICC-01/04-01/06 A 5, A. Ch., 1 December 2014, para 33. The ICTY Appeals Chamber held that deficient submissions by the parties do not need to be considered on the merits. When a submission is made regarding an alleged factual error, the accused must ensure that his submission is clear and not a repetition of arguments raised at trial. Cf. ICTY, Judgment, *Prosecutor v. Tolimir*, Case No.: IT-05-88/2-A, A. Ch., 8 April 2015, para 14.

[328] Rule 107 ICTY RPE and ICTR RPE state: 'the rules of procedure and evidence that govern proceedings in the Trial Chamber shall apply *mutatis mutandis* to proceedings in the Appeals Chamber.'

[329] Article 83(1) ICC Statute and Article 69(3) ICC Statute.

accurate fact-finding lies with the Trial Chamber.[330] A margin of deference is given to the Trial Chamber because the Trial Chamber hears, for example, witnesses and is therefore able to properly assess the reliability of the witness testimony and weigh this against the other evidence. The prominent position of the Trial Chamber regarding fact-finding also means that the parties may not use the appellate stage to remedy their mistakes or omissions made during the trial proceedings.[331] For example, additional evidence on appeal is not admissible if the evidence was already available during trial: counsel is expected to act diligently and present all relevant and available evidence before the Trial Chamber. Only when 'gross negligence is shown to exist' on the part of the counsel may the Appeals Chamber admit additional evidence that was already available during the trial proceedings.[332] Gross negligence of counsel should not be detrimental to the interests of the accused.

The Appeals Chamber in *Limaj* summed up which evidence the Appeals Chamber will consider during the appeal: evidence referred to by the Trial Chamber in the body of the judgment or in a footnote; evidence in the trial record, referred to by the parties; and any additional evidence admitted during the appeal.[333] Considering the volume of evidence presented during the trial proceedings, it makes sense to limit the amount of evidence that is considered in-depth on appeal: it is impossible to present and weigh all the evidence anew. This limitation can only be justified if the Trial Chamber has indicated in detail which evidence it finds reliable and supportive for the charges. In order to be an effective supervisory mechanism, marginal supervision regarding the facts requires a well-reasoned judgment of the Trial Chamber. It is hard, however, for Trial Chambers to fully comply with this requirement. As the Appeals Chamber held in *Brđanin*:

> Evidence before a Trial Chamber is notoriously voluminous: a Trial Chamber cannot be expected to refer to all of it. The Appeals Chamber has to presume that *all relevant evidence* was taken into consideration by the Trial Chamber even if not expressly referred to by it, as long as there is no indication that the Trial Chamber completely disregarded any particular piece of evidence. A Trial Chamber does not have to explain every decision it makes, as long as the decision, with a view to the evidence, is reasonable.[334]

---

330 ICTY, Judgment, *Prosecutor v. Vasiljević*, Case No.: IT-98-32-A, A. Ch., 25 February 2004, para 5. ICTY, Judgment, *Prosecutor v. Kordić & Čerkez*, Case No.: IT-95-14/2-A, A. Ch., 17 December 2004, para 19, 21. Cf the Appeals Chamber in *Krajišnik*: 'The Appeals Chamber will not review the entire trial record de novo. Rather, it will in principle only take into account evidence referred to by the Trial Chamber in the body of the judgment or in a related footnote, evidence contained in the trial record and referred to by the parties, and additional evidence admitted on appeal.' ICTY, Judgment, *Prosecutor v. Krajišnik*, Case No.: IT-00-39-A, A. Ch., 17 March 2009, para 13.

331 ICTY, Judgment, *Prosecutor v. Erdemović*, Case No.: IT-96-22-A, A. Ch., 7 October 1997, para 15.

332 ICTY, Judgment, *Prosecutor v. Kupreškić et al.*, Case No.: IT-95-16-A, A. Ch., 23 October 2001, paras 50–51.

333 ICTY, Judgment, *Prosecutor v. Limaj et al.*, Case No.: IT-03-66-A, A. Ch., 27 September 2007, para 10.

334 ICTY, Judgment, *Prosecutor v. Brđanin*, Case No.: IT-99-36-A, A. Ch., 3 April 2007, para 11. Emphasis added. It is noted that this quotation does not include *irrelevant* evidence: it is a matter of common sense that evidence which has no probative value or is irrelevant is not referred to in the judgment. Cf. ICTY, Judgment, *Prosecutor v. Hadžihasanović*, Case No.: IT-01-47-A, A. Ch., para 13.

The margin of deference regarding factual issues is then rather substantial: the parties, in particular the accused, have to specifically draw the Appeals Chamber's attention to contested factual issues.

At the ICC, two appeal judgments have been handed down so far. The Appeals Chamber referred to the similarities between the legal framework of the ad hoc Tribunals and the ICC with regard to appeal proceedings. The margin of deference that is given to the Trial Chambers of the ICTY and ICTR regarding factual issues will be applied by the ICC Appeals Chamber as well.[335]

4.3.5.3 Additional Evidence on Appeal

Rule 115 ICTY RPE and ICTR RPE allows for the admission of additional evidence on appeal. A party requesting additional evidence to be admitted during the appeal proceedings must indicate to which factual finding of the Trial Chamber the additional evidence is directed. If the evidence is relevant and credible and was not available at trial, the Appeals Chamber will determine whether the additional evidence, together with any evidence in rebuttal, could have been a decisive factor in the Trial Chamber's deliberations. If this is the case, the Appeals Chamber will consider the additional evidence together with the evidence already on the record. This provision is concerned with additional evidence regarding the guilt or innocence of the accused. If one of the parties wishes to challenge other matters, the general admissibility requirements of Rule 89(C) ICTY and ICTR RPE apply.[336]

Additional evidence may also be presented during appeal proceedings at the ICC: Article 83(1) ICC Statute and Rule 149 ICC RPE state that the Appeals Chamber has the same powers of the Trial Chamber. This means that additional evidence can be admitted. In the first appeal judgment on the merits, the Appeals Chamber observed that it 'will generally not admit additional evidence on appeal unless there are convincing reasons why such evidence was not presented at trial, including whether there was a lack of due diligence.'[337]

---

[335] ICC, Judgment on the Appeal of Mr Thomas Lubanga Dyilo Against his Conviction, *Prosecutor v. Lubanga Dyilo*, Case No.: ICC-01/04-01/06 A 5, A. Ch., 1 December 2014, para 27. ICC, Judgment on the Prosecutor's Appeal against the Decision of Trial Chamber II entitled "Judgment pursuant to Article 74 of the Statute"', *Prosecutor v. Ngudjolo Chui*, Case No.: ICC-01/04-02/12 A, A. Ch., 7 April 2015, paras 18–27.

[336] ICTY, Judgment, *Prosecutor v. Kupreškić et al.*, Case No.: IT-95-16-A, A. Ch., 23 October 2001, para 55 (with references to case law).

[337] ICC, Judgment on the Appeal of Mr Thomas Lubanga Dyilo Against his Conviction, *Prosecutor v. Lubanga Dyilo*, Case No.: ICC-01/04-01/06 A 5, A. Ch., 1 December 2014, para 58.

4.3.5.4 Standard of Review

The standard of factual review is the standard of reasonableness: the Trial Chamber's findings of fact will not be overturned lightly.[338] The Appeals Chamber will only 'substitute its own findings for that of the Trial Chamber when no reasonable trier of fact could have reached the original decision.'[339] The Appeals Chamber will only overturn the alleged error of fact when the error has resulted in a miscarriage of justice, which has been defined as 'a grossly unfair outcome in judicial proceedings, as when a defendant is convicted despite a lack of evidence on an essential element of the crime.'[340] The ICC Appeals Chamber held that:

> when a factual error is alleged, the Appeals Chamber will determine whether a reasonable Trial Chamber could have been satisfied beyond reasonable doubt as to the finding in question. The Appeals Chamber will not assess the evidence *de novo* with a view to determining whether it would have reached the same factual conclusions as the Trial Chamber.[341]

This entails that the Appeals Chamber accords the Trial Chamber a margin of deference regarding the determination of factual issues.

Standard of review and additional evidence on appeal

When additional evidence is admitted during the appeal proceedings, the Appeals Chamber has more evidence to consider than the Trial Chamber did. What are the consequences for the standard of review?

In the *Blaskić* appeal judgment, the Appeals Chamber made a distinction between two scenarios in which additional evidence has been admitted. If, in the first scenario, the Appeals Chamber comes to the conclusion that no reasonable trier of fact could have reached a finding of guilt based on the evidence before the Trial Chamber and the additional evidence, the Appeals Chamber must apply a deferential standard of review. It will not determine whether it is itself convinced beyond reasonable doubt, but will merely state that no reasonable trier of fact *could* be convinced beyond reasonable doubt. Although this reasoning is somewhat formalistic (if one states that no reasonable trier could be convinced of

---

[338] ICTY, Judgment, *Prosecutor v. Tolimir*, Case No.: IT-05-88/2-A, A. Ch., 8 April 2015, para 11. ICC, Judgment on the Prosecutor's Appeal Against the Decision of Trial Chamber II Entitled "Judgment Pursuant to Article 74 of the Statute"', *Prosecutor v. Ngudjolo Chui*, Case No.: ICC-01/04-02/12 A, A. Ch., 7 April 2015, para 23.

[339] ICTY, Judgment, *Prosecutor v. Hadžihasanović*, Case No.: IT-01-47-A, A. Ch., para 13. Cf. ICTY, Judgment, *Prosecutor v. Stakić*, Case No.: IT-97-24-A, A. Ch., paar 10.

[340] ICTY, Judgment, *Prosecutor v. Simić*, Case No.: IT-95-9-A, 28 November 2006, para 10 (with references to case law).

[341] ICC, Judgment on the Appeal of Mr Thomas Lubanga Dyilo Against his Conviction, *Prosecutor v. Lubanga Dyilo*, Case No.: ICC-01/04-01/06 A 5, A. Ch., 1 December 2014, para 27. See also ICC, Judgment on the Prosecutor's Appeal against the Decision of Trial Chamber II entitled "Judgment pursuant to Article 74 of the Statute"', *Prosecutor v. Ngudjolo Chui*, Case No.: ICC-01/04-02/12 A, A. Ch., 7 April 2015, para 23–27.

the guilt of the accused, one does not apply a deferential standard but the beyond reasonable doubt standard itself), it is instructive to compare it with the second scenario.

In the second scenario, the Appeals Chamber finds, on the basis of the evidence before the Trial Chamber and the additional evidence on appeal, that a reasonable trier of fact *could* reach a finding of guilt beyond reasonable doubt. In such cases, the Appeals Chamber will not apply a deferential standard, but will consider whether it is convinced beyond a reasonable doubt of the guilt of the accused. This way, the totality of the evidence has been properly weighed once. In practice, if an appeal is filed by the defence alleging that the Trial Chamber made an error of fact and additional evidence has been admitted, the Appeals Chamber will proceed as follows. It will first verify whether, on the basis of the trial record alone, a reasonable trier of fact could be convinced beyond reasonable doubt of the guilt of the accused. If not, no further examination of the additional evidence is needed: the Trial Chamber's judgment will be reversed. If, however, the Appeals Chamber concludes that a trier of fact could have reached a finding of guilt beyond reasonable doubt on the basis of the evidence presented to it, it will then consider the totality of the evidence and determine whether it is itself convinced of the guilt of the accused beyond reasonable doubt.[342]

In her dissenting opinion to the *Blaskić* appeal judgment, Judge Weinberg de Roca criticized the concept of 'the totality of the evidence'. She pointed out that the Appeals Chamber is not presented with the whole evidentiary record, but solely with the evidence the Trial Chamber has referred to in its judgment. Consequently, the Appeals Chamber is not in a position to consider the totality of the evidence of the case, she argued.[343]

The ability of the Appeals Chamber to consider the totality of the evidence can indeed be questioned. The evidence the Trial Chamber has referred to in its judgment is a selection from the total amount of evidence presented during the trial proceedings. Evidence the Trial Chamber deemed irrelevant or without probative value has been put aside, and the remaining evidence has been weighed holistically. Therefore, the only Chamber that has full knowledge of the total amount of evidence (besides, of course, the additional evidence presented on appeal) of the case is the Trial Chamber. Leaving patently clear cases aside, it is hard to see how the Appeals Chamber is able to actually weigh properly the totality of the

---

[342] ICTY, Judgment, *Prosecutor v. Blaškić*, Case No.: IT-95-14-A, A. Ch., 29 July 2004, paras 20–24. If the Appeals Chamber finds that the Trial Chamber applied a wrong legal standard to a factual finding, the Appeals Chamber will proceed in a similar manner. First, after pronouncing the correct legal standard, the Appeals Chamber determines whether it is itself convinced of the guilt of the accused beyond reasonable doubt. If it is, the Appeals Chamber will then determine whether it is *still* convinced beyond reasonable doubt when the additional evidence has been taken into account. See also: ICTY, Judgment, *Prosecutor v. Krajišnik*, Case No.: IT-00-39-A, A. Ch., 17 March 2009, paras 11–15.

[343] ICTY, Judgment, *Prosecutor v. Blaškić*, Case No.: IT-95-14-A, A. Ch., 29 July 2004, Partial Dissenting Opinion Weinberg de Roca para 7.

evidence. From an epistemological point of view, it would make more sense to refer the case back to the Trial Chamber to have it re-consider carefully the part of the judgment to which the additional evidence related. This would be in line with the deferential standard the Appeals Chamber normally applies concerning factual issues. Such a referral also allows the accused to challenge and comment on such additional evidence before the trier of fact that has all the evidence at his disposal.

The right to appeal the trial judgment is a principle of international criminal procedure.[344] It entails that the factual basis of the conviction or acquittal can be reviewed: the evidence on which the Trial Chamber relied can be challenged, and additional evidence can be admitted. This second stage of the proceedings does not, however, provide for a full rehearing and reassessing of all the evidence the Trial Chamber has been provided with. The deferential standard of the Appeals Chamber regarding factual issues precludes a 'fresh' determination of the facts of the case. In fact, the Appeals Chamber relies to a significant extent on the factual conclusions of the Trial Chamber. The specific character of the appeal proceedings results in a shortcut in which the accused must act diligently and actively in order to effectively participate during the appeal stage. Considering the fact that the Appeals Chamber is hesitant to reverse the factual findings of the Trial Chamber *proprio motu*, an informed and assertive accused is of the essence.

References

Ambos K (2009) The transnational use of torture evidence. Israel Law Rev 2:362–397

Anderson T, Schum D, Twining W (2005) Analysis of evidence. Cambridge University Press, Cambridge

Arendt H (1963) Eichmann in Jerusalem. A report on the banality of evil. Penguin Books, London (1963)

Boas G, Jackson J, Roche B, Taylor D (2013) Appeals, reviews, and reconsideration. In: Sluiter GK et al (eds) International criminal procedure: principles and rules. Oxford University Press, Oxford

Choo AL-T (2012) Evidence. Oxford University Press, Oxford

Damaška MR (1986) The faces of justice and state authority: a comparative approach to the legal process. Yale University Press, New Haven, London

Guariglia F, Hochmayr G (2008) Article 65. In: Triffterer O (ed) Commentary on the Rome Statute of the International Criminal Court. C.H. Beck/Hart/Nomos, Munich

Hall CK (2008) Article 7. In: Triffterer O (ed) Commentary on the Rome Statute of the International Criminal Court. C.H. Beck/Hart/Nomos, Munich

Heller KJ (2007) Prosecutor v. Karemera. Am J Int Law 101(1):157–163

Jacobs D (2013) Standard of proof and burden of proof. In: Sluiter GK et al (eds) International criminal procedure: principles and rules. Oxford University Press, Oxford

Jørgensen NHB, Zahar A (2013) Deliberation, dissent, judgment. In: Sluiter GK et al (eds) International criminal procedure: principles and rules. Oxford University Press, Oxford

Khan KAA, Dixon R (2009) Archbold International criminal courts practice, procedure and evidence. Sweet & Maxwell, London

[344] Boas et al. 2013, p. 1010.

Klamberg M (2013a) Evidence in International criminal trials. Confronting legal gaps and the reconstruction of disputed events. Martinus Nijhoff Publishers, Leiden/Boston
Klamberg M (2013b) General requirements for the admission of evidence. In: Sluiter GK et al (eds) International criminal procedure: principles and rules. Oxford University Press, Oxford
Kwon OG (2007) The challenge of an International criminal trial as seen from the bench. J Int Crim Justice 5(2):360–376
Laudan L (2006) Truth, error and criminal law. An essay in legal epistemology. Cambridge University Press, New York
Mamiya R (2007) Taking judicial notice of genocide? The problematic law and policy of the Karemera decision. Wisconsin Int Law J 25(1):1–22
Morgan EM (1943–1944) Judicial notice. Harvard Law Rev 57
Nerenberg M, Timmermann W (2011) Documentary evidence. In: Khan KAA, Buisman C, Gosnell C (eds) Principles of evidence in International criminal justice. Oxford University Press, Oxford
Piragoff DK (2008) Article 69. In: Triffterer O (ed) Commentary on the Rome Statute of the International Criminal Court. C.H. Beck/Hart/Nomos, Munich
Roberts P, Zuckerman A (2010) Criminal evidence. Oxford University Press, Oxford
Rohan CM (2010) Reasonable doubt standard of proof in International criminal trials. In: Khan KAA, Buisman C, Gosnell C (eds) Principles of evidence in International criminal justice. Oxford University Press, Oxford
Shahabuddeen M (2012) International criminal justice at the Yugoslav tribunal: a judge's recollection. Oxford University Press, Oxford
Shapiro BJ (1991) Beyond reasonable doubt and probable cause. University of California Press, Oakland
Sluiter GK (2009) Evidence. In: Cassese A (ed) Oxford companion to International criminal justice. Oxford University Press, Oxford
Stewart JG (2003) Judicial notice in International criminal law: a reconciliation of potential, peril and precedent. Int Criminal Law Rev 3:245–289
Tapper C (2010) Cross & Tapper on evidence. Oxford University Press, Oxford
Vasiliev SV (2014) International criminal trials: a normative theory. PhD-thesis, University of Amsterdam
Weigend T, Turner JI (2013) Negotiated justice. In: Sluiter GK et al (eds) International criminal procedure: principles and rules. Oxford University Press, Oxford
Wilson RA (2011) Writing history in international criminal trials. Cambridge University Press, Cambridge
Zappalà S (2013) Comparative models and the enduring relevance of the accusatorial—inquisitorial dichotomy. In: Sluiter GK et al (eds) International criminal procedure: principles and rules. Oxford University Press, Oxford

Chapter 5
Avoiding a Full Criminal Trial: Evading Fairness?

Abstract In this chapter the diversions and shortcuts, described in the previous chapters, are critically evaluated in light of the participatory model of proof. Each diversion and shortcut is analysed with the four elements of the participatory model as guidelines: non-compulsion, informed involvement, the ability to challenge the evidence and the element of a reasoned judgment. The main question of the chapter is whether the accused is able to participate effectively when the full criminal trial is avoided.

Keywords Fairness · Diversions · Shortcuts · Diversions · Shortcuts · Guilty plea · Admission of guilt · Agreed facts · Judicial notice · Facts of common knowledge · Adjudicated facts · Appeal proceedings · ICTY · ICTR · ICC · Dutch criminal proceedings

Contents

K. Vriend, *Avoiding a Full Criminal Trial*, International Criminal Justice Series 8, DOI 10.1007/978-94-6265-153-1_5

5.1 Introduction

In this chapter, the diversions and shortcuts that have been described in Chaps. 3 and 4 are evaluated. The participatory model of proof, as described in Chap. 2, is the normative framework. Each diversion and shortcut is analysed with the four elements of the participatory model as guidelines: non-compulsion, informed involvement, the ability to challenge the evidence and the element of a reasoned judgment. In this chapter, the elements are discussed in more detail, related to the particular diversions and shortcuts described in the previous chapters. The main question is whether the accused is able to participate effectively when the full criminal trial is avoided.

Certain elements of the participatory model, viewed in isolation, do not fit easily (or, not at all) to particular diversions or shortcuts. For example, the element of the reasoned judgment does not fit easily with diversions in which the decision is not handed down by the court.[1] Similarly, the element of non-compulsion does not seem to be a proper point of view when analysing the use of facts of common knowledge: the fact that the court identifies such facts *proprio motu* does not infringe in any way on the element of non-compulsion. It is precisely in these circumstances that the overall notion of participation is of the essence: certain elements may be not applicable or infringed, but it is vital that, overall, the accused is able to participate effectively.[2]

The European Court of Human Rights itself shows a flexible approach to the different elements of the model (for example by the Court's approach to jury trials and the right to a reasoned judgment). This testifies to the Court's holistic approach in the determination of whether the proceedings were fair: the Court considers the proceedings as a whole to determine whether the right to a fair trial has been infringed.

---

[1] The international practice on plea-bargaining provides for an interesting exception.

[2] Jackson and Summers make a similar point when they observe: 'The ECtHR has given states considerable leeway in translating these principles into national law in an attempt to accommodate established procedures within the two prevailing traditions. It may seem, for example, that jury trial offends against the principle of a reasoned judgment, but the ECtHR has accepted that one way of compensating for the lack of a reasoned judgment is by a carefully framed direction from the judge. It is also true that each principle may not in isolation measure up to the degree of participation permitted in one or other of the established traditions. For example, the right to examine witnesses in the adversarial tradition has not been confined only to decisive witnesses. By contrast, however, the second principle requiring informed defence participation before trial goes much further than traditional adversarial or inquisitorial procedure. Collectively, it may be said that the principles extend the boundaries of participation beyond those that have been traditionally permitted within each of the traditions and the established procedures have had to be realigned upon a more participatory footing.' Jackson and Summers 2012, p. 104.

As the Court's Grand Chamber held in *Al-Khawaya and Tahery*:

> The Court recalls that the guarantees in paragraph 3(d) of Article 6 are specific aspects of the right to a fair hearing set forth in paragraph 1 of this provision which must be taken into account in any assessment of the fairness of the proceedings,[3]

and,

> the Court has always interpreted Article 6 § 3 in the context of an overall examination of the fairness of the proceedings.[4]

Evaluating the fairness of diversions is particularly relevant, because the number of such out-of-court settlements is on the rise. This is not only the case in The Netherlands: this trend can be discerned all over the Continent.[5] Similarly, a substantial number of guilty pleas have been concluded before the international criminal tribunals. At first sight, it seems odd to take the case law of the European Court of Human Rights as the normative framework, particularly the Court's interpretation of Article 6. The Article protects the right to a fair trial: it does not protect the right to a fair out-of-court settlement. Nowadays, however, criminal law is to a very significant extent enforced outside the traditional trial context. In a state that promotes the rule of law, it is unacceptable to have diversions operate in a normative vacuum.

Regarding the Dutch context, Keulen argued that the rise of out-of-court settlements (predominantly in the form of punitive orders) may infringe on one of the fundamental pillars of the criminal justice system: accurate fact-finding.[6] The accuracy of the factual basis of out-of-court settlements is indeed important. A recent study conducted by the Procurator General of the Dutch Supreme Court concluded that punitive orders do not contain the means of proof on which they

[3] ECtHR (GC), 15 December 2011, App. No.: 26766/05 and 22228/06, (*Al-Khawaya and Tahery v. United Kingdom*), para 118.

[4] ECtHR (GC), 15 December 2011, App. No.: 26766/05 and 22228/06, (*Al-Khawaya and Tahery v. United Kingdom*), para 143. See also *Ibrahim and Others v. United Kingdom*, in which the Fourth Section of the Court held: 'The guarantees in para 3 of Article 6 are specific aspects of the right to a fair hearing set forth in Article 6 § 1 which must be taken into account in that evaluation. Their intrinsic aim is to contribute to ensuring the fairness of the criminal proceedings as a whole. But they are not an end in themselves; compliance with the requirements of a fair trial must be examined in each case having regard to the development of the proceedings as a whole, and not on the basis of the isolated consideration of one particular aspect or incident.' ECtHR, 16 December 2014, App. No.: 50541/08; 50571/08; 50573/08 and 40351/09, (*Ibrahim and Others v. United Kingdom*), para 191 (references omitted).

[5] See *Jaarbericht 2013 OM*. In 2013, a substantial number of cases result in a punitive order (34,300), a transaction (17,600) or conditional dismissal (9800). In the same year, the first-instance courts processed 110,050 cases. Weigend observed on the rise of out of court-settlements that 'The trial has become an accident in the smooth administration of criminal justice'. Weigend 2006, p. 209.

[6] Keulen 2014, p. 1.

are based.[7] This is troubling because it impedes the accused from determining easily whether the punitive order was issued correctly. Concerns regarding the use of plea-bargaining in the international context have been raised over the years: is it really desirable to avoid the trial context in case of international crimes?[8]

An important question is which procedural guarantees exist regarding diversion mechanisms. If the state (or an international court) wishes to exercise its *ius puniendi*, the accused should be able to derive protection from the basic and fundamental concept of fairness. Seen this way, the manner in which the Court has developed its 'trial concept' of fairness over the past decades reflects only in part what actually occurs in the member states regarding the enforcement of criminal law. Or, more specifically: the protection that the concept of fairness provides, does not apply to a significant part of the criminal justice system. A solid normative framework is indispensable because of the lack of transparency and public scrutiny of diversion mechanisms. We can evaluate such mechanisms by using the participation model and apply it by analogy: instead of asking ourselves to what extent the accused has been able to participate effectively during the trial proceedings, we ask ourselves how effectively the accused has been able to participate in the 'proceedings' resulting in the diversion from the full criminal trial.

5.1.1 Waiving Rights

One could argue that a normative framework for diversions already exists: the criteria for a valid waiver of the right to have the case brought before an independent and impartial tribunal protect the accused from undue interference by the prosecutor.[9] When the accused disagrees with the prosecutor on the facts of the case, the manner in which he is treated or the sentence that the prosecutor wants to impose, the accused may bring the case to court. In other words, the accused has a significant say regarding the use of the diversion mechanism: by not complying or by actively opposing the diversion mechanism, he can force the prosecutor to reconsider his intention to punish the accused. Should the prosecutor want to pursue the case, he must bring it to court, which means that all fair trial guarantees are applicable. Seen this way, the right of access to a court should then provide the

[7] Procureur-Generaal bij de Hoge Raad der Nederlanden 2014, p. 31. The report was conducted pursuant to Article 122(1) of the Judiciary Organization Act. This article gives the Procurator General the authority to inform the Minister of Security and Justice when the Procurator General finds that the prosecution service does not conduct its work properly.

[8] Weigend and Turner 2013, p. 1377.

[9] Jacobs and Van Kampen 2014, pp. 73–85.

necessary procedural guarantees for the diversion mechanism.[10] Complying with the terms of the diversion mechanism, in this view, is then to be regarded as a waiver of the fair trial guarantees that are applicable during trial proceedings.

Although the practice of diversion mechanisms has to comply with the Court's case law on waiving the right to access to a court and other fair trial rights, as a normative framework it does not suffice. Waiving the right of access to a court is the culmination of a process in which both the prosecutor and the accused operate in the shadow of trial proceedings. To focus solely on the final agreement of the parties ignores the process that has preceded it. The participatory model provides the normative framework required because it enables us to look at the process as a whole instead of looking at a single procedural moment.

5.1.2 Outline

The chapter is divided into two parts. In the first part, the manner in which the full criminal trial is avoided in the Dutch context is evaluated. The second part of the chapter is concerned with the international context.

5.2 Diversions and Shortcuts in Dutch Law of Criminal Procedure

5.2.1 Diversions and the Participatory Model of Proof

5.2.1.1 The Punitive Order

When the prosecutor wants to issue a punitive order consisting of community service, the prohibition to drive motor vehicles, the payment of a sum exceeding 2000 € (either as a fine or damages) or when the prosecutor wants to impose a measure, it is mandatory to hear the accused.[11] Hearing the accused aims, *inter*

---

[10] See for the right to access to a court: ECtHR, 27 February 1980, App. No.: 6903/75, (*Deweer v. Belgium*). For restrictions on this right, see for example, ECtHR (GC), 29 July 1998, App. No.: 51/1997/835/1041, (*Gúerin v. France*). In ECtHR, 21 February 1975, App. No.: 4451/70, (*Golder v. United Kingdom*), the Court for the first time recognized the right of access to a court in Article 6(1). The Court held in para 36: '(...) it follows that the right to access constitutes an element which is inherent in the right stated in Article 6 para 1. This is not an extensive interpretation forcing new obligations on the Contracting States: it is based on the very terms of the first sentence of Article 6 para 1 read in its context and having regard to the object and purpose of the Convention, a lawmaking treaty, and to general principles of law.'

[11] Article 257c CCP. In case of the payment of a sum exceeding 2000 € the accused must be accompanied by a lawyer.

alia, to improve the quality of the prosecutor's decision. Although hearing in this regard is not the same as an interrogation where the accused is under arrest, the accused must be warned that he has the right to remain silent during the hearing.[12] In this regard, the accused cannot be forced to incriminate himself, or, considering the character of the hearing, to contribute actively to the correct imposition of the punitive order. The recent report of the Procurator General shows that in almost all cases that were analysed, the accused was informed of his right to remain silent during the hearing.[13] The right of access to a lawyer before the hearing is respected in virtually all cases that were analysed.[14]

When the accused files a notice of disagreement against the punitive order, the case will be sent to court (unless the prosecutor withdraws the punitive order), and the provisions in the Code of Criminal Procedure on regular first-instance proceedings will apply. It is not uncommon that the prosecutor, when the case is sent to court, demands a higher sentence than the one stated in the punitive order. In the directive on the punitive order, issued by the Board of Procurator Generals, it is stated that the prosecutor may seek a higher penalty (with a maximum of 20 % above the initial sanction in the punitive order) in cases where the accused has not formulated the reasons for the complaint and fails to appear in court.[15] Similarly, when an accused does appear in court but refuses to explain the reasons for his complaint, the prosecutor may demand a higher penalty.

How does this relate to the element of non-compulsion? Kooijmans emphasized that the prosecutor is entrusted with the determination of the appropriate sentence for the accused. This requires him to ensure that the charge can be proven, that there are no legal impediments and that the accused cannot invoke any justification or excuse. Moreover, the initial sentence imposed by the prosecutor in the punitive order must be in conformity with standard sentencing guidelines.[16] Seen this way, to strive for a higher sentence because the accused files a complaint is not in conformity with the task the prosecutor has been entrusted with: imposing sentences.

Compared with the other diversions, the punitive order requires an active attitude from the accused. Whereas the transaction and conditional dismissal can only function properly when the accused agrees with the terms of both mechanisms, the punitive order becomes binding when the accused remains passive and does not file a notice of disagreement. The active attitude is closely related to the next element of the participatory model of proof: informed involvement.

---

[12] *Kamerstukken I*, 2005/06, 29849, C, p. 31.

[13] Procureur-Generaal bij de Hoge Raad der Nederlanden 2014, p. 33.

[14] Procureur-Generaal bij de Hoge Raad der Nederlanden 2014, p. 34.

[15] Aanwijzing OM-beschikking, para 4.1., *Stcrt*. 2015, 8971. See also *Kamerstukken II*, 2004/05, 29849, 3, p. 42.

[16] Kooijmans 2012, aant. 5.6.

The active attitude requires that the accused is sufficiently informed about the consequences of the issuance of the order. He has to be properly informed about his rights and the consequences of every procedural choice he may wish to make. Article 6(3)(a) of the Convention contains the right to be informed promptly of the nature and cause of the accusation. According to Article 257a(6)(b) CCP, the punitive order must contain the factual and legal aspects of the charge. 'Charge' has the same meaning as 'charge' in regular trial proceedings.[17] The Court has held that: 'in criminal matters the provision of full, detailed information concerning the charges against a defendant is an essential prerequisite for ensuring that the proceedings are fair'.[18] This encompasses both the factual basis and the legal characterization of the offence.[19] The right to be informed, however, is not concerned with providing the accused with information regarding his procedural rights. Nevertheless, Article 257(6)(f) CCP states that the punitive order must provide the accused with information on how to file a notice of disagreement against the punitive order. When the punitive order consists of a fine, the prosecutor (or a police officer) must inform the accused that the payment of the fine results in waiving the right to file a notice of disagreement.[20] When the accused is sufficiently informed of the consequences of paying and voluntarily decides to do so, he has validly waived his right to file a notice of disagreement. In response to the report of the Procurator General to the Supreme Court, the prosecution service decided to provide accused persons with a leaflet in which the legal framework of the punitive order is explained.[21] The accused is informed that he can only pay the fine or start with community service after he has consulted a lawyer, unless he waives his right to do so. Moreover, the accused is informed that when he pays, he can no longer file a notice of disagreement.

In case the punitive order is of a more serious character, the accused must be heard. He must also be informed explicitly of his right to a lawyer. In the most serious cases, a lawyer must accompany the accused when the prosecutor

---

[17] Article 257a(6)(b) CCP refers to Article 261(1) and (2) CCP on the requirements for charging the accused.

[18] ECtHR, 25 July 2000, App. No.: 23969/94, (*Mattoccia v. Italy*), para 59.

[19] ECtHR (GC), 25 March 1999, App. No.: 25444/94, (*Pélissier and Sassi v. France*), para 51. The Court observed in para 54 that '(…) as regards the complaint under Article 6 § 3(b) of the Convention, the Court considers that sub-paras (a) and (b) of Article 6 § 3 are connected and that the right to be informed of the nature and the cause of the accusation must be considered in the light of the accused's right to prepare his defence.'

[20] Aanwijzing OM-strafbeschikking, bijlage 2. *Stc.* 2013, 33003. These procedural guarantees are left out the most recent directive on the punitive order. This probably has to do with the reaction to the Procurator General's report on punitive orders. The Board of Procurators General decided that punitive orders that consist of a fine, may not be paid immediately any longer. https://www.om.nl/actueel/nieuwsberichten/@88117/reactie-rapport/ (last visit: 1 January 2016).

[21] https://www.om.nl/actueel/nieuwsberichten/@91271/aangepaste-werkwijze/ (last visit: 1 January 2016).

interrogates him. This way, the accused is provided with sufficient information on his procedural rights.

An important element concerns the factual basis of the punitive order: what is the evidence the prosecutor relies on?[22] And, more importantly, does the accused have access to the case file, and is he able to challenge any incriminating evidence? The right to challenge evidence is typically exercised during proper trial proceedings, where the prosecutor presents the evidence against the accused. Subsequently, the accused may challenge the evidence presented against him. Regarding the punitive order, no typical procedural moment is envisaged in which the evidence is presented with the possibility to challenge it: on the contrary, if the accused wishes to challenge the evidence, he should opt for the full criminal trial (in which the regular fair trial guarantees apply). Article 33 CCP states that as soon as the punitive order has been issued, the accused has the right to get acquainted with the case file.[23]

The prosecutor determines independently whether the accused is in fact guilty of the crime or infraction for which the punitive order is imposed. Thus, the prosecutor is obliged to disclose the incriminating evidence he has in his possession: the disclosure guarantees of Article 6 apply by analogy.[24] According to the Court, it is a 'requirement of fairness [...] that the prosecution authorities disclose to the defence all material evidence for or against the accused'.[25] This aspect of fairness is often linked to the principle of equality of arms and the right to have adequate time and facilities to prepare one's defence.[26] The obligation to provide the accused with all the relevant evidence after the punitive order has been issued was underlined by the Minister of Justice during the parliamentary debates on the punitive order.[27] In order to be effective, the evidence should be provided before the term to file a notice of disagreement has expired (that is, normally, within two weeks).

---

[22] In the report of the Procurator General examples are given of cases in which a considerable percentage (8 %) of the handled cases are based on an insufficient factual basis. Procureur-Generaal bij de Hoge Raad der Nederlanden 2014, pp. 59–60.

[23] Article 27c(3)(d) CCP states that accused that are *arrested* shall be notified of their right of access to the case file prior to the first interrogation. However, punitive orders may be issued without having arrested the accused. See also the directive on the punitive order, concerning the right to get acquainted with the case file. Aanwijzing OM-afdoening, *Stc.* nr. 11374, 29 April 2013.

[24] 'In addition Article 6(1) requires (...) that the prosecution authorities should disclose to the defence all material evidence in their possession for or against the accused.' ECtHR (GC), 16 February 2000, App. No.: 28901/95, (*Rowe and Davis v. United Kingdom*), para 60. See also ECtHR, 16 December 1992, App. No.: 13071/87, (*Edwards v. United Kingdom*), para 36.

[25] ECtHR, 16 December 1992, App. No.: 13071/87, (*Edwards v. United Kingdom*), para 36.

[26] Cf. ECtHR (GC), 16 February 2000, App. No.: 28901/95, (*Rowe and Davis v. United Kingdom*), para 60.

[27] *Kamerstukken II*, 2004/05, 29849, 3, p. 64.

The final element of the participatory model of proof concerns the right to a reasoned judgment that can be challenged. In the case of the punitive order it is more appropriate to speak of the right to a reasoned decision. There are multiple rationales for a reasoned decision. First, a reasoned decision allows the parties to verify whether the prosecutor has taken the decision in accordance with the applicable rules. Second, the requirement to account for the findings ensures that the prosecutor accounts for his findings: he has to explain how he determined the guilt of the accused. Third, reasoned decisions demonstrate to the public that criminal law is enforced in a proper and transparent manner. Finally, in case the accused has formulated objections against particular elements of the case, the prosecutor must explain why the objection was found unpersuasive.

One of the conclusions in the Procurator General's report concerned the contents of the punitive order. Article 257a(6)(b) CCP states that the punitive order must contain the facts of the case, including when and where the fact was committed. The Procurator General concluded that the factual description in the punitive order is normally rather brief and sometimes even cryptic.[28] This may leave the accused in the dark as to which particular fact the punitive order was issued. This is also problematic with regard to the *ne bis in idem* rule. When the fact for which the punitive order is issued cannot be identified with sufficient precision, the protection of the *ne bis in idem* rule may be jeopardized.[29]

The Minister of Justice stated during the parliamentary debates on the punitive order that it is within the prosecutor's discretion to provide a reasoned punitive order.[30] Article 257a CCP does not contain an obligation to do so. Only when the accused has specifically addressed certain issues during the hearing is the prosecutor obliged to provide reasons, if he disagrees with the accused. If, however, the prosecutor has given the reasons orally, there is no obligation to put them in writing.[31]

In order for the right to file a notice of disagreement to be effective, the accused has to be able to participate effectively: only when the accused has full knowledge of the reasons for issuing the punitive order (more specifically, the incriminating evidence the prosecutor relies on) and is fully aware of his procedural rights, he can determine freely whether or not to file a notice of disagreement.

5.2.1.2 The Transaction

The transaction is a diversion mechanism characterized by consensus: unlike the punitive order, a sentence is not imposed but agreed to by the accused. When

---

28 Procureur-Generaal bij de Hoge Raad der Nederlanden 2014, p. 58.

29 Procureur-Generaal bij de Hoge Raad der Nederlanden 2014, p. 58.

30 *Kamerstukken II*, 2004/05, 29849, 3, p. 69.

31 Article 257c(3) CCP.

discussing the transaction, it is important to make a clear distinction between transactions that are offered for minor offences and so-called special transactions.[32] The latter category consists of all transactions above 500,000 € and transactions above 50,000 € that are not included in the internal prosecutorial directive. Transactions that are offered in controversial cases, such as cases that have attracted substantial media coverage or which concern ethical issues, are also labelled as special transactions. With the implementation of the punitive order, it was envisaged that the transaction would be abolished gradually. It still remains unclear, however, whether the transaction will indeed be abolished completely: particularly in complex cases (such as fraud cases involving corporations), the transaction enables the prosecutor to reach an out-of-court settlement, thereby avoiding costly and lengthy trial proceedings with an uncertain outcome. In case of minor offences, the transaction has been replaced by the punitive order.

The transaction is based on consensus between the accused and the prosecutor and on the actual enforcement of the conditions contained in it: the accused has to consent to the conditions of the transaction, and those conditions have to be fulfilled.[33] The legal character of the transaction itself presupposes voluntariness: the prosecutor cannot enforce the transaction unilaterally but has to seek the cooperation or consent of the accused. Although in cases concerning minor offences the transaction was often perceived as an ordinary fine that is imposed, this perception should not detract from the consensual character of the transaction. Especially in more controversial cases, the consensual character of the transaction will be acknowledged by the accused: he will normally be assisted by counsel, who informs the accused of this consensual character.

Considering the element of non-compulsion, it can be concluded that the transaction does not have a compulsory character. Although some pressure will exist due to the mere fact that someone is accused of a criminal offence, the transaction is based on voluntariness and consensus. The accused can simply ignore the transaction, in which case the prosecutor must initiate regular trial proceedings and bring the case to court. The major difference with the punitive order is the fact that a passive attitude of the accused will not lead to the enforcement of the conditions in the transaction (whereas remaining passive in the framework of the punitive order will lead to the enforcement of the punitive order).

Considering the element of informed involvement, it is again important to distinguish clearly between transactions offered for minor offences (which have been replaced by the punitive order) and the transactions with a special character. The latter category is of primary interest when the element of informed involvement is discussed: it is common practice that such transactions are concluded after negotiations have been conducted between the prosecutor and the accused (often represented or assisted by counsel). It is safe to assume that an accused who enters

[32] Cf. Aanwijzing hoge transacties en bijzondere transacties, *Stcrt*. 2008, 209 and *Stcrt*. 2013, 22031.

[33] Cf. Crijns 2010, pp. 175–6.

into negotiations with the prosecutor is well aware of his legal position and of the consequences that his procedural choices may have.

Closely related is the element of challenging the evidence. The fact that transactions are offered or negotiated *inter partes* without any public scrutiny makes it hard to determine to what extent the accused is able to get acquainted with incriminating evidence and whether he is in a position to challenge such evidence.[34] However, it seems safe to assume that the prosecutor will present the evidence (or a summary thereof) he relies on during the negotiations: if he does not do so, he will probably not convince the accused that he has a case that can be brought successfully before the court. The result will be that the negotiations fail.

The element of a reasoned judgment that can be challenged is practically absent: there is no judgment that is pronounced in public (the press release for special transactions cannot be equated with a fully reasoned judgment). Moreover, there is no incentive for either party to bring the case to court, which means the transaction cannot be challenged. It is instructive in this regard to recall the rationale of reasoned judgments. The Court has stated that the reasoned judgments are a 'vital safeguard against arbitrariness'.[35] Moreover, the accused must be able to understand the reasons for his conviction.[36] The Court, however, also held that the 'extent of the duty to give reasons varies according to the nature of the decision and must be determined in the light of the circumstances of the case.'[37] In a jury trial where no reasons for the conviction are given, the Court held that the trial proceedings as such and the manner in which the jury answered the questions put to them complied with the right to a reasoned judgment. As long as the parties are aware of the 'framework on which the decision had been based', there will be no violation of the right to a reasoned judgment.[38] This entails that the proceedings as such, instead of the final judgment, can provide the reasons for the outcome.

It is clear that these judgments of the Court are concerned with proper trial proceedings, in which the applicant complained that the *court* failed to provide him with a reasoned judgment. Nevertheless, the rationale the Court discerns for providing reasons is instructive for out-of-court settlements as well. The Court allows for a differentiated approach regarding the obligation to provide reasons; this depends on the nature of the decision and the procedure that has been chosen. Although the Court is concerned here with decisions within the trial context, this should not detract us from the fundamental importance of avoiding arbitrariness

[34] It should be noted though, that special transactions are, as a rule, accompanied by a press release, in which the prosecutor explains with whom he has reached a transaction. The press release includes the factual basis for the transaction, as well as the amount of money the accused has to pay to avoid trial proceedings. Cf. Aanwijzing hoge transacties en bijzondere transacties, para 4.

[35] ECtHR (GC), 16 November 2010, App. No.: 926/05, (*Taxquet v. Belgium*), para 90.

[36] ECtHR (GC), 16 November 2010, App. No.: 926/05, (*Taxquet v. Belgium*), para 92.

[37] ECtHR, 9 December 1994, App. No.: 18390/91, (*Ruiz Torija v. Spain*), para 29.

[38] ECtHR (GC), 16 November 2010, App. No.: 926/05, (*Taxquet v. Belgium*), para 86.

and providing the accused with sufficient reasons for offering a transaction. The obligation for the prosecutor to provide reasons can then be regarded as a legitimate alternative for providing the accused with a reasoned decision.

In the leading textbook on Dutch criminal procedure, Borgers argued in favour of judicial supervision for special transactions: the court should approve such transactions after a public hearing.[39] This way, both the quality of the transaction (is there sufficient evidence, has the prosecutor acted in conformity with all the applicable rules and regulations?) and the public scrutiny of the enforcement of criminal law is guaranteed. This resembles the practice of plea-bargaining of the international tribunals, which is described in Chap. 4. Such judicial approval would ensure that the procedural guarantees have been observed and that sufficient evidence has been collected. Considering the importance of the rights of the accused and transparent criminal law enforcement, judicial approval of special transactions is to be welcomed.[40]

5.2.1.3 The Conditional Dismissal

Similar to the transaction, conditional dismissals are based on consensus: the prosecutor stipulates the conditions the accused has to comply with, and the accused consents to those conditions. The analysis on the conditional dismissal resembles the analysis on the transaction.[41]

The dismissal is based on the notion that the accused complies voluntarily with the conditions stipulated by the prosecutor. The prosecutor cannot enforce the conditional dismissal. In case the accused refuses to comply, he must bring the case to court if he wishes to have the conditions imposed on the accused.

If the accused complies with the conditions of the conditional dismissal, the prosecutor forfeits the right to bring the case to court. Seen in the light of the element of non-compulsion: the accused may at any time refuse to comply, or refuse to comply any longer, with the conditions. The prosecutor has no enforcement mechanisms to ensure the (continued) cooperation of the accused: the only possibility left is to initiate regular trial proceedings.

Similar to the transaction, the degree of informed involvement depends on the manner in which the prosecutor informs the accused of his procedural rights. In case of a non-represented accused, the prosecutor should make sure the accused is well aware of the non-coercive character of the dismissal. In addition to his procedural rights, the accused should also get acquainted with the incriminating

[39] Corstens and Borgers 2014, p. 985.

[40] Verschaeren and Schoonbeek argued against the judicial approval of transactions. According to these authors, judicial approval renders the transaction proceedings inefficient. Verschaeren and Schoonbeek 2015, pp. 190–205.

[41] The character of the transaction and the conditional dismissal resemble each other. Cf. Crijns 2010, p. 190.

evidence. This enables him to make an informed decision as to whether or not to comply with the dismissal: if the accused believes that the evidence is insufficient, unreliable or illegally obtained, he may choose to refuse to comply. Normally this would result in regular trial proceedings in which the accused can contest the incriminating evidence.

In regard to the ability to challenge the evidence before the case goes to court, the law is silent. However, it seems reasonable to assume that the prosecutor will inform the accused about the evidentiary basis for the dismissal. One could argue that merely facilitating the participation of the accused, in the sense that the accused is given the opportunity to put forward his arguments, does not suffice: the prosecutor must ensure that the accused can participate effectively and should, therefore, bring the incriminating evidence to the attention of the accused. Within the trial context, Jackson and Summers argued that 'in order to ensure effective defence participation, it is not enough to facilitate defence participation. Steps must be taken to see that it is exercised effectively and the court has an important role to play in this regard.'[42] It is argued that the prosecutor has a similar responsibility: in the context of diversion mechanisms, he is the one that must enable the accused to participate effectively.

Similar to the transaction, no reasoned decision will be handed down. The legitimacy of the dismissal mechanism is based on the manner in which the prosecutor provides the accused with sufficient information and reasons during the process of issuing the dismissal. Again, to avoid arbitrariness it is vital that the prosecutor provides sufficient information to the accused in order for him to make an informed and voluntary decision.

5.2.2 Shortcuts and the Participatory Model of Proof

As was described in the Introduction, shortcuts to proof are used during the trial proceedings to speed up the proceedings. The principle of *nulla poena sine iudicio* is fully adhered to: there is direct judicial supervision on the use and fairness of the shortcut to proof. The shortcuts that were discussed in Chap. 3 are evaluated in light of the participatory model of proof: was the accused able to participate effectively when the shortcut to proof was used?

5.2.2.1 Facts of Common Knowledge

The use of facts of common knowledge can have detrimental consequences for the manner in which the accused is able to participate during the proceedings.

[42] Jackson and Summers 2012, p. 303.

Although no issue arises concerning the element of non-compulsion (the accused is not in any way compelled to provide or to challenge facts of common knowledge), the other elements of the participatory model of proof may be infringed.

The element of informed involvement may be infringed when the accused does not expect the court will consider the use of a fact of common knowledge to 'prove' a part of the *probandum*. Normally, the accused can easily determine to which part of the charge the means of proof relate: for example, witness statements relate to specific parts of the *probandum*, a DNA match relates to the identification of the accused and the statement of the accused may relate to the accused's *mens rea*. If, however, the court does not require formal proof for the existence of a particular fact, the accused may not be properly informed about the evidence the court relies on. This is particularly the case when the accused is confronted with a fact of common knowledge for the first time in the judgment. As discussed in Chap. 3, in several cases the use of facts of common knowledge to prove contextual facts, such as the existence and character of an armed conflict, was revealed to the accused for the first time in the judgment.

Closely related is the right to challenge the evidence. It is evident that the accused is not in a position to properly challenge the existence of facts of common knowledge when he is confronted for the first time with such facts in the judgment. The Supreme Court held in the *A.C.A.B.*-case that, when the court is not sure whether a fact is indeed of common knowledge, the court is obliged to discuss such a fact with the accused and the prosecutor. This enables the parties to comment on or challenge such facts. If one of the parties seriously doubts that the fact is of common knowledge and provides reasons for this view, the court is obliged to specifically respond to such arguments when it still finds the fact to be of common knowledge.[43]

The obligation for the court to provide reasons regarding why it deemed a particular fact to be of common knowledge is, in fact, triggered by the parties. The nature of facts of common knowledge implies that, normally, the court is under no obligation to account for the use of facts that are not controversial and are undisputed. Accordingly, it suffices for the court to identify facts of common knowledge and include them in the judgment. This explains why the parties can be surprised when the judgment is handed down and they learn how the court has made use of facts of common knowledge.

From a procedural point of view, a distinction can thus be made between two types of facts of common knowledge: facts that are patently indisputable and facts that are most likely to be of common knowledge but which have to be discussed during the proceedings. From an epistemological point of view this distinction is absurd: a fact is either of common knowledge or it is not. Procedurally, however, it makes sense to distinguish between the two types. In the latter category, the court is obliged to account specifically for the conclusion that certain facts are

[43] HR, 11 January 2011, *NJ* 2011, 116, m.n. Mevis. Cf. Article 359(2) CCP.

of common knowledge. When we take the example of the post WWII cases, as described in Chap. 3, the contextual fact of the state of war has been regarded as a fact of common knowledge by the extraordinary courts and the Extraordinary Court of Cassation. Even in cases in which the accused explicitly argued that no state of war existed when he committed his acts, the courts held that the state of war was of common knowledge. In the more recent prosecutions under the Criminal Law in Wartime Act and the International Crimes Act, contextual elements have been proven (in part or in whole) by facts of common knowledge. The District Court in *Joseph M.*, and to a lesser degree in *Yvonne B.*, based the finding that a non-international armed conflict existed in Rwanda on the ICTR's conclusion that the existence and nature of an armed conflict are facts of common knowledge. On the basis of the judgments, it cannot be verified whether the court discussed these facts with the prosecution and the defence during the proceedings. Neither can it be verified whether the defence challenged the existence and nature of the armed conflict.

The Supreme Court ruling in the *A.C.A.B.*-case is primarily concerned with facts that are not *prima facie* of common knowledge. However, even if certain facts are *prima facie* of common knowledge, it can still be important to identify and discuss these facts with the parties. This is particularly the case when such facts relate directly to important contextual facts.[44] The argument that the existence and nature of an armed conflict in Rwanda in 1994 is a notorious historical fact not subject to reasonable dispute is true but irrelevant in this regard: procedural justice demands that such facts are discussed (briefly or *in extenso*, when the parties or the court wishes to do so) with a view to adversarial argument ('un débat contradictoire'). It is the fundamental right of the accused to participate effectively in the proceedings and challenge every piece of evidence and facts of common knowledge he wishes.

The examples above illustrate why it is important to identify facts of common knowledge as soon as possible. It provides the accused with the possibility to challenge such facts and to participate effectively in the proceedings. This is of paramount importance when facts of common knowledge are used to prove contextual elements.

The final element of the participatory model of proof, the right to a reasoned judgment, does not apply as such to the use of facts of common knowledge: the court is, normally, not obliged to explain why a particular fact is of common knowledge.[45] This is not problematic with regard to the *prima facie* facts of common knowledge: it would be pointless to account for facts that are beyond dispute. The other category, however, requires more reasoning: the court must account for

[44] This is the situation in which a *factum probandum* is proven by a fact of common knowledge, instead of a *factum probans*.

[45] It is recalled that the use of facts of common knowledge aims to expedite proceedings and to limit the reasoning in the judgment.

why a particular fact is of common knowledge, for example, by referring to reliable and publicly accessible sources.[46]

5.2.2.2 Chain Evidence

Chain evidence allows the court to rely on the evidence or conviction regarding other charges in proving a particular charge. The use of chain evidence in criminal proceedings and the compatibility of this shortcut to proof with the right to a fair trial, in particular the right to examine witnesses, has been addressed by the Court in the case of *Scheper v. The Netherlands*. Before we turn to the elements of the participatory model, this case will be discussed first.

The accused in this case faced three charges of rape. The victims, drug-addicted street prostitutes, all stated that they had been raped in a very aggressive, painful and even bizarre manner. The rapes were committed in three different towns, but, considering the similar *modus operandi*, the police were able to arrest the accused. The accused admitted that he had sexual intercourse with the three women but denied that he had raped them. As is not uncommon in sexual assault cases, the evidence consisted mainly of the statements of the victims. The defence requested to have the three witnesses testify in open court in order to challenge their statements. Attempts to locate the witnesses and have them appear in court were, however, fruitless.[47] The defence argued that the right of the accused to examine the witnesses against him, protected under Article 6(3)(d) of the Convention, had been violated. The Court concluded that the fair trial rights of the accused in this particular case were not violated, because the statements were not the sole or decisive evidence against the accused. The Court held:

> Indeed, the Court observes that the applicant's conviction of the rape of Ms A., Ms B. and Ms C. did not rest solely on the statements made by them to the police. A number of leads, with which these witnesses had provided the police, had been followed up and had resulted in supporting evidence. Bearing in mind that it concerned three nearly identical incidents with a similar modus operandi by the perpetrator and which occurred within a relatively short time span in three different towns, and having regard to all the material used in evidence against the applicant, including his own statements made before the police and the trial courts, the Court holds that the applicant's conviction cannot be said to have been based only or to a decisive extent on the statements given by Ms A., Ms B. and Ms C. to the police.[48]

---

[46] An example of what such reasoning may look like, can be found in the *Karemera* case. Reasons were given by the ICTR Appeals Chamber for why a particular fact was of common knowledge, with references to public sources. ICTR, *Prosecutor v. Karemera*, Decision on Prosecutor's Interlocutory Appeal of Decision on Judicial Notice, Case No.: ICTR-98-44-AR73(C), A. Ch., 16 June 2006.

[47] Ms. A did appear before the Court of Appeal, but the defence was not able to question her: she stated that she believed she was called as an injured party and not as a witness. After a short adjournment of the proceedings, Ms. A did not return: she was too traumatized to give evidence. ECtHR, 5 April 2005, App. No.: 39209/02, (*Scheper v. The Netherlands*), pp. 2–3.

[48] ECtHR, 5 April 2005, App. No.: 39209/02, (*Scheper v. The Netherlands*), p. 8.

Consistent with its established case law, in particular the fourth instance-doctrine, the Court did not assess the evidence that was presented before the domestic courts.[49] The statements were not regarded by the Court as the only or decisive evidence against the accused because of the similar *modus operandi*. The Court, in determining whether the witness statements were the sole or decisive evidence against the accused, took into account the similarities between these statements. When we look at the three charges in isolation, however, it appears that the statements of the three women were the decisive evidence regarding each particular charge. Decisive evidence, according to the Court's definition, is 'evidence of such significance or importance as is likely to be determinative of the outcome of the case'.[50]

In the case of Ms A., the evidence consisted of her statement that she had been raped in Arnhem; the statement of the accused that he had sexual intercourse with Ms A.; a medical report of Ms A.; a police report on similar rapes in Groningen and Amsterdam; the statement of a witness who identified the accused from a number of photos; and, finally, the identification of the accused by Ms A. from a number of photographs.[51] It is evident that the statement of Ms A. and her identification of the accused were decisive evidence for the outcome of the case.

In the case of Ms B., the evidence consisted of the statement of Ms B.; a police report on the similar rape of Ms C. and the statement of the accused that he had sexual intercourse with a prostitute in Groningen.[52] Similar to the case of Ms A., the statement of Ms B. has to be regarded as decisive evidence.

In the case of Ms C., the evidence consisted of the statement of Ms C. that she had been raped in a car in an aggressive and very painful manner and the statement of the accused that he had sexual intercourse with a prostitute in Amsterdam. Ms C. was able to provide the police with the license plate of the car, which matched the license plate of the car of the accused.[53] Again, the statement of Ms C. is the decisive evidence in her case.

When the cases would have been analysed in isolation, it would have resulted in the conclusion that the right to examine the witnesses was violated: decisive witness statements have not been challenged, and no counterbalancing measures were taken. The Court held, however, that due to the similarities between the three cases, the statements of the women were not decisive evidence. In fact, each statement corroborated the other two statements. From an epistemological point of view this is a solid line of argument. Nevertheless, the accused has been deprived

49 ECtHR, 12 July 1988, App. No.: 10862/84, (*Schenk v. Switzerland*).

50 ECtHR (GC), 15 December 2011, App. No.: 26766/05 and 22228/06, (*Al-Khawaya and Tahery v. United Kingdom*), para 131.

51 ECtHR, 5 April 2005, App. No.: 39209/02, (*Scheper v. The Netherlands*), pp. 4–5.

52 ECtHR, 5 April 2005, App. No.: 39209/02, (*Scheper v. The Netherlands*), p. 5.

53 ECtHR, 5 April 2005, App. No.: 39209/02, (*Scheper v. The Netherlands*), pp. 5–6.

of the right to examine the witnesses against him. The right to challenge the evidence and participate effectively in the proceedings were not counterbalanced by any procedural measures. The reasoning of the Court is problematic because in cases in which the evidence consists predominantly of statements of vulnerable witnesses that do not testify in open court, chain evidence can be used as a remedy for not being able to examine the witnesses. This can hardly be regarded as a proper way of compensating the defence. As the Court held in *Al-Khawaya and Tahery*, when the conviction is based:

> solely or decisively on the evidence of absent witnesses, the Court must subject the proceedings to the most searching scrutiny. (…) The question in each case is whether there are sufficient counterbalancing factors in place, including measures that permit a fair and proper assessment of the reliability of that evidence to take place. This would permit a conviction to be based on such evidence only if it is sufficiently reliable given its importance in the case.[54]

In *Scheper*, such an assessment of the reliability of the unchallenged witness statements did not occur: the Court held that the statements were not decisive evidence.[55] The reasoning of the Court is not persuasive: the unchallenged statements are, as such, decisive evidence. This is not altered by the fact that the statements are regarded as chain evidence in order to support each other. The perils of using chain evidence are exemplified by the reasoning of the Court: by using the statements as chain evidence, the domestic court was not obliged to provide for counterbalancing measures. This means that the accused was not able to challenge the evidence against him effectively: he has not had the opportunity to challenge the witnesses directly, and it is uncertain whether he has had the opportunity to comment on the use of the statements as chain evidence.

When the use of chain evidence is examined in light of the participatory model of proof, it becomes evident that the right to effectively challenge the evidence is infringed when the use of chain evidence is not explicitly discussed during the proceedings. Chain evidence is normally used in proceedings in which there is insufficient evidence to prove each charge separately.[56] The evidence in such cases consists predominantly of the specific *modus operandi* regarding the different charges.

From the perspective of the accused, it is important that the potential use of chain evidence is discussed during the proceedings and not *in camera* after the close of the proceedings. The prosecutor, when he presents the case, often requests

---

[54] ECtHR (GC), 15 December 2011, App. No.: 26766/05 and 22228/06, (*Al-Khawaya and Tahery v. United Kingdom*), para 147.

[55] This does of course not mean that the domestic courts did not assess the reliability of the statements as such: the reliability of each statement has to be assessed by the court. However, when the evidence exists solely or decisively of unchallenged witness statements, the court must 'subject the proceedings to the most searching scrutiny.' Arguably, this entails more than the general obligation of courts to assess the reliability of witness evidence.

[56] See Chap. 3 and Vriend 2013.

the court to consider the use of chain evidence.[57] The court itself can also discuss the use of chain evidence during the proceedings. The accused is then enabled to challenge any perceived similarities between the different charges. When the court concludes that the accused acted in a particular *modus*, it will have to provide sufficient reasons for this conclusion in the judgment. However, when the prosecutor does not specifically request the court to use chain evidence, it is unlikely that the court will bring up the possibility of chain evidence *proprio motu*. There is no rule that obliges the court to discuss the use of chain evidence: the court is not obliged to provide the parties during the proceedings with information on how it will reason in the judgment.[58] Chain evidence in this respect has to be regarded as a particular way of providing reasons for the use of the evidence in the judgment; it has, therefore, more to do with the manner in which the judgment is drafted than with the manner in which the court discusses the evidence during the proceedings.

The fact that the court is not obliged to inform the parties before the drafting of the final judgment on the possible use of chain evidence, means that the accused may be confronted for the first time with chain evidence in the judgment. Thus, the accused can only challenge the use of chain evidence when there is the possibility of an appeal.[59] In order to successfully challenge the use of chain evidence during the appeal proceedings, it is essential that the first-instance court provides the accused with a reasoned judgment that specifically addresses the use of chain evidence. Dutch judgments in which chain evidence has been used are, in general, properly reasoned and specifically address the use of chain evidence.[60] This means that in case of first-instance judgments, the accused is able to specifically challenge the use of chain evidence during the appeal proceedings. Most importantly, he is able to question the court's conclusion that the charges are characterized by a similar *modus operandi*.[61]

---

[57] Examples in which the prosecutor requested the court to use chain evidence: Rechtbank Rotterdam, 23 April 2013 *ECLI*:NL:RBROT:2013:BZ8269; Rechtbank Oost-Brabant, 6 March 2014 *ECLI*:NLRBOBR:2014:1025; Rechtbank Noord-Holland, 24 June 2014 *ECLI*:RBNHO:2014:5724; Rechtbank Zeeland-West-Brabant, 29 July 2014, *ECLI*: RBZWB:2014:5364. Rechtbank Rotterdam, 23 December 2014 *ECLI*:RBROT:2014:10545; Rechtbank Amsterdam, 24 December 2013 *ECLI*:NL:RBAMS:2013:9339.

[58] Cf. De Wilde 2009, note 74.

[59] Although the accused can also complain before the Supreme Court on the use of chain evidence, the chances of success are greater during the appeal proceedings: the accused can challenge the factual and legal conclusions of the court. Before the Supreme Court, the accused can only file legal objections against the appeal judgment.

[60] E.g. Rechtbank Amsterdam, 21 March 2012 *ECLI*:NL:RBAMS:2012:BX0593; Gerechtshof Amsterdam, 21 December 2012 *ECLI*:NL:GHAMS:2012:BY7123; Rechtbank Breda, 2 September 2010, *ECLI*:NL:RBBRE:2010:BN5835; Gerechtshof Den Bosch, 11 October 2011, *ECLI*:NL:GHSHE:2011:BT7167. See also: Vriend 2013.

[61] More specifically: he may question the intra-individual and inter-individual variation of the behavior. See Chap. 3 for a more detailed discussion of these two notions.

5.2.2.3 Confessions and Cases Ad Informandum

The archetypical way of avoiding a full criminal trial is the confession. Depending on the characteristics of a particular criminal justice system, the confession is regarded as either a diversion or a shortcut to proof. Thus, when we evaluate confessions and *ad informandum* cases, it is important to distinguish clearly between the character of confessions in Dutch criminal proceedings and the character of confessions in international criminal proceedings. In the terminology of the Dutch Code of Criminal Procedure, a confession, as such, does not exist: Article 341(1) CCP holds that the *statement* of the accused can be used as evidence. In international criminal law, a confession is to be regarded as a procedural fact: the accused waives his right to trial proceedings and diverts the case from the court. Provided that the court regards the confession of the accused as a valid guilty plea or admission of guilt, the proceedings enter into the sentencing stage. As described in Chap. 3, the difference has important procedural consequences: in general, a guilty plea or an admission of guilt will significantly change the procedural context. In Dutch trial proceedings, the procedural context remains the same (although the proceedings will, most likely, no longer be concentrated on the determination of the guilt of the accused). Accordingly, the confession is regarded as a shortcut to proof in the Dutch context.

Confessions and the element of non-compulsion constitute a well-known pair and have attracted considerable scholarly attention. The Court itself has often ruled on the question of whether or not an accused has been compelled to testify. In the famous *Gäfgen* case, the Court held that:

> As regards the use of evidence obtained in breach of the right to silence and the privilege against self-incrimination, the Court reiterates that these are generally recognized international standards which lie at the heart of the notion of fair procedures under Article 6.[62]

As long as the coercion does not infringe the very essence of the right to self-incrimination, the use of coercive measures is allowed. In *Jalloh*, the Court held that in order to determine whether any compulsion was improper, it took into account the nature and the degree of the compulsion, the existence of any procedural safeguards and the use to which any material so obtained was put.[63] In case of confessions obtained during the investigations, issues may arise regarding the right not to be compelled to provide self-incriminatory statements.

Considering confessions and the participatory model of proof, the following observations can be made. First, as was stated above, it is important to verify that the accused was not in any way forced or compelled to confess to the charges. Regarding the element of informed involvement, it is important that the accused is fully aware of the consequences of his confession. This is particularly the case with regard to the other two elements: the ability to effectively challenge the evidence and the right to a reasoned judgment. Normally, the accused does not want to challenge any incriminating evidence: by confessing to the charges, he

62 ECtHR (GC), 1 June 2010, App. No.: 22978/05, (*Gäfgen v. Germany*), para 168.

63 ECtHR (GC), 11 July 2006, App. No.: 54810/00, (*Jalloh v. Germany*), para 101.

implicitly waives the right to challenge the evidence against him. This waiver, however, can be withdrawn during the proceedings: if the accused wishes to alter his confession or to challenge particular pieces of evidence, the court will have to conduct more rigorous fact-finding. According to Article 359(3) CCP, in cases in which the accused has confessed, it suffices to just list the means of proof instead of giving a fully reasoned judgment.[64] This is an example of a 'contest-orientated' approach: when the accused acknowledges his guilt, there is no contested issue left, which obviates the need for the court to provide a fully reasoned judgment.[65]

Regarding the *ad informandum* cases, the following observations can be made. It is highly unlikely that in such cases issues will arise regarding the element of non-compulsion. The accused is informed before the start of trial proceedings of the *ad informandum* cases, and he has to acknowledge in court that he has committed those facts. In general, the accused will have an incentive to do so: the cases are dismissed, no formal proceedings can be initiated for these facts anymore and the sentence will be more moderate than when the fact would be prosecuted separately. In Chap. 3, the situation was discussed in which, in the absence of the accused, the court could nevertheless take the *ad informandum* cases into consideration.[66] Considering the element of non-compulsion, the Code of Criminal Procedure explicitly states that the accused may not be compelled to provide self-incriminatory statements. This applies to the investigation phase and to the trial proceedings.[67]

Considering the element of informed involvement, it is important to emphasize that cases *ad informandum* are not formal charges. This means that the provisions on the indictment are not, as such, applicable. Article 6(3)(a) ECHR states that the accused must be informed in detail of the nature and cause of the accusation against him. However, when this provision is considered together with the right to a fair hearing and the right to prepare a defence, it follows that the accused must be informed in detail of the nature and cause of the proceedings initiated against him.[68] Although these are not formal charges, the accused is expected to comment

---

[64] For a case law analysis, see Duker 2012.

[65] This resembles the manner in which appeal proceedings are conducted: the proceedings are normally concentrated on contested issues. Cf. *Kamerstukken II*, 2003/04, 29255, 3, p. 7.

[66] See also, for example, HR, 24 March 2009, *ECLI*:NL:HR:2009:BH1784, para 2.4.

[67] Article 29(1) and Article 271(1) CCP.

[68] On the relationship between Article 6(3)(a) and Article 6(1) see, *inter alia*, the Grand Chamber's judgment in *Pélissier and Sassi v. France*: 'Article 6 § 3(a) of the Convention affords the defendant the right to be informed not only of the cause of the accusation, that is to say the acts he is alleged to have committed and on which the accusation is based, but also the legal characterization given to those acts. That information should, as the Commission rightly stated, be detailed. The scope of the above provision must in particular be assessed in the light of the more general right to a fair hearing guaranteed by Article 6 § 1 of the Convention [...]. The Court considers that in criminal matters the provision of full, detailed information concerning the charges against a defendant, and consequently the legal characterization that the court might adopt in the matter, is an essential prerequisite for ensuring that the proceedings are fair.' ECtHR (GC), 25 March 1999, App. No.: 25444/94, (*Pélissier and Sassi v. France*), para 51–52.

on them during the proceedings and, when he confesses, the court will take the *ad informandum* cases into account in sentencing. This means that the accused must be informed in sufficient detail of those facts. The accused has to be informed of the *ad informandum* case, but this may be done in a very rudimentary manner (such as a short description of the fact, with an indication of the time and place). When the accused is not willing to confess to the fact, the court cannot take it into account in sentencing. When the accused is not present during the proceedings, the court can still take the *ad informandum* case into consideration. This is possible when the accused has confessed at an earlier stage, for example during police interrogation, that he has committed the *ad informandum* case. The Supreme Court held that the *Salduz* criteria, as such, do not apply for such 'out-of-court confessions': the court may take these cases into consideration regarding the sentence, even if the accused has not been able to consult a lawyer.[69] From an informed involvement perspective, this is unacceptable: the accused is not sufficiently informed about the possible consequences of his out-of-court confession. In his advisory opinion, the Advocate General to the Supreme Court argued that such out-of-court confessions would have been excluded from the evidence when the prosecutor would have filed formal charges.[70] Consequently, the protection that the accused derives from *Salduz* is circumvented when the out-of-court confessions are used to present a case *ad informandum*.

Considering the possibility to challenge the evidence, the accused can simply deny the facts or remain silent. This way, the court cannot take the *ad informandum* facts into consideration. Moreover, the prosecutor will not present any evidence, which means that challenging the evidence is pointless. It is important for the accused to have the *ad informandum* cases mentioned in the judgment (or in the transcript of the proceedings). Only in this way will he be able to demonstrate that the cases have been disposed of. Should the prosecutor initiate formal proceedings for such cases, the accused can invoke the protection of due process considerations and the *ne bis in idem*-principle.

The final element of the participatory model of proof, the right to a reasoned judgment, is, as such, not applicable to *ad informandum* cases. Such cases are only mentioned in the judgment, more specifically in the part on sentencing.[71] The court does not provide reasons for taking these cases into account, but merely refers to the confession of the accused. This resembles the abbreviated judgment when the accused confesses to a formal charge: it suffices, according to Article 359(3) CCP, to list the means of proof instead of providing a fully reasoned judgment.

---

[69] HR, 22 May 2012, *ECLI*:NL:HR:2012:BW6174, para 2.3.3.

[70] Advisory Opinion of the Advocate General, HR 22 May 2012, *ECLI*:NL:HR:2012:BW6174.

[71] E.g. *ECLI*:NL:RBUTR:2010:BO5058; *ECLI*:NL:RBZLY:2010:BM2073; *ECLI*:NL:RBNNE:2015:810; *ECLI*:NL:GHARL:2014:6902; *ECLI*:NL:GHARL:2014:5115.

5.2.2.4 Appeal Proceedings

Appeal proceedings provide for a full review of both conviction and sentence: the court of appeal is not bound by any part of the first-instance judgment and conducts fact-finding autonomously.[72] However, the findings of the court of first instance and the objections of the parties against the first-instance judgment are relevant to the manner in which the appeal proceedings are conducted. The court of appeal may take into account the transcript of the first-instance proceedings.[73] It was concluded in Chap. 3 that appeal proceedings are significantly influenced by the case strategy of the parties, in particular by the objections they file against the first-instance judgment. When the accused, with or without the assistance of defence counsel, objects to particular elements of the first-instance judgment, the court of appeal will normally focus the proceedings on those elements. The same holds true for the prosecutor: he can direct the court of appeal to those elements of the judgment he disagrees with. Although the court of appeal can, out of its own motion, direct the proceedings to elements of the case it deems relevant itself, the parties have a significant say in the course of the appeal proceedings. More than in the first-instance proceedings, the appeal stage requires an active attitude from the accused: he must specifically challenge the legal and factual elements of the judgment he disagrees with.

The character of the appeal proceedings has the following consequences for the ability of the accused to participate effectively. First, it is noted that the element of non-compulsion is not applicable here: there is no compulsion whatsoever to initiate and participate in the appeal proceedings.[74] The element of informed involvement, however, is essential with regard to appeal proceedings: the accused must be informed of the manner in which appeal proceedings are conducted and how he can challenge the evidence effectively. When he does not formulate his objections against the first-instance judgment at the moment he files his appeal, nor presents his objections at the beginning of the appeal proceedings, the court of appeal may declare the case inadmissible.[75] This normally means that the court of appeal will

[72] It is noted that it is not possible to file an appeal against a conviction for an infraction, when the sentence does not exceed 50 €. (Article 404(2) CCP. See Article 404(3) CCP for an exception to this rule). Cases consisting of infractions or crimes punishable by a maximum of 4 years require a leave to appeal when the sentence does not exceed 500 € (Article 410a CCP). In all other cases, an appeal can be filed, except for an accused who was acquitted in the first-instance proceedings (Article 404(1) CCP).

[73] Article 422(2) CCP.

[74] Except in case the court of appeal orders that the accused should be present during the proceedings (Article 278(2) CCP, which applies also in the appeal stage, pursuant to Article 415(1) CCP). However, even in such cases, the accused is not forced to participate: he may remain silent during the proceedings.

[75] The court of appeal may, *proprio motu*, consider the evidence in case no objections against the first-instance judgment were filed or presented. However, in the majority of cases in which no objections are filed, the court of appeal declares the case inadmissible. The Supreme Court leaves the courts of appeal considerable discretion to declare inadmissible cases in which no objections were filed. HR, 2 October 2010, *ECLI*:NL:HR:2010:BK0910.

not consider the evidence: the first-instance judgment becomes final and can no longer be challenged.[76]

The character of the appeal proceedings requires an active attitude of the accused. Apart from the requirement that objections are filed timely, the accused must also file requests for new evidence in a timely manner. Article 414 CCP states that new evidence may be presented during the appeal proceedings: both the prosecutor and the accused may request the hearing of new witnesses and expert witnesses. Other means of proof may also be included in the appeal proceedings.[77] It is important to file requests to hear (new) witnesses and expert witnesses as soon as possible: when the request is filed together with the appeal brief, the court will determine whether hearing the witness is in the interest of the defence. When such a request is made at the beginning of the appeal proceedings, the court of appeal will determine whether hearing the witness is necessary. Although a clear distinction between these two criteria is hard to make in practice, it is common understanding that the court has more discretion to refuse to hear the witness under the last criterion.[78] This entails that, in order to be able to challenge witness statements effectively, the accused should file his request to do so as soon as possible. Before the start of the appeal proceedings, the accused can request the investigating judge to conduct further investigations.[79] This enables the accused, when the request is granted, to obtain new evidence that can be taken into account in the appeal proceedings.

The need for an active attitude of the accused is particularly important with regard to the possibility for the accused to challenge the evidence: it is not necessary to discuss particular pieces of evidence again when none of the parties, or the court of appeal itself, requires it. In Chap. 3, it was concluded that the court of appeal will, in general, direct the appeal proceedings to the objections of the accused (or the prosecutor) against particular elements of the first-instance judgment. During the parliamentary debates on the new appeal proceedings it was envisaged that when an appeal is filed (either by the accused or the prosecutor), the complaints against the first-instance judgment would be sent to the court of appeal.[80]

---

[76] According to Article 416(2) CCP, the court of appeal *may* declare the appeal inadmissible. When the court concludes that the appeal proceedings should be continued, although no objections have been filed, it is free to do so. This happens only in cases where the court of appeal identifies a fundamental defect in the first-instance judgment.

[77] The Supreme Court held that the court of appeal, when deliberating on the admission of new evidence, should determine whether admission of the new evidence is in conformity with the principle of due process. The nature of the new evidence is relevant in this regard. When the new evidence consists of incriminating evidence, regard must be had to the type of case and the timing of the request. HR, 29 June 2010, *ECLI*:NL:HR:2010:BL7709, para 2.3.

[78] This was acknowledged by the Supreme Court in HR, 19 June 2007, *ECLI*:NL:HR:2007:AZ1702. The two criteria have resulted in detailed case law on the applicability of each criterion in particular phases of the proceedings. The Supreme Court has recently clarified the applicability of each criterion in several distinct phases of the trial and appeal proceedings. HR, 1 July 2014, *ECLI*:NL:HR:2014:1496.

[79] Article 411a CCP (further investigations may be conducted by the investigating judge or justice).

[80] *Kamerstukken II*, 30320, 2005/06, 3, p. 11.

The European Court of Human Rights has held that, in order to determine whether appeal proceedings are in conformity with Article 6 of the Convention, the character of the appeal proceedings should be taken into account. This means, for example, that the right to a hearing before the appellate court may be restricted when a hearing has taken place before the first-instance court.[81] The guarantees of Article 6 during appeal proceedings have to be seen in light of the proceedings as a whole, including the manner in which trial proceedings were conducted.[82] The Court acknowledged that the trial stage can influence the application of Article 6 during the appeal proceedings. The Court did, however, make a distinction between appeal proceedings concerning questions of law and proceedings concerning questions of fact. Restrictions on the right to be present during the appeal proceedings are permissible in case of leave-to-appeal proceedings and in case of appeal proceedings that involve questions of law (provided, however, that there has been a hearing before the trial court).[83] In case the accused wishes to challenge the factual conclusions of the trial court and the appeal proceedings allow for such questions of fact to be considered, the court of appeal must enable the accused to effectively challenge the conclusions of the trial court.

Dutch appeal proceedings allow for a full review of the facts: the trial judgment can be challenged on both factual and legal issues. Considering the character of the appeal proceedings, it is essential that the accused is able to participate effectively and to be able to challenge the evidence. In this regard, the elements of informed involvement and the ability to challenge the evidence interact: when the accused wishes to challenge the factual conclusions of the court of first instance effectively, he must be sufficiently aware of the particularities of the appeal proceedings. This applies in particular to the right to call (new) witnesses and experts, to have additional investigations conducted and the manner in which objections against the trial judgment have to be formulated.[84]

The right to a reasoned judgment has to be respected at the appeal stage as well: Article 415(1) CCP provides that the provisions on the obligation to provide

[81] ECtHR, 12 November 2002, App. No.: 28394/95, (*Döry v. Sweden*), para 39.

[82] ECtHR, 26 May 1988, App. No.: 10563/83, (*Ekbatani v. Sweden*), para 27: 'The manner of application of Article 6 to proceedings before courts of appeal does, however, depend on the special features of the proceedings involved; account must be taken of the entirety of the proceedings in the domestic legal order and of the role of the appellate court therein.'

[83] ECtHR, 26 May 1988, App. No.: 10563/83, (*Ekbatani v. Sweden*), para 31. It is noted that the Human Rights Committee held that the right to appeal, protected under Article 14(5) of the ICCPR, requires 'a review by a higher tribunal of the conviction and the sentence.' HRC, 24 August 2010, Communication No. 1797/2008, U.N. Doc. CCPR/C/99/D/1797/2008 (2010), (*Mennen v. The Netherlands*), para 8.3.

[84] This is essential: appeal proceedings are often the final stage of the proceedings. Cassation proceedings, which are focused on points of law, are not the forum to address factual complaints of the accused (although the Supreme Court can, to a certain extent, address factual issues via the obligation to provide sufficient reasons for the judgment). Cf. Crijns and Schoep, who emphasize that courts of appeal should be aware of the fact that they are often the final court in the proceedings. Crijns and Schoep 2014, p. 259.

reasons are also applicable to appeal proceedings. The obligation for the domestic courts to state reasons requires that they must 'indicate with sufficient clarity the grounds on which they based their decision.'[85] Thus, the accused is able to verify whether his arguments have been taken into account by the court. This is important for the decision to make use of any available remedy.[86]

The Court has specifically addressed the right to a reasoned judgment in appeal proceedings. Courts of appeal are not obliged to give a detailed answer to every argument (nor are courts of first instance, for that matter) and they may endorse the findings of the courts of first instance[87] as long as the essential issues of the case have been addressed by the court of appeal.[88] More generally, Article 6(1) obliges the domestic courts to 'conduct a proper examination of the submissions, arguments and evidence adduced by the parties, without prejudice to its assessment of whether they are relevant to its decision.'[89]

The court of appeal may, according to Article 423(1) CCP, confirm or quash the first-instance judgment, either in whole or in part. When it confirms the judgment, the court of appeal may also adopt the reasons the first-instance court provided. When the court of appeal disagrees with the reasoning, it can replace it with its own reasoning. This article exemplifies that the appeal proceedings are not trials *de novo* (although every aspect of the case may become part of the proceedings), but a second stage of the proceedings.[90] Considering the importance that is attached in the appeal proceedings to the objections against the first-instance judgment, the court of appeal will have to respond to those objections (in particular, when the court of appeal disagrees with them).[91] The Supreme Court endorsed this view.[92]

---

[85] ECtHR, 16 December 1992, App. No.: 12945/87, (*Hadjianastassiou v. Greece*), para 33.

[86] ECtHR, 22 February 2007, App. No.: 1509/02, (*Tatishvili v. Russia*), para 58.

[87] ECtHR (GC), 21 January 1999, App. No.: 30544/96 (*Garcia Ruiz v. Spain*), para 26; ECtHR, 19 April 1994, App. No.: 16034/90, (*Van de Hurk v. The Netherlands*), para 61.

[88] ECtHR, 19 December 1997, App. No.: 157/1996/776/977, (*Helle v. Finland*), para 60: '[...] the Court would emphasize that the notion of a fair procedure requires that a national court which has given sparse reasons for its decisions, whether by incorporating the reasons of a lower court or otherwise, did in fact address the essential issues which were submitted to its jurisdiction and did not merely endorse without further ado the findings reached by a lower court.' See also para 27 of ECtHR, 9 December 1994, App. No.: 18064/91, (*Hiro Balani v. Spain*), in which the Court emphasized that the obligation to provide reasons is case specific: 'The extent to which this duty to give reasons applies may vary according to the nature of the decision. It is moreover necessary to take into account, inter alia, the diversity of the submissions that a litigant may bring before the courts and the differences existing in the Contracting States with regard to statutory provisions, customary rules, legal opinion and the presentation and drafting of judgments.'

[89] ECtHR, 19 April 1993, App. No.: 13942/88, (*Kraska v. Switzerland*), para 30.

[90] Damaška argued that in such a model of criminal procedure, the first-instance judgment 'acquires an aura of provisionality.' Damaška 1986, p. 49.

[91] During the parliamentary debates on the new appeal proceedings, the Minister of Justice argued that the new appeal proceedings are based on the idea of a contest ('oppositie'). This implies, he argued, that the court of appeal is obliged to respond to the objections. *Kamerstukken II*, 2005/06, 30320, 3, p. 30. See also Crijns and Schoep 2014, p. 261.

[92] HR 13 July 2010, *ECLI*:NL:HR:2010:BM0256, para 2.6.

Regarding the participatory model of proof and appeal proceedings, it is essential that the accused is properly informed about the manner in which appeal proceedings are conducted. The accused must be aware of the procedural outlook of the appeal proceedings, in particular of the manner in which he can challenge the evidence.

5.3 Diversions and Shortcuts in the Law of International Criminal Procedure

5.3.1 Introduction

Diversions and shortcuts in international criminal proceedings are important tools to avoid or speed up the trial proceedings. A full criminal trial, in which all the evidence is presented in open court and challenged by the defence, will last for years. Criticism on the effectiveness of international criminal proceedings often involves the length and costs of the proceedings.[93] Any mechanism that can facilitate a more expeditious trial or which obviates the need to conduct a trial at all is to be welcomed, as long as the accused is still provided with a fair determination of his criminal responsibility. The diversions and shortcuts that are used by the *ad hoc* Tribunals and the ICC will be evaluated in this chapter. The elements of the participatory model of proof will function as guidelines to answer the question of whether the accused was able to participate effectively.

5.3.2 Diversions and the Participatory Model of Proof

5.3.2.1 *Guilty Pleas and Admissions of Guilt*[94]

The guilty plea is the archetypical diversion from the full criminal trial: by pleading guilty, the accused does not contest the charges, which obviates the need for a contested trial altogether. When the prosecutor and the accused agree on the factual basis of the plea and the legal characterization of the facts, there is no need for a detailed presentation and discussion of the evidence in open court. The guilty plea is typically regarded as a procedural fact: the accused does not wish to challenge the evidence collected and waives his right to a trial before an independent and impartial court. In such an approach to pleading guilty, the notion of

[93] Damaška observed that the practice of plea bargaining at the international courts was rooted in the need for more efficiency. Damaška 2004, p. 1035.

[94] Considering their similarity, the two concepts are discussed under the same heading. Cf. Weigend and Turner 2013, p. 1389.

voluntariness is prominent: when the accused, out of his own free will, decides not to have the prosecutor prove his guilt before a court, this is to be respected. It should not come as a surprise that the practice of guilty pleas is often associated with contract law theories, in which the notion of party autonomy is very prominent. Although instructive, such an approach does not do justice to the public law character of criminal law.[95] Therefore, it cannot function as a proper normative framework.

The normative framework in which agreements are reached on the guilt of the accused (in particular when the plea involves international crimes) is not just a matter for the parties involved: there is a clear public interest in the manner in which such agreements are reached. This explains why the plea agreement must be submitted to the Chamber for judicial approval. This entails that the normative framework for plea-bargaining cannot be the fact that the bargaining process is conducted in the shadow of full trial proceedings. In such a view, the fairness of the bargaining process is guaranteed by the fact that the accused is always able to bring the case to court. This prospect, the argument goes, will ensure that the prosecutor acts in a fair and decent manner: he acts as if he were a judge himself. From a rule of law perspective, this is an untenable approach, though: as an organ of an international court, the prosecutor cannot operate in a normative vacuum in which the *possibility* of trial proceedings functions as the required framework.[96]

The first element to be discussed is the element of non-compulsion: the accused may not be forced to enter into plea negotiations with the prosecutor or compelled to enter a guilty plea. In other words, entering a plea must be voluntary. At the ICC, an admission of guilt can only be made by the accused after sufficient consultation with defence counsel.[97] In their Separate Opinion to the *Erdemovic* Appeals Chamber's judgment, judges McDonald and Vohrah argued that voluntariness consists of two elements: first, the accused must be mentally competent to enter a plea. Second, the plea must not be the result of threats or inducements, other than a reduced sentence.[98] The expectation of a moderate sentence after a guilty plea or admission of guilt may well function as a strong inducement to confess: it is not in the interest of the accused to opt for a contested trial, which may result in a higher sentence. The 'discount' that the accused receives is sometimes regarded as an improper way of forcing an accused to comply with the conditions in the plea agreement.[99]

---

95 See for example: Scott and Stuntz 1992.

96 The same holds true for a prosecutor acting as an agent of the state: a prosecutor is not a random party that enters into an agreement with an accused to avoid trial proceedings.

97 Article 65(1)(b) ICC Statute.

98 ICTY, Joint Separate Opinion of Judge McDonald and Judge Vohra, *Prosecutor v. Erdemović*, Case No.: IT-96-22, A. Ch., 7 October 1997, para 10.

99 For an in-depth discussion of the distinction between 'waiver rewards' and 'trial penalties', see: Lippke 2011, pp. 10–37.

In most cases, the Trial Chamber sentences within the sentencing range recommended by the prosecutor.[100] This means that the accused can predict fairly accurately what the outcome of the sentencing hearing will be. In case the accused opts for a contested trial, he remains in uncertainty for a prolonged period of time on the sentence that will be imposed. Normally, Trial Chambers do not indicate the scope of the sentence reduction after the accused entered a guilty plea. This makes it hard to say anything concrete on the inducement that the prospect of a reduced sentence may entail. In the plea agreement itself, the prosecutor normally emphasizes that the Trial Chamber is not in any way bound by the recommended sentencing range and can impose a sentence of life imprisonment. In the agreement, no references are made to sentences that have been imposed in similar cases in which the accused contested the charges. This would have allowed for a fruitful comparison of sentences handed down after contested trials and after a plea agreement has been submitted. Unlike some domestic criminal justice systems, no sentencing guidelines exist that stipulate the credit an accused receives when he pleads guilty to the charges.[101]

Although the precise extent of the sentence reduction is unknown, the mere fact that the sentence is normally reduced is an important inducement for the accused to plead guilty. Inducing the accused with the expectation of a lower sentence does not mean that he is compelled to enter into negotiations with the prosecutor.[102] Of significant importance is whether the accused is able to predict whether a Trial Chamber would convict him after a contested trial: in other words, is there sufficient evidence in the case file for a conviction? This refers to the element of informed involvement. Weigend and Turner argued that a plea can only be regarded as informed when the accused had 'access to all evidence that is exculpatory or otherwise material to his defence.'[103] These authors refer solely to the right of the accused to get acquainted with exculpatory evidence. However, the decision to plead guilty is only truly informed when the accused knows which incriminatory evidence the prosecutor has obtained.[104] This allows the accused to determine the strength of the case and to make an informed choice between a diversion and a contested trial.[105]

---

100 The exceptions are discussed in Chap. 4.

101 Cf the guidelines of the Sentencing Council for England and Wales: *Reduction in Sentence for a Guilty Plea*, Definitive Guideline (Rev. 2007), accessed via https://www.sentencingcouncil.org.uk/wp-content/uploads/Reduction_in_Sentence_for_a_Guilty_Plea_-Revised_2007.pdf (latest visit: 1 January 2016).

102 Considering the ECtHR's position in *Deweer*, the mere *expectation* of a moderate sentence does not mean that the accused is compelled to waive his fair trial rights. ECtHR, 27 February 1980, App. No.: 6903/75, (*Deweer v. Belgium*).

103 Weigend and Turner 2013, p. 1381.

104 Turner refers to plea bargaining practice in Germany and Bulgaria, where the accused is provided with the entire case file. Turner 2009, pp. 116, 152.

105 Normally, accused are assisted by counsel when they enter into a plea agreement in order to make an informed decision. Article 65(1)(b) ICC Statute even requires that an admission of guilt is made after 'sufficient consultation' with defence counsel. The legal framework of the *ad hoc* Tribunals does not contain a similar provision.

At the *ad hoc* Tribunals, the element of informed involvement regarding a guilty plea is often related to the question of whether the accused understands the nature of the charges and the consequences of pleading guilty. It is indeed important that the accused is fully aware that by pleading guilty he waives the right to a contested trial in which he can challenge the evidence. Informed involvement does, however, not only entail knowledge of the procedural consequences of pleading guilty but also of the factual basis underlying the charges. This entails that the accused must be provided with the evidence the prosecutor has collected, or a summary thereof. Only in this way can the accused make a truly informed decision regarding his plea.

When the accused is provided with the incriminatory evidence against him, the question arises as to what extent he can challenge or comment upon such evidence. At first sight, this seems an anomaly: diversions of the full criminal trial are mechanisms to avoid the contested trial in which the evidence can be challenged. In order to be able to challenge the evidence, one must opt for regular trial proceedings. However, in the context of plea-bargaining, the possibility to become acquainted with the evidence and to comment upon such evidence may be indispensable. The prosecutor presents his case in order to persuade the accused to plead guilty: without any incriminating material there is no incentive for the accused to enter into plea negotiations in the first place. Challenging particular pieces of evidence allows the accused to participate effectively in the bargaining process.[106] In fact, such participation is required to avoid a 'take-it-or-leave-it' situation in which the prosecutor merely presents a plea agreement to be signed by the accused.

When the parties reach an agreement, the result is submitted to the Chamber for judicial approval: as described in Chap. 4, the parties do not have a determinative say as to whether the full criminal trial will be avoided. When the criteria for a valid plea have not been observed, when there is no factual basis for the plea, or when a full contested trial would be in the interest of justice (more particular: in the interest of the victims) the agreement will not be approved.[107] The approval of the Chamber cannot in any way be equated with independent fact-finding in the setting of a contested trial.[108] When the agreement is approved, the accused is provided with an abbreviated reasoned judgment in which the Chamber sums up the facts and legal qualifications that have been agreed upon. Most importantly, the Chamber accounts for the sentence that it imposes: the aggravating and mitigating circumstances and the recommended sentencing range are discussed. Regarding the possibility to challenge the sentencing judgment of the Chamber, the accused has normally waived his right to appeal the sentencing judgment when the sentence falls within the recommended sentencing range.

---

[106] This possibility seems inevitable in case of factual and charge bargains.

[107] It rarely occurs that plea agreements are not approved by the Chamber, however.

[108] This is the reason why no judicial notice may be taken of facts that are based upon a plea agreement: such facts have not been truly adjudicated.

Diverting a case from the full criminal trial, in which evidence is properly presented and challenged, comes at a price: the accused must be provided with a decent and fair out-of-court procedure in which he can determine freely to consent to the diversion of his case. This means that the accused must be enabled to participate effectively during the plea negotiations: this includes providing the accused with sufficient information regarding the procedural consequences and allowing him to present his arguments regarding the evidence.

5.3.3 Shortcuts and the Participatory Model of Proof

5.3.3.1 Agreed Facts

The use of agreed facts occurs within the trial context: the *nulla poena sine iudicio* principle is fully adhered to. There are, however, similarities between agreed facts as a shortcut to proof and the manner in which Chambers have considered the validity of guilty pleas. In order to accept the plea of the accused, thereby diverting the case from a full criminal trial, several criteria have to be fulfilled. These criteria are based on the rich common law case law on guilty pleas: a plea must be made voluntarily, the accused must be sufficiently informed on the content and consequences of the plea and the plea must not be equivocal. Moreover, in international criminal proceedings, the Chamber can only accept the plea when there is a sufficient factual basis for the crimes involved.

An agreement on particular facts can be regarded as a partial guilty plea, particularly when the prosecutor and accused agree on the existence and accuracy of incriminating facts. Agreements on factual issues are normally regarded as sufficient proof for the existence and accuracy of the facts concerned. In this way, parts of the *probandum* are proven based on the consensus of the parties: whereas in case of a guilty plea the accused pleads guilty to all facts contained in the *probandum*, an agreement of fact concerns only a part of the *probandum*. The similarities between agreed facts and guilty pleas can be discerned in the reasoning of the Trial Chamber in *Blagojevic & Jokić*. In an interlocutory decision, the Chamber held that, as the 'guarantor of the rights of the accused', it must ensure that the accused has entered into the agreement voluntarily and is aware of the consequences of such an agreement.[109]

Considering whether the accused has been able to participate effectively regarding this shortcut to proof, one has to take into account both the number and the character of the agreed facts. In cases in which only a modest number of facts is

[109] ICTY, Decision on Prosecution's Motion for Judicial Notice of Adjudicated Facts and Documentary Evidence, *Prosecutor v. Blagojević & Jokić*, Case No.: IT-02-60-T, T. Ch. I, 19 December 2003, para 14.

agreed upon and where those facts relate to uncontroversial issues, such as the place and date of birth of the accused, no issue arises regarding the ability to participate. In such cases, it is completely clear that the parties agree on rather trivial issues that do not even remotely bear upon the criminal responsibility of the accused. If, however, the facts stated in the agreement concern parts of the *probandum*, it is vital that the rights of the accused are respected. As mentioned in Chap. 4, the Trial Chamber in *Stanišić & Simatović* noted that the parties agreed on the existence of an armed conflict throughout the period in which the accused had, allegedly, committed their crimes.[110] The agreement, together with adjudicated facts, resulted in conclusive proof of the *chapeau* element of the existence of an armed conflict. When the agreed fact is an important and even indispensable fact that has to be proven in order to convict, the guarantees discussed regarding a guilty plea apply fully. The accused must agree voluntarily that the particular fact occurred after being sufficiently informed on any evidence regarding the fact and of the consequences the agreement in terms of probative value may have.

In the case of *Nourain & Jerbo Jamus*, concerning war crimes committed against African Union peacekeepers in Darfur, the prosecutor and the defence agreed that only three issues remained contested between them:

i) Whether the attack on the MGS Haskanita on 29 September 2007 was unlawful;
ii) If the attack is deemed unlawful, whether the Accused persons were aware of the factual circumstances that established the unlawful nature of the attack; and
iii) Whether AMIS was a peacekeeping mission in accordance with the Charter of the United Nations.[111]

ICC Trial Chamber IV noted the agreement and stated that the agreement would significantly narrow the contested issues at trial, which is in the interest of an expeditious trial.[112] In such cases, it is vital that the accused is sufficiently informed on the consequences of the agreement in terms of the scope of the trial proceedings.

Before an agreement on factual issues is submitted to a Chamber, the parties have negotiated about the precise wording and number of facts they agree upon. In such negotiations, the evidence upon which the prosecutor relies can be disclosed to the accused.[113] Thus, he is informed of parts of the case against him and can make an informed decision regarding whether or not to agree to the accuracy of

---

110 ICTY, Judgment, *Prosecutor v. Stanišić & Simatović*, Case No.: IT-03-69-T, T. Ch. I, 30 May 2013, para 958.

111 ICC, Decision on the Joint Submission regarding the Contested Issues and the Agreed Facts, *Prosecutor v. Abdallah Banda Abakaer Nourain & Saleh Mohammed Jerbo Jamus*, Case No.: ICC-02/05-03/09, T. Ch. IV, 28 September 2011, para 3.

112 ICC, Decision on the Joint Submission regarding the Contested Issues and the Agreed Facts, *Prosecutor v. Abdallah Banda Abakaer Nourain & Saleh Mohammed Jerbo Jamus*, Case No.: ICC-02/05-03/09, T. Ch. IV, 28 September 2011, para 44.

113 E.g. ICC, The Prosecution's Submission Concerning the Status of Negotiations on Agreed Facts, *Prosecutor v. Bemba Gombo*, Case No.: ICC-01/05-01/08, T. Ch. III, 20 January 2010, para 2–3.

the facts. When the accused challenges, for example, the probative value of the disclosed evidence, he is able to comment upon the evidence and to decide whether or not to agree on the accuracy of the fact. The agreed facts that are noted by the Chamber are normally included in the judgment: no additional evidence is required, and the facts are regarded as proven.

The use of agreed facts is, as was already shown in Chap. 4, rather limited at the *ad hoc* Tribunals. Considering the extensive use that has been made at these tribunals of the possibility to notice adjudicated facts (which does not require the consent of the parties), there is simply no strong incentive to agree on factual issues. At the ICC, however, the use of agreements of factual issues may become an important shortcut in order to speed up the trial proceedings. The legal framework of the ICC does not provide for taking judicial notice of adjudicated facts, which has functioned as an effective tool to speed up the trial proceedings at the ICTY.[114] Compared to the *ad hoc* Tribunals, the number of *Serienprozesse* will be modest at the ICC: both the ICTY and ICTR deal with cases that often involve the same crime base, which means that the number of adjudicated facts that can be noticed by the Chambers is substantial. At the ICC, it is unlikely that a similar number of cases will be processed *seriatim*. Thus, the use of agreements as to evidence may become an indispensable shortcut to proof.

Agreements on the facts of the case, similar to the criteria for a valid guilty plea, must be entered into voluntary, based on sufficient information and be concluded in a setting in which the accused is able to comment upon the evidence the prosecutor has collected.

5.3.3.2 Facts of Common Knowledge

In Chap. 4, the use of facts of common knowledge in international criminal proceedings was discussed. It was shown that such facts are sometimes used to prove contextual elements, in particular in cases conducted before the ICTR. This is similar to the manner in which several Dutch courts handled cases in the post-WWII period. How does the use of facts of common knowledge in international criminal proceedings relate to the participatory model? Is the accused able to participate effectively in the proceedings when facts of common knowledge are included in the Chamber's judgment?

Trial Chambers must take judicial notice of facts of common knowledge: they have no discretion to refuse to take judicial notice of facts that are indisputable. The provisions in the Rules of Procedure and Evidence of the *ad hoc* Tribunals

[114] At the ICTR, much less use has been made of adjudicated facts, probably because of the liberal use that has been made of noticing facts of common knowledge.

and the ICC Statute oblige the Chamber to act *proprio motu*.[115] In practice, however, it is normally the prosecutor who files a motion in which the Trial Chamber is requested to take judicial notice of particular facts of common knowledge. This is advantageous for the accused: he is able to file a response in which he can object to the prosecution's motion. Chambers may also take judicial notice of facts pursuant to Rule 94(A) *proprio motu* without hearing the parties on the particular facts. In *Dragomir Milošević*, for example, the Trial Chamber considered first whether the facts for which the prosecutor requested judicial notice be taken pursuant to Rule 94(B) could be noticed pursuant to Rule 94(A).[116] Consequently, the accused was not able to comment upon the notoriety of the facts included in the prosecution's motion.

To take judicial notice of facts of common knowledge after a motion has been filed has two important procedural consequences. First, the accused is properly informed of the facts the prosecutor deems to be of common knowledge. Considering the probative value that is attributed to facts of common knowledge after they are judicially noticed (i.e. conclusive evidence, without the possibility to present evidence in rebuttal), it is vital that the accused is fully aware of those facts. Second, considering that the accused cannot present evidence in rebuttal after the Chamber has decided to notice such facts, the accused can only challenge these facts by filing a response to the prosecutor's motion or file a motion for reconsideration (this seems, however, a mere theoretical possibility: it would require the accused to present such an amount of credible evidence that the Chamber will have to reconsider its earlier decision).

Facts of common knowledge must, according to Rule 89(C) ICTY and ICTR RPE, be relevant to the proceedings: the basic criterion of relevancy applies also to facts that are deemed indisputable. As the Appeals Chamber held in *Semanza*, judicially noticed facts may not clutter the evidentiary record with irrelevant facts.[117] This approach makes sense and prevents the Chamber from having to decide on facts that are unrelated to the case at hand. The relevancy criterion does, however, also have a reverse side: when a fact of common knowledge is relevant to the proceedings, the question must be asked whether the particular fact relates in any (remote) way to the criminal responsibility of the accused. In other words: does the fact of common knowledge prove a part of the *probandum*?

---

[115] The wording in the ICC Statute is a bit ambiguous and less imperative than Rule 94(A) of the Rules of Procedure and Evidence of the *ad hoc* Tribunals: 'The Court shall not require proof of facts of common knowledge but may take judicial notice of them.'

[116] ICTY, Decision on Prosecution's Motion for Judicial Notice of Adjudicated Facts and Prosecution's Catalogue of Agreed Facts with Dissenting Opinion of Judge Harhoff, *Prosecutor v. Milošević*, ICTY-IT-98-29/1-T, T. Ch. III, 10 April 2007, para 25.

[117] ICTR, Judgment, *Prosecutor v. Semanza*, ICTR-97-20-A, A. Ch., 20 May 2005, para 189.

In this respect, the important decision of the Appeals Chamber in *Karemera* must be mentioned here again. In this interlocutory decision, the Appeals Chamber declared the context in which the accused committed his acts to be common knowledge.[118] The Appeals Chamber held that 'it is not relevant that these facts constitute elements of some of the crimes charged and that such elements must ordinarily be proven by the Prosecution. There is no exception to Rule 94(A) for elements of offences.'[119]

A significant part of the *probandum* is proven this way: the contested issue left for the Chamber to decide on is the personal involvement of the accused in the atrocities. It is important to understand that the Appeals Chamber ruled that the facts of common knowledge can also refer to legal terms:

> It is true that 'widespread and systematic attack against a civilian population' and 'armed conflict not of an international character' are phrases with legal meanings, but they nonetheless describe factual situations and thus can constitute 'facts of common knowledge'. The question is not whether a proposition is put in legal or layman's terms (so long as the terms are sufficiently well defined such that the accuracy of their application to the described situation is not reasonably in doubt). The question is whether the proposition can reasonably be disputed.[120]

This is the crucial difference with Rule 94(B): judicial notice of legal characterizations cannot be taken pursuant to this Rule. Thus, the Chamber has to decide for itself whether the facts constitute, for example, an armed conflict or a widespread and systematic attack. Judicial notice of contextual elements pursuant to Rule 94(A) means that, similar to the Dutch post-WWII cases, the context in which the accused operated is conclusively proven by indisputable facts of common knowledge. The Appeals Chamber held in *Semanza* that to proceed in this way is just an alternative manner of proving the charges.[121]

The accused is, in practice, only able to challenge the facts of common knowledge in a response to a motion of the prosecutor.[122] At the ICTR, however, filing a response can be futile: the Appeals Chamber has held that facts that are considered to be of common knowledge by the Appeals Chamber *must* be noticed by the trial

---

[118] For the facts of which the Appeals Chamber took judicial notice pursuant to Rule 94(A), see Chap. 4.

[119] ICTR, Decision on Prosecutor's Interlocutory Appeal of Decision on Judicial Notice, *Prosecutor v. Karemera et al.*, Case No.: ICTR-98-44-73(C), A. Ch., 16 June 2006, para 30.

[120] ICTR, Decision on Prosecutor's Interlocutory Appeal of Decision on Judicial Notice, *Prosecutor v. Karemera et al.*, Case No.: ICTR-98-44-73(C), A. Ch., 16 June 2006, para 29.

[121] 'The Appeals Chamber finds that these judicially noticed facts did not relieve the Prosecution of its burden of proof: they went only to the manner in which the Prosecution could discharge that burden in respect of the production of certain evidence which did not concern the acts done by the Appellant. When determining the Appellant's personal responsibility, the Trial Chamber relied on the facts it found on the basis of the evidence adduced at trial.' ICTR, Judgment, *Prosecutor v. Semanza*, Case No.: ICTR-97-20-A, A. Ch., 20 May 2005, para 192.

[122] Or by filing a motion of reconsideration. As stated, this is a mere theoretical possibility.

chambers, when the fact is relevant to the proceedings.[123] At the Special Court for Sierra Leone, which operates under similar Rules of Procedure and Evidence as the ICTR, Judge Robertson commented on the probative value of facts of common knowledge and the manner in which a judicially noticed fact can be reversed:

> The only exception – and it will rarely if ever arise – is if fresh information subsequently comes into the hands of a party or to the notice of the court suggesting that the fact is questionable after all. Were such a situation ever to arise, the chamber should exercise its inherent power to reconsider its original decision.[124]

When the prosecutor requests judicial notice of facts that have already been noticed by the Appeals Chamber, filing a response is superfluous: the fact is already conclusively established. Should a Chamber take judicial notice of a fact *proprio motu*, the accused cannot challenge the fact at all: it is likely that such a fact will be mentioned for the first time in the judgment after the close of the proceedings. The determination of a fact of common knowledge is a legal question, which entails that the accused can request the Appeals Chamber to determine whether the Trial Chamber correctly applied the criteria for taking judicial notice.[125]

Considering the possibility to participate effectively and to challenge the evidence, the accused may be unable to challenge facts that are used to prove the charges. In case of this particular shortcut to proof, the court declares parts of the *probandum* proven by relying on facts of common knowledge. In this way, the court effectively reduces the number of contested issues in the case. The decisions in which notice is taken are, in general, duly reasoned: the accused is provided with reasons as to why the Chamber considered a particular fact to be common knowledge. When the Trial Chamber grants certification, the decision is open to interlocutory appeal: the accused can try to challenge the decision of the Trial Chamber.[126]

---

[123] ICTR, Decision on Prosecutor's Interlocutory Appeal of Decision on Judicial Notice, *Prosecutor v. Karemera et al.*, Case No.: ICTR-98-44-73(C), A. Ch., 16 June 2006, para 23; A similar approach can be discerned at the ICTY. See e.g. ICTY, Decision on Prosecution Motion for Judicial Notice of Facts of Common Knowledge Pursuant to Rule 94(A), *Prosecutor v. Popović et al.*, Case No.: IT-05-88-T, T. Ch. II, 26 September 2006, para 12.

[124] SCSL, Separate Opinion of Justice Robertson to Fofana-Decision on Appeal against "Decision on Prosecution's Motion for Judicial Notice and Admission of Evidence", *Prosecutor v. Norman et al.*, SCSL-2004-14-AR73, A. Ch., 16 May 2005, para 8.

[125] ICTR, Decision on Motion for Reconsideration, *Prosecutor v. Karemera et al.*, Case No.: ICTR-98-44-AR73(C), A. Ch., 1 December 2006, para 8; ICTR, Decision on Prosecutor's Interlocutory Appeal of Decision on Judicial Notice, *Prosecutor v. Karemera et al.*, ICTR-98-44-AR73(C), A. Ch., 16 June 2006, para 23.

[126] According to Rule 73(B) ICTY and ICTR RPE, the Trial Chamber may grant certification 'if the decision involves an issue that would significantly affect the fair and expeditious conduct of the proceedings or the outcome of the trial, and for which, in the opinion of the Trial Chamber, an immediate resolution by the Appeals Chamber may materially advance the proceedings.' The wording of Article 82 ICC Statute on interlocutory appeals is similar.

Taking judicial notice of facts of common knowledge obviates the need to admit evidence in order to prove patently indisputable facts. This is the main rationale for judicial notice of this category of facts. Typically, facts of common knowledge include basic factual notions, such as the names of geographical regions, the laws of nature or historical facts. The type of facts that have been noticed by the ICTR is unprecedented, though: legal terms that are part of the charges and that refer to the core crimes in the Statute itself, are regarded as indisputable and cannot be challenged by the accused. This should not be misunderstood: the argument is not that no atrocities, including genocide, were committed in Rwanda in the spring and early summer of 1994. However, in a legal forum in which the right to a fair trial is respected and in which the accused should be able to challenge the charges and the evidence presented, there is no place to declare important contextual facts as indisputable facts.

From the perspective of the accused and his ability to participate effectively, the Appeals Chamber should have required formal evidence or should have noticed the facts pursuant to Rule 94(B) instead. This would allow the accused to challenge these facts: during the regular trial proceedings, by filing a response or by filing a motion of reconsideration. It is noted that judicial notice of adjudicated facts is prohibited if the facts contain, or consist of, legal characterizations. Chambers should carefully select which facts may be judicially noticed, without importing legal conclusions from other trials.[127] To conclude, Chambers should be cautious when they use this shortcut to proof: the adversarial character of the full criminal trial may be infringed by declaring facts indisputable.

5.3.3.3 Judicial Notice of Adjudicated Facts

At the ICTY and ICTR, judicial notice can be taken of adjudicated facts and documentary evidence.[128] The Chamber can do so *proprio motu* or at the request of one of the parties. This shortcut to proof allows the Chamber to rely on the factual conclusions of another Chamber. Evidence does not have to be presented and discussed extensively: the full criminal trial is avoided by importing facts from other, related, cases.

The accused may request the Trial Chamber to take judicial notice of certain adjudicated facts. Thus, the accused can import exonerating facts that have been established in other cases and which are relevant for his case. Not much use has been made of this possibility: it does not occur often that exonerating facts are proven in the context of another case. The accused is, of course, in no way

[127] Although the distinction between factual and legal terms is rather blurred, as was discussed in Chap. 4.

[128] The legal framework of the ICC does not provide for a similar provision.

compelled to provide the Chamber with exonerating facts from other cases: the presumption of innocence is infringed when the accused must provide the Chamber with exonerating evidence.

In order to be able to challenge the evidence effectively, the accused must be well informed: he must know which adjudicated facts the prosecutor or the Chamber want to have judicially noticed. Therefore, the accused must be provided with a detailed description of the facts, including the sources for these facts. In the case law of both the ICTY and ICTR this requirement is encapsulated in several of the criteria for judicial notice:

b) The fact must be distinct, concrete, and identifiable;
c) The fact, as formulated by the moving party, must not differ in any substantial way from the formulation of the original judgment;
d) The fact must not be unclear or misleading in the context in which it is placed in the moving party's motion. In addition, the fact must be denied judicial notice 'if it will become unclear or misleading because one or more of the surrounding pur-ported facts will be denied judicial notice';
e) The fact must be identified with adequate precision by the moving party.[129]

These criteria ensure that the facts for which judicial notice is requested by the prosecutor, or proposed by the Chamber, are identified in detail. This enables the accused to file a detailed response to the prosecutor's motion on judicial notice: the accused can formulate his objections against a particular fact before the Chamber has noticed the fact.

It is important that the accused is also aware of the consequences when facts are judicially noticed. The effect in terms of probative value and the role such facts can play in the final judgment is considerable: judicially noticed facts are regarded as well-founded presumptions for the accuracy of these facts, and they may become conclusive evidence in the final judgment. Therefore, the accused must be informed of the possibility to challenge these facts during the proceedings by presenting evidence in rebuttal. In the interlocutory decisions of the Chambers, reference is normally made to the possibility for the defence to challenge the facts by 'introducing reliable and credible evidence'.[130] This allows the accused to challenge any incriminating evidence: the Chamber has concluded that the judicially noticed facts are presumably accurate, but it is willing to hear any evidence to the contrary.

Although the possibility to present exonerating evidence exists, it can be questioned whether the accused is able to challenge the facts effectively in practice.

---

[129] ICTY, Decision on Accused's Motion for Judicial Notice of Adjudicated Facts Related to Count One, *Prosecutor v. Karadžić*, ICTY-IT-95-5/18-T, T. Ch., 21 January 2014, para 6.

[130] See, for example: ICTY, Decision on Prosecution Motion for Judicial Notice of Adjudicated Facts and Documents, *Prosecutor v. Hadzić*, ICTY-04-75-T, T. Ch., 23 May 2013, para 10.

The number of judicially noticed facts has risen over the years, resulting in cases in which thousands of facts are imported via Rule 94(B).[131] Trial Chambers have acknowledged that the 'volume or type of evidence the Accused can be expected to present in rebuttal may place such significant burden on him that it jeopardizes his right to a fair trial.'[132] Normally, the accused challenges the facts in its response to the motion of the prosecutor: particular facts for which the prosecutor requests judicial notice are challenged on the basis of the admissibility requirements for Rule 94(B). The hearing requirement ensures that the parties are enabled to express their views on the matter. Moreover, accused often refer to the discretionary power of the Chamber to refuse judicial notice in the interest of justice. However, these responses are not often successful: in general, Chambers take judicial notice of the facts presented by the prosecutor. This means that those facts will, in principle, not be discussed anymore during the proceedings. The prosecutor does not have to present evidence for these facts. If the defence does not specifically challenge these facts by presenting evidence in rebuttal, the facts will be left uncontested.

In the case law, references are made to the fair trial implications of taking judicial notice of adjudicated facts. The importance of the right to challenge the adjudicated fact by presenting evidence in rebuttal is referred to by Judge Shahabuddeen in his Separate Opinion to an interlocutory decision in *Milošević*:

> If there is no right of rebuttal, the consequence is that, as a result of the judicial notice, the opposing party would be bound by the adjudicated fact without an opportunity to dispute it with new evidence. The undesirability of this, particularly in a criminal case, cannot be overstated. The adjudicated fact may be important for the outcome of the case. As is sought to be shown below, it may well relate to a matter which is in reasonable dispute between the parties. There would, therefore, be ground for objecting that there is an encroachment on the presumption of innocence.[133]

The accused can exercise this right to rebuttal by requesting the Chamber to reconsider its earlier decision on judicial notice.[134] He may also present evidence

---

[131] In *Stanišić and Župljanin*, judicial notice was taken of more than 1000 facts; in *Karadžić* the Trial Chamber took notice of more than 2300 facts. See Vriend 2012.

[132] ICTY, Decision on Prosecutor's Motion for Judicial Notice of Adjudicated Facts Pursuant to Rule 94(B), *Prosecutor v. Tolimir*, ICTY-IT-05-88/2-PT, T. Ch.II, 17 December 2009, para 32. See also *Prosecutor v. Mejakić et al.*, in which the Trial Chamber held: 'Considering that this Trial Chamber has recently held that, in the exercise of its discretion pursuant to Rule 94(B), factors that may be taken into account include: (a) whether the facts, when taken together, will result in such a large number as to compromise the principle of a fair and expeditious trial;' ICTY, Decision on Prosecution Motion for Judicial Notice pursuant to Rule 94(B), *Prosecutor v. Mejakić et al.*, Case No. IT-02-65-PT, T. Ch., 1 April 204, p. 5.

[133] ICTY, Separate Opinion of Judge Shahabuddeen Appended to the Appeals Chamber's Decision Dated 28 October 2003 on the Prosecution's Interlocutory Appeal Against the Trial Chamber's 10 April 2003 Decision on Prosecution Motion for Judicial Notice of Adjudicated Facts, *Prosecutor v. Milošević*, IT-02-54-AR73.5, A. Ch., 31 October 2003, para 14–15.

[134] E.g. ICTY, Decision on Three Accused's Motions for Reconsideration of Decisions on Judicial Notice of Adjudicated Facts, *Prosecutor v. Karadžić*, IT-95-5-/18-T, T. Ch., 4 May 2012.

during the proceedings that would render the previously noticed fact disputable: the Chamber is then invited to make its own factual finding, based upon the evidence presented. It is necessary, however, to provide the Chamber with sufficient evidence to reconsider its earlier decision: a mere objection against particular facts or the concept of judicial notice as such will not suffice. The accused must, in other words, substantiate his request for reconsideration.[135]

Considering the element of being able to effectively challenge the evidence, the number of judicially noticed facts in certain cases is of particular concern. It is doubtful whether the accused is truly able to participate effectively when he has to present evidence in rebuttal regarding thousands of facts that were established in other trials, before other judges. It is recalled here that the facts of which judicial notice is taken have been established in other proceedings in which the accused might not have had a particular interest in challenging these facts. Although the fact is 'adjudicated' (another Chamber has indeed weighed the evidence regarding the fact), this does not necessarily mean that the fact was truly contested. When the accused wants to challenge only a small number of judicially noticed facts in his case, no issues arise regarding the fairness of the proceedings. The accused is allowed to present his views on the facts when the motion for judicial notice is heard, and he can present evidence in rebuttal afterwards. In this way, the accused can properly participate and challenge the evidence against him. However, the sheer number of facts that are imported by Rule 94(B) does raise an issue regarding the ability of the accused to effectively challenge those facts. The Trial Chamber in *Krajišnik* acknowledged this: the Chamber held that a high number of adjudicated facts might be 'oppressive' to the defence.[136]

It is a distinctive feature of international criminal proceedings that the narrative of a particular armed conflict, a genocidal campaign or other atrocities is written over the years: only after a certain number of trials have been conducted and completed does a detailed version of the historical events emerge. The factual conclusions of the early trials function as the basis upon which subsequent trials are founded. Accused that enter the dock after proceedings against others (often low-ranking officials) have been concluded, find themselves in a procedural setting in which a lot of the relevant factual background to the conflict has been established already. Accused often claim that they are tried under a 'presumption of guilt', which means that the judges are only trying to place the accused within the context

---

[135] Cf. the observations of the Trial Chamber in *Mladić*: 'The Chamber [...] considers that even if the challenging party notifies the proposing party of its intention to challenge certain judicially noticed facts, the proposing party may still rely on the legal effect of being relieved of its initial burden to produce evidence on the point, until the moment that the challenging party puts the adjudicated fact into question by *introducing* evidence to the contrary.' ICTY, Fourth Decision on Prosecution Motion for Judicial Notice of Adjudicated Facts Concerning the Rebuttal Evidence Procedure, *Prosecutor v. Mladić*, Case No. IT-09-92-T, T. Ch. I, 2 May 2012, para 17 (emphasis in original).

[136] ICTY, Decision on Third and Fourth Prosecution Motions for Judicial Notice of Adjudicated Facts, *Prosecutor v. Krajišnik*, Case No. IT-00-39-T, T. Ch. I., 24 March 2005, para 22.

of a war or genocidal campaign. The burden of proof shifts from the prosecutor to the accused, who has to demonstrate his innocence, the argument goes.[137]

What should be made of this? It is important that Chambers, when they consider a judicial notice motion from the prosecutor, carefully assess whether the facts do not touch upon the personal criminal responsibility of the accused. This is one of the admissibility criteria developed in the Tribunals' case law and it is worth emphasizing: facts that are rather remote in proceedings against low-ranking officials (such as facts regarding a country's military or political structure) can be essential for cases in which high-ranking accused stand trial. Moreover, the cumulative effect of taking judicial notice of adjudicated facts may be detrimental to the case at hand. The discretionary power of the Chamber to refuse notice in the interest of justice allows the Chamber to refuse the import of a huge number of facts, when this would be too oppressive to the accused.

The Chamber should provide solid reasoning regarding the use of adjudicated facts: not only in the interlocutory decisions on judicial notice, but also in the final judgment. It was shown in Chap. 4 that not all judicially noticed facts are included in the final judgment: it is important that the Chamber indicates why this is the case and accounts for the adjudicated facts that are included in the judgment. Thereby, the accused is enabled to determine whether he can successfully challenge these factual conclusions during the appeal proceedings. Detailed references to the original judgments from which the adjudicated facts are derived, are essential in this regard.

In international criminal proceedings accused are often standing trial consecutively regarding the same factual basis. However, the individual criminal responsibility of the accused differs. Military and political structures are mirrored in the charges: some accused are charged with having committed the atrocities themselves (e.g. murder, looting, rape etc.), while others are charged for their role as superiors (either military or political). The accused operated in the same context in which the atrocities were committed: it would indeed be a waste of time and resources to establish in every single case the factual background from scratch. The proceedings should be focused on their personal involvement in the crimes. Judicial notice of adjudicated facts facilitates clearly focused proceedings in which evidence is presented and challenged regarding the personal involvement of the accused.

'Well-founded' presumptions of fact are, both from an epistemological perspective as well as from the perspective of the law of criminal evidence, something to be suspicious about. The standard of proof is not met by presumptions, but by facts that are established convincingly and conclusively. Accurate fact-finding requires the Chamber to be sure about the factual conclusions it draws from the

---

[137] Cf. ICTY, Response to First Prosecution Motion for Judicial Notice of Adjudicated Facts, *Prosecutor v. Karadžić*, Case No.: IT-96-05/18-PT, T. Ch. III, 30 March 2009; ICTY, Professor Vojislav Šešelj's Response to the Prosecution's Motion to Take Judicial Notice of Documentary Evidence Pursuant to Rule 94(B) With Annex A., *Prosecutor v. Šešelj*, Case No.: IT-03-67-PT, T. Ch. III, 2 November 2007; ICTY, Response of General Miletic to the Prosecution Motion for Judicial Notice of Adjudicated Facts, *Prosecutor v. Popović et al.*, Case No.: IT-05-88-PT, T. Ch. II, 30 June 2006.

evidence presented. In other words, a solid justification has to be provided for this shortcut to proof. How do we justify that the factual conclusions of a Trial Chamber have a wider scope than the proceedings before the Chamber itself?

It is argued that the distinctive character of international criminal proceedings justifies the use of this shortcut. The tribunals are specialized courts that were set up to try persons regarding atrocities committed in a particular region during a particular period of time. Specifically, the *ad hoc* Tribunals are handling cases that are similar to others regarding the factual context in which the accused operate. No other criminal courts have been confronted with this prolonged display of *Serienprozesse*: a tailored approach for processing huge quantities of evidence, regarding a very complex and detailed factual context is inevitable. The accused must be allowed to challenge the adjudicated facts by presenting evidence in rebuttal and be provided with a carefully reasoned judgment in which the Chamber accounts in detail for the use of the adjudicated facts. Finally, it is essential that Chambers are aware of the use other Chambers can make of their factual conclusions: this underlines the importance of accurate fact-finding.

5.3.3.4 Appeal Proceedings

Taking judicial notice of adjudicated facts is a shortcut to proof that allows Chambers to rely on the factual conclusions of other Chambers. There is a striking similarity with the manner in which appeal proceedings are conducted: the appeals chambers in international criminal proceedings rely to a significant extent on the factual conclusions of trial chambers. Appeal proceedings are not trials *de novo*, but a second stage in the proceedings in which errors of fact will only be remedied when they have resulted in a miscarriage of justice. This means that appeal proceedings are another example of a shortcut: not all the evidence is presented and discussed before the second trier of fact. Appeal proceedings are regarded as corrective, which allows for a more deferential standard of review. Consequently, the primary responsibility for accurate fact-finding lies with the Trial Chamber:

> Pursuant to the jurisprudence of the Tribunal, the task of hearing, assessing and weighing the evidence presented at trial is left primarily to the Trial Chamber. Thus, the Appeals Chamber must give a margin of deference to a finding of fact reached by a Trial Chamber.[138]

The ICC Appeals Chamber held in this regard:

> Regarding factual errors, the Appeals Chamber has held that it will not interfere with factual findings of the first-instance Chamber unless it is shown that the Chamber committed a clear error, namely, misappreciated the facts, took into account irrelevant facts, or failed to take into account relevant facts. As to the "misappreciation of facts", the Appeals Chamber has also stated that it 'will not disturb a Pre-Trial or Trial Chamber's evaluation of the facts just because the Appeals Chamber might have come to a different conclusion.

[138] ICTY, Appeal Judgment, *Prosecutor v. Kupreškić et al.*, Case No.: IT-95-16-A, A. Ch., 23 October 2001, para 30.

> It will interfere only in the case where it cannot discern how the Chamber's conclusion could have reasonably been reached from the evidence before it.[139]

As was discussed in Chap. 4, the parties have a significant say in the manner in which the appeal proceedings are conducted: the Appeals Chamber will normally concentrate the proceedings on the issues that the parties deem relevant for their case.

The relationship between the Trial Chamber and Appeals Chamber regarding questions of fact and the manner in which appeal proceedings are conducted are important to understand the position of the accused during the appeal proceedings. The European Court of Human Rights has held that the specific features of a particular appeal procedure may influence the scope and applicability of Article 6 of the Convention: appeal proceedings must indeed be fair, but in the determination of fairness, the Court takes into account the proceedings as a whole.[140] This means that the trial proceedings are relevant for the assessment of the fairness of the proceedings as a whole.

The Statutes of the *ad hoc* Tribunals and the ICC allow for appeals on both errors of law and errors of fact.[141] The latter category is of particular interest here: how can the accused address alleged errors of fact made by the Trial Chamber? In order to effectively challenge the factual findings of the Trial Chamber, it is vital that the accused is provided with a duly reasoned trial judgment, where the manner in which the evidence has been weighed is accounted for in detail. Trial judgments often consist of a general part in which the approach to certain categories of evidence is described (such as statements of traumatized witnesses or statements and reports of expert witnesses).[142] The Appeals Chamber held that it must 'lend some credibility' to the methods the Trial Chamber used to assess the evidence presented to it. Only in case the Trial Chamber assessed the evidence in an unreasonable way, the Appeals Chamber will have to consider the evidence itself and indicate the proper method of assessing the evidence.[143]

---

139 ICC, Judgment on the Appeal of Mr Thomas Lubanga Dyilo Against his Conviction, *Prosecutor v. Thomas Lubanga Dyilo*, Case No.: ICC-01/04-01/06 A 5, A. Ch., 1 December 2014, para 21.

140 'The manner in which para 1, as well as para 3(c), of Article 6 is to be applied in relation to appellate or cassation proceedings depends upon the special features of the proceedings involved. Account must be taken of the entirety of the proceedings conducted in the domestic legal order and of the role of the appellate or cassation court therein.' ECtHR, 2 March 1987, App. No.: 9562/81 and 9818/82, (*Monnell and Morris v. United Kingdom*), para 56. Cf ECtHR (GC), 18 October 2006, App. No.: 18114/02, (*Hermi v. Italy*), para 60.

141 Article 25 ICTY Statute; Article 24 ICTR Statute; Article 81 ICC Statute.

142 Cf. ICC, Judgment Pursuant to Article 74 of the Statute, *Prosecutor v. Thomas Lubanga Dyilo*, Case No.: ICC-01/04-01/06, T. Ch. I, 14 March 2012, para 102–123.

143 ICTR, Appeal Judgment, *Prosecutor v. Kayishema and Ruzindana*, Case No.: ICTR-95-1-A, A. Ch., 1 June 2001, para 119. In a similar manner: ICC, Judgment on the Prosecutor's Appeal Against the Decision of Trial Chamber II entitled "Judgment pursuant to Article 74 of the Statute", *Prosecutor v. Mathieu Ngudjolo Chui*, Case No.: ICC-01/04-02/12 A, A. Ch., 7 April 2015, para 18–27.

The factual findings are generally presented as a narrative with footnotes referring to the particular sources from which the facts are derived. Issues that have been addressed explicitly during the trial proceedings will be accounted for in the judgment. The judgments must provide the accused with sufficiently detailed reasons in order to formulate well-reasoned grounds of appeal and to prepare for the appeal proceedings.

The amount of evidence that the trial chambers have to weigh is immense: if the Chamber should have to account for each and every piece of evidence that has been presented in proceedings that have lasted for several years, the judgments would become even longer and more detailed. It can be seriously doubted whether an extremely detailed analysis provides more solid reasoning as to why the accused was found guilty or not.[144] Trial Chambers weigh the evidence holistically: every piece of evidence is assessed in light of the entire body of evidence. The ICC Appeals Chamber emphasized that any other approach to the evidence by the Trial Chamber would be 'incorrect'.[145]

This has consequences for the reasoning of the Chamber in the judgment because no detailed analysis is provided for the assessment of each and every piece of evidence. The general framework at the beginning of the judgment provides, however, some guidance regarding the assessment of the evidence by the Trial Chamber. This general framework on how a Chamber has assessed the evidence is to be welcomed, because it allows the accused during the appeal proceedings to challenge the particular method the Trial Chamber has chosen regarding a certain category of evidence and the manner in which the method was applied. The Trial Chamber in *Perišić*, for example, stated that in the assessment of expert evidence it considered the:

> professional competence of the expert, the material at his disposal, the methodology used, the credibility of the findings made in light of these factors and other evidence, the proximity of the expert to the party offering him or her as an expert, as well as whether the opposing party opposed some of the expert evidence and/or reports.[146]

When the accused wants to challenge a particular witness or expert, he has to be aware of the fact that the Appeals Chamber will only reverse the factual findings of the Trial Chamber when the misinterpretation of the witness or expert statement has resulted in a miscarriage of justice. In other words, the accused must substantiate his grounds of appeal regarding factual issues: the disqualification of a particular witness or expert as such does not suffice.

---

[144] Cf. the Trial Chamber in *Perišić*: 'The Trial Chamber underlines that the right of an accused to a reasoned opinion in writing, as set forth in Article 23(2) of the Statute and Rule 98*ter*(C), in no way imposes an obligation to explain every detail of its assessment of the evidence adduced during the trial.' ICTY, Judgment, *Prosecutor v. Perišić*, Case No.: IT-04-91-T, T. Ch. I, 6 September 2011, para 23.

[145] ICC, Judgment on the Appeal oAf Mr Thomas Lubanga Dyilo against his conviction, *Prosecutor v. Thomas Lubanga Dyilo*, Case No.: ICC-01/04-01/06 A 5, A. Ch., 1 December 2014, para 22.

[146] ICTY, Judgment, *Prosecutor v. Perišić*, Case No.: IT-04-91-T, T. Ch. I, 6 September 2011, para 48.

To participate effectively during the appeal proceedings, it is essential that the accused is able to challenge the evidence on which the Trial Chamber relied, including any additional evidence that is presented before the Appeals Chamber.[147] Similar to the Dutch appeal proceedings, an active attitude is required from the accused: he has to draw the attention of the Appeals Chamber to particular factual elements in the trial judgment with which he disagrees.[148] In order to do so it is vital that the accused is informed in detail about the scope and character of the appeal proceedings. In virtually all cases, the accused is represented or assisted by counsel during the appeal: competent counsel will have informed the accused about the procedural outlook of the appeal proceedings.

The ability to participate effectively in the appeal proceedings depends to a significant degree on the manner in which the Trial Chamber has provided detailed reasons for its factual conclusions. Only in this way can the accused effectively challenge the facts before the Appeals Chamber: normally, evidence will not be reheard before the Appeals Chamber. As the Appeals Chamber held in *Kupreškić*, this deference to the Trial Chamber's factual conclusions is 'tempered by the Trial Chamber's duty to provide a reasoned opinion.'[149] In other words, the discretion the Trial Chamber enjoys must be accounted for.[150]

When additional evidence has been presented before the Appeals Chamber of the *ad hoc* Tribunals, the Appeals Chamber will determine first whether a reasonable trier of fact could have reached a finding of guilt based on the trial record. If

---

[147] This may also include the possibility to present evidence in rebuttal. Cf. Bianchi and Onsea 2010, p. 747.

[148] Cf. the ICC Appeals Chamber in *Lubanga Dyilo*: 'Appellants alleging factual errors need to set out in particular why the Trial Chamber's findings were unreasonable. In that respect, repetitions of submissions made before the Trial Chamber as to how the evidence should be assessed are insufficient if such submissions merely put forward a different interpretation of the evidence.' ICC, Judgment on the Appeal of Mr Thomas Lubanga Dyilo against his conviction, *Prosecutor v. Thomas Lubanga Dyilo*, Case No.: ICC-01/04-01/06 A 5, A. Ch., 1 December 2014, para 33. The Appeals Chamber in *Limaj et al.* held: 'In order for the Appeals Chamber to assess a party's arguments on appeal, the appealing party is expected to provide precise references to relevant transcript pages or paragraphs in the Trial Judgment to which the challenges are being made. Further, "the Appeals Chamber cannot be expected to consider a party's submissions in detail if they are obscure, contradictory, vague or suffer from other formal and obvious insufficiencies."' ICTY, Judgment, *Prosecutor v. Limaj et al.*, Case No.: IT-03-66-A, A. Ch., 27 September 2007, para 15.

[149] ICTY, Appeal Judgment, *Prosecutor v. Kupreškić et al.*, Case No.: IT-95-16-A, A. Ch., 23 October 2001, para 32.

[150] Judge Ušacka observed in her Dissenting Opinion to the appeals judgment in *Lubanga Dyilo*: 'Although the Trial Chamber is not required to articulate every step of its reasoning or to address every piece of evidence for each particular finding, a conviction decision nevertheless must enable both the convicted person and the Appeals Chamber to understand *how* the Trial Chamber made its findings based on the evidence before it, to ensure that the accused can exercise his or her right to appeal and for the Appeals Chamber to conduct a meaningful review.' ICC, Dissenting Opinion of Judge Anita Ušacka to the Judgment on the Appeal of Mr Thomas Lubanga Dyilo against his Conviction, *Prosecutor v. Lubanga Dyilo*, Case No.: ICC-01/04-01/06A 5 A. Ch., 1 December 2014, para 26 (emphasis in original).

this is the case, the Appeals Chamber will assess whether it is itself convinced of the guilt of the accused, taking into account both the trial record and the additional evidence presented during the appeal.[151] At the ICC, the Appeals Chamber has not formulated detailed criteria for the admissibility and weighing of additional evidence on appeal. It has, however, indicated that, regarding the similarities between the legal frameworks of the ICC and the *ad hoc* Tribunals, the case law of those tribunals may provide guidance in this respect.[152]

Finally, the question as to what extent the Appeals Chamber is obliged to provide reasons in the appeal judgment is of interest. Rule 117(B) ICTY RPE, Rule 118(B) ICTR RPE and Article 83(4) ICC Statute state that the appeal judgment must contain the reasons on which it is based. The European Court held that appellate courts are allowed to simply endorse the findings of the trial court as long as the 'essential issues which were submitted to its jurisdiction' have been addressed.[153] This means that grounds of appeal that have been presented by the accused must be specifically addressed in the appeal judgment. The Appeals Chamber held in *Kunarac*:

> The rationale of a judgment of the Appeals Chamber must be clearly explained. There is a significant difference from the standard of reasoning before a Trial Chamber. Article 25 of the Statute does not require the Appeals Chamber to provide a reasoned opinion such as that required of the Trial Chamber. Only Rule 117(B) of the Rules calls for a 'reasoned opinion in writing'. The purpose of a reasoned opinion under Rule 117(B) of the Rules is not to provide access to all the deliberations of the Appeals Chamber in order to enable a review of its ultimate findings and conclusions. The Appeals Chamber must indicate with sufficient clarity the grounds on which a decision has been based. However, this obligation cannot be understood as requiring a detailed response to every argument.[154]

It becomes evident from the appeal judgments of the *ad hoc* Tribunals and the ICC that the appeal chambers provide detailed reasons regarding the grounds of appeal in relation to alleged factual errors.[155] In practice, the Appeals Chamber will only address factual errors when the Chamber has been invited to do so by one of the parties in a duly reasoned notice or brief of appeal.

---

[151] ICTY, Judgment, *Prosecutor v. Blaškić*, Case No.: IT-95-14-A, A. Ch., 29 July 2004, para 24.

[152] ICC, Judgment on the Appeal of Mr Thomas Lubanga Dyilo against his Conviction, *Prosecutor v. Lubanga Dyilo*, Case No.: ICC-01/04-01/06A 5 A. Ch., 1 December 2014, para 27, 53.

[153] ECtHR, 19 December 1997, App. No.: 157/1996/776/977, (*Helle v. Finland*), para 60.

[154] ICTY, Judgment, *Prosecutor v. Kunarac et al.*, Case No.:IT-96-23 & IT-96-23/1-A, A. Ch., 12 June 2002, para 42.

[155] See for example the reasoning of the ICC Appeals Chamber in *Lubanga Dyilo* and *Nugudjolo Chui*. ICC, Judgment on the Appeal of Mr Thomas Lubanga Dyilo against his Conviction, *Prosecutor v. Lubanga Dyilo*, Case No.: ICC-01/04-01/06A 5 A. Ch., 1 December 2014; ICC, Judgment on the Prosecutor's Appeal against the Decision of Trial Chamber II entitled "Judgment pursuant to Article 74 of the Statute, *Prosecutor v. Ngudjolo Chui*, Case No.:ICC-01/04-02/12 A, A. Ch., 7 April 2015. Similar judgments have been handed down by the ICTY and ICTR Appeals Chamber. E.g. ICTY, Judgment, *Prosecutor v. Tolimir*, Case no.: IT-05-88/2-A, A.Ch., 8 April 2015; ICTR, Judgment, *Prosecutor v. Gatete*, Case No.: ICTR-00-61-A, A. Ch., 9 October 2012.

5.4 Conclusion

In this chapter, the diversions and shortcuts that have been identified in the Dutch and international criminal justice systems were evaluated. The question was asked to what extent the accused is able to participate effectively when his case is diverted from the full criminal trial altogether, or when a shortcut to proof is used. The ability of the accused to participate depends on the extent to which the (out-of-court) proceedings allow for adversarial argument ('débat contradictoire'). In this respect it is important to emphasize that the prosecutor, in case of diversions, and the court, in case of shortcuts, are responsible for ensuring that the accused is encouraged and invited to present his views on his case. In other words, the prosecutor and court should stimulate an adversarial setting in which the accused can exercise his fair trial rights to the best of his abilities.

References

Bianchi L, Onsea I (2010) Additional evidence on appeal, review proceedings, and reconsideration. In: Khan KAA, Buisman C, Gosnell C (eds) Principles of evidence in international criminal justice. Oxford University Press, Oxford

Corstens GJM, Borgers MJ (2014) Het Nederlands strafprocesrecht. Kluwer, Deventer

Crijns JH (2010) De strafrechtelijke overeenkomst. De rechtsbetrekking met het Openbaar Ministerie op het grensvlak van publiek- en privaatrecht. Kluwer, Deventer

Crijns JH, Schoep GK (2014) De motivering in strafzaken in hoger beroep. In: Van Kempen PHPHMC et al. (eds) Hoger beroep: renovatie en innovatie. Het appel in het burgerlijk, straf- en bestuursprocesrecht. Kluwer, Deventer

Damaška MR (1986) The faces of justice and state authority: a comparative approach to the legal process. Yale University Press, New Haven, London

Damaška MR (2004) Negotiated justice in international criminal courts. J Int Crim Justice 2:1018–1039

De Wilde B (2009) Schakelconstructies in bewijsmotiveringen. Delikt en Delinkwent 6:563–588

Duker MJA (2012) De verkorte bewijsmotivering bij bekennende verdachten: is er nog een toekomst?'. Delikt en Delinkwent 6:550–567

Jackson JD, Summers SJ (2012) The internationalisation of criminal evidence: beyond the common law and civil law traditions. Cambridge University Press, Cambridge

Jacobs P, Van Kampen PTC (2014) Dutch 'ZSM Settlements' in the face of procedural justice: the sooner the better? Utrecht Law Rev 10:73–85

Keulen BF (2014) Strafrechter en consensualiteit. Delikt en Delinkwent 10:739–749

Kooijmans T, In: Melai/Groenhuijsen (eds), Wetboek van Strafvordering, aant. 5.6., artt. 257a-257 h Sv, (online, revised 18 September 2012)

Lippke RL (2011) The ethics of plea bargaining. Oxford University Press, Oxford

Procureur-Generaal bij de Hoge Raad der Nederlanden (2014) Beschikt en gewogen. Over de naleving van de wet door het Openbaar Ministerie bij het uitvaardigen van strafbeschikkingen. The Hague

Scott RE, Stuntz WJ (1992) Plea bargaining as contract. Yale Law J 101(8):1909–1968

Turner JI (2009) Plea bargaining across borders. Aspen Publishers

Verschaeren NGH, Schoonbeek AB (2015) Geschikt en gewogen: streeft roep om rechterlijke toetsing van transacties doel voorbij? Tijdschrift voor Bijzonder Strafrecht en Handhaving 1(5):190–205

Vriend KCJ (2012) Commentary. In: Klip/Sluiter, Annotated Leading Cases of International Criminal Tribunals, XXX:175–180. Intersentia, Antwerp

Vriend KCJ (2013) Inzichtelijk gebruik van schakelbewijs in strafzaken: een Bayesiaans perspectief. Expertise en Recht 4:130–134

Weigend T (2006) Why have a trial when you can have a bargain? In: Duff A, Farmer L, Marshall S, Tadros V (eds) The trial on trial vol. 2: judgment and calling to account. Hart Publishing, Oxford

Weigend T, Turner JI (2013) Negotiated justice. In: Sluiter GK et al (eds) International criminal procedure: principles and rules. Oxford University Press, Oxford

Chapter 6
Why Fairness Matters

Keywords Fairness · Participation · Non-compulsion · Informed involvement · Reasoned judgment · Challenging evidence · Diversions · Shortcuts

Contents

6.1 Conclusion

The aim of this study was to analyse how the concept of fairness regulates and limits the use of avoidance mechanisms in the enforcement of criminal law. The archetypical trial context was explored and functioned as the starting point of the analysis. Any derogation from this ideal type must be accounted for in terms of fairness. In the Introduction, a distinction was made between avoidance mechanisms that operate outside the trial context (the diversions) and those that operate within the trial context (the shortcuts to proof). They have in common that they infringe on the concept of the full criminal trial in which incriminating evidence is both presented and discussed or challenged. The avoidance mechanisms were derived from the Dutch and international criminal justice systems. Avoidance mechanisms can be discerned in all types of criminal cases, including the handling of minor offences as well as cases involving the most serious violations of (international) criminal law. The systems discussed provided for a good overview of manners to avoid the full criminal trial. They also show the great diversity of these avoidance mechanisms.

K. Vriend, *Avoiding a Full Criminal Trial*, International Criminal Justice Series 8, DOI 10.1007/978-94-6265-153-1_6

Avoiding the full criminal trial can have detrimental consequences for accurate fact-finding. The accuracy of a judgment or out-of-court settlement is normally enhanced when the evidence has been contested by the accused. Therefore, it is vital that the accused can still challenge the evidence against him when the full criminal trial is avoided. As stated in the Introduction, the accuracy of the avoidance mechanisms in terms of fact-finding was not chosen as the normative framework. Such an analysis would require an objective standard of factual accuracy to which the avoidance mechanisms are juxtaposed. Such a standard does not exist: we cannot, for example, assess the factual accuracy of a punitive order or guilty plea. What we can do, however, is assess the conditions under which such avoidance mechanisms operate. Accurate fact-finding is improved in an adversarial setting in which the evidence is critically assessed. The concept of fairness, in particular the ability of the accused to participate effectively in his own case, was chosen as the proper normative framework for this study.

In Chap. 2, the concept of fairness in criminal proceedings was explored in more detail. Fairness in criminal proceedings is normally associated with the trial context as such. When the accused is charged with a criminal offence and his case is handled before the court, he is entitled to receive a fair trial. The interpretation of Article 6 of the European Convention on Human Rights is almost exclusively concerned with matters *in foro*: the relevant case law addresses infringements of particular rights of the accused within the archetypical setting of the criminal trial. This has resulted in an unprecedented amount of case law in which the right to a fair trial has been defined in great detail. Although the Court has, in a limited number of cases, addressed the out-of-court context in relation to the waiver of particular fair trial rights, the Court itself has not formulated a detailed normative framework for the enforcement of criminal law outside the regular trial context.

The second chapter presented the normative framework of the study. The concept of fairness was analysed, in particular the importance of effective participation of the accused in criminal proceedings. In their analysis of the ECtHR case law on fairness in criminal proceedings, Jackson and Summers argued that the Court has developed a normative framework to assess the fairness of the proceedings, which transcends the dichotomy between common law and civil law criminal justice systems. This model, the participatory model of proof, consists of four elements: non-compulsion, informed involvement, the ability to challenge the evidence and the right to a reasoned opinion of the court. These aspects of the model were discussed in detail.

The normative framework applies without more to the shortcuts to proof: these avoidance mechanisms operate within the trial context. This means that they cannot escape the test of fairness, because the trial context entails that the fairness of such avoidance mechanisms can be assessed. It was argued that the normative framework applies to diversions as well. Avoidance mechanisms that operate outside the trial context can also be evaluated in the light of fairness. Both from the perspective of the Court's autonomous interpretation of the concept of the criminal charge and the perspective of the rule of law, the notion of fairness applies to diversions as well as to shortcuts to proof.

In Chap. 3, diversions and shortcuts to proof in Dutch law of criminal procedure were discussed. The chapter started with an outline of the characteristics of the full criminal trial, followed by avoidance mechanisms that can be discerned in the Dutch criminal justice system. Three diversions were discussed: the punitive order, the transaction and the conditional dismissal. The prosecutor can issue a punitive order when he concludes that a particular offence (infractions and minor crimes) has been committed. The punitive order does not require the consent of the accused: when the accused does not file a notice of disagreement, the order becomes binding. This entails that no judicial supervision exists, unless the accused files a notice of disagreement. The other diversions (i.e. the transaction and the conditional dismissal) do require the consent of the accused and cannot be enforced without his cooperation. In the final part of the chapter, shortcuts to proof were discussed. The use of facts of common knowledge, chain evidence and confessions (including the cases *ad informandum*) was outlined. Finally, the chapter concluded with a discussion of the manner in which appeal proceedings are conducted.

Chapter 4 was concerned with the diversions and shortcuts to proof in international criminal proceedings. Similar to the previous chapter, the concept of the full criminal trial was explored first by exploring what this entails in the context of international criminal proceedings. Subsequently, the diversions from the full criminal trial were discussed. The legal framework and practice of guilty pleas before the ICTY and ICTR were outlined, followed by the analysis of the admission of guilt within the context of the ICC. These diversions are quite similar to each other, apart from the prominent position of victims at the ICC regarding the approval of such an admission of guilt. The shortcuts to proof concerned the use of agreed facts, facts of common knowledge, judicial notice of adjudicated facts and the manner in which appeal proceedings are conducted before the international courts.

In Chap. 5, the diversions and shortcuts to proof were critically assessed in light of the normative framework presented in Chap. 2. Regarding the diversions, three categories were discerned: diversions based on consensus which are not subject to judicial approval (the transaction and the conditional dismissal); diversions based on consensus which are subject to judicial approval (the guilty plea and the admission of guilt); and the diversion that can be imposed, regardless of any consensus between the parties (the punitive order). It was argued that, when judicial approval is absent or limited, it is vital that the accused is still able to participate effectively regarding the determination of his criminal responsibility. This provides the required legitimacy regarding these avoidance mechanisms. A similar argument was made regarding the use of shortcuts to proof. The different shortcuts operate in front of the court which guarantees judicial supervision. The court must ensure that when the full criminal trial is avoided the possibility for the accused to participate effectively is respected. This entails, *inter alia*, that the accused is sufficiently informed of his procedural rights and that he is able to challenge any incriminating evidence against him.

6.2 A Case for Fairness

The focus on the trial context in relation to fairness in criminal proceedings obscures the fact that the enforcement of criminal law in present-day criminal justice systems is, to a significant degree, conducted outside the archetypical trial context. Out-of-court settlements and the imposition of sentences occur regularly and are regarded as a necessary tool for efficient criminal law enforcement. The diversions discussed in this study exemplify this trend and show that the type or category of criminal offences that are diverted from the full criminal trial is immaterial: diversions are used in the handling of both minor offences as well as the most serious violations of international criminal law. When the case is handled by a court, shortcuts to proof can be discerned that aim to speed up the proceedings. These shortcuts are characterized by their great diversity. What they have in common is that they, to a greater or lesser extent, infringe on the full criminal trial in which the evidence is presented in order to enable the accused to effectively challenge the incriminating evidence.

The diversions and shortcuts to proof that were discussed are examples of ways to avoid a full criminal trial. The legitimacy of these avoidance mechanisms was assessed in light of the concept of fairness in criminal proceedings; in the examination, the ability of the accused to participate effectively regarding the handling of his own case provided the normative framework. The avoidance mechanisms have in common that the accused is expected to be able to take care of his interests and to be diligent and assertive regarding his procedural rights. It is evident that this can be a burdensome task for accused that are not assisted by defence counsel. In such circumstances, the prosecutor, in case of diversions, or the court, in case of shortcuts to proof, must consider carefully the procedural interests of the accused. It is important in this regard to emphasize that criminal proceedings are not a battle between equal opponents: the accused is confronted with the criminal enforcement apparatus of the state or the international prosecutor. When the accused is not able to effectively exercise his procedural rights, this should be of true concern to the court or the prosecutor.

In his contribution to *The Trial on Trial*, Thomas Weigend wrote:

> Will trials survive? Or will they become the dinosaurs of criminal procedure, eventually extinguished because they no longer fit into an environment geared toward efficient crime control rather than a dramatic presentation of guilt and punishment?[1]

Weigend observed that, over the last decades, the criminal trial is in decline: out-of-court settlements are on the rise and the efficient enforcement of criminal law has become more important. This to the detriment of due process considerations. He envisaged that the trial will remain but that it will lose much of its prominence.[2] The trial context is no longer regarded as the exclusive or preferred

---

[1] Weigend 2006, p. 208.

[2] Weigend 2006, p. 222.

context in which the guilt of the accused is determined; instead, the trial is but one of the options available within a criminal justice system.

The decline of the full criminal trial is worrying, both from an epistemological perspective and the perspective of fairness. Although a full criminal trial does not guarantee accurate factual outcomes, it does provide the best conditions to critically assess the evidence. A procedural context that promotes adversarial argument ('un débat contradictoire') is essential when it comes to accurate fact-finding. Avoiding this context has consequences for the fairness of the handling of the case as well: just as the trial context is the optimal context to conduct fact-finding, it also provides the proper context to ensure that the case is processed in a fair and decent manner. Criminal proceedings conducted before an independent and impartial court is the best guarantee that the fair trial rights of the accused are observed.

The Introduction explained that this study was based on the archetypical criminal trial in which the charges against the accused are examined, the evidence is presented and challenged and a reasoned judgment from the court represents the conclusion. It was argued that, when this archetypical setting is abandoned and the full criminal trial is avoided, it is important that the accused can still properly participate in the handling of his case. Avoiding the full criminal trial is, in fact, legitimate only when the accused is able or enabled to do so effectively. This entails that he is not compelled to waive his right to the full criminal trial, that he is properly informed about the procedural outlook of the diversion or shortcut to proof, that he is able to challenge the evidence that is presented against him and that he is provided with a reasoned decision or judgment that can be challenged.

Present-day criminal justice systems will continue to provide for ways to avoid the full criminal trial; for many different reasons, they simply must have mechanisms that administer criminal cases in a smooth and efficient manner. This study is not a plea for the unconditional re-instalment of full criminal proceedings. Instead, it signals the trend of the avoidance of the full criminal trial and the implications in terms of fairness. The desirability and legitimacy of diversions and shortcuts to proof should not be based on efficiency considerations, but on a proper normative framework. The concept of fairness in criminal proceedings transcends the trial context and permeates the criminal justice system as such: processing criminal cases must be conducted in a fair manner. In this regard, the concept of fairness has an autonomous meaning or scope, which is not limited to the full criminal trial. The notion of an 'ethics of conflict', adversarial proceedings and effective participation are important and indispensable standards in this respect. Criminal trials are typically a display of conflicting interests of the parties involved. Therefore, it is vital that the accused is able to present his arguments, to challenge the evidence and to be regarded as a participant whose interests must be taken seriously. This applies equally to the full criminal trial as well as to diversions and shortcuts to proof.

This study analysed the workings of these mechanisms and the proper normative framework for such avoidance mechanisms. The concept of fairness in its traditional meaning has been developed within the context of the full criminal trial. The European Court of Human Rights has, in its interpretation of Article 6 of the

Convention, interpreted the right to a fair *trial*. It is not surprising that the concept of fairness is first and foremost associated with the trial context as such. However, the developments in terms of enforcement of criminal law and the rise of avoidance mechanisms have resulted in a paradox: the right to a fair trial has been interpreted and discussed in great detail, whereas the significance of the trial as such has gradually diminished.

The decline of the full criminal trial is generally perceived as an intolerable trend towards more efficiency in the handling of criminal cases. The old dichotomy between efficiency and due process considerations is often referenced, at times with a sort of nostalgia when arguing that proper and legitimate criminal law enforcement should be conducted before an independent and impartial court that takes the proceedings seriously, not hampered by any efficiency considerations. However, the decline of the full criminal trial does not have to result in a similar decline of due process or fairness. In this regard, it is essential that the concept of fairness in criminal proceedings is regarded as an autonomous concept that transcends the context of the full criminal trial. When the concept of fairness is regarded as a principle underlying the enforcement of criminal law, it regulates and limits the use of avoidance mechanisms. Moreover, it provides the required legitimacy when a case is handled in a diverted or abbreviated manner.

When the concept of fairness is regarded as a principle that applies, regardless of the procedural context in which the case is processed, the criticism on the decline of the full criminal trial can be properly addressed. In every case in which the full criminal trial is avoided, the consequences for the fair handling of the case must be assessed. The different elements of the participatory model of proof provide guidelines that have to be taken into account: can the accused still opt for a full criminal trial? Is he properly informed of the outlook of the proceedings? Is he able to effectively challenge the evidence? Is he provided with a reasoned decision that can be challenged? Questioning the desirability of avoidance mechanisms as such is obsolete because these mechanisms will remain. In fact, they are expected to become more prominent, particularly in uncontested cases. What is of interest is the question of how avoidance mechanisms can be developed that are legitimate, in terms of fairness, in current criminal justice systems. This requires an approach in which fairness is regarded as a fundamental principle of criminal law enforcement, which has to be operationalized regarding particular diversions and shortcuts to proof. The diversions suffer from insufficient regulation in this respect; for obvious reasons, the focus has been on issues of fairness within the trial context. The analysis presented in this study provides useful guidelines with respect to an effective and legitimate way of processing criminal cases. In this sense, the search for more efficiency does not have to be detrimental for the participation rights of the accused. What is essential is that, when the full criminal trial is avoided, any possible consequences in terms of fairness are acknowledged and properly remedied by providing the accused the opportunity to participate effectively in the handling of his case.

6.3 Recommendations

If fairness is taken seriously in the enforcement of criminal law, the following recommendations must be made. A division is made between the Dutch and international context. Within the Dutch context, three diversions were discussed: the punitive order, the transaction and the conditional dismissal. When the accused files a notice of disagreement against the punitive order, regular first-instance proceedings will follow. The punitive order as such and the manner in which the punitive order was issued are normally not part of the deliberations of the court. It has been argued in the literature that any irregularities that have occurred in the imposition of the punitive order can be regarded as irregularities that have occurred during the pre-trial phase. As a result, the regular regime of addressing procedural violations applies. However, because the prosecutor can impose sentences unilaterally (traditionally the prerogative of the court), more robust and explicit safeguards are indispensable. This can be achieved by amending Article 257f(3) CCP, which concerns the manner in which proceedings are conducted after a notice of disagreement has been filed. The amendment should give the court the specific authority to include in its deliberations the manner in which the punitive order was imposed. This authority can be exercised *proprio motu*, or at the request of one of the parties.

Regarding the transaction, judicial approval of special transactions can be a useful safeguard for the fairness of the negotiating process that preceded the transaction. Party autonomy should be respected as much as possible in that the court should limit itself to determine whether the process resulting in the transaction has been conducted in a fair manner. The practice of plea-bargaining in the international criminal law context provides useful guidelines in this respect. The court can determine whether the accused has entered into the negotiations voluntarily, whether he has been informed properly of his procedural rights and incriminating evidence, whether he has agreed unequivocally to the terms in the transaction and whether the transaction has a sufficient factual basis. Considering the character of the transaction, judicial approval should focus on the procedural aspects of this diversion: was the procedure, resulting in a transaction, fair? Similar safeguards can be envisaged regarding conditional dismissals. In cases in which no punitive order can be imposed, no transaction can be offered (the case concerns a crime punishable by more than 6 years' imprisonment) and no regular first-instance proceedings are initiated by the prosecutor, a conditional dismissal can be an appropriate avoidance mechanism. Although the number of cases that fall into this category will be low, the extraordinary character of such cases warrants judicial approval. Similar to the special transactions, the court determines in these cases whether the procedural safeguards have been complied with, and whether the accused was treated fairly by the prosecutor.

Irrespective of which diversion is used by the prosecutor, he should enable the accused to participate as effectively as possible in the process that results in a particular diversion. It has been stated before: diverting a case from the full criminal trial, in which evidence is properly presented and challenged, comes at a price. The accused must be provided with a decent and fair out-of-court procedure in which he can determine freely to consent to the diversion of his case.

In respect of the shortcuts to proof, similar observations can be made: the accused must be provided with a fair trial in which he is enabled to participate effectively. In case of shortcuts, the main responsibility for providing the accused with this opportunity lies with the court. When the court considers the use of facts of common knowledge, it must determine whether such facts have to be discussed with the parties. The distinction made by the Dutch Supreme Court between patently indisputable facts of common knowledge and *prima facie* facts of common knowledge may be rather absurd from an epistemological point of view; however, procedurally this distinction makes sense. Discussing the latter category with the parties during the proceedings enables them to comment on such facts. Effective participation is then guaranteed.

Considering the use of chain evidence, a similar line of argument can be followed: when neither the prosecutor nor the defence has referred to the possible use of chain evidence, the court should invite the parties to share their view on this matter. This way, the parties, particularly the defence, are able to challenge any possible use of chain evidence during the proceedings.

The use of confessions and in particular the *ad informandum* cases have been categorized as a shortcut in the Dutch context. Confessing to the charges has significant consequences for the proceedings, although the case will not be diverted from the court. The right to challenge the evidence is (implicitly) waived when the accused confesses, and he will normally not be provided with a reasoned judgment. This is, as such, not problematic because a waiver of the right to challenge the evidence is legitimate if, and only if, the accused acts out of his own free will and is properly informed of the consequences of his procedural choices.

Regarding appeal proceedings in the Dutch context, it is essential that the accused is aware of the specific procedural outlook of the appeal proceedings. The more active role that is required from the accused regarding challenging the evidence is of particular interest here. As was stated in Chap. 5, the court of appeal can direct the proceedings to any aspect of the case *proprio motu*. The accused is well-advised to be active and put forward his objections against the first-instance judgment as early as possible. In case of unrepresented accused, the court of appeal must ensure that the accused is informed of his rights and is given the opportunity to challenge any part of the first-instance judgment he wants. Such accused should be informed that aspects of the case that the accused does not challenge may be left undiscussed, if the court of appeal does not discuss them *proprio motu*.

The diversions discussed within the international context are the guilty plea and the admission of guilt. Both diversions, which are quite similar to each other, are embedded in a solid procedural framework that ensures that the accused is aware of the consequences of his choice to admit guilt. Only when the accused is well-informed and enters his plea voluntarily may the Chamber consider and accept the plea. The ICC Statute states explicitly that the accused may enter an admission of guilt only after sufficient consultation with defence counsel. Considering the protection the accused can derive from this legal framework, it is remarkable that no admission of guilt has been filed at the ICC so far. Combined with the length of regular proceedings before the ICC, it is advisable for both the prosecutor and the accused to seriously explore the possibilities of diverting the case from regular proceedings. This includes disclosure of incriminating evidence, or a summary thereof, by the prosecutor in order to convince the accused that the prosecutor has indeed a case against him.

The use of shortcuts can significantly shorten the proceedings, if applied properly and fairly. Particularly the use of agreed facts may speed up the proceedings considerably. Within the context of the ICC, the prosecutor and defence are encouraged by the Chamber to reach agreement on as many facts of the case as possible. Unlike the legal framework of the *ad hoc* Tribunals, the ICC legal framework does not provide for the possibility to take judicial notice of adjudicated facts. Therefore, the agreement of the parties on parts of the factual basis of the charges is an important tool to speed up the proceedings. As stated in Chap. 5, this is acceptable only if the accused agrees to particular facts on a voluntary and informed basis. The safeguards regarding guilty pleas and admissions of guilt apply by analogy. The use of judicial notice of adjudicated facts at the ICTY in particular has resulted in more expeditious trials in which the proceedings are focused on the contested issues of the case. Although this shortcut has proven its potential at the ICTY, it is unlikely that an amendment of the Rules of Procedure and Evidence of the ICC to include this shortcut would be really helpful. The ICC's case-load differs considerably from the case-load at the ICTY; in particular, a significant number of cases at the ICTY concerned the same factual basis. In such cases, the use of judicial notice can indeed speed up the proceedings: the individual criminal responsibility of the accused has to be determined against the background of facts that have been established in other proceedings. At the ICC, the use of agreed facts is to be encouraged by the Chamber in order to provide for more expeditious trials.

Considering judicial notice of facts of common knowledge at the ICC, Chambers should carefully assess the character of the facts of common knowledge. When those facts concern or relate to contextual elements of the crimes alleged, the Chamber should make sure that the accused is able to comment upon those facts. Ideally, contextual elements of the crime are proven by 'ordinary' means of proof which the accused can challenge during the proceedings.

The particular procedural context in which appeal proceedings are conducted in international criminal law requires an active attitude from the accused. Appeal proceedings are not trials *de novo* but are normally concentrated on the objections of the parties against the judgment of the Trial Chamber. This entails that the accused must be sufficiently aware of the procedural outlook of the appeal proceedings and of the fact that he must formulate his objections as precisely and timely as possible.

Reference

Weigend (2006) Why have a trial when you can have a bargain? In: Duff A, Farmer L, Marshall S, Tadros V (eds) The trial on trial vol. 2: judgment and calling to account. Hart Publishing, Oxford

Index

K. Vriend, *Avoiding a Full Criminal Trial*, International Criminal Justice Series 8, DOI 10.1007/978-94-6265-153-1

FSC
www.fsc.org
MIX
Papier | Fördert
gute Waldnutzung
FSC® C083411

Kolibri 360 GmbH
Ferdinand-Jühlke-Straße 7
99095 Erfurt, Deutschland
produktsicherheit@kolibri360.de